MASTERING THE APPLE IIGS TOOLBOX

Dan Gookin and Morgan Davis

Greensboro, North Carolina

Printed in the United States of America

10 9 8 7 6 5 4 3 2 1

ISBN 0-87455-120-X

COMPUTE! Publications, Inc., Post Office Box 5406, Greensboro, NC 27403, (919) 275-9809, is part of ABC Consumer Magazines, Inc., one of the ABC Publishing Companies, and is not associated with any manufacturer of personal computers. Apple is a registered trademark and Apple IIGS is a trademark of Apple Computer, Inc.

Contents

Foreword .... *v*

Chapters

1. How to Use This Book 1

2. Things You Should Know 9

3. Toolbox Specifics 23

4. Calling the Toolbox 33

5. Converting to Other Language Formats 47

6. Elementary Toolbox Examples 61

7. Designing Applications 75

8. Memory Management 93

9. The Tool Sets 109

10. Strings and Things 127

11. Error Handling Routines 139

12. The Event Manager 149

13. QuickDraw II—Pens, Colors, and Patterns 171

14. QuickDraw II and the Mouse 201

15. Windows 233

16. Pull-Down Menus 263

17. Dialog Boxes 293

18. Sound 323

19. Short Cuts 351

Tool Sets 363

Appendices

A. ASCII Character Codes 583

B. Firmware Entry Points and Vectors 585

C. Hardware Registers and Softswitches 590

D. ProDOS 16 Function Calls 595

E. Error Codes 599

F. 65816 Opcode Chart 603

G. Apple IIGS Monitor Command Summary 610

H. Apple Desktop Bus Keycodes 613

I. Tool Set Cross Reference 614

J. ProDOS Filetypes 618

K. List of Tools by Function Name 620

Index 639

Foreword

Just when you thought the venerable 6502 chip was running out of surprises, along comes the 65816 and the first computer to be based on this new generation chip: the Apple IIGS.

With a bus 16 bits wide, able to address up to eight megabytes, and a marvel of speed and flexibility, the IIGS promises to keep the Apple II name alive for years to come. A natural descendant of both the Apple II and the Macintosh, it combines the programmability of the former with the friendly user interface of the latter.

The Apple IIGS toolbox is nearly as revolutionary as the chip that supports it. Virtually every function imaginable has been packed into this library of routines, along with the advanced sound and graphics capabilities that gave the IIGS its initials.

But what good is a library without a card catalog? Although mountains of paper have been published about the toolbox, very little of it has been organized in a usable manner for the programmer.

The authors of this book gathered the necessary information and organized it into a usable format. They brought to this work not only the existing documentation, but also their willingness to experiment. Some sections of the toolbox are not as well documented by the manufacturer as others. Information on the sound capabilities of the IIGS, for instance, can be found in this book and nowhere else.

For the beginning machine language programmer, this book provides many programming examples on string handling, graphics, memory management, error handling, and good programming practices. More advanced programmers can make use of the tool set documentation which comprises the latter half of the book. Any programmer will appreciate the lists of firmware entry points, error codes, 65816 opcodes, and the tool set cross reference in the Appendices which make this the complete reference to the Apple IIGS.

Chapter 1

How to Use This Book

This book is about the Apple IIGS toolbox—what it is, what it does and how it works. The purpose of the book is to teach you how to use the toolbox, and ultimately the Apple IIGS, to your best advantage.

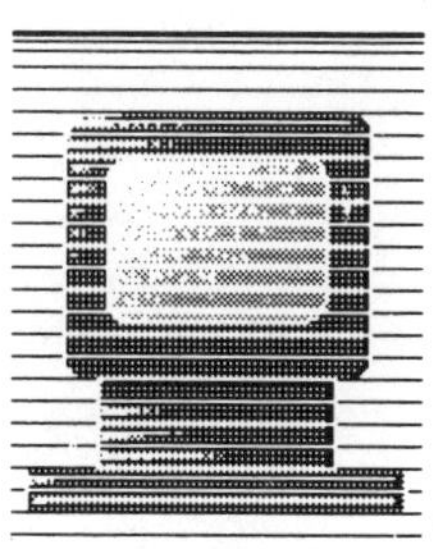

Before deciding this chapter isn't worth reading, it should be pointed out that this book makes a few assumptions about you, the reader. The toolbox is not a simple thing to master. So before you attempt anything, a few points should be made clear.

First, this book is written with the assumption that you know a little bit about the Apple computer or programming in general, or both. Anyone familiar with the way a computer works will probably be comfortable with this book.

Second, knowing a programming language is a must. Knowing machine language or C langauge is almost a necessity, though not a requirement. It's assumed that not everyone using this book will be writing and distributing programs for the Apple IIGS; some readers might simply use this book as a reference or insight to their machines. However, without some programming knowledge, many of the concepts expressed here will be difficult or impossible to understand.

When possible, a complete and fully commented machine language program is provided to illustrate a toolbox concept. Otherwise, due to space considerations, only a small snippet of a program (the most important part) is used. In Chapter 5, an example of translating machine language listings to other language formats is illustrated.

And finally, this book is written for several types of readers: the Apple computer hacker, the programmer, the computer whiz, and the computing enthusiast. All of you were kept in mind as these words were typed and programming examples entered. After all, the Apple is a fun computer, and any book about it should carry the same light and honest attitude.

Finding Your Way Around

This book is laid out in a linear fashion. If you're a beginner at programming the Apple IIGS, you should read this book straight through. Intermediate to advanced users should probably read this and the next chapter, then pick up wherever your interest lies.

Because this book couldn't possibly cover every aspect of the Apple IIGS toolbox and still maintain a managable size and reasonable price, a compromise was made. *Mastering the Apple IIGS Toolbox* falls halfway between a comprehensive tutorial and a complete reference work. After all, why buy two very heavy books when you can buy this one and sample the waters?

The first part of this book is designed to familiarize you with the toolbox, using examples and sample programs. Chapters 1–5 will tell you everything you need to know before tackling the toolbox. These chapters should give you the background you need to use the rest of the book. Chapter 6 contains some quick and easy toolbox programs.

The second part of this book is about programming the toolbox. Chapters 7–11 cover five separate areas of the toolbox: designing applications, memory management, setting up the tool sets, dealing with strings, and error handling routines.

The third part of this book deals directly with using the toolbox and the desktop environment. Subjects like how the toolbox intercepts events; the mouse; creating graphics and sound; and using windows, pull-down menus, and dialog boxes are covered in this part. Each chapter contains a complete toolbox program and/or program examples.

The last part of this book is a reference. It contains a listing of the complete Apple IIGS toolbox, tool by tool. An index to all tools using their function names is also provided. This is followed by ten useful appendices.

About the Program Listings

This book uses several conventions to provide consistency within this book and with Apple's documentation. The program listings you see in this book are generated using the *Apple Programmer's Workshop (APW)* environment and its various tools.

The assembler included with *APW* is the *ORCA/M* macro assembler from Byte Works. It can be purchased separately from *APW*, though serious Apple IIGS programmers will probably want the entire *APW* package.

Great care was taken to insure that every routine listed in each chapter works as documented. You will find no complex macros, no assumed setup routines, or any other "Gotchas!" in this book.

Numbers and the Like

The majority of the numbers you'll see in this book are in *hexadecimal* (base 16) notation. It is assumed you are familiar with hexadecimal notation. Before everyone goes screaming for the door, this was done for several reasons.

Hexadecimal *(hex)* is the numbering system used by Apple in all its documentation. It is a more logical approach to programming applications than decimal (what everyone on the planet is already used to), and it's more convenient than binary. (Hex is almost a shorthand method for jotting down binary numbers.)

All hex numbers are preceded by a $ (dollar sign). They contain the numerals 1–9 and the capital letters *A, B, C, D, E* and *F.* (See Appendix A for a comparison of equivalent hex, binary, and decimal numbers.)

By using Hex, an extra level of confusion has been avoided. The hex numbers $2A0F and $2C0F both end in the value $0F. In toolbox notation, this means they're both part of the same tool set (which is discussed later in this book). Because both numbers end in $0F, it's easy to identify them as part of the same tool set. Had 10,767 and 11,279 (their decimal equivalents) been used, this relationship would not be as obvious.

There are three types of hex numbers used in this book: *bytes, words,* and *long words.*

Bytes. A byte value (B) is a two-digit hex number. It ranges from $00 through $FF (0–255 decimal). A byte is composed of two *nibbles.* In the byte value $E1, $E is the upper nibble and $1 is the lower nibble.

Words. A word value (W) is a four-digit hex number. Word values rangefrom $0000 through $FFFF (0–65535 decimal). Words are composed of two bytes: the *most significant byte (MSB)* and the *least significant byte (LSB).* In the word value $A095, $A0 is the MSB and $95 is the LSB.

Long Words. A long word (L) is an eight-digit hex number. It is equivalent to two words or four bytes. Long word values range from $00000000 through $FFFFFFFF (0–4,294,967,295 decimal). Long words are composed of two words: the *high order word (HOW)* and the *low order word (LOW).* In the long word value $00E100A8, $00E1 is the high order word and $00A8 is the low order word.

With the Apple IIGS , all long word addresses are typically expressed as $000000 (three bytes). The most significant byte of the high order word is always set to $00. Or, using the handy baffling abbreviations, the MSB of the HOW is always $00.

```
Long Word: $00E065A8
      HOW: $00E0
      LOW: $65A8
 HOW, MSB: $00
 HOW, LSB: $E0
 LOW, MSB: $65
 LOW, LSB: $A8
```

It's Logical

Occasionally, the toolbox may deal with a logical, or *Boolean,* value. These are numbers which represent the true or false result of a certain action. A *true value* is any value not equal to zero. Commonly, a true value is understood to be the hex word $8000. A *false value* is zero.

Logical True = $8000 or any non-zero value
Logical False = $0000

When the toolbox returns a logical true or false value, the actual numbers returned are as listed above.

Type of Equipment You'll Need

This is an active book where your participation is essential. It's assumed that you have access to an Apple IIGS. It is further assumed that you're sitting in front of it, waiting to begin programming.

Your Apple IIGS comes with 256K of memory installed. To take full advantage of this book, you should have at least 768K of memory in your computer. This means you'll need to purchase a memory expansion card with at least 512K of RAM on it. Because memory is so inexpensive, it's suggested that you pack your memory board with as many chips as will fit.

If upgrading memory is not possible, a 256K Apple IIGS will get you by. But to take full advantage of this book and the toolbox, a memory upgrade is strongly recommended.

If you have the extra memory, you might want to use some of it as a ramdisk. If you have more than one megabyte of RAM in your Apple IIGS and only one disk drive, installing an 800K ramdisk gives you the equivalent of two disk drives.

The information you put in the ramdisk stays there as long as your computer is running. Even if you reset the machine, the files and programs stored in the ramdisk will remain intact. However, turning off the computer erases the ramdisk.

The ramdisk can be accessed through the computer's control

panel. Refer to your Apple IIGS owner's guide for assistance. (Press Control-Apple-ESC to access the control panel.)

Other Things Worth Noting

Tackling the toolbox is a tough job. In order to make your journey little easier, the following reference books are recommended:

Eyes/Lichty. *Programming the 65816*. New Jersey: Prentice Hall Press, 1986. ISBN 0-89303-789-3.

Fischer, Michael. *Apple IIGS Technical Reference*. New York: McGraw-Hill, 1986/1987. ISBN 0-07-881009-4.

Sanders, William B. *Sound and Graphics on the Apple IIGS*. Greensboro: Compute! Publications, 1987. ISBN 0-87455-096-3.

Wagner, Roger. *Compute!'s Apple IIGS ML for Beginners*. Greensboro: Compute! Publications, 1987. ISBN 0-87455-097-1.

Worth/Lechner. *Beneath Apple ProDOS*. New Jersey: Prentice Hall Press, 1985. ISBN 0-8359-0463-6.

Chapter 2

Things You Should Know

It would be nice to just sit down and begin accomplishing something. Many people would love to simply sit down at a piano keyboard, think of a tune, and play it. But it just doesn't work that way.

The same can be said about computer programming. Sure,

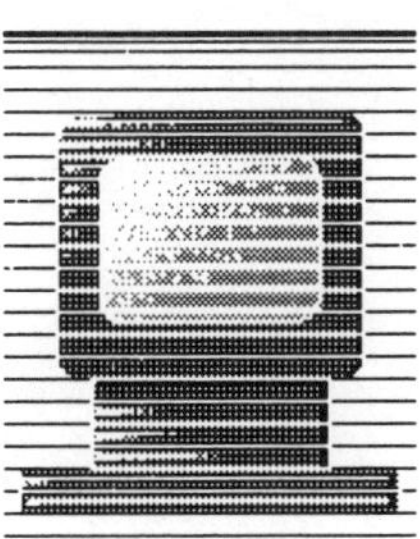

most of us would like to be able to sit down at the keyboard, think of a program, and write it. Or better yet, wouldn't it be nice if you could stare at the computer, pore over the manuals and absorb the information (the *osmosis* approach).

The truth is, you need some ground work before taking off. That's what this chapter is for. Here the Apple IIGS's microprocessor, its RAM, and how the toolbox works are all discussed.

The Processor

The brain of the Apple IIGS is the 65816 microprocessor chip. It's also referred to as the Central Processing Unit (CPU), or sometimes just *the processor.*

The 65816 chip is the offspring of the 65C02 chip found in the Apple IIe and IIc computers, but much more powerful. Though it's not at all the same chip, the 65816 can be told to imitate, or *emulate,* the 65C02 chip. This emulation is what keeps the Apple IIGS compatible with its ancestors.

The 65C02 chip was also an improvement, this time over the 6502 microprocessor originally found in the Apple II, Apple II+, and original Apple IIe (see Figure 2-1). The differences between the 65C02 and the 6502 were mainly in speed and several new machine code instructions. The 6502 has a single accumulator register (A), and two index registers (X and Y). Each register could only hold eight bits of data. The 65C02 looks exactly the same.

All of these chips are considered part of the same family. Generally speaking, programs written for the older chips will still work on the 65816 (see Figure 2-2). But programs written specifically for the 65816 cannot work on the older chips. When the 65816 is told to emulate the functions of the 65C02, it can run programs just as if it were the 65C02. The 65816 looks similar to the 6502. The major difference is that the A, X, and Y registers are twice as wide—16 bits instead of 8. Also, a Direct Page register and Data Bank Register have been added.

Figure 2-1. Diagram of 6502

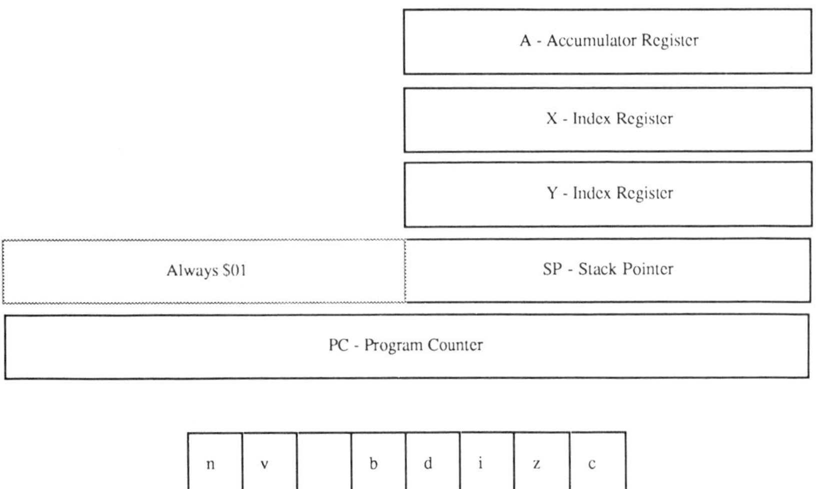

Figure 2-2. Diagram of 65816

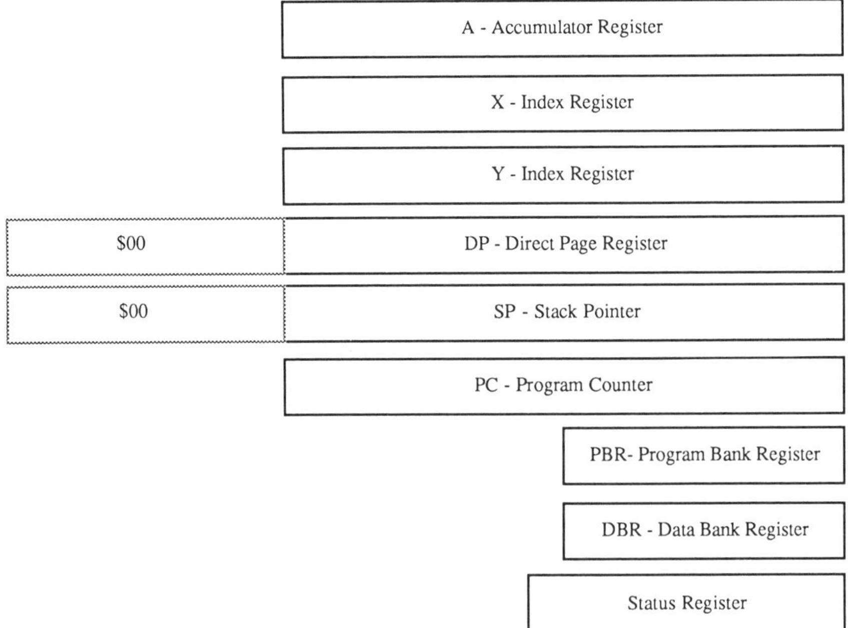

Emulation and Register Widths

The 65816 can be very clever in the way it deals with data. In its native 16-bit mode, all information is transferred using 16-bit values. However, to maintain compatibility with the 65C02 and just to be interesting, the 65816 has several other modes, all of which need to be understood to use the Apple IIGS toolbox routines.

There are three special bits in the 65816's status, or flags, register. Two of these bits control the size of the 65816's registers, whether they are 16 bits or 8 bits wide. The third bit turns 65C02 emulation on and off. See Figure 2-3.

Figure 2-3. Diagram of 65816 Status Register

e	n	v	m	x	d	i	z	c

The *E flag* controls emulation. When this flag is set, or equal to one, the microprocessor is in emulation mode and the 65816 behaves exactly like the 65C02. When the E flag is reset, or equal to zero, the 65816 is not in emulation and is said to be in its native mode.

E = 1 65C02 emulation is ON
E = 0 65C02 emulation is OFF

Turning off 65C02 emulation is done with two machine code instructions: the *Clear Carry Flag (CLC)* instruction, and a new 65816-only instruction, *XCE.* The XCE intruction exchanges the carry and emulation flags. If the carry flag has been cleared using the CLC instruction, XCE will indirectly clear the emulation flag by swapping the two. This indirect procedure is necessary because there is no direct method of modifying the E flag.

The machine language instructions to turn off emulation are

```
CLC     ;CLEAR THE CARRY FLAG,
        ;RESETTING IT TO 0
XCE     ;EXCHANGE CARRY/EMULATION FLAG.
        ;NOW, 65816 MODE IS ACTIVE
```

Figure 2-4. To Clear the E Flag, CLC then XCE.

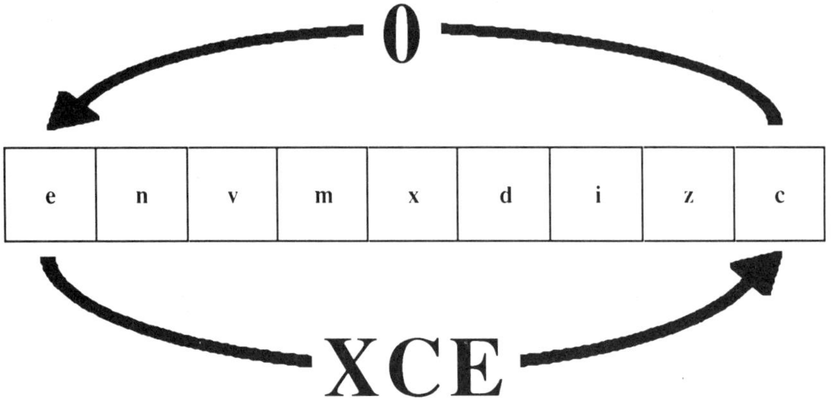

To turn on 65C02 emulation, the E flag must be set. This is similar to turning off emulation, except the carry flag is first set to one, then swapped with the E flag (Figure 2-5).

```
SEC     ;SET CARRY FLAG TO 1
XCE     ;SWAP CARRY AND EMULATION FLAGS
        ;NOW, THE E FLAG EQUALS 1
        ; EMULATION IS ON.
```

Figure 2-5. To Set the E Flag, SEC then XCE.

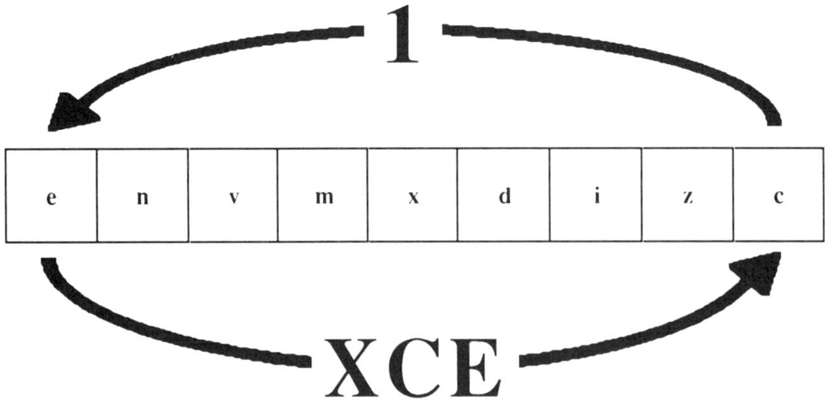

With 65C02 emulation turned on, the size of all the 65816's registers is set at 8 bits. When emulation is turned off (the E flag is reset to zero), the size of the 65816's registers can be 8 bits or 16 bits wide. The width of these registers is controlled by the M and X status flags.

The *M flag* controls the width of the A register, also known as the *accumulator.* When this flag is set, or equal to one, the A register is only 8 bits wide. All the instructions which deal with the A register will do so in 8-bit-wide values. When the M flag is reset, or equal to zero, the A register returns to a 16-bit width.

M = 1 accumulator is 8 bits wide
M = 0 accumulator is 16 bits wide

The M flag actually stands for *Memory.* Besides changing the width of the A register, it also changes the way certain machine language instructions deal with memory. When M is equal to zero, the 65816's memory functions all work with 16-bit values. EOR, AND, CMP, DEC, INC are all 16-bit instructions when M equals zero.

The *X flag* controls the width of the X and Y index registers. When the X flag is set, or equal to one, the X and Y registers are only 8 bits wide—just as the A register is only 8 bits wide when the M flag is set. All machine code instructions now deal with the X and Y registers in 8-bit-wide values. When the X flag is reset, or equal to zero, the X and Y index registers return to a 16-bit width, just as the A register returns to a 16-bit width when the M flag is reset.

X = 1 X and Y index registers are 8 bits wide
X = 0 X and Y index registers are 16 bits wide

There might be many reasons for changing the width of a register—for example, if your program requires manipulating 8-bit values for some specific reason. When this happens, the appropriate status flag, either M or X, should be set to one. However, under normal operations, the 65816's registers can be kept at 16-bit widths (both the M and X flags reset to zero).

Two special opcodes were introduced with the 65816 to control the status flags. The *REP* instruction resets bits in the status register to zero. The *SEP* instruction sets bits in the status register to one. By using SEP and REP you can control the width of the registers by individually turning on and off the M and X flags.

The following instruction turns the M and X flags in the status register off, making the width of all registers 16 bits.

```
REP   #$30    ;RESET BITS X AS IN: 00XX0000 TO 0.
              ;THE SAME BIT POSITIONS AS
              ; IN THE STATUS REGISTER
```

Figure 2-6. REP #$30 resets the status of flags M and X to zero.

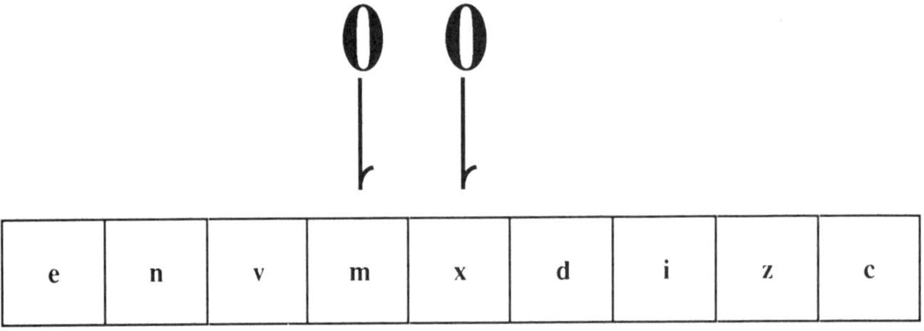

The following instruction turns on the M and X flags, making the width of all registers 8 bits.

```
SEP   #$30    ;SET BITS X AS IN 00XX0000 TO 1.
```

Figure 2-7. SEP #$30 sets the status of flags M and X to one.

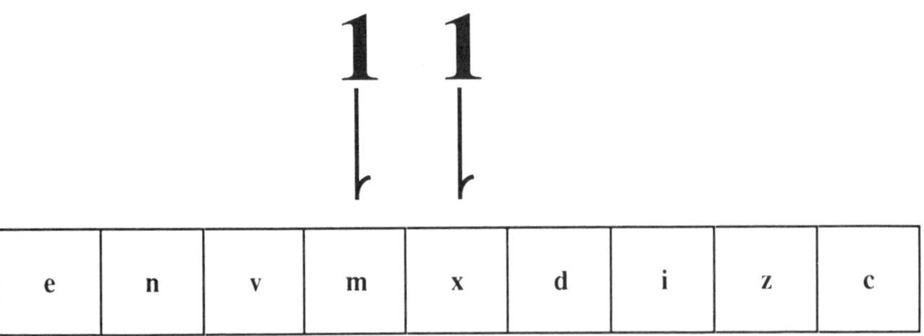

The size of the A or X and Y registers can also be set individually. The following instruction sets the A register to 8 bits, but doesn't change the status of the X and Y registers.

```
SEP   #$20    ;SET ONLY THE M FLAG,
              ;POSITION: 00X00000
              ;A REGISTER IS NOW 8 BITS WIDE
```

Figure 2-8. SEP #$20 sets only the M flag to one, making the A register 8 bits wide.

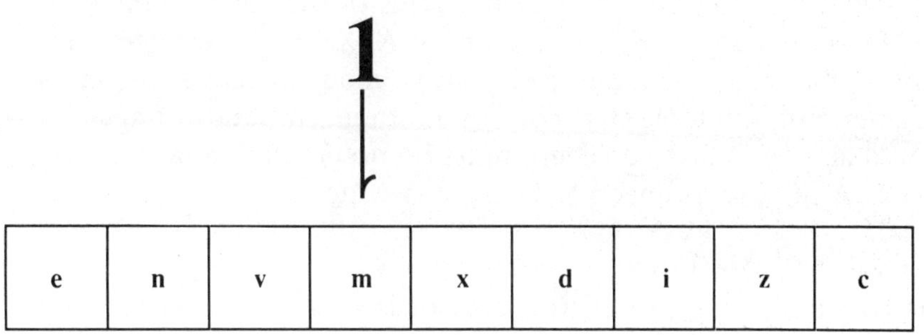

The following pair of instructions set the width of the A register to 16 bits, then set the width of the X and Y registers to 8 bits.

```
REP    #$20    ;RESET M FLAG TO 0 FOR 16 BIT A REG.
SEP    #$10    ;SET X FLAG TO 1 FOR 8 BIT Y AND X
               ;A IS NOW 16 BITS
               ;X AND Y ARE NOW 8 BITS
```

Figure 2-9. REP #$20, then SEP #$10 sets up a 16-bit A register and 8-bit Y and X registers.

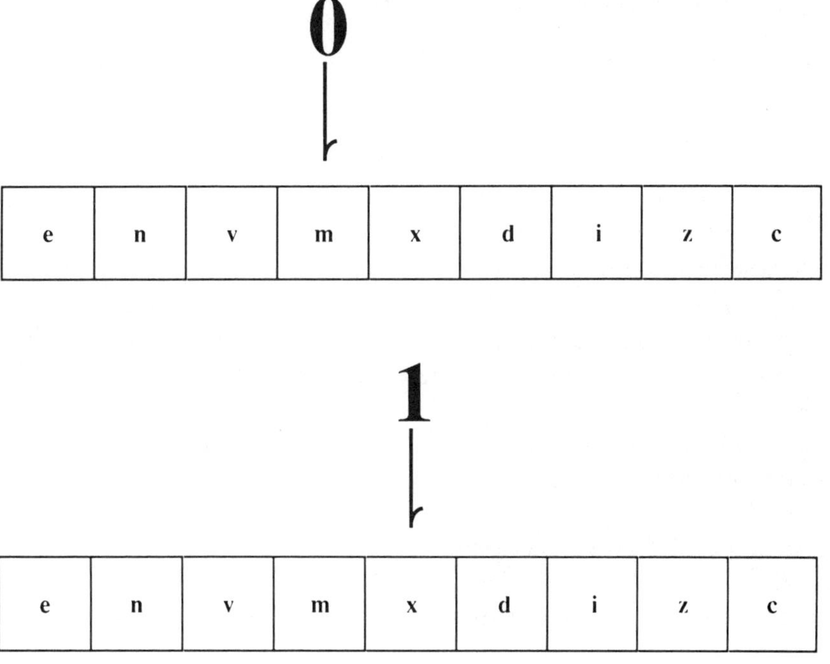

The width of these registers cannot be adjusted when 65C02 emulation is on (the E flag is set to one). The REP and SEP op codes will function and change the status of the 65C02's flags while in emulation. But, the size of the A, X, and Y registers can only be changed when the 65816 native mode is active. As far as programming the toolbox is concerned, the E, M, and X flags should all be set to zero. There must be no emulation, and all registers—A, X, and Y—need to be 16 bits wide.

A Matter of Memory

The Apple IIGS's 65816 microprocessor is capable of accessing up to 16 megabytes of memory. In the current design of the system, only half of that, or roughly 8 megabytes, can be used.

The memory locations in the Apple IIGS are not accessed contiguously. Instead, the 65816 divides the total memory up into 64K segments.

For example, consider the amount of memory potential of the 65816 as a 256-story building. Each story is a bank of 64K of RAM. The total RAM in the building is 16 megabytes. The processor uses RAM, one 64K floor at a time.

In the 65816 there are four registers which are associated with the 64K banks of memory (Table 2-1).

Table 2-1. Four Registers Associated with the 64K Banks of Memory

Register	Full Name
S	Stack Pointer
D	Direct Page Register
PBR	Program Bank Register
DBR	Data Bank Register

Using the building example, the *stack pointer (S)* and *direct page (D)* registers can only use the bottom story (the first 64K bank) of the building. The stack and direct page can be placed anywhere within the first 64K bank, but they cannot be located in another bank.

The *program bank register* determines which floor of the building contains the machine level programming instructions. This register can have its own floor all to itself—totally independent from the stack pointer and direct page registers.

The *data bank register* can also use its own floor for storing and accessing data. Again, this can be a floor separate from the stack and direct page floor, as well as separate from the program bank's floor.

Figure 2-10. 65816 DBR and PBR Registers Using Different Banks of Memory

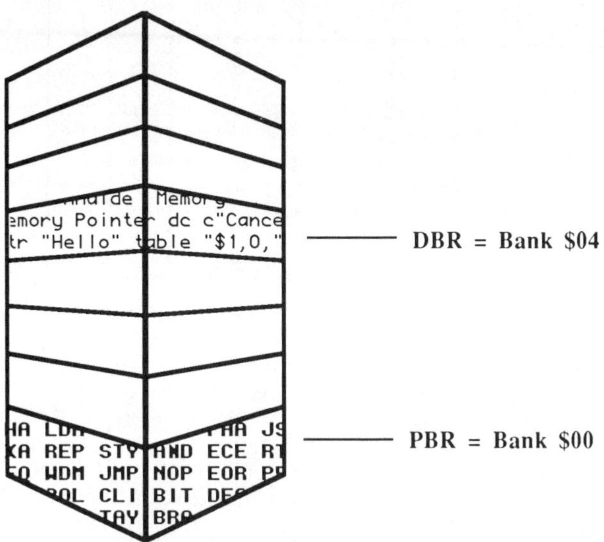

The *PBR* and *DBR* registers allow programs to use up to 128K of memory for programming instructions and data at one time. These registers can also be changed to different banks in memory, allowing as much memory as possible to be used. (When doing this, you must be very careful. Jumping from one program bank to another can have disastrous effects if not done correctly.)

The 256 banks of 64K which came with your Apple IIGS are shown in Figure 2-11.

Banks $00 and $01 are configured the same as an enhanced Apple IIe while the Apple IIGS is in emulation mode. The monitor and Applesoft BASIC are in ROM. The 80-column screen, soft switches, and all ROM entry points are the same as for the Apple IIe. This area of RAM is referred to as Mega II in some documentation. This is because it all sits on one big flat chip in your Apple IIGS. The Mega II is essentially an Apple IIe all on one computer chip.

Banks $E0 and $E1 (224 and 225 decimal) are referred to as the *shadow banks* of memory. They're mirror images of banks $00 and $01, respectively.

Figure 2-11. Layout of the 256K (Five Banks) of Memory Provided with the Base Model Apple IIGS

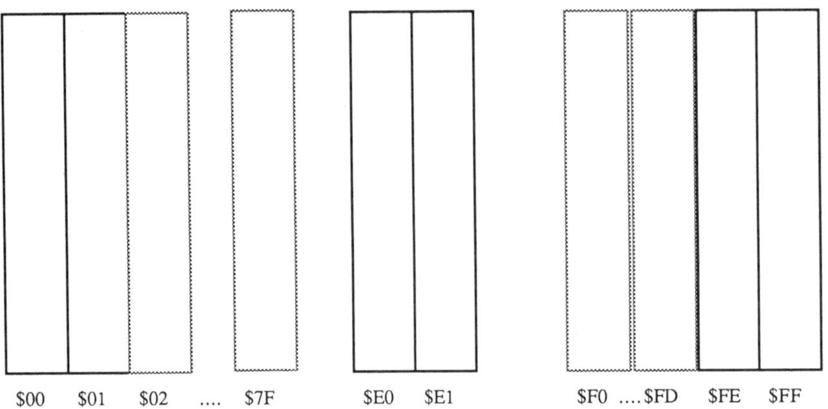

Banks $FE and $FF contain the Apple IIGS's system ROM. This is where the toolbox and all its routines are located.

Apple has supplied ample room for expansion of the IIGS. Starting with bank $02, you can add extra RAM to your computer. Each 64K chunk of RAM adds another bank. Therefore, a 1.5 megabyte RAM card adds 24 64K banks from bank $02 to bank $19. The Apple IIGS can have up to bank $7F filled with RAM for a total of 8.25 megabytes of memory.

ROM expansion starts at bank $FD and moves downward 13 banks to bank $F0. At present, nothing is available as ROM expansion. But Apple isn't short on surprises, and besides, even with a full complement of RAM there's plenty of room in the IIGS for interesting additions.

The Toolbox

The operation and use of the toolbox are discussed in the next two chapters. But, keeping in mind the title of this chapter,"Things You Should Know," here's one thing that is often assumed and rarely explained.

Quite a few of the toolbox routines are documented with the caution, "This call should not be made by an application." While this sounds a bit odd, there is a reason for it.

Out of all the many toolbox calls, the average program may contain only a handful. Even the most complex programs might wind up using only a dozen toolbox calls. Yet, Apple was very thorough in its documentation of the toolbox; it even included toolbox calls that are made internally by the IIGS. In some cases, these toolbox calls use other toolbox calls.

If you see a toolbox function that claims it should never be used by an application, it means that function is used internally by some other toolbox routine. For example, whenever you reset your IIGS by pressing Control-Reset, it calls some of these special "don't touch" functions.

In most cases, you should use another similar toolbox function. This second function will probably internally incorporate the first forbidden function.

The important thing to remember is that when the documentation says, "This call should not be made by an application," that's what it means. This book references all toolbox calls and points out which ones should never be used.

Chapter 3

Toolbox Specifics

Why a toolbox? Many programmers prefer to program a computer on the lowest, crudest level. They want absolute control over the machine.

Of course, this approach leads to extra work developing standard routines for performing

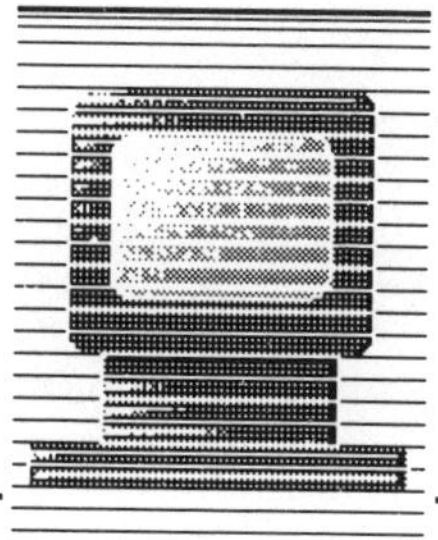

even the most simple operation. Much of the work involved in this type of approach is spent "reinventing the wheel."

The Apple IIGS toolbox is an assortment of routines and functions ready for use in a variety of programs. You should take advantage of them; that's the primary reason for having a toolbox. Many of the routines you'll need have already been written. As a programmer, all you need to do is *call* them.

This doesn't mean that everything in the Apple IIGS toolbox is the last word in coding. For example, the text tool routines in the toolbox are perhaps the best ever written for a computer, but they just aren't fast enough for some applications.

For specific, special applications, some programmers may proceed to do the forbidden: They access the machine at its lowest, most fundamental level. But for learning about the computer, and for 98 percent of the programs you'll write, everything you need is furnished in the toolbox.

Routines, Tools, Tool Sets, and Functions

The Apple IIGS toolbox contains a variety of routines, all of which make it easier to program the computer. These routines are grouped into similar sets called *tools,* or *tool sets.* Some tools are also referred to as *Managers.*

Within each tool set are the individual routines, or *functions.* For example, the QuickDraw II tool set is actually a group of drawing and graphics functions. Each function is referred to by a specific function name.

The function names are used to reference the toolbox routine. For example, QDStartup is a specific function within the Quickdraw II tool set. This can be a bit confusing since not every function incorporates the name of its tool set.

For example, the GetNewUserID function changes a programmer's User IDentification value. The routine to set this value is in the Memory Management tool set. However, GetNewUserID is in the Miscellaneous tool set. There is no way to tell where the function is located simply by looking at it's name.

A complete list of function names is provided at the end of Chapter 14. If you encounter an unknown function name, look it up there and use the cross reference to find out its tool set and function number.

Tool Set and Function Numbers

Tool sets and functions are numbered; each tool set is given a value as is each function within the tool set. These values are used to access specific toolbox routines. Tool set and function numbers are expressed in hexadecimal with the function number coming first followed by the tool set number.

For instance, tool set number $03 is the Miscellaneous tool set. Function number $0F is ReadASCIITime. This is expressed as function $0F of tool set $03:

$0F03 = ReadASCIITime, Misc Tools

Function $10 is SetVector. It looks like this:

$1003 = SetVector, Misc Tools

It's important to remember that this notation is backward from what you would expect: Function number comes first, then tool set.

Table 3-1 is a complete list of all the tools presently available in the Apple IIGS toolbox, along with a brief description of each.

Table 3-1. Toolbox Tools

Number	Name	Brief Description
$01	Tool Locator	Loads RAM-based tools from disk, locates tools into memory.
$02	Memory Manager	Assigns, deletes, and organizes blocks of memory.
$03	Miscellaneous	Contains routines which do not fit elsewhere; mouse routines.
$04	QuickDraw II	Drawing, graphics, and graphic text-related routines.
$05	Desk Manager	Controls Desk Accessories. These are found in a pull-down menu or from the Classic Desk Accessory menu (press Control-Apple-ESC).
$06	Event Manager	Used to monitor *events* such as mouse movement and key presses.
$07	Scheduler	Controls access and timing of certain desk accessories.
$08	Sound Manager	Accesses the Apple IIGS's sound capabilities.
$09	Apple Desktop Bus	Controls devices connected to the ADB, joystick, mouse, keyboard, and so forth.

$0A	SANE	(Standard Apple Numeric Environment) Controls numerous floating-point and real number arithmetic operations.
$0B	Integer Math	Contains arithmetic routines: division and multiplication, for example.
$0C	Text Tool Set	Deals with standard input/output, reading the keyboard, writing to the screen, and so forth.
$0D	Reserved	Internal use.
$0E	Window Manager	Deals with windows on the screen and the desktop.
$0F	Menu Manager	Controls pull-down menus.
$10	Control Manager	Deals with check boxes, buttons, dials, scroll bars—any "control" manipulated by the mouse.
$11	Loader	Loads applications and overlays into memory.
$12	QuickDraw Aux.	Additional, RAM-based drawing routines.
$13	Print Manager	Controls the printer, printing screens, printing text, and so forth.
$14	LineEdit	Contains basic text editing utilities; insert, delete, highlight, and so forth.
$15	Dialog Manager	Allows the creation of dialog and alert boxes.
$16	Scrap Manager	Controls cutting, pasting, copying, and the Clipboard.
$17	Standard File	Gives access to file operations using special dialog boxes.
$18	Disk Utilities	Not available.
$19	Note Synthesizer	No information.
$1A	Note Sequencer	Not available.
$1B	Font Manager	Controls the style of type used by the Apple IIGS with QuickDraw II.
$1C	List Manager	Manages a list of items in a scrollable window.

Some of these tool sets are located in the IIGS's firmware (ROM). Others are on disk and are loaded into memory (RAM) when the computer starts, or as your program requires them.

Any tool sets not already in ROM, referred to as the disk- or RAM-based tools, are put in the prefix /SYSTEM/TOOLS/ of your boot disk. From there they can be loaded into memory as they are needed. Table 3-2 indicates where each tool set is located.

Table 3-2. Tool Set Locations

Tool Set		ROM	On Disk	Filename
$01	Tool Locator	•		
$02	Memory Manager	•		
$03	Misc. Tool Set	•		
$04	QuickDraw II	•		
$05	Desk Manager	•		
$06	Event Manager	•		
$07	Scheduler	•		
$08	Sound Manager	•		
$09	Apple Desktop Bus	•		
$0A	SANE	•		
$0B	Integer Math	•		
$0C	Text Tool Set	•		
$0D	Internal Use	•		
$0E	Window Manager		•	TOOL014
$0F	Menu Manager		•	TOOL015
$10	Control Manager		•	TOOL016
$11	Loader		•	TOOL017
$12	QuickDraw II Aux.		•	TOOL018
$13	Print Manager		•	TOOL019
$14	Line Edit		•	TOOL020
$15	Dialog Manager		•	TOOL021
$16	Scrap Manager		•	TOOL022
$17	Standard File		•	TOOL023
$18	Disk Utilities		•	TOOL024
$19	Note Synthesizer		•	TOOL025
$1A	Note Sequencer		•	TOOL026
$1B	Font Manager		•	TOOL027
$1C	List Manager		•	TOOL028

Common Toolbox Functions

The first six functions are the same for every tool in the toolbox. These are referred to as the Housekeeping Routines. They are:

$01	BootInit	This call initializes or installs the tool set. It's made by the Apple IIGS at boot time so there's no need to call it from your program.
$02	StartUp	Your application makes this call to ready the tool set for use. Often, none of the other functions work until this one is called. With some tool sets there is no need to call this function.
$03	ShutDown	This call is made after your application is finished. This should be part of your program's "quit code." As with StartUp, some tool sets don't need to make this call.

$04	Version	Using this call, the major and minor release numbers of the tool set are returned. This comes in handy with future releases of the Apple IIGS as far as toolbox and program compatibility is concerned.
$05	Reset	This call is made only by the Apple IIGS when the computer is RESET (Control-Reset). This is an example of a call your application should never make.
$06	Status	This call determines whether the tool set is active or not. A tool set must be active before you can use any of its routines. Function 2 is called to start up the tool set.

The rest of the function numbers vary within each tool set.

Out of these six common functions, only four are for use by your programs: StartUp, ShutDown, Version, and Status. The other two, BootInit and Reset, are only used by the computer during boot time and when the machine is reset.

The Version function returns a two-byte value (word) containing the major and minor release numbers, and also indicates if the tool set is a final release or a Beta version. The most significant byte (MSB) indicates the major release number and the least significant byte (LSB) is the minor release. If bit 7 of the major release is set (bit 15 of the word), the release is a beta version. For example,

$0101 (binary 0000 0001 0000 0001)

indicates version 1.1.

$0301 (binary 0000 0011 0000 0001)

indicates version 3.1.

$8101 (binary 1000 0001 0000 0001)

indicates beta (pre-release) version 1.1.

The Status function returns a two-byte value (word). If the value returned is $0000, the tool set is loaded into memory and ready to go. If the value is not $0000 (typically $FFFF), the tool set has not been initialized or loaded into memory.

The Location of the Toolbox

The actual location of the toolbox in memory is ROM banks $FE and $FF. And, as mentioned earlier, other parts of the toolbox are loaded into RAM. The exact location of the toolbox is unimportant as far as programming is concerned.

Specific memory locations in the toolbox may change as the

Apple IIGS matures and grows. Therefore, the toolbox is accessed in a unique way to help keep it compatible with future releases. Though at a future date, some enterprising Apple enthusiast will probably publish a list of "secret locations" inside the toolbox memory, these locations shouldn't be used since they could change. By using the toolbox as documented here, you shouldn't have any problems. (Programmers acquainted with the Macintosh will find some of this familiar).

The toolbox is accessed through a special vector. All calls to the toolbox pass through this single gate. Accessing the toolbox is discussed in greater detail in the next chapter.

The Meaning of the Error Codes

If you've done a lot of programming, you know that it's rare to have a program run right the first time. It's possible to make mistakes when using the toolbox. When this happens, the Apple IIGS will let you know. Fortunately, in most cases it will not let you know by turning itself off, resetting, or beeping.

Errors returned from the toolbox all follow a specific pattern. They're typically a word-sized (16-bit) value. (You might have seen them displayed in hexadecimal if you've ever crashed your machine.) The first byte of the word is the tool set number. The second byte is the error number.

Tool Set—Error Number

The LineEdit Tool Set is number $14. Errors occurring in the LineEdit Tool Set would all start with $14. For example,

$14xx

The second byte of the word indicates the *error code.* These are numbered sequentially from $01 on up through $FF, or as many errors as can be produced from a certain tool set.

For example, the Text Tool Set is number $0C. Error number $08 is the disk full error. If this error occurred, the toolbox would return the following error:

$0C08

This means the error occurred in tool set $0C, the Text Tool Set, and it was error $08. Note that this is opposite from the way the toolbox is called. When you call the toolbox, the tool set is listed last. When an error is returned, the tool set is listed first.

Unlike the tool set functions, there are few common error codes. In fact only one is consistent for all toolbox calls:

$0000

This error code means no error occurred. Otherwise, the error code can be examined to determine which tool set it belongs to and which error number it is.

See Appendix E for a list of all error codes.

Chapter 4

Calling the Toolbox

This book's programs access the toolbox using machine language. Another method would be to use the C programming language. Several C examples have been included to illustrate the differences between the two languages.

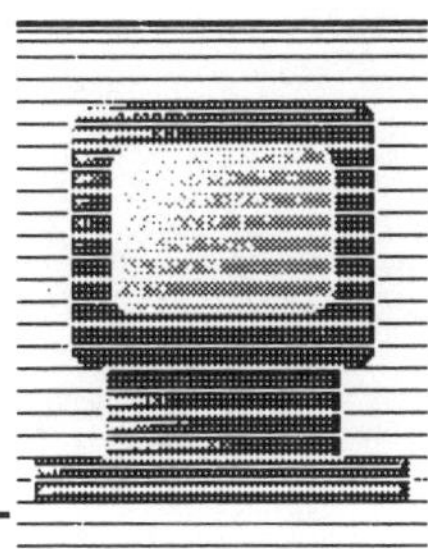

Machine language is a low-level language which controls the 65816 directly. C uses a library of subroutines which contain the 65816 instructions. The C subroutines do the same thing as the 65816 machine language, but are easier to read, maintain, and update.

Each language has its fans. C provides a quick and easy method of toolbox access. Machine language shows the details. At the writing of this book, neither language has achieved dominance in the programs written for the Apple IIGS. (Although machine language is preferred simply because the C compilers have yet to be written.) The Apple IIGS has no "official" programming language. Quite a few programs are written in machine language, with C gaining ground day by day.

This chapter shows how each programming language is used to access toolbox routines. While C is a little easier to read and understand, machine language is currently more popular. The next chapter deals with using the toolbox with other languages and the computer's Monitor program.

Machine Language

The toolbox is called, or accessed, by making a long jump to a subroutine in memory bank $E1, at location $0000. This location, or vector, is referred to as the long word address $E10000. (The most significant byte of the high order word is ignored, therefore $E10000 is the same as $00E10000.)

The 65816 instruction JSL, for Jump-Subroutine-Long, is used to pass program control to the toolbox. The operand of the JSL instruction is a memory bank and offset within that memory bank.

```
JSL    $E10000    ;CALL THE TOOLBOX
```

The vector for accessing the toolbox is in memory bank $E1, offset $0000. After executing the above JSL instruction, execution continues at memory location $E10000, the toolbox.

Every toolbox call is done this way.

Calling Individual Tools

Before the toolbox is called, the number of the tool set and function are loaded into the X register. (The tool set and function number were discussed in the last chapter.)

For example, tool $03 is the Miscellaneous tool set, function $0F is ReadASCIITime. This function returns the current time and date as a string and places it at a specified address in memory. To make this toolbox call, the following 65816 instructions are used:

```
LDX   #$0F03    ;LOAD MISC TOOL/READASCIITIME INTO X
JSL   $E10000   ;CALL THE TOOLBOX
```

The function number and tool set are loaded into the X register. All registers must be 16 bits wide and the 65816 cannot be in emulation mode when the toolbox is accessed.

After the X register is loaded, the long jump to the subroutine in bank $E1 at memory location $0000 is made.

Passing Arguments

Arguments are values sent to and received from the toolbox. They are used to communicate with the toolbox.

Information passed to and received from the toolbox is placed on the stack. Those not familiar with what a stack is and how it works should turn to a 65816 reference book. Briefly, the *stack* is a temporary storage area most commonly used to keep track of return addresses when a JSR or JSL instruction is received, but is also used in toolbox calls to send messages back and forth.

Information sent to the toolbox is pushed onto the stack.

Information returned from the toolbox is pulled from the stack.

Suppose a hypothetical toolbox routine requires you to give it a word-sized value and it returns that value, plus one. Pretend this is function $45 of the Mythical tool set, $FF.

The instructions to call the toolbox are:

```
LDX   #$45FF    ;FUNCTION $45 OF TOOL SET $FF
JSL   $E10000   ;CALL THE TOOLBOX
```

Before calling the toolbox, push the value onto the stack. After the toolbox returns execution to your routine, the result is on the stack. To access the result, pull that word from the stack.

```
        LDA    #$0001     ;LOAD A WITH THE VALUE TO SEND
        PHA               ;PUSH THE A REGISTER ON THE STACK
;                         ;NOW VALUE IS ON THE STACK, READY
;                         ;FOR THE TOOLBOX
        LDX    #$45FF     ;FUNCTION NUMBER $45 OF TOOL SET $FF
        JSL    $E10000    ;CALL THE TOOLBOX
;                         ;THE TOOLBOX HAS THE RESULT VALUE
;                         ;ON THE STACK
        PLA               ;PULL THE RESULT FROM THE STACK
```

The A register now contains $0002—the original value plus one.

The toolbox took the argument—the value $0001—from the stack, performed whatever operations are required to add one to that value, then placed the result back on the stack. The value is then retrieved into the A register with the PLA instruction.

Another way to push a value to the stack is with the *PEA (Push Effect Address).* This instruction simply pushes the word value listed after it on the stack. There's no need to specify a # sign; the value after the PEA instruction, and not the memory location, is pushed to the stack.

Using PEA, the above toolbox call can be rewritten as

```
        PEA    #$0001     ;PUSH 1 TO THE STACK
        LDX    #$45FF     ;FUNCTION NUMBER $45 OF TOOL SET $FF
        JSL    $E10000    ;CALL THE TOOLBOX
        PLA               ;PULL THE RESULT FROM THE STACK
```

If function $45 of tool set $FF existed it would be documented as:

Function: $45FF
Name: AddOne
Adds one to the value sent to the toolbox.
Push: Value (W)
Pull: Result Value (W)
Errors: none
Comments: This is an example.

AddOne is the name of function $45 in Mythical tool set $FF. This shows that a word value is pushed on the stack before the call is made. After the call, a word value is pulled from the stack. No errors are possible.

Sending, But Not Receiving

Some functions require information, but do not return it. For example, hypothetical function $1D of tool set $FF prints a number of Zs on the screen. To tell it how many Zs to print, you push that value on the stack.

```
LDA   #$0FA0   ;LOAD A TO PRINT 4,000 Z'S
PHA            ;PUSH IT ON THE STACK
LDX   #$1DFF   ;PRINT Z'S FUNCTION AND TOOL SET
JSL   $E10000  ;CALL THE TOOLBOX—DO IT!
```

This routine prints the number of Zs specified. Nothing is returned on the stack.

Quite a few toolbox functions require input on the stack, but do not return values. This means there's nothing to pull from the stack after the call. As with the above routine, all the function requires is a value. After control returns to your program, that number of Zs are printed on the screen. The stack and stack pointer will be the same as before the call.

This toolbox call would appear as follows in the index.

Function: $1DFF
Name: PrintZs
Prints a number of Zs on the screen.
Push: Count (W)
Pull: nothing
Errors: none
Comments: Count is any value up to $FFFF.

The name of function $1D in tool set $FF is PrintZs. A word-sized value representing the number of Zs to print is pushed onto the stack. Nothing is pulled from the stack after the call, and no errors are possible.

Result Space

Some routines return information on the stack, but don't require any for input. When this happens, you must create room on the stack by pushing *result space* on the stack. Result space consists of empty, or *worthless* values. It is into these positions that the toolbox places the results it returns. (The result space acts as a place holder on the stack.)

Pushing dummy values for result space onto the stack can be

done with one of two methods.

```
PHA                 ;PUSH CONTENTS OF THE ACCUMULATOR
```

This pushes whatever value is in the accumulator on the stack. Because all we need to do is create space on the stack, the contents of the A register are unimportant.

Or

```
PEA    $0000        ;PUSH THE VALUE $0000 ON THE STACK
```

The PEA instruction pushes the word-sized value specified onto the stack. Because $0000 is specified, it is pushed onto the stack. Actually, any value would work. What's important is that there is now a place on the stack for the function to return a value.

Function $06 of tool set $FF returns the status of tool set $FF. This is one of the Housekeeping functions common to all tool sets, even the Mythical tool set. To make room for the word-sized status, a word-sized result space needs to be pushed onto the stack before the call.

```
PEA    $0000        ;PUSH EMPTY RESULT SPACE
LDX    #$06FF       ;GET THE STATUS OF TOOL SET $FF
JSL    $E10000      ;CALL THE TOOLBOX
PLA                 ;PULL THE STATUS, $0000 = ACTIVE
```

After the toolbox is called, the status of the tool set is on the stack. This value is pulled into the A register for examination. The PEA instruction could be replaced by

```
PHA                 ;PUSH WHATEVER'S IN THE A REGISTER
```

or any other push instruction—just as long as a word-sized result space is pushed to the stack. It should also be pointed out, for the byte-conscious among you, that PHA takes only one byte of code where PEA takes three. When you're just pushing dead air onto the stack, it makes sense to use PHA instead of PEA. This function would appear as follows in the index:

Function: $06FF
Name: MythStatus
Returns the status of the Mythical tool set.
Push: Result Space (W)
Pull: Status (W)
Errors: none
Comments: If the status is $0000, the tool set is active.

Function $06 of the Mythical tool set returns its status. A word of result space is pushed, and after the call, the status is pulled. If the status is any value other than $0000, the Mythical tool set is not active.

Long Result Space

When the toolbox returns a long word (two word) value, then a long word result space needs to be pushed. For example, suppose function $0D of the Mythical tool set returns a long word indicating if the computer is happy. The following routine pushes a long word result space onto the stack. It then pulls that result from the stack and stores it in the memory location MOOD.

```
PEA   $0000     ;PUSH A LONG RESULT SPACE
PEA   $0000     ;ONTO THE STACK
LDX   #$0DFF    ;GET THE COMPUTER'S MOOD FUNCTION
JSL   $E10000   ;CALL THE TOOLBOX
PLA             ;PULL THE LOW ORDER WORD
STA   MOOD      ;STORE IT AT THE MOOD LOCATION
PLA             ;PULL THE HIGH ORDER WORD
STA   MOOD+2    ;STORE IT AT THE MOOD PLUS 2
```

Note that the long word is pulled low order word first. This is followed by the high order word. If this function were returning a memory location, the offset would be pulled first, followed by the bank number.

Figure 4-1. Pulling a Long Word from the Stack

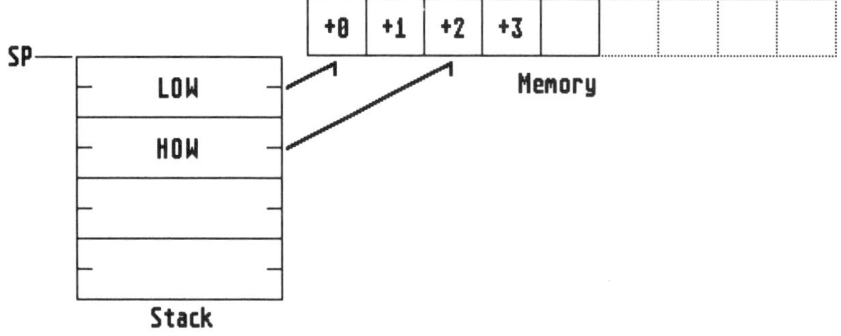

Keep in mind your Apple IIGS is a 16-bit computer and the MOOD value is two words, or four bytes, long. MOOD + 2 is used to reference the high order word of a long word stored at the address MOOD.

This is the opposite of how long words are pushed onto the stack; the high order word is pushed first, followed by the low order word. (Dealing with long word values is covered extensively in Chapter 10.)

Figure 4-2. Pushing a Long Word to the Stack

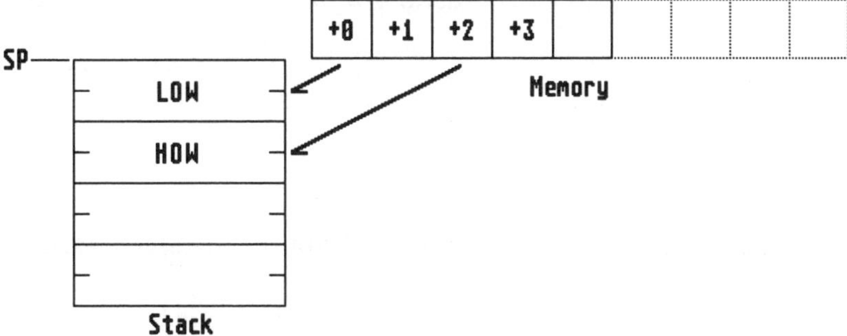

Function: $0DFF
Name: MythMood
Returns a long word indicating the computer's mood.
Push: Result Space (L)
Pull: Mood value (L)
Errors: none
Comments: The value $AAA00EEE is the happiest the computer gets.

A Real Example

The ReadASCIITime function in the Miscellaneous tool set returns the current date and time as a string of characters. It places this string at a specific location in memory. ReadASCIITime is function $0F of the Miscellaneous tool set, $03.

From the toolbox index, this function looks like

Function: $0F03
Name: ReadASCIITime
Reads a time string into a 20-character buffer.
Push: Buffer Address (L)
Pull: nothing
Errors: none
Comments: Text returned has the high bit set.

To call this function, the toolbox needs to know the address of a memory buffer where the time string will be stored. This information is sent to the toolbox by pushing a long word (L) onto the stack.

The following two-word values can be used to compose the long word value needed by ReadASCIITime.

$00E0 Store the string in bank E0
$0400 At memory location $400 (the text screen)

This toolbox call does not return anything on the stack, so after the call is done nothing needs to be pulled.

To make the ReadASCIITime call using 65816 machine language, the following routine could be used.

```
        PEA     $00E0       ;PUSH BANK NUMBER FOR CALL (BANK E0)
        PEA     $0400       ;PUSH MEMORY LOCATION (400 HEX)
;                           ;(THAT'S A LONG WORD)
        LDX     #$0F03      ;MISC TOOL/READASCIITIME INTO X
        JSL     $E10000     ;CALL THE TOOLBOX
```

That gets the job done. The 20 bytes at memory location $0400 in RAM bank $E0 will contain the current date and time (Figure 4-3).

Figure 4-3. Memory Bytes with Time Value

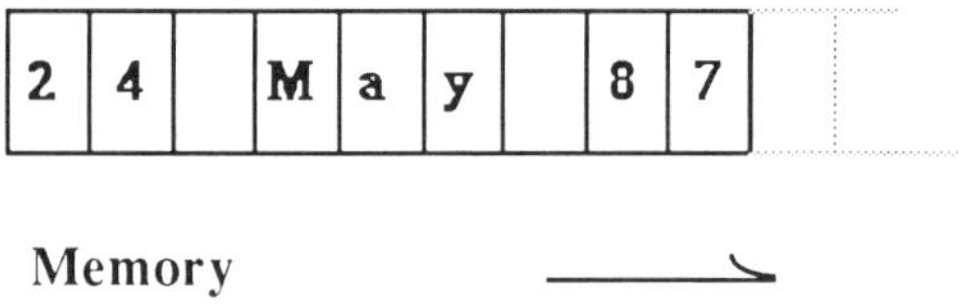

2	4		M	a	y		8	7		

Memory ———→

Before making this toolbox call, it might be a good idea to establish the width of the X register as 16 bits, as well as insure that the 65816 is not in emulation mode. This depends on the assembler and the computer's environment (the circumstances under which the program was run).

If the *APW* or *ORCA/M* assembler is used, there's no need to establish the size of the registers and turn off emulation; all this is done by *APW*. However, if the program is being run under less certain circumstances, the following instructions should be added to the program (described earlier).

```
        CLC              ;CLEAR CARRY FLAG, RESET IT TO 0
        XCE              ;EXCHANGE CARRY AND EMULATION FLAG
                         ;THE E FLAG IS 0 FOR NATIVE MODE
        REP    #$30      ;TURN ON ALL 16 BITS REGISTERS
;                        ;(RESET M AND X FLAGS TO 0)
```

One more instruction needs to be added: *a return from this subroutine to the calling program.* For now, the following instruction can be used:

```
        RTS              ;RETURN FROM THIS ROUTINE TO CALLER
```

In the *APW* environment, the RTL (ReTurn from subroutine Long) is used. This is just an *APW* convention, and when using *APW* to assemble brief routines such as this, RTL is the best way of doing things.

```
        RTL              ;RETURN TO APW
```

So the whole thing is

```
        CLC              ;CLEAR CARRY FLAG, RESET IT TO 0
        XCE              ;EXCHANGE CARRY AND EMULATION FLAG
;                        ;THE E FLAG IS 0 FOR NATIVE MODE
        REP    #$30      ;TURN ON ALL 16 BITS REGISTERS
                         ;(RESET M AND X FLAGS TO 0)
        PEA    $00E0     ;PUSH BANK NUMBER FOR CALL (BANK E0)
        PEA    $0400     ;PUSH MEMORY LOCATION (400 HEX)
        LDX    #$0F03    ;MISC TOOL/READASCIITIME INTO X
        JSL    $E10000   ;CALL THE TOOLBOX
        RTS              ;RETURN FROM THIS ROUTINE TO CALLER
```

This routine can now be assembled and run under any Apple IIGS environment. It can even be typed into the system's Monitor and run from there. (This is discussed in detail in the next chapter.)

If written with *APW*, the routine is

```
        KEEP   TIMEDATE  ;CREATE AN EXECUTABLE FILE, PROG1
MAIN    START            ;START THE PROGRAM HERE
        PEA    $00E0     ;PUSH BANK NUMBER FOR CALL (BANK E0)
        PEA    $0400     ;PUSH MEMORY LOCATION (400 HEX)
        LDX    #$0F03    ;MISC TOOL/READASCIITIME INTO X
        JSL    $E10000   ;CALL THE TOOLBOX
        RTL              ;RETURN TO APW
        END              ;ASSEMBLER END DIRECTIVE
```

Under *APW*, if assembled and linked, the above code produces an executable program, TIMEDATE. Refer to your *APW* manual if you need additional information.

After either routine is assembled and run, it places the current date and time on the top line of the 40-column display screen.

Errors

After a toolbox call is made, an error code is returned in the A register. If the A register contains a zero, there was no error. Also, if the C (carry) flag in the status register is reset (equals zero) no error occurred. If the C flag is set to one after making a toolbox call, then the A register contains a 16-bit error code.

For example, the following code is used after a toolbox call to determine if there was an error.

```
...              ;TOOLBOX CALL PREPARATIONS
JSL    $E10000   ;CALL THE TOOLBOX
BCS    OOPS      ;BRANCH CARRY SET TO OOPS ROUTINE
...              ;NO ERROR—CODE CONTINUES HERE
```

The above routine has the *BCS (Branch if Carry flag Set)* instruction following the JSL toolbox call. If the carry flag is set, meaning an error has occurred, execution branches to the routine labeled OOPS.

Because 65816 machine language allows many variations on a theme, the following code also works for error detection.

```
...              ;TOOLBOX CALL PREPARATIONS
JSL    $E10000   ;CALL THE TOOLBOX
BCC    OKAY      ;BRANCH CARRY CLEAR TO OKAY ROUTINE
...              ;ERROR ROUTINE, ERROR IS IN A REG.
```

This routine uses the *BCC (Branch if Carry Clear)* instruction. If the carry flag is clear, meaning no error, execution branches to the OKAY routine. If the carry flag is set, execution continues with the instruction after BCC. The program could then evaluate the error code in the A register and take action based on the result.

A complete study of error handling routines is offered in Chapter 11.

One final, important note: Don't perform any error testing unless the toolbox call indicates a possibility of an error.

Some toolbox calls alter the value of the A register and may return with the carry flag set. Even so, an error may not have occurred. The only way to be certain is to use the toolbox reference. If the function shows that no errors are possible, then don't test for them.

Alterations

The toolbox does not leave everything unscathed upon return. In fact, you can pretty much guarantee the toolbox will obliterate any values in any register after it returns. Unless you've extensively debugged your toolbox calls and are absolutely positive they don't alter the contents of the 65816's registers, assume nothing.

As a general summary, the following things will happen to the 65816, its registers and flags, after a toolbox call is made. (Tables 4-1 and 4-2.)

Table 4-1. Status Register Flags:

Flag	Name	Effect of Call
E	Emulation	Not changed (still zero)
N	Negative	Set or reset according to the routine
V	Overflow	Set or reset according to the routine
M	Accumulator width	Not changed (still zero)
X	Index width	Not changed (still zero)
D	Decimal	Reset (is zero on return)
I	Interrupt	Not changed
Z	Zero	Set or reset according to the routine
C	Carry	Set or reset according to the routine

Table 4-2. 65816 Registers

Register	Name	Effect of Call
A	Accumulator	Equal to $0000 or error code (is changed)
DBR	Data bank	Not changed
X	X index	Changed according to the routine
Y	Y index	Changed according to the routine
D	Direct page	Not changed
S	Stack pointer	Varies with the routine
PBR	Program bank	Not changed
PC	Program counter	Address of JSL $E10000 call plus 3 (the next instruction)

The X and Y registers may or may not be changed by the toolbox call. The X register contains the function and tool set number and its value is only occasionally preserved. Of all the toolbox calls tested for this book, 50 percent altered the contents of the Y register. Because there is no hard information on when this happens, or any guarantee that future versions of the toolbox may change the effect on the X and Y registers, it's wise to assume they will be altered for each call.

If the value returned in the A register does not equal $0000, and the C flag is set, an error has occurred. The error number is in the A register. Remember from the previous section that this only holds true if the toolbox function is capable of producing an error. Refer to the reference for which functions can produce errors.

The stack pointer may or may not be changed according to the routine. Some routines require a value be pulled from the stack to even things up again. These values should be pulled and stored before any further processing is done.

Chapter 5

Converting to Other Language Formats

Machine language has its drawbacks. It is hard to update, tedious to debug, and the time required to produce workable code is much longer than other languages. However, a lot of Apple's own documentation

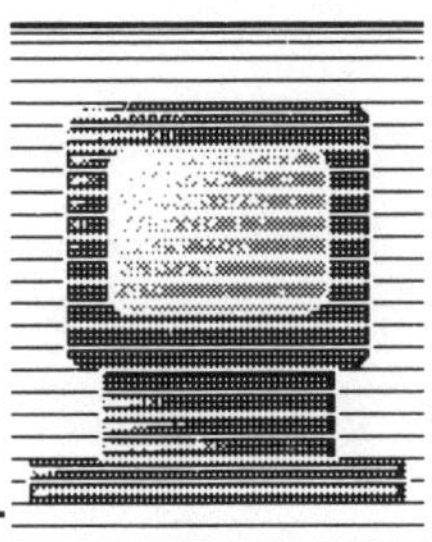

uses machine language. So to be compatible, this book uses machine language to some extent.

The C language is the language of choice among developers, but it has drawbacks as well. C is a midlevel language which uses a few shortcuts to access machine language. These shortcuts cut the programmer off from the mechanics of the toolbox.

There are several alternative ways of programming the toolbox without using machine language or C. One way is using the BASIC interpreter built into the Apple IIGS's ROM. Another way is using the Apple IIGS's monitor program. The methods for doing this are discussed in this chapter.

BASIC Language Formats

The BASIC computer language is the most popular microcomputer language. When the Apple II computer came out, BASIC was one of the only pieces of software available. Using it, Apple enthusiasts wrote thousands of programs enabling the Apple computer to do things previously unheard of.

BASIC, which stands for the Beginner's All-purpose Symbolic Instruction Code, is a simple and easy language to learn and use. However, it just doesn't pack the power needed to access the toolbox. If anyone is serious about using the toolbox, they should not consider programming it with BASIC.

For example, each toolbox routine would need to be placed into memory either by POKEing it (individually creating the routine in memory, byte by byte), or by BLOADing a prewritten routine from disk into memory. Either way, accessing the toolbox via BASIC would be cumbersome and time-consuming—especially for a high-level language.

For example, to POKE a routine into memory, you must first create it using an assembler. From the assembler's object code, the routine must be taken apart byte by byte. Each of these bytes must be translated into a decimal value, then POKEd into a memory location, and finally, CALLed from BASIC. It's a lot of work.

The following is a BASIC program which uses a machine language example from the last chapter to display the current date and time on the screen.

```
10  HOME
20  PRINT CHR$ (21)
30  FOR N = 1 TO 20
40  READ V
50  POKE 767 + N,V
60  NEXT N
70  CALL 768
80  VTAB 2
90  END
100 DATA 24,251,194,48,244,0,0
110 DATA 244,0,4,162,3,15,34,0
120 DATA 0,225,56,251,96
```

The program first clears the screen in line 10, then sets the Apple IIGS to 40-column mode with the PRINT CHR$(21) instruction in line 20.

Next, the machine language code is read from the DATA statements in lines 100 to 120 and POKEd into memory locations 768 ($300) through 788 (the loop between lines 30 and 60).

Finally, the routine is executed by the CALL 768 instruction in line 70. Line 80 moves the cursor to line 3 and line 90 ENDs the program.

The values POKEd into memory location 768 come from the following source code. The values are listed on the left side of the page next to their hex memory locations.

```
0300  18              CLC             ;CLEAR CARRY FLAG
0301  FB              XCE             ;EXCHANGE CARRY/EMULATION
0302  C2  30          REP  #$30       ;ALL 16 BITS REGISTERS
0304  F4  00  00      PEA  $0000      ;BANK NUMBER (BANK 0)
0307  F4  00  04      PEA  $0400      ;MEMORY LOCATION
030A  A2  03  0F      LDX  #$0F03     ;READASCIITIME
030D  22  00  00  E1  JSL  $E10000    ;CALL TOOLBOX
0311  38              SEC             ;SET CARRY FLAG
0312  FB              XCE             ;TURNING EMULATION FOR
0313  60              RTS             ;RETURN TO BASIC
```

Because Applesoft BASIC operates in 65816 emulation mode, the processor must be directed to use native mode (the CLC and XCE instructions). The registers must be set to 16 bits (the REP

#$30 instruction) before calling the toolbox.

When the toolbox call is finished, emulation mode needs to be reset. This is done with the SEC and XCE instructions.

The BASIC program received its DATA statement values from the hex numbers in the above object listing. Each hex value was converted into its decimal equivalent, then placed into the DATA statements.

All in all, it's rather messy but it can be done. For simple toolbox calls such as this, POKEing a routine into memory with BASIC is an easy way to access the toolbox. However, for complex programs, coding in C or machine language is recommended.

Tips on Assembler Macros

Macro is short for *macroinstruction.* It refers to a single programming instruction which represents a series of other instructions. All the same instructions are executed simply by using, or invoking, the macro statement.

An assembler macro is a common set of programming instructions, or *op-codes.* Much Apple IIGS machine language source code makes extensive use of macros. For example,

```
PUSHLONG ADDRESS
_READASCIITIME
```

Believe it or not, that's machine language.

Because one of the jobs of this book is to teach the toolbox using machine language, macros as shown above are not used. While they are handy and make debugging easier, they're not a good visual teaching aid. This does not mean that their use is discouraged.

Programmers use assembler macros to replace redundancies which occur in programming. Or, as in the previous example, as a form of simple notation. For example, the following statements define the macro SetNative (using the *APW* assembler):

```
       MACRO                  ;START THE MACRO DEFINITION
&LAB   SETNATIVE              ;MACRO NAME FOLLOWS MACRO STATEMENT
&LAB   CLC                    ;CLEAR CARRY FLAG
       XCE                    ;RESET E FLAG TO 0, NATIVE MODE
       REP        #$30        ;RESET M & X FLAGS, 16 BIT REGS
       MEND                   ;END OF MACRO
```

The macro contains three machine language instructions.

```
CLC                 ;CLEAR CARRY FLAG
XCE                 ;RESET E FLAG TO 0, NATIVE MODE
REP       #$30      ;RESET M & X FLAGS, 16 BIT REGS
```

Recalling from Chapter 2, these instructions set the 65816 microprocessor to its native 16-bit mode. Now, each time the macro SetNative is mentioned in a program listing, the assembler replaces it with the above machine language instructions. For example,

```
          ...       ;START OF YOUR PROGRAM
          ...       ;INTERESTING CODE PROBABLY GOES HERE
          SETNATIVE ;INSERT MACRO INSTRUCTIONS HERE
          ...       ;THE REST OF YOUR PROGRAM
```

The assembler would expand the macro instructions at the time of assembly to the following:

```
     ...                      ;START OF YOUR PROGRAM
     ...                      ;INTERESTING CODE PROBABLY GOES HERE
     SETNATIVE                ;INSERT MACRO INSTRUCTIONS HERE
+    CLC
+    XCE
+    REP         #$30
     ...                      ;THE REST OF YOUR PROGRAM
```

Note that using a macro does not condense your code, nor will it make the program run any faster. It's simply a handy way of abbreviating commonly used instructions.

The macro example below calls the toolbox. It uses a variable, or symbolic parameter. This adds versatility to the macro.

```
     MACRO                    ;START THE MACRO DEFINITION
&LAB TOOLCALL  &TOOL          ;THIS MACRO IS CALLED TOOLCALL
&LAB LDX       &TOOL          ;LOAD X WITH SYMB. PARA. &TOOL
     JSL       $E10000        ;CALL THE TOOLBOX
     MEND                     ;END OF MACRO
```

This macro, ToolCall, uses the symbolic parameter &Tool. This parameter is used in the LDX instruction before a jump is made to the toolbox. In practice, it would be used as follows:

```
     ...                      ;START OF YOUR PROGRAM
     TOOLCALL  #$200C         ;CALL TOOL SET $0C, FUNCTION $20
     ...                      ;THE REST OF YOUR PROGRAM
```

The assembler expands the above macro into the following:

```
        ...                          ;START OF YOUR PROGRAM
        TOOLCALL     #$200C          ;TOOL SET $0C, FUNCTION $20
+       LDX          #$200C
+       JSL          $E10000
        ...                          ;THE REST OF YOUR PROGRAM
```

Because every toolbox call is done the same way, this macro saves typing. To make a toolbox call using the ToolCall macro, all you need to know is the tool set and function number. The assembler will expand the ToolCall macro into the proper instructions for you.

Most often you'll see the tool calls used as follows:

```
_NEWMENU
```

These macros incorporate the name of the tool function they execute. Apple is guilty of doing this in most of its own documentation. However, it is consistent by prefixing all toolbox macros with an underscore, _.

The above macro expands to

```
       MACRO
&LAB   _NEWMENU
&LAB   LDX        #$2D0F     ;CREATE A NEW MENU ON THE MENU BAR
       JSL        $E10000    ;CALL THE TOOLBOX
       MEND
```

Because quite a few programmers, and book authors, have descended to this level of accessing the toolbox, this book has a complete list of all toolbox functions at the end of the toolbox reference. If you happen upon a program or reference book which contains a series of toolbox call macros, refer to the reference.

Two other types of macros are popular with toolbox programmers:

```
PUSHWORD
```

and

```
PUSHLONG
```

These macros simply push a word or long word value onto the stack. The macros themselves are quite complex. Therefore, it's recommended you use the methods for pushing words and long words onto the stack as described in this book before you venture off into macroland. Once you feel comfortable with the concepts of pushing words and long words onto the stack, then you should try macros.

A Final Macro Note

Each assembler implements macros differently. Most assemblers allow you to include the macros along with the rest of the source code. For example, you could create and list all your macros at the start of your source listing. Other assemblers allow macros to be listed in a separate file. Refer to your own assembler for additional information.

Tips on the C Language

The C programming language is currently one of the most popular languages among serious software developers. With the advent of the 16-bit Apple IIGS, C is a practical language choice for Apple programmers. One of C's greatest assets is that it combines the attributes of a high-level programming language with the power and flexibility of machine language.

In fact, when C falls short of providing a necessary function, programmers can write machine language instructions into their C language programs.

The *Apple Programmer's Workshop* for the C language (*APW C*), allows you to create C programs for your computer with complete access to the entire toolbox. This, when coupled with the high-level language "look and feel," and C's ability to use machine language instructions when necessary, provides a powerful tool for the programmer.

Making a toolbox call from C is easy because all the information required to perform a function resides in a C *library.* A library is collection of subroutines, sometimes called *procedures* or *functions,* which can be accessed by the programmer. For example, to call the Miscellaneous tool set's ReadASCIITime function from C, the following statement is used:

```
ReadASCIITime(Address);
```

Address is an input parameter which is required in order to make the function call. It points to a location in memory where the ReadASCIITime function will place a 20-character string of time and date information.

The *APW C* compiler translates the ReadASCIITime( ) function into a series of machine language instructions for use by the *APW* assembler. It's even possible that the C compiler might convert ReadASCIITime(Address) into the following machine language statements:

```
PUSHLONG ADDRESS
_READASCIITIME
```

These lines should look familiar. When the assembler reads these two macro calls, it expands them into the appropriate assembler opcodes as discussed in the previous section. Here the correspondence between C and machine language (especially under *APW C*) becomes apparent.

Not so obvious are the following bits of information.

Some of the standard housekeeping functions, such as MTStartUp, do not need to be called by a C program. Your program should not use the first six functions of a tool set, except for the Status and Version calls, unless otherwise specified.

The tradeoff to all of this automation is that a C program must include the following lines before any toolbox calls are made:

```
#INCLUDE  <TYPES.H>
#INCLUDE  <MISCTOOL.H>
```

The first line instructs the C compiler to insert an *include* file called *types.h* into the compilation at that point in the source file. This file contains definitions for certain C data types that are used by other include files.

The second line is shown as an example and is not required by a C program unless calls to the Miscellaneous tool set are made. This is the law for all toolbox calls your program might include. For example, if your C program uses the PaintOval( ) function, it would require the following C compiler directive:

```
#INCLUDE <QUICKDRAW.H>
```

This is because PaintOval( ) is a function of the QuickDraw II tool set; the quickdraw.h include file needs to be added to your C source code.

The following is an example illustrated earlier in this chapter using BASIC. This C code displays the date and time on the screen, but from the *APW C* shell and not BASIC.

```
#INCLUDE  <TYPES.H>                  /* NECESSARY HEADER FILE */
#INCLUDE  <MISCTOOL.H>               /* USING THE MISCELLANEOUS TOOL
                                     SET */

#DEFINE   BUFFER    0X000413         /* SCREEN LOCATION ADDRESS */
MAIN()
{
          ReadASCIITime(BUFFER);     /* CALL READASCIITIME*/
          EXIT(0);                   /* AND RETURN TO APW */
}
```

This source code would be saved on disk as TIME.C. The extended file type under *APW* should be CC and the file type should be SRC. (These are all *APW* conventions. Other C compilers will differ.)

To make an executable program, type in the following:

```
RUN TIME.C KEEP=TIME
```

This compiles, links, and executes the file. What's created is a 17-block file named TIME which displays the time in the upper right corner of your screen. (The reason the file is so big is that the entire *misctool* library is loaded as part of the code.)

To fully describe C's interaction with the toolbox would fill another book. The high-level tool calls from C avoid the important details. They provide a buffer between the inner workings of the toolbox and the user, masking the procedures. In order to clarify the Apple IIGS toolbox, the use of C programming examples in this book are few and far between.

Accessing the Toolbox from the Monitor

The monitor is a low-level interface between the user and the computer. It contains routines that display (or *dump*) memory, alter memory contents, and execute and debug programs. The monitor also contains a miniassembler program for writing and testing quick routines.

The Apple IIGS monitor offers a way to access the toolbox while in the monitor. This method allows arguments to be pushed and pulled from the stack, and it allows the function and tool set number to be specified all on one line.

This is not a practical way to access the toolbox, but it's an excellent way to experiment with the various toolbox calls one at a time. Many of the toolbox calls illustrated in this book can quickly be demonstrated using the monitor and the method described below.

There are a number of ways to get to the monitor. From Applesoft BASIC (the BASIC.SYSTEM file on your system disk), type

```
]call −151
```

From the Apple Programmer's Workshop (APW), the monitor can be accessed from DEBUG. At the APW prompt, type

```
#DEBUG
```

Then from Debug's prompt type

```
:mon
```

The monitor's prompt is an asterisk, *. To set the screen to 80 columns, press Esc and then the 8 key. (Or to set the screen to a 40-column width, press Esc followed by the 4 key.)

The general format for calling the toolbox from the monitor is

```
*\TO-STACK FROM-STACK VALUES... FUNCTION TOOL SET\U
```

\	Identifies the following numbers for use as a toolbox call.
to-stack	The number of bytes pushed onto the stack. If six bytes (three words, or one word and a long word) are pushed, the hex number $06 is listed.
from-stack	The number of bytes pulled from the stack. If two bytes (a word) are pulled, the hex number $02 is listed.
values...	The bytes pushed to the stack. Words and long words are listed in MSB/LSB order and each byte of the word or long word is separated by a space. (See below.)
function	The function number of the tool set. It's listed as a single hex byte, followed by a space.
tool set	The number of the tool set, also listed as a single hex byte.
\u	Immediately follows the tool set value; *u* is the monitor's tool locator function.

All values are listed as hexadecimal bytes separated by spaces. And contrary to the way values are stored in memory (with the least significant byte coming first), here the words and long words are just as you would expect. For example, 00 00 20 00 is the long word $00002000, indicating memory location $2000 in bank $00.

Other than that oddity, the tool locator is a great way to test those toolbox routines for which you are uncertain. For example, the following routine returns the version number of the Text tool set:

```
\02 02 00 00 04 0C\U
```

The first value, 02 is the number of bytes pushed on the stack. In this case, a word is pushed on the stack which allows space for the version number to be returned.

The second value is also 02 because two bytes (a word) are pulled from the stack.

This is followed by 00 00 which is just space for the result. And finally, the function number 04 and the tool set 0C.

If expressed in machine language, the tool call would look like this:

```
PEA   $0000     ;ALLOW SPACE FOR THE RESULT
LDX   #$040C    ;TOOL SET AND FUNCTION NUMBER
JSL   $E10000   ;TOOLBOX CALL
```

After execution, the result (the version number of the Text tool set) would now be on the stack. (It can be retrieved using the PLA opcode in machine language.) When using the monitor, it displays the values found on the stack to the screen.

```
\02 02 00 00 04 0C\U
TOOL ERROR-> 0000
02 01
```

The version number is 1.2. The value $0102 was pulled from the stack and displayed on the screen. Byte values are listed LSB, MSB—the least significant byte is pulled from the stack and displayed first. Therefore "02 01" is the word value $0102.

TOOL ERROR-> indicates any error which might have occurred. $0000 means no error. Two common errors which may occur at this point are $0002 or $0001: $0002 means the tool is not loaded into memory or has not been initialized; $0001 indicates an internal error with the call—either the values on the stack are wrong or an incorrect number of values was passed.

As mentioned before, values returned from the toolbox are pulled from the stack in the order they appear, from left to right. For example,

```
TOOL ERROR-> 0000
34 12
```

is actually the word value $1234. The LSB, $34, is pulled first, followed by the MSB, $12.

For practice, enter the monitor. Type CALL-151 at the BASIC prompt, or *mon* from *APW*'s DEBUG program.

The following routine calls the Integer Math tool set, $0B, Function $2A. This function, called HexIt, takes a word value and returns it as a four-byte hexadecimal ASCII string. So the value $013E is returned on the stack as the four characters 013E.

The HexIt call pushes two values to the stack. First, a long word allowing space for the four characters returned is pushed. The next number pushed is the value to be converted to ASCII. The function returns a long word which is actually the four ASCII characters in sequence.

Function:	$2A0B
Name:	HexIt
	Returns ASCII string representing 16-bit integer.
Push:	Result Space (L); Integer Value (W)
Pull:	String (L)
Errors:	none
Comments:	The String actually contains the ASCII characters starting with the LSB of the low-order word.

Using the monitor, an example of this call would appear as follows:

```
\06 04 00 00 00 00 12 34 2A 0B\U
```

06	Push six bytes on the stack.
04	Pull four bytes from the stack.
00 00 00 00	A long word (four bytes) allowing space for the result.
12 34	The word value to convert ($1234).
2A	The tool function, HexIt.
0B	The tool set, Integer Math.

After pressing RETURN, the following is displayed:

```
TOOL ERROR-> 0000
31 32 33 34
```

31, 32, 33, and 34 are the hex values for the characters 1, 2, 3, and 4. The actual long word pulled from the stack is

$34333231

or the two word values

$3433 $3231

It's important to remember that the monitor displays the bytes as they are pulled from the stack, which is the opposite of the way the values would appear in a machine language program.

The monitor can be an interesting tool for debugging and testing toolbox routines. For real applications, however, it is quite limited.

Chapter 6

Elementary Toolbox Examples

This chapter will feature some quick and easy toolbox routines. These sample programs are designed to get your feet wet and to get you in the mood for programming. They do not represent the actual way many

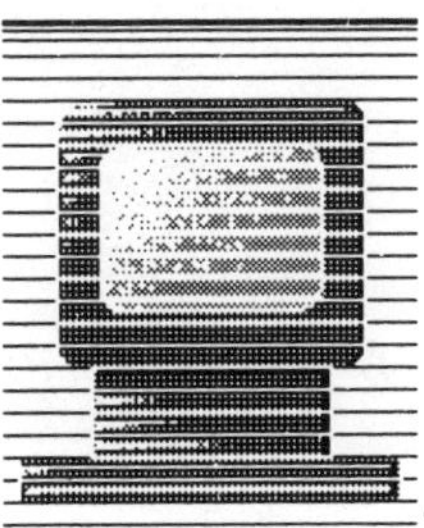

toolbox calls are made. In fact, these routines make some assumptions many applications should never make, but they do provide some insights into the operation of the toolbox and introduce some common concepts. The next part of this book gives a more detailed picture of writing toolbox applications.

The assembler package used for the machine language programs is either the *APW* or *ORCA/M* assembler. The programs can be entered using either the *APW* editor or an editor of your choice. Remember to change the file types if using a text editor other than *APW*'s editor, as stated in the *APW* reference manual. The line numbers appearing in the program listings are for reference only; you should not type them in when entering the programs.

BeepBeep

This routine reads a key from the keyboard. It checks for any number key, 1–9. When one of these keys is pressed, the computer will beep that number of times. This routine uses the Text tool set and the Miscellaneous tool set. (Neither of these tool sets require detailed initialization.)

Related functions (from the reference section):

Function: $220C
Name: ReadChar (Text tool set)
Reads one character from the input device.
Push: Result Space (W); Echo flag (W);
Pull: ASCII Character (W)
Errors: Possible Pascal errors
Comments: Echo flag is $0001 to echo, $0000 no echo; the character returned is the LSB of the word, its high bit is clear; the character is affected by the AND and OR masks of function 09.

Function: $2C03
Name: SysBeep (Misc. Tools)
Beep!
Push: nothing
Pull: nothing
Errors: none
Comments: Makes a call to the system's bell vector.

Program Code:

```
1  ;THIS PROGRAM WAS WRITTEN FOR THE APW ASSEMBLER
2
3           KEEP    BEEPBEEP
4  MAIN     START
5
6  GETKEY   PEA     $0000       ;PUSH RESULT SPACE (W)
7           PEA     $0000       ;0 = DON'T ECHO CHARACTER
8           LDX     #$220C      ;READCHAR/TEXTTOOLS
9           JSL     $E10000     ;CALL TOOLBOX
10
11          PLA                 ;GET CHARACTER FROM STACK
12          AND     #$00FF      ;GET RID OF HIGH BYTE
13          CMP     #$0031      ;"1" KEY
14          BCC     GETKEY      ;IF LESS THAN, READ AGAIN
15
16          CMP     #$003A      ;"0" KEY
17          BCS     GETKEY      ;AGAIN IF 0 KEY OR MORE
18
19          AND     #$000F      ;MAKE IT A BINARY VALUE
20
21 LOOP     PHA                 ;PUSH IT ON THE STACK
22
23          LDX     #$2C03      ;SYSBEEP/MISC TOOLS
24          JSL     $E10000     ;CALL THE TOOLBOX
25
26          PLA                 ;GET COUNT BYTE BACK
27          DEC     A           ;TICK ONE OFF
28          BNE     LOOP        ;AND KEEP LOOPING
29
30          RTL                 ;LEAVE
31
32          END
```

The ReadChar function in the Text tool set reads one character from the keyboard. Two items are pushed to the stack: a word of result space and an echo flag. If the echo flag is $0000, the character typed is not displayed. If the echo flag is $0001, the character is displayed. The character is returned on the stack in the low byte of the result.

Lines 12–17 determine if the character typed was in the range of $31–$39, the ASCII character codes for the numbers 1–9. First, the high byte (which could be anything) is stripped from the number (line 12); then, it is compared with $31. If the value is less than $31, execution branches back to the getkey function and another key is read. If the key entered is equal to or greater than $31, it is next compared with $3A (the value for the 0 key). If the key is greater than or equal to $3A, execution branches back to getkey and another key is read (lines 16 and 17). Otherwise, it's assumed a number key was pressed. The AND statement in line 19 is used to get the binary value of the key typed (rather than its ASCII value).

This program uses the stack to save the value of the key in lines 21 and 26. The SysBeep call (which simply sounds the beeper) does not require any arguments on the stack. Don't confuse the pushing and pulling of the count value in the A register with any parameters required by SysBeep.

Once the routine has cycled through a given number of beeps, the program ceases operation in line 30. If it was called with a JSL from another routine, it will return operation to that routine.

Bombs Away!

This program produces results that may be familiar to you. It uses the SysFailMgr (System Failure Manager) to display an error message and lock up the computer in a loop. Most applications use this routine as their standard fatal error handler. The SysFailMgr is part of the Miscellaneous tool set. No initialization is required to make the call.

Related functions:

Function: $1503
Name: SysFailMgr (Misc Tools)
Halt program and display an error message.
Push: Error Code (W); String Address (L)
Pull: nothing
Errors: none
Comments: String starts with a count byte. If String Address is 0, the standard message is used.

Program code:

```
1   ;THIS PROGRAM USES THE APW ASSEMBLER
2
3              KEEP     BOMBER
4   MAIN       START                              ;START OF THIS PROGRAM
5
6              PEA      $FACE                     ;PUSH ERROR NUMBER VALUE
7              PEA      MSG|-16                   ;DATA BANK OF MESSAGE
8              PEA      MSG                       ;THE MESSAGE ITSELF
9              LDX      #$1503                    ;TOOL $03, FUNCTION $15
10             JSL      $E10000                   ;CALL THE TOOLBOX
11
12  MSG        DC       I1"39"                    ;STRING COUNT BYTE
13             DC       C"THAT'S A BIG OOPS!"     ;MESSAGE
14             DC       I1"10,13,10,10"           ;A FEW LINE FEEDS
15             DC       C"ERROR NUMBER -> $"
16
17             END                                ;END OF THIS PROGRAM
```

This program makes a call to the SysFailMgr function number $15 of the Miscellaneous tool set. Two things must be pushed onto the stack: an error number and a long-word pointer to an error message string. The error number in this program is the hex value $FACE (SysFailMgr displays the error numbers in hex). The string is at memory location MSG.

The bar character (|) in line 7 is used to rotate the memory location of MSG 16 bits to the right, effectively dividing the value of the long word by 65536, or moving the high order word into position to be pushed onto the stack. You probably recall that when pushing words onto the stack, they must be in the sequence high order word, then low order word. When pulling them from the stack, they are in low order word/high order word sequence. The instruction PEA MSG|-16 gives the memory bank of the string—the first part of the long word pushed to the stack. It is important to remember that whenever a long-word pointer is pushed to the stack, the first word (the memory bank) is calculated this way.

If a long word of zero is pushed to the stack instead of a memory location, the standard message "Fatal System Error" is displayed.

Another thing to notice about this program is its lack of a return statement. Because SysFailMgr branches to the system failure screen and stays there, a return is not necessary.

Incidently, if you would like to see the names of the Apple IIGS Design Team members, press Control-Option-Apple-N while the Apple character bounces from side to side on your screen.

Greetings

The following program asks for input from the keyboard and then echoes the input back as part of a greeting. It uses three methods for displaying text on the screen: *Pascal, C,* and *Block.* These methods are further discussed in Chapter 10, but briefly, Pascal strings all start with a count byte. The count byte is a value between 0–255 which describes the length of the string immediately following.

C strings are delimited by a terminating character. Rather than use an initial count byte, a C string is considered to be all the characters appearing before a special end-byte value, the End Of Line (EOL) character. In the Apple IIGS toolbox, the byte value $00 is used as the EOL character for a C string.

Block strings can appear anywhere within a block. Their lengths are determined by a block address, an offset which indicates how far the beginning of the string is from the beginning of the block, and a third value indicating the length of the string.

This program uses only the Text tool set.

Related functions:

Function: $1C0C
Name: WriteString (Text tool set)
Displays a line of text to the output device.
Push: String Pointer (L)
Pull: nothing
Errors: Possible Pascal errors
Comments: First character of the string is a count byte; characters in the string are affected by the AND and OR masks of function 0A; no carriage return is added.

Function: $1E0C
Name: WriteBlock (Text tool set)
Displays characters at a given address and offset.
Push: Text Address (L); Offset (W); Length (W)
Pull: nothing
Errors: Possible Pascal errors
Comments: Characters in the block are affected by the AND and OR masks of function 0A.

Function: $200C
Name: WriteCString (Text tool set)
Displays a string of text to the output device
Push: String Address (L)
Pull: nothing
Errors: Possible Pascal errors
Comments: The string ends with the byte $00; characters in the string are affected by the AND and OR masks of function 0A.

Function: $240C
Name: ReadLine (Text tool set)
Reads a string from the input device
Push: Result Space (W); Buffer Address (L); Line length (W)
End of line (EOL) character (W) Echo Flag (W)
Pull: Character Count (W)
Errors: Possible Pascal errors
Comments: EOL character is in LSB of word pushed; EOL is not written to buffer; Echo flag is $0001 to echo, $0000 no echo.

Program code:

```
;THIS PROGRAM ALSO USES THE APW ASSEMBLER

          KEEP    GREETINGS
MAIN      START

          PEA     ASK|-16                  ;BANK ADDRESS
          PEA     ASK                      ;OFFSET OF STRING
          LDX     #$1C0C                   ;WRITESTRING
          JSL     $E10000

          PEA     $0000                    ;RESULT SPACE (W)
          PEA     BUFFER|-16               ;CHARACTER INPUT
          PEA     BUFFER                   ;BUFFER (L)
          PEA     $0014                    ;MAXIMUM CHARACTERS
          PEA     $000D                    ;END OF LINE CHAR.
          PEA     $0001                    ;ECHO IS ON
          LDX     #$240C                   ;READLINE
          JSL     $E10000

          PLA                              ;GET INPUT COUNT
          STA     COUNT                    ;AND SAVE IT

          PEA     GREET|-16                ;DISPLAY GREETINGS
          PEA     GREET
          LDX     #$200C                   ;WRITECSTRING
```

```
26              JSL     $E10000
27
28              PEA     BUFFER|-16                  ;DISPLAY INPUT BACK
29              PEA     BUFFER
30              PEA     $0000                       ;OFFSET WITHIN BLOCK
31              LDA     COUNT                       ;LENGTH OF STRING
32              PHA                                 ;PUSH ON STACK
33              LDX     #$1E0C                      ;WRITEBLOCK
34              JSL     $E10000
35
36              RTL                                 ;EXIT
37
38  ASK         DC      I1'A02-A01'
39  A01         DC      C'WHAT IS YOUR NAME?'
40  A02         ANOP
41
42  COUNT       DS      2
43  BUFFER      DS      20
44
45  GREET       DC      I1'13,10'
46              DC      C'GOOD TO MEET YOU, '
47              DC      I1'0'
48
49              END
```

Lines 6–9 display the initial message on the screen. A long pointer to the string *ask* is pushed on the stack, then a call is made to function $1C (WriteString) of the Text tool set. The WriteString function requires that the string start with a one-byte count value (a Pascal string). This is calculated by the *APW* assembler using the statements in lines 38–40. The first value is a one-byte integer value arrived at by subtracting the memory location of A01 from A02. This gives the length of the string. The ANOP instruction is used to give a label to an address. In line 40, ANOP gives the address of the memory location just after the string.

Lines 11–18 read a string of characters from the keyboard using the ReadLine function. First, a word of result space is pushed onto the stack (line 11), followed by a long pointer to the input buffer (using the familiar |-16 technique). In line 14, the maximum number of characters allowed—$14, or 20 decimal—is pushed onto the stack. Line 15 pushes the End of Line (EOL) character—$0D, or 13 decimal (the code for the Return key). When this character is typed, ReadLine stops reading characters. The final value pushed onto the stack is the echo flag. The value $0001 instructs the toolbox to echo (or print) characters to the screen.

Once a string is entered (the user either typed the maximum number of characters or pressed the Return key), the number of characters entered is pulled from the stack and stored in the memory location *count* (lines 20 and 21).

After the text is entered, a greeting string is displayed using the WriteCString call. Strings displayed by WriteCString end in $00 (a C string). First, a long pointer to the string's address, at *greet*, is pushed onto the stack in lines 23 and 24. Next, the call is made to WriteCString. Notice how the greet string starts with a carriage return and line-feed character (line 45), and then ends in the one-byte value zero (line 47). The carriage return and line feed are needed because ReadLine does not echo it to the screen after a string is input.

Finally, the text entered is displayed on the screen using the WriteBlock function. Write block displays a string at a given offset from a certain memory location. Block strings require three things: the address of the block, the offset within the block, and the length of the string. These are pushed to the stack in lines 28–32.

The program returns to *APW* with the RTL instruction in line 36.

Memsize

This program uses the Memory Manager tool set to return the status of your IIGS's memory. The total amount of RAM in your computer is returned, as are the number of bytes available for programs (minus any ramdisks you may have) and the total bytes available. The Integer Math and Text tool sets are also used.

Related functions:

Function: $1B02
Name: FreeMem
Returns memory available for programs
Push: Result Space (L)
Pull: Integer Value (L)
Errors: none
Comments: Returns the total number of bytes in memory, not counting ramdisks or other allocated blocks.

Function: $1C02
Name: MaxBlock
Returns memory available to programs
Push: Result Space (L)
Pull: Integer Value (L)
Errors: none
Comments: Returns the largest free block in memory.

Function: $1D02
Name: TotalMem
Returns total RAM in the System
Push: Result Space (L)
Pull: Integer Value (L)
Errors: none
Comments: Returns all RAM in your II, including the basic 256K, any ramdisks, and so on.

Function: $270B
Name: Long2Dec (Integer Math)
Produces a string of ASCII numeric characters for a 32-bit integer input
Push: Integer Value (L); String Address (L);
String Length (W); Sign (W)
Pull: nothing
Errors: $0B04
Comments: See function 26.

Function: $1C0C
Name: WriteString (Text tool set)
Displays a line of text on the output device
Push: String Pointer (L)
Pull: nothing
Errors: Possible Pascal errors
Comments: First character of the string is a count byte; characters in the string are affected by the AND and OR masks of function 0A; no carriage return is added.

Program code:

```
;THIS PROGRAM WAS WRITTEN FOR THE APW ASSEMBLER
            KEEP    MEMSIZE
MAIN        START
            PEA     $0000                       ;RESULT SPACE (L)
            PEA     $0000
            LDX     #$1D02                      ;TOTALMEM FUNCTION
```

```
         JSL     $E10000              ; TO GET ALL OF RAM
         PEA     TMSTR|-16            ;STORE VALUE HERE
         PEA     TMSTR
         PEA     $0007                ;LENGTH OF STRING
         PEA     $0000                ;VALUE IS UNSIGNED
         LDX     #$270B               ;LONG2DEC
         JSL     $E10000
         PEA     $0000                ;RESULT SPACE (L)
         PEA     $0000
         LDX     #$1B02               ;FREEMEM FUNCTION
         JSL     $E10000              ;FOR USABLE RAM
         PEA     FMSTR|-16            ;LONG WORD POINTER TO
         PEA     FMSTR                ;PLACE TO STORE NUMB.
         PEA     $0007                ;LENGTH OF STRING
         PEA     $0000                ;VALUE IS UNSIGNED
         LDX     #$270B               ;LONG2DEC
         JSL     $E10000
         PHA                          ;RESULT SPACE (L)
         PHA
         LDX     #$1C02               ;MAXBLOCK FUNCTION
         JSL     $E10000
         PEA     MBSTR|-16            ;STORE NUMBER HERE
         PEA     MBSTR
         PEA     $0007                ;LENGTH OF STRING
         PEA     $0000                ;UNSIGNED VALUE
         LDX     #$270B               ;LONG2DEC
         JSL     $E10000
         PEA     TEXT|-16             ;DISPLAY RESULTS
         PEA     TEXT
         LDX     #$1C0C               ;WRITESTRING
         JSL     $E10000
         RTL                          ;EXIT
TEXT     DC      I1'ENDTEXT-STEXT'    ;SIZE OF TEXT
STEXT    DC      C'TOTAL MEMORY = '
TMSTR    DC      C'       ',I1'13,10' ;(7 SPACES)
         DC      C' FREE MEMORY = '
```

```
53 FMSTR   DC      C'   ',I1'13,10'
54         DC      C'AVAILABLE MEM = '
56 MBSTR   DC      C'   '
57 ENDTEXT ANOP
58
59         END
```

This program may appear a bit long, but it consists of three routines, each of which is structured similarly. Lines 6–16 contain the first routine. With only subtle differences, lines 18–28 and 30–40 contain almost exactly the same code.

Each routine first calls the Memory Manager to return either the total memory, free memory, or available memory. This is done by pushing a long word of result space to the stack and then making the appropriate call. Note how the last routine uses two PHA statements to push a long word onto the stack. Result space can be any value, so PHA works as well (in fact, better, because the code is shorter) than a PEA $0000.

After the call to the memory manager, the long word result is on the stack. To convert this long unsigned integer to a string of characters, a call is made to the Integer Math tool set's function $27, Long2Dec. This function requires four items pushed to the stack: the value to convert, the memory location to place the text, the length of the text, and whether the value is signed or unsigned.

Because the number is already on the stack, there's no need to pull if off and push it again, so skip to the next step. The next step is to push the memory location of the string onto the stack (lines 11–12, 23–24, and 35–36). This is followed by the length of the string, which is set to $07. Long2Hex will left-justify the number within those seven places and pad the remainder with space characters. Finally, a word of zero is pushed to indicate that the result is to be unsigned. All memory values are unsigned.

The strings returned from the Long2Dec function are placed into assigned spaces in the Text string, lines 49–56. (Remember, they will be left-justified within those areas.) Lines 42–45 set up a WriteString function call to display the results. Line 47 returns to the *APW* shell.

Chapter 7

Designing Applications

Designing applications is what programming the toolbox is all about. Fortunately, the procedures for using the toolbox are fairly standard. This means that when you understand the basic steps, building toolbox applications will be a snap.

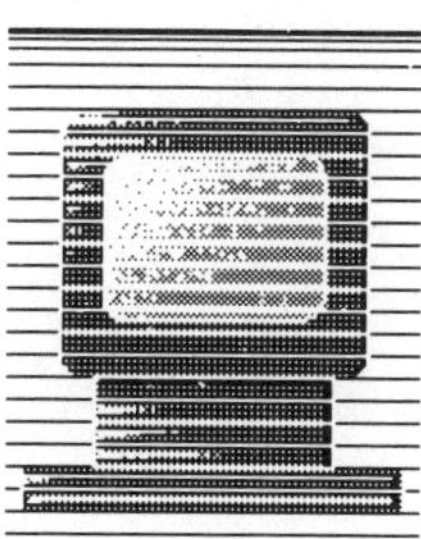

Because of the way the toolbox is implemented, there are certain steps which should be taken by every program using the toolbox. This chapter covers a general outline of those steps, describing which procedures are used and why. By following these steps, you'll be able to set up and run any toolbox program with few complications.

Program Outline

Every major program or application you write for the toolbox will probably use an outline similar to the following.

- Set up the environment
- Set up/initialize needed tool sets
- Prepare tools/establish parameters
- Do something (accept input, process information, or whatever the program does)
- Shut down

This outline gives a general idea of the steps needed to set up and use the toolbox. There are no hard and fast rules about any of these steps. Instead, they provide a logical approach to writing toolbox applications.

The first part of your program should be to set up a programming environment. This is where you could define where your stack pointer, program, and data banks are located. This step can be a very complex set of instructions, or it can be simple or nonexistent. It all depends on the length of your code and what your program does.

Once the environment is established, you should initialize, or set up, each of the tool sets your program needs. If the tool sets are on disk, they need to be loaded into RAM. Some tool sets require extensive setups, others require only a call to their StartUp function. (These are detailed in Chapter 9.)

Finally, your program needs to prepare for each of the tools it uses. For example, if your program uses menus, dialog boxes, and windows, you need to define each of them; if your program uses graphics, various ports need to be defined and initialized; and if your program uses sound, sound wave data needs to be loaded into memory or created by the program.

After everything is set, your actual program begins (the part that does the work). Comparatively speaking, the code to set up and initialize the tools might be longer than the code that does the work. In fact, most programs will consist of a *main loop* and a bunch of *subroutines.* In time, setting up and initializing the toolbox (the first three steps) will become old hat; then, you'll really appreciate how easily you can write sophisticated programs using the toolbox.

After your application is finished, it needs to turn itself off, or go through a *shutdown procedure.* Long gone are the days of the simple RTS instruction to end a program, and this brings up an interesting point.

It's easy for an experienced programmer to ignore proper shutdown procedures. These shutdown procedures enable your program to return to the previous program—whether it's the *APW* shell, the Apple IIGS Program Launcher, or whatever—with no loose strings. If you simply end your program without switching off the necessary tools and properly releasing your program's memory, you're programming yourself into a hole.

Program Skeleton Example

The majority of the routines documented in this book follow a pattern based on the outline in the previous section. Each program accomplishes specific tasks in a general order. The only difference is in the fourth step, in which the actual work of the program is done.

The following goes into a little more detail on the outline.

Set up environment. For some applications, this step may not be needed—it depends on the program. Generally speaking, most programs (especially smaller ones) will not need extensive setting up of the environment. Major applications—such as spreadsheets, word processors, and the like—may need to set up a complex interbank memory scheme. But for programmers just starting out with the toolbox, setting up the environment is not a complicated procedure.

A simple example of setting the environment is to assert that both the program code bank register and data bank register are set for the same memory bank. You may recall from Chapter 2 that these two registers define which banks in memory are used for executing code and which are used for accessing data. Your programs should not assume both these registers are pointing at the same bank when the program starts.

To assert that the data bank is equal to the program bank, use the following code (also used in the example near the end of this chapter):

```
PHK         ;PUT THE CODE BANK ON THE STACK
PLB         ;PULL THAT BANK INTO THE DBR
```

Now, the code bank is equal to the data bank. If you write your program assuming that data and code will be in the same bank (which is the way most code will be written), these two instructions define your environment.

Other environment instructions might include defining a stack for your program or simply asserting that the processor is in its full native mode.

Setup/initialize needed tool sets. This step usually contains several smaller steps. It just isn't as easy as calling the StartUp function of each tool set. For example, the Memory Manager must allocate space if you're using tool sets which require their own direct page. Also, certain tools are on disk and need to be loaded into RAM. This step takes care of those procedures, using the following five substeps.

- Start the Tool Locator and Memory Manager
- Establish space for a direct page (if needed)
- Set up ROM (nondisk-based) tools
- Load disk-based tools
- Set up the disk-based tools

Start the Tool Locator and Memory Manager. The ToolLocator must be the first tool set used by your program. Next, the Memory Manager is started up to give your application a UserIdentification, or *User ID.* The User ID is used by other tools in assigning memory to your application. These two tools are always started up first.

Establish space for a direct page (if needed). Direct-page space needs to be established if your program uses tools that require their own direct page. For example, the MenuManager requires its own direct page. If your application makes use of pull-down menus, you'll need to establish direct-page space for your program and then assign a direct page to the MenuManager. (This is covered in Chapters 9 and 16.)

Set up ROM (nondisk-based) tools. Other ROM tools are started next. This way, if any of the tool sets requires a direct page, that space will have been established by the previous step.

Load disk-based tools. Disk-based tools are loaded with the LoadTools function of the Tool Locator. The Tool Locator scans your startup disk for the prefix /SYSTEM/TOOLS. It will then load any tool sets into memory that you have specified.

Set up the disk-based tools. Setting up the rest of the tools simply implies starting them up with a call to their StartUp function. (They should all be loaded from disk at this point.)

Of these five substeps, the first is the most important. The others can be carried out in just about any order, or in some cases, not at all. It all depends on your type of application and which tools you need. A variety of programs provided in this book illustrate many different approaches.

Set up tool set parameters. Some tool sets require a little more work than just calling their StartUp function. For example, if your program uses menus, windows, dialog boxes, or the mouse, each of these needs further definition. If your program uses pull-down menus, each of those menus needs to be defined and placed on the menu bar. If your program uses graphics, the graphics ports and regions need to be defined. And if your program uses the mouse, you need to tell the mouse where it can and can't go, then display the mouse pointer on the screen.

Do something. This is the section which actually does the work. What happens here depends on the application. For some desktop applications, this section may only consist of a loop which scans for activity. As activity is detected, the program branches to various subroutines to handle the activity.

Most activity, especially with graphics–based window and pull–down menu programs, is monitored by the Event Manager tool set. Programs like text editors, which use only the text screen, use more traditional programming methods, but for mouse-based applications, all the mouse monitoring, window dragging, and menu pulling is monitored by the Event Manager (and it's cousin, the TaskMaster). There will be more about these two later.

Shutdown. This part of your program turns off all tool sets initialized and set up in step 2. Some tools can be shut down in any order; however, the final two tools shut down must be the Memory Manager and the Tool Locator. This adds the following substeps to step 5.

- Shut down tools
- Release memory

- Shut down Memory Manager and Tool Locator
- Quit via ProDOS

Shut down tools. Shutting down the tool sets used by your program is as simple as calling the tool set's ShutDown function. You should keep track of the tool sets used by your program and remember to turn them off when your program is done. Otherwise, the toolbox keeps the tool set active and if you run another program, it could crash when it attempts to set up an active tool set.

The only two tool sets not shut down in this step are the Memory Manager and Tool Locator.

Release memory. The memory used by the program (associated with the program's User ID) is released in this step. Again, this depends on the application. Some unique things can be done by leaving programs in memory, but for most applications, all the program's memory should be released.

Shut down Memory Manager and Tool Locator. The last two tools shut down are the first two started up: the Memory Manager and the Tool Locator. The Memory Manager is shut down first, followed by the Tool Locator. This is the exact opposite of the way they were started up.

Quit via ProDOS. Finally, a call is made to ProDOS to quit the program and return to whatever program was running before. This way, your program returns control to the Program Launcher, or to a specialized shell program from which your program was called.

If you follow all of these steps, your programs will be compatible with all other programs (assuming they, too, follow these steps) as well as future releases of both the Apple IIGS and the toolbox.

Applying the Example

All the steps discussed so far are used in the following assembly language example. PROG1 follows each of the steps just outlined.

- Set up environment
- Set up/initialize needed tool sets
- Start the Tool Locator and Memory Manager
- Establish space for a direct page (if needed)
- Set up ROM (nondisk-based) tools
- Load disk-based tools
- Set up the disk-based tools
- Prepare tools/set parameters
- Do something

- Shut down
- Shut down tools
- Release memory
- Shut down Memory Manager and Tool Locator
- Quit via ProDOS

Basically, PROG1 sets up a mouse pointer on the screen. You press a key and the program ends. Later in this chapter, you'll add some code to make the mouse pointer moveable, but for demonstration purposes, PROG1 is sufficient.

Here is how PROG1 follows the steps.

Set up environment. PROG1 lacks any need for a complex environment. The only thing done in this step is to make sure the program bank and data bank are the same. PROG1 was written assuming everything happens in the same bank of RAM.

Set up/initialize needed tool sets.

Start the Tool Locator and Memory Manager. The first two tool sets initialized are the Tool Locator and Memory Manager. When the Memory Manager is started, it returns the program's User ID.

Establish space for a direct page (if needed). Three direct pages are set up by PROG1 for the QuickDraw II tool set. This program doesn't make direct use of QuickDraw II, yet it requires the direct pages.

Set up ROM (nondisk-based) tools. Two ROM tool sets are used by PROG1, the Miscellaneous tool set and QuickDraw II. Although this program uses the Text tool set, it does not need to be initialized.

Load disk-based tools. PROG1 does not need or load any disk-based tools.

Set up the disk-based tools. Since no disk-based tools are loaded, there is no need to set them up.

Prepare tools/set parameters. Nothing this program does requires any further preparation. The only thing done in this step is to display the mouse pointer on the screen. In a modified version of the program, you can move the pointer around.

Do something. The actual program consists of a call to the function ReadChar in the Text tool set. Once a key is pressed, the program is done.

Shut down.

Shut down tools. QuickDraw II and the Miscellaneous tool set are both shut down in this step. Again, the Text tool set, though used, does not need to be shut down.

Release memory. The program releases its memory with a call to the function DisposeHandle in the Memory Manager.

Shut down Memory Manager and Tool Locator. Finally, the Memory Manager and Tool Locator are shut down.

Quit via ProDOS. PROG1 ends with a call to ProDOS's Quit function, $29. This returns you to whichever program you were running before.

PROG1 incorporates two other areas besides the above parts. One is a simple data storage area, the second is an error handling routine. The error handling routine is a simple test to see if the carry flag is set after calling the toolbox. If it is, the program halts and displays the standard system error message "Fatal System Error" and the error number. Otherwise, the error handler returns to the main routine. (Error handlers are discussed in detail in Chapter 11.)

PROG1 Assembly Source

The following is the source code for the PROG1 program. It was written for use with the *APW* assembler and named PROG1.ASM. The final executable file, PROG1, can be run from the *APW* shell. Line numbers have been provided for reference purposes only. You should not type them into your editor.

Make sure the filetype and subtype of PROG1.ASM are SRC and ASM65816, respectively. Refer to the *APW* manual for details on changing the filetype and subtype if they are different.

To assemble and link this program under *APW*, at the *APW* prompt, type

```
#asml prog1.asm
```

To run the program, type

```
#prog1
```

You will see a black mouse pointer in the upper left-hand corner of a black screen. Type any key to exit.

```
*****************************************************************************
* PROG1.ASM A SIMPLE TOOLBOX DEMO PROGRAM
*****************************************************************************

            ABSADDR   ON                      ;ABSOLUTE ADDRESSING IS ON
            KEEP      PROG1                   ;EXE FILE WILL BE PROG1

MAIN        START

            PHK                               ;ASSERT CODE BANK ==
                                              ;DATA BANK
            PLB

*****************************************************************************
* THIS SECTION INITIALIZES AND STARTS
* UP VARIOUS TOOLBOX ROUTINES NEEDED
* FOR THIS PROGRAM
*
* IN ORDER:
*         TOOL LOCATOR
*         MEMORY MANAGER
*         MISC. TOOLS
*         QUICK DRAW II
*
*    NOTE: THE TEXT TOOL SET (USED HERE)
*       DOES NOT NEED TO BE STARTED OR SHUT DOWN.
*
*****************************************************************************

;-----------------------------------
; START THE TOOL LOCATOR

            LDX       #$0201                  ;TLSTARTUP
            JSL       $E10000                 ;BUMP START THE TOOL
                                              ;LOCATOR

;-----------------------------------
; START THE MEMORY MANAGER AND RETURN
; A USERID FOR THIS PROGRAM

            PEA       $0000                   ;RESULT SPACE
            LDX       #$0202                  ;MMSTARTUP
            JSL       $E10000                 ;GET A USERID & SOME
                                              ;MEMORY
```

```
            JSR       ERRORH             ;CHECK FOR ERRORS

            PLA                          ;GET OUR USERID
            STA       USERID             ;SAVE IT

;----------------------------------
; START THE MISC TOOLS TOOL SET

            LDX       #$0203             ;MTSTARTUP
            JSL       $E10000            ;BUMP START MISC. TOOLS
            JSR       ERRORH             ;CHECK FOR ERRORS

;----------------------------------
; ESTABLISH AND INITIALIZE A DIRECT PAGE
; FOR THIS PROGRAM

            PEA       $0000              ;LONG RESULT SPACE
            PEA       $0000
            PEA       $0000              ;CREATE A THREE PAGE BLOCK
            PEA       $0300              ; FOR ZERO PAGES
            LDA       USERID             ;OUR PROGRAM'S ID
            PHA
            PEA       $C005              ;ATTRIBUTES
            PEA       $0000              ;WHERE OUR BLOCK BEGINS
            PEA       $0000              ; IN MEMORY
            LDX       #$0902             ;NEWHANDLE
            JSL       $E10000
            JSR       ERRORH             ;CHECK FOR ERRORS
            PLA                          ;GET HANDLE OF NEW BLOCK
            STA       0                  ;CREATE A ZERO PAGE
            STA       HANDLE             ;AND COPY THE RESULT TO
                                         ;HANDLE
            PLA
            STA       2
            STA       HANDLE+2           ;THE HIGH ORDER WORD
            LDA       [0]
            STA       4

;----------------------------------
; SET UP AND START QUICK DRAW II

            LDA       4
            PHA                          ;STARTING ADDRESS OF 0 PAGE
            PEA       $0000              ;SCREEN MODE
```

```
          PEA     $0000               ;PIXEL MAP SIZE
          LDA     USERID              ;OUR PROGRAM'S ID
          PHA
          LDX     #$0204              ;QDSTARTUP
          JSL     $E10000             ;FIRE UP QUICK DRAW II
          JSR     ERRORH

;---------------------------------
; DISPLAY THE MOUSE POINTER

          LDX     #$9104              ;SHOWCURSOR
          JSL     $E10000             ;DISPLAY THE MOUSE

;---------------------------------
; WAIT FOR A KEYPRESS

          PEA     $0000               ;RESULT SPACE
          PEA     $0000               ;DON'T SHOW CHARACTER
                                      ;INPUT
          LDX     #$220C              ;READCHAR (TEXT TOOLS)
          JSL     $E10000
          PLA                         ;READ THE CHARACTER

;---------------------------------
; END OF PROGRAM: SHUT DOWN ALL ROUTINES
; THIS IS PART OF A "GRACEFUL EXIT."


          LDX     #$0304              ;QDSHUTDOWN
          JSL     $E10000             ;SHUTDOWN QUICK DRAW II

          LDX     #$0303              ;MTSHUTDOWN
          JSL     $E10000             ;SHUT DOWN MISC TOOLS

          LDA     HANDLE+2            ;PUSH HANDLE
          PHA                         ;TO FREE MEMORY TAKEN
          LDA     HANDLE              ;BY THIS PROGRAM
          PHA
          LDX     #$1002              ;DISPOSE HANDLE
          JSL     $E10000

          LDA     USERID              ;SHUT DOWN THIS PROGRAM
          PHA
          LDX     #$0302              ;MMSHUTDOWN
```

```
            JSL     $E10000         ;SHUT DOWN MEMORY
                                    ;MANAGER

            LDX     #$0301          ;TLSHUTDOWN
            JSL     $E10000         ;SHUT DOWN TOOL LOCATOR

;---------------------------------
; EXIT VIA PRODOS 16 MLI CALL $29

            JSL     $E100A8         ;PRODOS 16 CALL
            DC      I2'$29'         ;QUIT FUNCTION
            DC      I4'QPARAMS'     ;QUIT PARAMETERS

********************************************************************************
* ERROR HANDLER
********************************************************************************
ERRORH      BCS     UHOH            ;CARRY SET IF ERROR
            RTS                     ;ELSE, RETURN

UHOH        ANOP
            PHA                     ;TOOLBOX RETURNS ERROR
                                    ;IN A
            PEA     $0000           ;0 IS SPECIFIED, SO USE
            PEA     $0000           ; DEFAULT ERROR MESSAGE
            LDX     #$1503          ;SYSFAILMGR
            JSL     $E10000         ;SHUT THIS SUCKER DOWN!
                                    ;NO RETURN, NO ERRORS,
                                    ;NOTHING

********************************************************************************
* DATA STORAGE
********************************************************************************

USERID      DS      2               ;THIS PROGRAM'S USER ID
HANDLE      DS      4               ;ZERO PAGE HANDLE

                                    ;QUIT PARAMETERS:

QPARAMS     ANOP
            DC      I4'$0'          ;RETURN TO PREVIOUS
                                    ;PROGRAM
            DC      I'$0000'

            END
```

Description of PROG1

Many of the concepts and programming examples used in PROG1 are explained in the next few chapters. There is a good chance that some of the features will be difficult to follow. If something doesn't make sense, continue reading and turn back to this example as you work your way through the book. It will make more sense as your knowledge grows.

Lines 5 and 6 in the program are *APW* assembler directives. Though the manual suggests that you not use absolute addressing (line 5), absolute addressing serves to make the program more compatible with other programs when it's running. The KEEP directive instructs the linker to save the EXEcutable file as PROG1 (line 6).

Lines 10 and 11 define the environment for this program. By pushing the code bank number on the stack and pulling the data bank, both will be equal. Otherwise, there's no way to know which bank of memory they might be pointing to. Because PROG1 maintains its data in the same bank as its code, the data bank must be changed to equal the code bank and not the other way around.

Lines 32 and 33 set up the Tool Locator. No error is possible.

Lines 39–45 start the Memory Manager. First, a word-sized result space is put on the stack (line 39). Then, a call is made to the MMStartUp function (lines 40 and 41). Because there is a possibility of an error, a call is made to the ErrorH (Error Handler) routines (lines 140–151). If no error occurred, execution would return to line 44 where this program's User ID is pulled from the stack. Line 45 has the User ID put in the memory location labeled UserID (found in the data storage area, line 158).

Lines 50–52 start the Miscellaneous tool set. This is done with a call to the function MTStartUp. The Error Handler routine is called here to test for errors.

From lines 58–77 a direct page and *handle* to the direct page are established. (Handles are discussed in Chapter 8.) The NewHandle function requires a number of parameters, all of which are pushed to the stack: a long word result space (lines 58 and 59); the size of the block to reserve (lines 60 and 61); the program's User ID (lines 62 and 63); the attributes describing the block (line 64); and a pointer where the block begins in memory, or $000000 for the next available block (lines 65 and 66). The NewHandle call is made in lines 67 and 68, followed by a call to the Error Handler in line 69.

After a successful call, the handle of the new block is pulled and stored at location 0 (zero) in the zero page, as well as in the memory location *Handle* (at line 159). The value pointed to by the pointer at location 0 is then stored in memory location 4 (lines 76 and 77). This address is then used by QuickDraw and any other tools that require a direct page. Creation of direct pages begins at this address and moves upward in 256-byte increments each time a direct page is required.

Lines 82–90 start up QuickDraw II. First, the direct page pointer is pushed onto the stack (lines 82 and 83); $0000 is pushed on the stack to set the screen mode to 320 (line 84); the pixel map size is then set by pushing $0000 to the stack (line 85); and finally, the User ID returned by the Memory Manager is pushed on the stack (lines 86 and 87). The QDStartUp function is called, and any possible errors are checked in lines 88–90.

Lines 95 and 96 call the ShowCursor function in QuickDraw II. This displays the mouse pointer on the screen.

The main program consists of a call to the function ReadChar in the Text tool set in lines 101–105. A result space is first pushed to the stack line (101). Next, the value $0000 is pushed, causing ReadChar not to display the character typed (line 102). Then, the call is made to ReadChar (lines 103 and 104) and the computer waits for a key press. The value of the pressed key is pulled from the stack (line 105). Nothing is done with the value, yet the stack needs to be adjusted back to normal (so the PLA instruction was included).

The program shuts down with the instructions from lines 112–131. First, QuickDraw II is shut down (lines 112 and 113), followed by the Miscellaneous tool set (lines 115 and 116). To free the memory used by this program, the direct page handle (a long word) is pushed to the stack (lines 118–121) and a call is made to the DisposeHandle function of the Memory Manager (lines 122 and 123).

To officially turn off the program, the User ID is returned to the Memory Manager (lines 125 and 126) for the MMShutDown function (lines 127 and 128). This also turns off the Memory Manager.

The Tool Locator is then shut down in lines 130 and 131.

The ProDOS Quit call is made in lines 136–138. The ProDOS vector is at $E100A8. This is followed by the byte value of the function (line 137) and the location of its parameters (line 138; the parameters are listed in lines 164 and 165).

The Error Handler is in lines 143–151. Line 143 tests to see if the carry flag is set, indicating an error. If not, the subroutine returns to the caller (line 144); otherwise, the "uhoh" routine (line 146) is executed. Because the error code is in the A register, it's pushed on the stack in line 147. This is followed by the long word value $000000 which causes the SysFailMgr function to display the standard fatal error message. The SysFailMgr call is made in lines 150 and 151. There is no return from that call.

Lines 158–165 contain this program's data. Line 158 is storage for this program's User ID. Line 159 is storage for this program's direct page handle. The ProDOS quit parameters are listed in lines 164 and 165.

Modifying PROG1

Adding the following routines to PROG1 enables the mouse pointer to be moved around on the screen. The program still ends after you press any key.

To activate mouse movement, the Event Manager must be added to the code. Any time you modify a program by adding another tool set you should do four things:

- Set aside space for the tool's direct page (if needed)
- Start up the tool set
- Initialize any parameters or tables
- When finished, include the tool set's shutdown function in your programs' quit code.

For this program, the Event Manager does not need any parameters or tables. To incorporate it into the PROG1, three things must be done: First, room must be made for a direct page, because the Event Manager requires one; second, the Event Manager must be initialized (this is a bit more complex than initializing QuickDraw II or the Miscellaneous Tools); and third, the Event Manager must be shut down in the program's quit code.
To make room for the Event Manager's direct page, modify line 61 to

```
PEA    $0400
```

The long word that's pushed to the stack is changed from $00000300 to $00000400. This reserves another 256 bytes (one page) in memory for the Event Manager's direct page.

From the toolbox index, the Event Manager StartUp routine is

Function: $0206
Name: EMStartUp
Starts the Event Manager
Push: Direct Page (W); Event Queue Size (W); Minimum X (W); Maximum X (W); Minimum Y (W); Maximum Y (W); UserID (W)
Pull: nothing
Errors: $0601, $0606, $0607
Comments: X and Y values refer to mouse *clamps* (limits).

To start the Event Manager quite a few things need to be pushed to the stack. All of the following are words.

- The event manager's direct page
- The event queue size
- The minimum X (left) value for the mouse
- The maximum X (right) value for the mouse
- The minimum Y (top) value for the mouse
- The maximum Y (bottom) value for the mouse
- This program's User ID

The direct page for use by PROG1 has been saved in memory location 4. The offset of a new direct page needs to be added to this value. For example, since the Event Manager is the first new program requiring a direct page after QuickDraw II, its direct page will start at the address stored in location 4, plus $300. (QuickDraw is already using a 768-byte ($300) area, starting at the address stored at location 4.)

To create a direct page location and then push it to the stack, the following instructions are used. Insert them at line 92.

```
LDA   4        ;GET OUR DIRECT PAGE LOCATION
CLC            ;CLEAR THE CARRY FLAG
ADC   #$300    ;START THE EM'S DIRECT PAGE AT OFFSET $300
PHA            ;PUSH THE VALUE (IN A)
```

After this is done, you must push the Event Queue size, the four *clamping* (limiting) values for the mouse, and this program's User ID. Continue inserting

```
PEA   $0014    ;USE A 20-ELEMENT EVENTQUEUE
PEA   $0000    ;MINIMUM X
PEA   $0140    ;MAXIMUM X = 320
PEA   $0000    ;MINIMUM Y
```

```
PEA   $00C8      ;MAXIMUM Y = 200
LDA   USERID     ;GET THIS PROGRAM'S USER ID
PHA              ;AND PUSH IT ON THE STACK
```

Finally, the call is made to EMStartUp, function $0206. Because there is a possibility of an error, this is followed by a call to PROG1's Error Handler.

```
LDX   #$0206     ;EMSTARTUP
JSL   $E10000
JSR   ERRORH     ;TEST FOR ERRORS
```

The Event Manager is initialized and the mouse is free to roam around.

The last step required is to shut down the Event Manager in PROG1's quit code section. Insert the following at line 111.

```
LDX   #$0306     ;EMSHUTDOWN
JSL   $E10000    ;TURN OFF THE EVENT MANAGER
```

Now you're done. Assemble and link the program. When PROG1 is run again, the mouse pointer on the screen will move as you move the mouse on the desktop. As before, pressing any key ends the program.

If you're interested in experimenting with the program, change the X and Y clamp values when the Event Manager is started. If you *halve* the X Maximum clamp to $00A0 (160 decimal) from $0140 (320 decimal), the mouse will only be able to move the cursor on the left side of the screen.

Succeeding chapters will explain the above procedures in greater detail.

Chapter 8

Memory Management

Memory allocation is an important part of the Apple IIGS. When you look at the problems and confusion other computers have with memory (for instance, the old Apple II, MS-DOS machines, and so on) you will appreciate the thought that went into the Apple IIGS's Memory Manager.

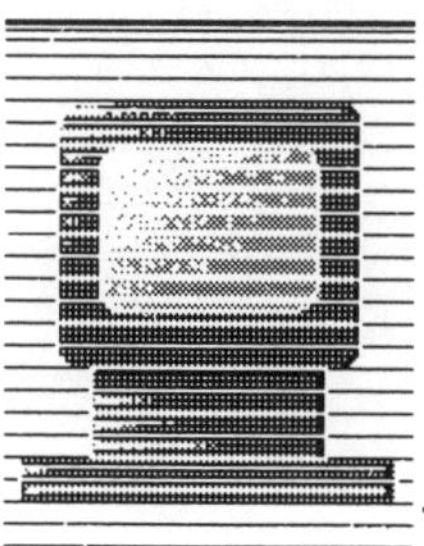

The Apple IIGS can have up to eight megabytes of RAM installed. Its designers wanted to make sure that memory would be used in a logical, sensible manner. The job of the Memory Manager tool set is to control memory by allocating, assigning, organizing, and purging various blocks of memory. This chapter covers the Memory Manager and how it can be used with your applications.

Memory Blocks

All memory in your Apple IIGS is controlled by the Memory Manager. Each time memory is used, a request is made to the Memory Manager for a certain sized *block* of memory. The Memory Manager is responsible for locating that block in memory and assigning it to your program.

The blocks of memory can be used for anything. Some blocks will contain data while other blocks might contain programming code. Applications you're using or writing will also occupy blocks of memory.

Also, the block may be located anywhere in memory. The days of indicating specific memory locations for your program code and data are history. With the Memory Manager in charge, memory is used as it is available. You cannot be certain where in memory the block may be, as the Memory Manager may change the block's location as part of its RAM organization duties.

The Memory Manager can assign blocks to certain areas of memory. It's also able to set certain protection levels on the block of memory. But for general memory use, the block will go wherever the Memory Manager finds the neatest fit.

Aside from allocating or assigning blocks of memory, the Memory Manager can organize the blocks. It does this by deleting certain blocks marked as *temporary,* or *purgeable,* and then moving other blocks which can be relocated. As your program assigns and disposes memory blocks, the Memory Manager makes sure memory is used efficiently.

Figure 8-1. Diagram of Memory Blocks, Some Marked Purgeable

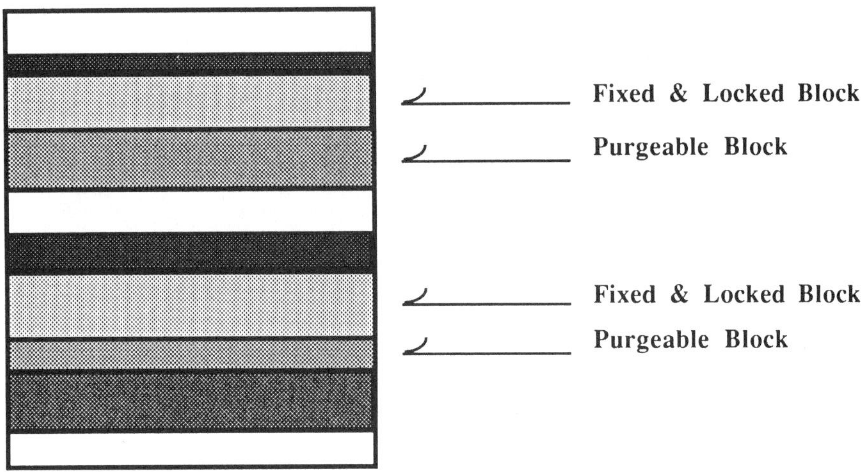

Figure 8-2. Diagram of Relocated Blocks After Housekeeping

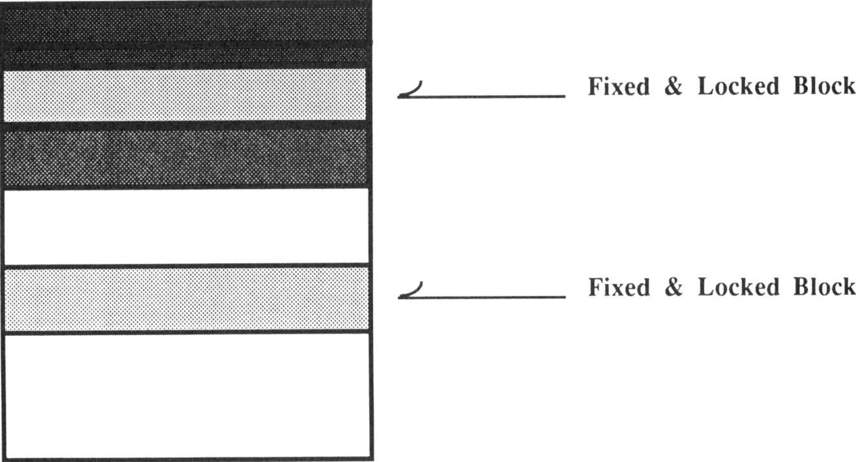

Handles

Because the location of a memory block can change, it's accessed using a *handle*. Handles are convenient references to things such as memory blocks or structures. Because the memory location of the block could change, or the contents of a structure could be altered, a handle provides a consistent reference.

A handle is often defined as a pointer to a pointer. This means the handle references an area of memory which contains a reference to another area of memory. While this definition is accurate, it's a little confusing. Maybe it would be easier to imagine the handle as if it were a handle on a suitcase. If you want to move the suitcase, you pick it up using the handle rather than wrapping your arms around it. The handle is quickly found and easy to grasp, and is always attached to the suitcase. In the Apple IIGS, a handle performs similar functions in providing easy access to a memory block or structure.

A handle is a long-word pointer. It points to a location in memory which contains information about what the handle is connected to. In the case of a block of memory, the handle points to a structure which, in turn, points to the actual block of memory.

Figure 8-3. Handle Pointing to a Memory Block

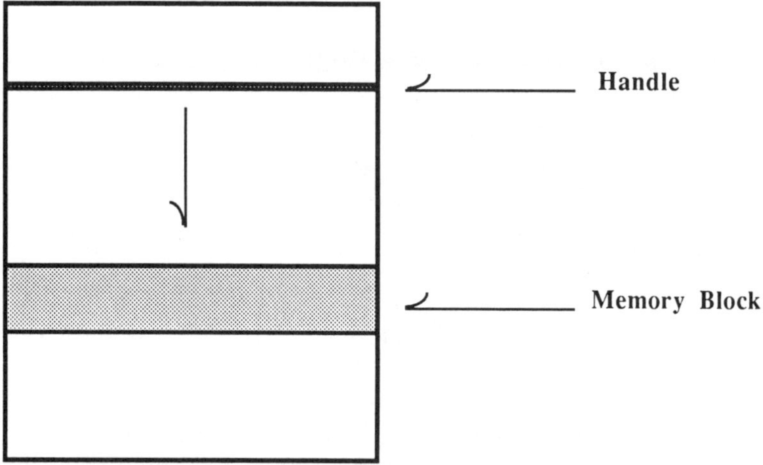

If the block of memory is moved by the Memory Manager, only the location in the structure is changed. Your handle still points to the same structure, but now the structure points to the new address of the block.

A handle points to a 20-byte memory structure containing six items that describe the memory block and give additional information to the Memory Manager regarding other blocks in memory.

If the handle of your block is $00E06550, the values at memory location $6550 in bank $E0 contain information about your

Figure 8-4. Handle Pointing to Memory Block's New Location (Handle's Location Doesn't Change)

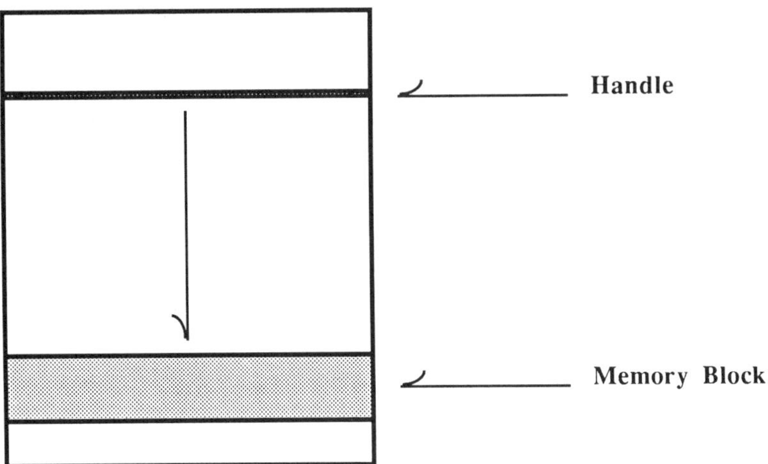

block of memory. The values at this address are

Location of Block	(long word)
Block's Attributes	(word)
Owner's User ID	(word)
Block Size	(long word)
Next handle	(long word)
Previous handle	(long word)

The Location of Block is a long word address pointing to the physical block of memory. As stated before, if your block is moved by the Memory Manager, this value will change.

The Block's Attributes is a word which describes the block in memory. Specific attributes are covered in the next section.

The Owner's User ID is a word identifying the program which owns this block. Each application has its own unique User ID.

The Block Size is a long-word value representing the physical size of the block, as specified when the block was allocated.

The Next Handle is a long-word pointer to the next available memory location for a block of memory. When another handle is allocated, it will use the memory at this location. (This is not the value of the next block's handle, but the actual address where the block will be located.)

The Previous Handle is the value of the last handle assigned by the Memory Manager. Because each structure takes 20 bytes, this value is often 20 bytes less the value of the current handle.

All these values in the memory block structure are assigned when you allocate the block of memory using function $09 of the Memory Manager, NewHandle. Other functions can modify and change the values in this structure, so it's not necessary for you to manually alter memory (while it can be done, it is frowned upon).

Block Attributes

Each block the Memory Manager allocates has certain attributes associated with it. These tell the Memory Manager information about the block and whether it can be relocated or purged. The Memory Manager uses the attribute information when it reorganizes memory and when it places a block in memory.

The attributes for the block are stored in a word called *MemAttributes.* This word is pushed to the stack when the block is allocated by the NewHandle function in the Memory Manager. MemAttributes later becomes part of the block's structure. The bits in this word describe the attributes of the allocated memory block (see Table 8-1).

Table 8-1. Meaning of MemAttributes' Bits

Bit	If Set (1)
0	Block must be in a particular memory bank
1	Block must be loaded at a specific address
2	Block must be aligned on a page boundary
3	Block can be located in special memory $00, $01, $E0, and $E1
4	Block cannot cross a bank boundary
5	Not used (should be reset to 0)
6	Not used
7	Not used
8	Purge level (low bit)
9	Purge level (high bit)
10	Not used
11	Not used
12	Not used
13	Not used
14	Block is fixed and cannot be moved
15	Block is locked, temporarily fixed, and not purgeable

Bit 0. Controls whether or not the block will be located in bank $00. When allocating a block for use as your program's direct page, this bit must be set.

Bit 1. Specifies if the block must be at a specific memory address. If set, the Memory Manager will assign the block to the memory address indicated by the NewHandle function call (see below). A reason for setting this bit would be to place a graphics screen image into graphics memory.

Bit 2. Indicates if the block is to be page-aligned. If this bit is set, the block will start on a 256-byte page boundary (a memory location ending in $00). With some programs, there are certain timing advantages to locating blocks of memory on a page boundary.

Bit 3. Allows the block to be located in special memory. If set, your block can be located in banks $00 and $01, or in the reserved memory locations of banks $E0 and $E1. Normally, blocks shouldn't be allocated in the special memory locations.

Bit 4. Controls whether or not the block may cross a *bank boundary.* If set, the block allocated will fit all within one bank of memory. Otherwise, a block may start in one bank and end in another. Blocks containing programs and code should not cross bank boundaries.

Bits 8 and 9. Set the block's *purge level.* The purge level can be one of four values, 0–3, depending on how bits 8 and 9 are set (see below). Program code should have a purge level of zero.

Bit 14. Determines if the block is *fixed,* or *moveable,* in memory. If set, the block is fixed and the Memory Manager cannot move it. Program code should be fixed (bit 14 is set), although data and other storage blocks need not be.

Bit 15. Controls whether or not the block is *locked.* If bit 15 is set, the block is locked and is temporarily considered fixed and not purgeable—regardless of the settings of bits 14, 8, and 9. Memory blocks can be temporarily locked and unlocked depending on which actions you perform on them.

The purge level of a block controls whether or not the block will be disposed when the Memory Manager does housekeeping. During housekeeping, and when the Memory Manager is running low on available memory, the attributes of memory blocks are examined. If the purge level is set low enough, those blocks will be purged to allow other blocks to be moved, or room for larger blocks to be created.

The purge level is set by bits 8 and 9 of the attribute word as shown in Table 8-2.

Table 8-2. Purge Level and Priority

Bit	8	9	Purge Level
	0	0	0 - Block cannot be purged
	0	1	1 - Lowest purge priority
	1	0	2 - Second-lowest purge priority
	1	1	3 - The block will be purged first

Purge level 3 is reserved for use by the System Loader. The other levels can be used to set the purge level for your blocks of memory.

When a block of memory is purged, the handle to that block is reset to all zeros. The block itself still exists in memory, but its contents are destroyed. By using certain Memory Manager function calls, the block could be revived but its contents would still be empty. Your program must reassign or recreate the information inside the block.

Purgeable blocks can be assigned, for example, if your program requires temporary memory for storage of a graphics image or other data. The purge level of any block of memory, and its locked or unlocked status, can be changed by various Memory Manager functions.

How Memory Is Allocated

To allocate a block of memory, a call is made to NewHandle, function $09 of the Memory Manager.

Function: $0902
Name: NewHandle
Makes a block of memory available to your program.
Push: Result Space (L); Block Size (L); UserID (W); Attributes (W); Address of Block (L)
Pull: Block's Handle (L)
Errors: $0201, $0204, $0207
Comments: See Chapter 8 for Attributes and other information.

To allocate a 256-byte block for use by your program, the following code could be used. This code assumes the program has already obtained a User ID from the Memory Manager and is storing that value at a memory location called UserID.

```
PEA   $0000     ;PUSH LONG WORD RESULT SPACE
PEA   $0000
PEA   $0000     ;PUSH SIZE OF BLOCK (LONG)
PEA   $0100     ;($00000100 = 256 BYTE BLOCK)
LDA   USERID    ;GET YOUR PROGRAM'S USERID VALUE
PHA             ;AND PUSH IT TO THE STACK
PEA   $0000     ;ATTRIBUTES FOR THIS BLOCK (NONE)
PEA   $0000     ;LOCATION OF BLOCK (LONG WORD)
PEA   $0000
LDX   #$0902    ;NEWHANDLE
JSL   $E10000
```

The following values were used by the NewHandle function:

$00000100 The size of the block to allocate.

UserID This is the value returned by the Memory Manager StartUp function at the start of the program. It shows that this program owns the memory block.

$0000 No attributes were specified for this block. It can be placed anywhere in memory and the purge level is set to zero (or *not purgeable*).

$00000000 Because the location of the block is not important, the Memory Manager places the block wherever is convenient in memory (or, if it is a large block, wherever it fits). Had a specific address been specified in the Attribute word (bit 1), this would be the address of the block.

If all goes well with the call, meaning there's memory to allocate and all the other parameters are good, a 256-byte block is established in memory and the toolbox returns a handle to that block. All further access to the block is then done using the handle as a reference.

Using Memory Blocks

Memory blocks can be used for any type of storage. Some tool sets require them, in which case the block is defined and the handle is passed to a particular routine. Other times, your program will need the block for storing information. For some specific items, such as icons in a dialog box, the toolbox will need to access the icon's data, but you must first move it into a memory block.

To move information into a memory block, two things must be done. You must first lock the block so the Memory Manager will not move it while you're copying data; and second, you must transfer your information to the block. Fortunately, two Memory Manager functions do all the work.

Function: $2002
Name: HLock
Locks and sets a specific handle to a purge level of 0
Push: Handle (L)
Pull: nothing
Errors: $0206
Comments:

The HLock function sets the Lock and Purge attributes on the block so that it will not be moved or deleted. This is the same as setting bit 15 of the attribute byte when the block is created. But just in case, you can push the block's handle on the stack and call the HLock function to set the Lock and Purge attributes to locked and unpurgeable.

```
LDA   BLOCKHANDLE+2        ;HOW OF BLOCK'S HANDLE
PHA                        ;ON THE STACK
LDA   BLOCKHANDLE          ;LOW OF BLOCK'S HANDLE
PHA                        ;ON STACK
LDX   #$2002               ;HLOCK THIS HANDLE
JSL   $E10000
```

The error which could be returned by this call, $0206, only pops up if the block's handle is invalid—meaning the block was not created by NewHandle, does not exist, or has been purged.

The reason for locking a block is simple: You don't want the Memory Manager to move the block while you're filling it with information. If the block is not locked, there's a remote chance the Memory Manager may relocate it, in which case, the information you're transferring may wind up elsewhere.

To move a chunk of memory to the block, the PtrToHand function is used. It copies a specific number of bytes from a memory address (a pointer) to a memory block via the block's handle. By using this function you don't need to mess with obtaining the actual location of the block from within the block handle's structure (which Apple forbids anyway).

Function: $2802
Name: PtrToHand
Copies a number of bytes from a specific memory address to a handle.
Push: Source address (L); Destination handle (L); Length (L)
Pull: nothing
Errors: $0202, $0206
Comments:

The first item to push on the stack is the long word address of the data you're moving to the memory block. Next, the handle of the memory block is pushed. This is followed by a long word value specifying the number of bytes to move.

For example, assume you're moving a $100-byte data structure to a $100-byte block of memory. The handle to the block was established by the Memory Manager and it is a locked (immobile) block. (The locked status can be set either when the block is created or by the HLock function call above.)

To move your $100 bytes to the memory block, the following code could be used.

```
PEA   MYDATA|-16       ;LONG POINTER TO YOUR DATA
PEA   MYDATA           ;IN MEMORY
LDA   BLOCKHANDLE+2    ;GET THE HOW OF THE BLOCK'S
PHA                    ;HANDLE ON THE STACK
LDA   BLOCKHANDLE      ;PUSH THE LOW OF THE BLOCK'S
PHA                    ;HANDLE ON THE STACK
PEA   $0000            ;PUSH THE LONG WORD LENGTH SHOWING
PEA   $0100            ;$100 BYTES TO BE COPIED
LDX   #$2802           ;PTRTOHAND - MOVE THE BYTES
JSL   $E10000
```

The only error which can occur here is $0206, which indicates an invalid BlockHandle. Otherwise, the number of bytes from your location in memory is copied into the block. Now a toolbox function can manipulate those bytes via a handle.

You might use this call to transfer an icon's image from your program's code to a memory block, or to transfer data loaded from disk to a memory block. Toolbox calls that only deal with data by the block, and thus, require a Handle and not a memory location, can take advantage of the PtrToHand function.

Disposing of Memory Blocks

Setting a block's purge level is done at the time the block is created. Two additional Memory Manager functions allow the purge level to be set after the block is established: Function $24, SetPurge, and function $25, SetPurgeAll, can reset the purge for all or a number of memory blocks.

By resetting a block's purge level, or initially establishing a block's purge level as highly purgeable, that block can be removed from memory to make room for larger blocks, or it can be removed when the Memory Manager performs housekeeping operations.

The CompactMem function ($1F) of the Memory Manager works like garbage collection routines in BASIC. When CompactMem is called, it scans all allocated blocks in memory. Purgeable blocks are removed according to the purge level. Moveable blocks are moved together and the dead space between them is made free for other purposes. CompactMem juggles memory blocks to allow larger blocks to be placed in memory more easily.

Purgeable memory blocks can be removed without calling CompactMem. Two other Memory Manager functions allow for the purging of specific blocks, or all blocks associated with a specific User ID.

Function: $1202
Name: PurgeHandle
Purges a block of memory.
Push: Block's Handle (L)
Pull: nothing
Errors: $0204, $0205, $0206
Comments: The block must be purgeable and unlocked. The block's handle is not deallocated by this call.

Function: $1302
Name: PurgeAll
Purges all blocks associated with a UserID.
Push: UserID (W)
Pull: nothing
Errors: $0204, $0205, $0207
Comments: The blocks must all be purgeable and unlocked.

After one of these functions is called, the purgeable blocks will have their handles reset to all zeros.

Disposing handles is more ruthless than purging. There's no way to reaccess the block after it's been disposed. Generally speaking, once your program is through using a block, you should dispose of it. These disposal routines remove blocks regardless of their locked or purge status:

Function: $1002
Name: DisposeHandle
Deallocates a block and releases its memory.
Push: Block's Handle (L)
Pull: nothing
Errors: $0206
Comments: The block is deleted regardless of its locked status or purge level.

Function: $1102
Name: DisposeAll
Releases all blocks associated with a UserID.
Push: UserID (W)
Pull: nothing
Errors: $0207
Comments:

At the end of each program, just before the Memory Manager is shut down, it's a good idea to call the DisposeAll function. This insures that the handles associated with blocks your program used are made free for use by other programs.

User IDs

When your application starts the Memory Manager, a *User ID* is returned. Everything associated with your program and the memory it uses is identified with this number. For example, the User ID is used to identify which blocks of memory are owned by your program. It's also used to release your program's memory when your program shuts down.

When the program is done, it passes the User ID back to the Memory Manager to help release your program's memory. (These functions, MMStartUp and MMShutDown, are covered in the next chapter.)

The User ID word contains three parts, or fields, which describe the program. They are the Type Field, AUX ID Field, and Main ID Field. The first two fields are the upper and lower nybble of the User ID's most significant byte (MSB). The Main ID field is the least significant byte (LSB) of the User ID word.

Bit:	15	14	13	12	11	10	9	8	7	6	5	4	3	2	1	0
User ID:	☐	☐	☐	☐	☐	☐	☐	☐	☐	☐	☐	☐	☐	☐	☐	☐
	Type				**AUX ID**				**Main ID**							

The *Type* field describes what type of program the User ID belongs to: straight application, desk accessory, setup file, and so on. Type is any value from $0 through $F (see Table 8-3). This value, although set by the MMStartUp call, can be altered (see below).

Table 8-3. Meaning of Values in the Type Field

Value	Program Type
$0	Memory Manager
$1	User Application
$2	Control Program

$3	ProDOS
$4	tool set
$5	Desk Accessory
$6	Runtime Library
$7	System Loader
$8	Firmware
$9	Tool Locator
$A	Setup File
$B	not defined
$C	not defined
$D	not defined
$E	not defined
$F	not defined

Normally, the Memory Manager assigns your application a type of $1. This can, however, be changed with a call to the GetNewUserID function in the Miscellaneous tool set.

The AUX ID Field has no special significance. The Memory Manager typically sets its value to $0, though your program can change it to any value from $0 to $F.

The Main ID Field is assigned by the Memory Manager when your program starts. It is any value from $01 to $FF, with $00 reserved. With each subsequent program started, the value of the Main ID Field increases by 1.

Suppose your program is being run under the *APW* shell, and further suppose that the *APW* shell is run under the ProDOS 16 launcher. In this case, the following User IDs might have already been allocated by the Memory Manager:

$A001	The TOOL.SETUP file from the /SYSTEM/SYSTEM.SETUP prefix of your system disk.
$A002	The ATLOAD.0 file from the same prefix.
$5001	A classic desk accessory from the /SYSTEM/DESK.ACCS/ prefix.
$5002	Another classic desk accessory.
$1001	The START file from your system disk (the Launcher in this case).
$400E	A tool set required by the START file
$400F	Another tool set required by START
$4010	Another tool set
$4014	Another tool set
$4015	Another tool set
$4017	Another tool set
$1002	The *APW* shell
$1003	Your program currently running in the *APW* shell

As each program is started, or loaded, the Memory Manager assigns it a new, unique User ID. Even the tool sets required by the program launcher (User ID = $1001) are given User IDs. Incidentally, the tool set's type field is always $4, but the Main ID is the actual number of the tool set. User ID $400E is tool set $0E, the Window Manager; $400F is the Menu Manager; and so on.

The value of your program's User ID can be changed by a function in the Miscellaneous tool set, $20, GetNewID. This call creates a new User ID for your program using different Type and Aux ID fields. The Main ID field, which was assigned by the Memory Manager, cannot be altered.

Function: $2003
Name: GetNewID
Install a new User ID.
Push: Result Space (W); Type/Aux ID fields (W)
Pull: New User ID (W)
Errors: $030B
Comments: Type and AUX ID values are discussed in Chapter 8.

The value pushed for Type/Aux ID fields are the same as shown in the chart above. The low order byte of the word pushed (where the Main ID Field would go) must be set to $00. You can alter the Type and Aux ID fields as necessary.

```
PHA              ;PUSH ONE WORD OF RESULT SPACE
PEA    $6000     ;CHANGE THE TYPE TO "RUNTIME LIB."
LDX    #$2003    ;GETNEWID FUNCTION
JSL    $E10000
JSR    ERRORH    ;CALL THE ERROR HANDLER

PLA              ;PULL THE NEW USER ID
STA    USERID    ;AND SAVE IT
```

This would change your program's User ID Type field to $6, meaning *runtime library.* The new User ID should be saved to a memory variable for use by further Memory Manager function calls.

Chapter 9

The Tool Sets

Each tool set your program uses requires some preparation before it can be started. Some tool sets require little preparation while others require a certain amount of ceremony before they can start. Some tool sets require their own direct-page space, other tools don't, and still other tools share

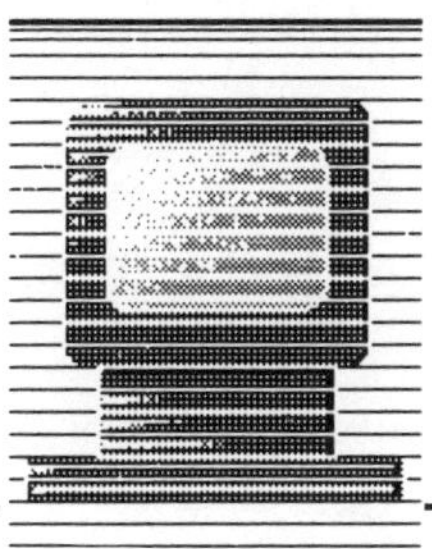

direct-page space. All this needs to be known before you set up a toolbox application.

This chapter covers the requirements of the various tool sets. These requirements should be checked any time your program accomplishes a given task, or needs to use a specific tool set. This chapter provides the background details required for each tool set to be setup and run properly.

Tool Set Categories

All tool sets in the Apple IIGS toolbox are grouped into the following categories according to the functions they perform. The most important tool sets, those required by almost every application, are listed in the Basic tool set category (Table 9-1). Nearly all toolbox applications will use these five tool sets.

Table 9-1. Basic Tool Sets (Called "The Big Five" by Apple)

Tool Set Number	Name
$01	Tool Locator
$02	Memory Manager
$03	Miscellaneous tool set
$04	QuickDraw II
$06	Event Manager

Programs that use pull-down menus, the mouse, windows, and other desktop features will probably use one or several of the tool sets in Table 9-2. A program does not need to load all of these to take advantage of the desktop interface—only those which are required should be activated.

Table 9-2. Mouse/Desktop Interface Tool Sets

Tool Set Number	Name
$05	Desk Manager
$0E	Window Manager
$0F	Menu Manager
$10	Control Manager
$12	QuickDraw II Aux.
$14	LineEdit tool set
$15	Dialog Manager

Tool Set Number	Name
$16	Scrap Manager
$17	Standard File Operations
$1B	Font Manager
$1C	List Manager

The rest of the tool sets are divided into three categories (Table 9-3): Mathematical tool sets cover basic math operations, converting numbers from one type to another, and performing arithmetic operations; the Sound tool sets are those routines used to generate music on the Apple IIGS; and the Specialty tool sets cover particular operations, including printing text, sending graphics and text to the printer, and other things.

Table 9-3. Mathematical, Sound, and Specialty Tool Sets

Mathematical tool sets

Tool Set Number	Name
$0A	SANE
$0B	Integer Math

Sound Tool Sets

Tool Set Number	Name
$08	Sound Manager
$19	Note Synthesizer
$1A	Note Sequencer

Specialty Tool Sets

Tool Set Number	Name
$07	Scheduler
$09	Apple Desktop Bus
$0C	Text tool set
$11	Loader
$13	Print Manager
$18	Disk Utilities

Starting Each Tool Set

To activate a tool set, enabling its functions to be used by your program, a call is made to the tool set's StartUp function. The StartUp function is always function number $02 in a given tool set. For each tool set, the work performed by the StartUp function differs. Some tool sets only require a call to the StartUp function. For example,

```
LDX  #$0201   ;TLSTARTUP
JSL  $E10000  ;START THE TOOL LOCATOR
```

Incidentally, TLStartUp is the first call your application should make.

The Memory Manager is different. It's StartUp routine returns a value which is used as the program's User ID. (Refer to the previous chapter on User ID's.)

Function: $0202
Name: MMStartUp
Starts the Memory Manager.
Push: Result Space (W)
Pull: UserID (W)
Errors: $0207
Comments: One of the first calls made by an application.

To call the Memory Manager, the following code could be used.

```
PHA              ;PUSH A WORD OF RESULT SPACE
LDX   #$0202     ;MMSTARTUP
JSL   $E10000
PLA              ;PULL THE USER ID VALUE
STA   USERID     ;AND STORE IT
```

First a word of result space is pushed to the stack, then the call is made to MMStartUp. The toolbox returns a number which is used as your application's User ID. This value must be saved for further use by your program and by other tool sets. It is also used when the Memory Manager assigns blocks of memory. MMStartUp should be the second toolbox call your application makes.

If your application is using an undefined block of memory, a possible error can occur when calling MMStartUp. As long as your programs are running from the Program Launcher, or the *APW* or similar shell program, this shouldn't be a problem.

Direct Pages

Many tool sets require only a call to function $02, the StartUp function, as shown above with the Tool Locator. Other tool sets require additional information to get up and running. Most commonly, they need their own work space (direct page), or the program's User ID number, or both.

A *direct page* is typically a 256-byte (one page) area of memory, assigned by the Memory Manager. It's used as a scratch pad for performing certain operations as well as for storing information. Some tool sets don't require a direct page, or they may "borrow" another tool's direct page. Most tool sets require only one direct page. The Print Manager needs two direct pages and QuickDraw II requires three.

After figuring out which tool sets your program needs, you should determine which ones require a direct page and calculate the total amount of direct-page space needed. Next, a call is made to the Memory Manager to allocate space for all the tool sets' direct pages.

You must allocate space for a direct page before you start the tool sets. (It should be done even before additional tool sets are loaded from disk.) It's assumed that the Memory Manager and Tool Locator tool sets have already been started at this point. The Miscellaneous tool set can also be started. It does not require a direct-page space, only a call to its StartUp function, $02.

Table 9-4 lists all the tool sets and shows which ones require a direct page.

Table 9-4. Which Tool Sets Require a Direct Page

Tool Set Number	Name	D Page	Comments
$01	Tool Locator	No	
$02	Memory Manager	No	
$03	Miscellaneous tool set	No	
$04	QuickDraw II	Yes	Requires $300 bytes
$05	Desk Manager	No	
$06	Event Manager	Yes	Requires $100 bytes
$07	Scheduler	No	
$08	Sound Manager	Yes	Requires $100 bytes
$09	Apple Desktop Bus	No	
$0A	SANE	Yes	Requires $100 bytes
$0B	Integer Math	No	
$0C	Text tool set	No	
$0E	Window Manager	No	Uses the Event Manager's Direct Page
$0F	Menu Manager	Yes	Requires $100 bytes
$10	Control Manager	Yes	Requires $100 bytes
$11	Loader	No	
$12	QuickDraw II Aux.	No	Uses QuickDraw II's Direct Pages
$13	Print Manager	Yes	Requires $200 bytes
$14	LineEdit	Yes	Requires $100 bytes
$15	Dialog Manager	No	Uses the Control Manager's Direct Page

Tool Set Number	Name	D Page	Comments
$16	Scrap Manager	No	
$17	Standard File	Yes	Requires $100 bytes
$18	Disk Utilities	Unknown	
$19	Note Synthesizer	Unknown	
$1A	Note Sequencer	Unknown	
$1B	Font Manager	Yes	Requires $100 bytes
$1C	List Manager	No	

Once the total direct-page space is calculated, your program should ask the Memory Manager for a block of memory to use as space for direct pages. The block should be on a page boundary to satisfy the requirements of certain tool sets. It also needs to be locked and fixed and must have bit 0 set to place the block in memory bank $00.

As an example, suppose a program uses the tool sets listed in Table 9-5.

Table 9-5. Tool Sets Utilized by Hypothetical Program

Tool Set Name	Direct Page Size
Tool Locator	
Memory Manager	
Miscellaneous tool set	
QuickDraw II	$300 bytes
Event Manager	$100 bytes
Window Manager	
Menu Manager	$100 bytes
Control Manager	$100 bytes
LineEdit	$100 bytes
Dialog Manager	
Standard File	$100 bytes
Total	$800 bytes

After the Tool Locator, Memory Manager, and Miscellaneous tool set are started up, your program needs to ask the Memory Manager for an eight-page block of memory to use as direct-page space.

```
PEA    $0000     ;LONG WORD RESULT SPACE
PEA    $0000
PEA    $0000     ;SIZE OF BLOCK (LONG)
PEA    $0800     ;$800 BYTES OF DIRECT PAGE
LDA    USERID    ;PUSH THIS PROGRAM'S USERID VALUE
PHA              ;(THE USERID WAS OBTAINED BY MMSTARTUP)
PEA    $C005     ;ATTRIBUTES (SEE BELOW)
```

```
PEA    $0000       ;LOCATION OF BLOCK ($0 = WHEREVER)
PEA    $0000
LDX    #$0902      ;NEWHANDLE FUNCTION CALL/MEMORY MANAGER
JSL    $E10000
```

The bits set in the block's attribute byte are

0 Block must be in a particular memory bank ($00)
2 Block must be aligned on a page boundary
14 Block is fixed and cannot be moved
15 Block is locked, temporarily fixed, and not purgeable

Also, the purge level (bits 8 and 9) is set to 0, meaning the block cannot be purged.

The NewHandle function call returns a long-word handle pointing to the memory block structure. This value needs to be pulled from the stack and stored in a four-byte variable. Additionally, the exact memory location of the direct page needs to be obtained so that each tool set can take advantage of it.

The following code pulls the direct page's memory block from the stack and places it into the handle DPage. It also stores the handle in the program's zero page. From the zero page, the exact location of the direct page's memory block can be obtained and examined by using indirect addressing. This code should immediately follow the previous routine.

```
PLA                 ;GET LOW OF HANDLE
STA    HANDLE       ;STORE IT HERE
STA    0            ;AND IN THE PROGRAM'S ZERO PAGE
PLA                 ;GET HOW OF HANDLE
STA    HANDLE+2     ;AND STORE IT HERE
STA    2            ;AND IN THE ZERO PAGE
```

The handle to the direct page is now stored in the four-byte variable, Handle. This handle is used again when the program quits in order to deallocate the space used. Additionally, the handle was placed at location 0 in this program's zero page. By taking advantage of the zero page, it's possible to peek into the memory handle's contents and get the exact location of this program's direct page.

```
LDA    [0]          ;GET MEMORY ADDRESS FROM HANDLE
STA    DPAGE        ;SAVE IT HERE
```

This code takes advantage of the handle returned by the Memory Manager and saved at location 0 in memory. The LDA [0] instruction reads a word-sized value at the memory location pointed to by the long word at location 0. The value in register A after the LDA [0] instruction is the actual memory address of the direct page in bank 0. This value is then saved in DPage for use by each tool set which requires a direct page.

DPage (the memory location in bank $00) is the start of the memory block the Memory Manager assigned as this program's direct-page space. Each tool set which requires a direct page will obtain its direct page location from the DPage variable.

Figure 9-1. How the Zero Page is Used to Indirectly Reference a Memory Block

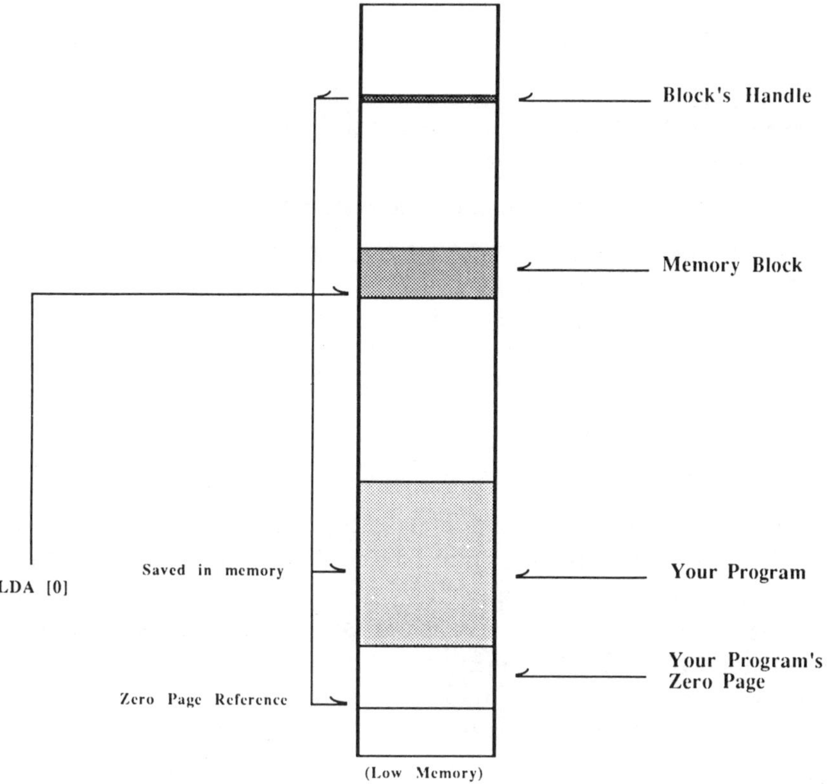

For a graphic depiction of the process, see Figure 9-1. The handle (which points to a structure) is saved in two spots. The value of the location pointed to by the handle is put into the A register with LDA [0]. That value is the actual location in bank $00 of the direct page memory block.

The tool sets which require a direct page will always push the location of their direct page on the stack as part of their StartUp call. Tool sets which also require the User ID will push that value as well. Because direct pages are always in bank $00, only a word value (the location of the page the tool set can use) is pushed.

For example, QuickDraw II requires three pages of direct-page space.

Function: $0204
Name: QDStartUp
Starts QuickDraw II.
Push: Direct Page (W); Master SCB (W); Pixel Map Size (W); UserID (W)
Pull: nothing
Errors: $0401, $0410, Memory Manager Errors
Comments: Clears the Screen as well.

To set up QuickDraw II, the following code could be used:

```
LDA   DPAGE      ;GET THE DIRECT PAGE ADDRESS
PHA              ;ONTO THE STACK
PEA   $0000      ;MASTER SCB VALUE (SEE CHAPTER 13)
PEA   $0000      ;PIXEL MAP (COVERED IN CHAPTER 13)
LDA   USERID     ;THIS PROGRAM'S USER ID
PHA              ;ONTO THE STACK
LDX   #$0204     ;QDSTARTUP
JSL   $E10000
```

The value stored in DPage is used as direct-page space for QuickDraw II. Also, this program's User ID is pushed, as are other values important to QuickDraw II.

Another example is the Event Manager (which does not need to be loaded from disk). The Event Manager requires one page of direct-page space. Because QuickDraw II is already using $300 bytes, the Event Manager's direct page needs to start at the location stored in DPage plus $300 bytes.

Function: $0206
Name: EMStartUp
Starts the Event Manager.
Push: Direct Page (W); Event Queue Size (W); Minimum X (W); Maximum X (W); Minimum Y (W); Maximum Y (W); UserID (W)
Pull: nothing
Errors: $0601, $0606, $0607
Comments: X and Y values refer to mouse clamps.

The code to start the Event Manager could be:

```
LDA   DPAGE        ;GET THE DIRECT PAGE ADDRESS
CLC                ;CLEAR CARRY FLAG FOR ADC INST.
ADC   #$300        ;DIRECT PAGE+$300
PHA                ;PUSH ONTO THE STACK
PEA   20           ;20 ELEMENT EVENT QUEUE
PEA   0            ;MINIMUM X CLAMP
PEA   320          ;MAXIMUM X CLAMP
PEA   0            ;MINIMUM Y CLAMP
PEA   200          ;MAXIMUM Y CLAMP
LDA   USERID       ;THIS PROGRAM'S USER ID
PHA                ;ONTO THE STACK
LDX   #$0206       ;EMSTARTUP
JSL   $E10000
```

Clamping values and the event queue are discussed in Chapter 12.

Because QuickDraw already used $300 bytes of direct-page space, the Event Manager's direct page needs to start at the base value, DPage, plus $300. The next tool started places its direct page at DPage plus $400, and so on.

For example, assume the next tool started is the Menu Manager. (It first needs to be loaded from disk, which is covered in the next section.)

Function: $020F
Name: MMStartUp
Starts the Menu Manager.
Push: UserID (W); Direct Page (W)
Pull: nothing
Errors: none
Comments:

The code to start up the Menu Manager could be

```
LDA   USERID     ;THIS PROGRAM'S USER ID
PHA              ;ONTO THE STACK
LDA   DPAGE      ;GET THE DIRECT PAGE ADDRESS
CLC              ;CLEAR CARRY FLAG FOR ADC INST.
ADC   #$400      ;DIRECT PAGE+$400
PHA              ;PUSH ONTO THE STACK
LDX   #$020F     ;MMSTARTUP
JSL   $E10000
```

Again, the Menu Manager's direct page starts a DPage plus $400 because QuickDraw II's direct page takes $300 bytes and the Event Manager's direct page takes $100.

Each succeeding toolbox StartUp function requiring a direct page should follow the above examples, each time adding $100 bytes to the location of its direct page.

Loading Tools from Disk

After the direct-page space is allotted, and perhaps a few ROM-based tools have been started, the disk-based tools can be loaded. These tool sets must be loaded into memory before their StartUp or any other functions can be used.

The disk-based tools are located on your system disk in the prefix /SYSTEM/TOOLS. If your program uses any of the tool sets in table 9-6, it must first load them into memory from disk.

Table 9-6. Tool Sets Which Must Be Loaded from Disk

$0E	Window Manager
$0F	Menu Manager
$10	Control Manager
$11	Loader
$12	QuickDraw II Aux.
$13	Print Manager
$14	LineEdit
$15	Dialog Manager
$16	Scrap Manager
$17	Standard File
$18	Disk Utilities
$19	Note Synthesizer
$1A	Note Sequencer
$1B	Font Manager
$1C	List Manager

To load a group of tools into memory, the Tool Locator's LoadTools function is used. The LoadTools function passes a long word pointer to the toolbox. The pointer is the memory address of a tool table containing a list of tools your program wants loaded from disk. LoadTools takes care of all the mechanics of loading the tools into memory. You just supply it with a list.

Function: $0E01
Name: LoadTools
Loads a list of tool sets into memory.
Push: Pointer to tool table (L)
Pull: nothing
Errors: $0110
Comments: See Chapter 9 for an example.

The Pointer is the memory address of a tool table. Your program's tool table is a list of each tool you want loaded from disk. The tool table uses the structure in Table 9-7.

Table 9-7. Structure of Tool Table

Tool Table	Value
Number of tools	Word value
Tool set	Word
Version number	Word
Tool set	Word
Version number	Word
and so on. . . .	

The Number of Tools is the number of tools you're loading from disk, as well as the number of tools in the list. If you're loading 3 tools, $0003 should be entered. For loading only one tool, the Tool Locator function LoadOneTool can be used instead of LoadTools.

The tool set value is the number of the tool set to load from disk. The Version Number can be used to specify a certain minimum version of the tool. For example, if your program requires version 1.3 of a tool set, $0103 is specified. Otherwise $0000 is a good value. A tool set's version number is obtained with function $04 of each tool set.

Say, for example, that you wish to load the following tools: $0E Window Manager, $0F Menu Manager, $10 Control Manager, $14 LineEdit, $15 Dialog Manager, $17 Standard File tool set. The tool table would appear as follows:

```
DC      I'6'        ;LOAD SIX TOOLS
DC      I'$0E'      ;WINDOW MANAGER
DC      I'0'        ;VERSION NUMBER ($0=DON'T CARE)
DC      I'$0F'      ;MENU MANAGER
DC      I'0'        ;VERSION
DC      I'$10'      ;CONTROL MANAGER
DC      I'0'        ;VERSION
DC      I'$14'      ;LINEEDIT
DC      I'0'        ;VERSION
DC      I'$15'      ;DIALOG MANAGER
DC      I'0'        ;VERSION
DC      I'$17'      ;STANDARD FILE TOOL SET
DC      I'0'        ;VERSION
```

Six tool sets need to be loaded from disk. This is followed by 12 sets of two-word values, each representing the tool set number and the minimum version number. Because this program doesn't care about a tool set's version number, $0000 is used.

After the LoadTools call is complete, your program can proceed by starting up each of the disk-based tools. As with the ROM-based tools, these tools might require a direct page, the program's User ID, or just a call to function $02—StartUp.

Shutting Down the Tool Sets

When your program is done, it needs to turn off each tool set. Generally speaking, it's a good idea and good programming practice to shut off the tools in the order they were started. However, that is not a rule. The only two tool sets which need to be shut off in a particular order are the Memory Manager and Tool Locator. Also, Apple suggests the Window Manager be shut down before the Control Manager if you're using both tool sets.

Shutting down each tool set is as easy as calling its ShutDown function, $03. This is the same for each tool set.

```
LDX     #$03XX      ;REPLACE XX WITH THE TOOL SET NUMBER
JSL     $E10000     ;SHUTDOWN THAT TOOL
```

A series of routines such as these can shut down all tool sets except the Memory Manager and Tool Locator.

Before the Memory Manager is shut down, your program should dispose of any memory blocks it has allocated. For example, if your program allocated a block of memory to use as a direct page (as above), the DisposeHandle function should be included to get rid of it.

Function: $1002
Name: Dispose
Deallocates a block and releases its memory.
Push: Block's Handle (L)
Pull: nothing
Errors: $0206
Comments: The block is deleted regardless of its locked status or purge level.

The following code would free the memory used by the handle *Handle,* the program's direct-page area.

```
LDA   HANDLE+2     ;GET HOW OF HANDLE
PHA                ;AND PUSH IT TO THE STACK
LDA   HANDLE       ;GET LOW OF HANDLE
PHA                ;AND PUSH IT
LDX   #$1002       ;DISPOSEHANDLE
JSL   $E10000
```

This code could be placed in a program just before the Memory Manager is shut down (and after the other tools are shut down).

If the program uses more than one memory block, the DisposeAll function is used to eliminate all blocks of memory.

Function: $1102
Name: DisposeAll
Releases all blocks associated with a UserID.
Push: UserID (W)
Pull: nothing
Errors: $0207
Comments:

In this case, the program's User ID is pushed to the stack to get rid of the memory blocks owned by the program. Because each block of memory is tied directly to the User ID, this function safely eliminates all the blocks. The following code could be used to eliminate all memory blocks associated with a program.

```
LDA   USERID       ;GET THIS PROGRAM'S USER ID
PHA                ;AND PUSH IT TO THE STACK
LDX   #$1102       ;DISPOSEALL
JSL   $E10000
```

Now all memory blocks associated with this program are gone.

The Memory Manager can be shut down once all blocks of memory have been disposed. This shutdown procedure requires only the User ID be pushed to the stack.

Function: $0302
Name: MMShutDown
Shuts down the Memory Manager.
Push: UserID (W)
Pull: nothing
Errors: none
Comments: Make this call when your application is finished.

The following code could be used to shut down the Memory Manager.

```
LDA    USERID        ;GET THIS PROGRAM'S USER ID
PHA                  ;AND PUSH IT TO THE STACK
LDX    #$0302        ;MMSHUTDOWN
JSL    $E10000
```

The final tool set to shut down is the Tool Locator. Its shutdown procedure is straightforward.

Function: $0301
Name: TLShutDown
Shuts down the Tool Locator.
Push: nothing
Pull: nothing
Errors: none
Comments:

And for the code:

```
LDX    #$0301        ;TLSHUTDOWN
JSL    $E10000
```

Now your program is through with the toolbox and all tools are safely shut down.

An option at this point is to exit the program via ProDOS. This code is presented and commented below; however, this is not a ProDOS 16 tutorial. Those desiring additional information on ProDOS 16 should consult their local bookstore.

```
JSL    $E100A8                 ;PRODOS VECTOR
DC     I2'$29'                 ;$0029 = PRODOS QUIT FUNCTION
DC     I4'QUITPARAMETERS'      ;A LONG WORD POINTING TO PARAMETERS
QUITPARAMTERS  ANOP            ;THE LOCATION OF YOUR QUIT PARAMS.
DC     I4'$0'                  ;A LONG WORD OF ZERO
DC     I2'$0'                  ;A WORD OF ZERO
```

ProDOS 16 functions are executed by jumping to a vector at address $E100A8. The JSL instruction is followed by six bytes: The

first two bytes define the function code; the next four bytes are a long pointer to a parameter list.

Function $29 requires a parameter list with two items.

Pathname (long pointer)
Flag value (word)

The Pathname is a pointer to the name of the next program to run after this one. The program's name is a complete pathname, in ASCII, with a leading count byte. If the Pathname pointer is a long word of zero, you are returned to the program shell, or the program which launched your application.

The Flag value does a few things based on how its bits are set. Only bits 15 and 14 of the word value hold any significance; the other bits should be reset to zero.

Bit 15 If set places your program's User ID on the stack. This way, the next program could do something with that value.
Bit 14 If set instructs the next program that your program can be restarted from memory.

For additional information on this and other ProDOS calls, consult your ProDOS reference.

Special Cases

There are a few tool sets which lack StartUp and ShutDown functions. These tool sets don't require the StartUp function to be called—they're always active. Likewise, the ShutDown function need never be called.

A call to these tool sets' StartUp or ShutDown functions won't hurt anything; the toolbox dispatcher simply returns your request unfulfilled.

The tool sets listed in Table 9-8 either have no StartUp function or don't require their StartUp function to be called. Likewise, the ShutDown function need never be used.

Table 9-8. Tool Sets Which Do Not Require StartUp or ShutDown

Tool Set Number	Name
$03	Miscellaneous
$07	Scheduler
$09	Apple Desktop Bus
$0B	Integer Math
$0C	Text Tools
$11	Loader
$1C	List Manager

Chapter 10

Strings and Things

When you're working with the toolbox, you'll be concerned with three major items: *Pointers, Handles,* and *Graphics.* Knowing the difference between each, and especially how the toolbox deals with them, is important. A lot of professional

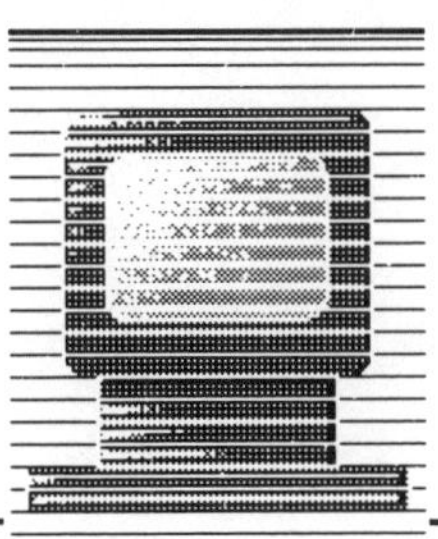

programmers make silly mistakes by confusing handles and pointers.

This chapter discusses the differences between pointers, handles, and graphics and how to use each with the toolbox. Additionally, the various types of strings used by the toolbox are covered. At the end of this chapter is a summary for pushing and pulling Pointers and Handles from the stack, which should help you avoid confusion.

The following briefly describes Pointers, Handles, and Graphics Pointers.

Pointers. A pointer is a memory location that points to other memory locations—it contains an address in which a string, structure, or table might be found.

Handles. Handles are pointers to pointers. A handle points to a memory location that contains additional information about what the handle is connected to—another memory address, structure, or combination of each.

Graphics. Graphics use a special type of pointer. The graphics pointer is the memory address of a series of values which define a rectangle or point on the screen. For all practical purposes, graphics pointers are the same as any other type of pointer. However, they deserve special mention because they point to a memory locations which are also structures.

How the Toolbox Works with Pointers

A pointer is a *memory address.* It points to a specific bank and offset within that bank where some type of information is or will be located. An example of a pointer is the value $00E0655C. This pointer points at offset $655C in memory bank $E0.

When the toolbox requires a pointer, you push the pointer's long word value onto the stack. The High Order Word (HOW) is pushed first, followed by the Low Order Word (LOW). In the case of pointers, the HOW is the memory bank and the LOW is an offset within that bank. The Most Significant Byte (MSB) of the HOW is always set to $00. (It is ignored by the toolbox.)

The following code pushes the pointer Text on the stack. Text points at the text characters listed in the example.

```
PEA   TEXT|-16      ;PUSH THE HOW
PEA   TEXT          ;THE LOW
TEXT  DC C'HELLO'   ;THE STRING IN MEMORY
```

In the *APW* assembler, |-16 shifts the value of Text right 16 bits. PEA TEXT|-16 pushes the bank number the label Text is located in. If Text's address is $020805, $0002 is pushed. A following PEA instruction would push Text's offset within the bank, or $0805. The important thing to remember is the bank number is pushed first.

A second way to do this is to push the Data Bank Register directly to the stack. The Data Bank Register already points to the bank where the string (or whatever the pointer is pointing at) is located. The only caution here is that the Data Bank Register is an eight-bit value and only one byte is pushed to the stack. Therefore, it must be done twice.

```
PHB                 ;PUSH AN 8 BIT VALUE
PHB                 ;PUSH THE DATA BANK
PEA   TEXT          ;AND NOW THE MEMORY OFFSET
```

This works because the toolbox ignores the MSB of the High Order Word pushed. So if the pointer Text is at memory location $020805, the following values are pushed to the stack:

$02	the PHB, an 8-bit value (ignored by the toolbox)
$02	the PHB again
$0805	the offset within bank $02

A word value, $0202, is still pushed to the stack. However, the toolbox ignores the MSB of this value, so pushing the Data Bank Register twice does the job. The only limitations to this trick is that you must be certain the Data Bank Register happens to be the same as where your data is located, or equal to your Program Bank Register. Otherwise, you might not be pointing to the proper bank of memory.

Occasionally the toolbox returns a pointer after a function is called. When it does, the following code can be used to pull the pointer's value from the stack and place it into the variable, Pointer.

```
PLA                     ;PULL LOW FIRST
STA     POINTER         ;STORE IT
PLA                     ;PULL HOW
STA     POINTER+2       ;STORE IT TOO
POINTER DS 4            ;STORAGE FOR THE POINTER
```

Now the pointer, or memory address, is stored in the four-byte variable, Pointer. The value stored points to a memory location which could contain a value, structure, or string of text.

Because a pointer returned by a tool set probably points at something you're interested in, it would be nice to examine that area of memory. This is done by taking advantage of your program's zero page. (Those not familiar with the zero page of the 65xx chips should refer to a programming manual.)

By placing the pointer pulled from the stack into the zero page as well as into a variable, the information the pointer is pointing to can be indirectly accessed. The following code places the pointer into location 0 of the zero page, as well as in the variable Pointer (this only works with the zero page).

```
PLA                     ;PULL LOW FIRST
STA     POINTER         ;STORE IT HERE
STA     0               ;AND IN THE ZERO PAGE
PLA                     ;PULL HOW
STA     POINTER+2
STA     2               ;AND HERE IN THE ZERO PAGE
```

The long word at memory location 0 points to the same location as the long word pointer returned from the toolbox. This location can be accessed using the long indirect addressing mode.

```
LDA     [0]
```

After the above instruction, the A register contains the word value at the memory location Pointer is pointing at. (This technique is graphically illustrated in the previous chapter.) If Pointer is pointing at a table or other data structure, after LDA [0], the A register contains the first word in the table.

How the Toolbox Works with Handles

A *handle* is a pointer to a pointer. The location the handle points to contains another pointer, a structure, or other interesting information. (Handles were discussed in Chapter 8.)

Like pointers, handles contain a memory location. But unlike pointers, the memory location a handle contains is not the information the handle is concerned with. While a valid handle may be $E0655C, the information at that location (which points to another location in memory) is what's important.

Most often, handles are created by the toolbox. You pass certain values on the stack to a function and it creates a handle and returns it to you. The handle then provides the convenient access by which you can use whatever you've created, a memory block, graphic shape, window, icon, and so on.

When the toolbox returns a handle, you pull the value of the handle from the stack and place it into a variable. For example,

```
PLA                 ;PULL LOW OF HANDLE
STA    HANDLE       ;PUT IT INTO STORAGE
PLA                 ;PULL HOW OF HANDLE
STA    HANDLE+2     ;AND PUT IT INTO STORAGE
```

The handle the toolbox returned is now stored in the four-byte variable, Handle. If your program wishes to examine the values stored in the memory location pointed at by Handle, you will have to use the zero page trick discussed earlier in this chapter. (It's also demonstrated in Chapter 9, in the section that discusses obtaining the direct page location.)

When a toolbox function requires that you push a handle to the stack, you push the value of the handle. This differs from pushing a pointer on the stack because a value and not a memory location is pushed.

For example, suppose a handle is stored at the four-byte memory location Handle. The following code pushes the handle to the stack:

```
LDA    HANDLE+2     ;PUSH HOW FIRST (THIS IS THE
PHA                 ;OPPOSITE OF HOW IT WAS PULLED)
LDA    HANDLE       ;PUSH LOW LAST
PHA
```

Now the handle has been put on the stack. Keep in mind how this is different from pushing a pointer; the pointer's memory location is pushed, often using PEA instructions. When pushing a Handle to the stack, it's value is pushed.

How the Toolbox Works with Graphics

When the toolbox deals with graphics, it's referencing a set of coordinate values. As far as the toolbox is concerned, these coordinates are treated as a pointer—they correspond to a memory location where something is stored. There are two major types of graphics: Rectangles and Points.

Rectangles. When the toolbox asks for a rectangle pointer, or any similar pointer, it's treated the same as the pointers described earlier in this chapter. For example, the following code pushes the pointer to the memory location Square on the stack.

```
PEA    SQUARE|-16       ;PUSH SQUARE'S MEMORY BANK
PEA    SQUARE           ;PUSH SQUARE'S LOCATION
```

As with other pointers, first the memory bank is pushed, then the address within that bank. Pointers to graphics are simply the memory locations of that particular graphic's set of coordinates.

Rectangles contain four word values. These values define the upper left and lower right corner of the rectangle. When a toolbox function requires a pointer to a rectangle, the structure is

```
RECTANGLE    DS  2         ;UPPER LEFT Y LOCATION, 1 WORD
             DS  2         ;UPPER LEFT X LOCATION, 1 WORD
             DS  2         ;LOWER RIGHT Y LOCATION, 1 WORD
             DS  2         ;LOWER RIGHT X LOCATION, 1 WORD
```

Notice that this notation is different from the standard X1, Y1, X2, Y2 notations used in certain high-level languages. In the toolbox reference, the coordinates are listed as Min Y, Min X, Max Y, Max X, for the Upper Left and Lower Right coordinates, respectively.

The toolbox only needs the locations of two of the rectangle's corners. It figures out the other corners as shown in Figure 10-1.

Passing a pointer to a rectangle to the toolbox is as simple as pushing the pointer to the stack. For the above example, the following will work.

```
PEA    RECTANGLE|-16 ;PUSH THE MEMORY BANK
PEA    RECTANGLE     ;PUSH THE LOCATION
```

If the toolbox returns a pointer to a rectangle, the location that pointer references contains the exact structure as above. Oftentimes, however, toolbox functions which return information about a rectangle first ask you to push a pointer on the stack. In these cases, your pointer should contain the memory address of an

Figure 10-1. How a Rectangle's Corners Are Labeled

empty structure. The toolbox function then fills the structure with the requested coordinates.

Rectangles may also be referred to as *Bounds, Rectangles,* or *Regions.* All use the same structure as noted above. The coordinates are considered *global* (which means they are relative to the upper left corner of the screen) unless they are labeled as local. Local coordinates are measured from the upper left corner of the window, dialog box, graphics rectangle, or other shape they are contained within.

Points. Points describe a coordinate location—the X and Y values which define where the point is located on the graphics screen. When a toolbox function requires a pointer to a point, the point structure is

```
POINT   DS  2        ;THE Y LOCATION, 1 WORD
        DS  2        ;THE X LOCATION, 1 WORD
```

Both X and Y are integer values. Each represents a specific number of pixels from the upper left corner of the graphics display. The Y value is the vertical and the X value is the horizontal displacement.

When the toolbox returns a pointer to a point, the address that pointer references contains the same structure (two words) as above.

How the Toolbox Works with Strings

The toolbox deals with three types of *strings.* Each of these strings is stored differently in memory, and for each type there is a corresponding toolbox function. They are:

- Pascal strings
- C strings
- Text blocks

All types of strings contain printable ASCII characters which are displayed as text. The difference between each type is in how the toolbox determines the length of the string.

Pascal strings. Pascal strings all start with a *count byte.* These are the most common types of strings used in the toolbox. The count byte is a value 0–255 which describes the length of the string immediately following. For example,

5,"Hello"

The byte 5 is the count byte. It is followed by five text characters, H-E-L-L-O. If the characters H-E-L-L-O-L-L-Y-P-O-P followed the count byte, only the first five would be considered part of the string.

The length of Pascal strings can be stated directly, as above, or calculated by your assembler. In the *APW* assembler, the above Pascal string could be written as

```
    DC    I1'5'        ;DEFINE A BYTE VALUE OF 5
    DC    C'HELLO'     ;DEFINE THE CHARACTER STRING
```

While this is accurate, it makes updating the code more difficult. A better way is to make the assembler calculate the string's length as follows.

```
STRING       DC     I1'STREND-STRSTART'
STRSTART     DC     C'HELLO'
STREND       ANOP
```

String is calculated as the length of *strend* (at the end of the string) minus *strstart.* Now the string size can be adjusted, characters can be added, and the assembler will always accurately calculate the length of the string at assembly time.

C strings. The length of a C string is determined by a terminating character. Rather than use an initial count byte, a C string is considered to be all the characters appearing before a special end-byte value, the *End Of Line (EOL)* character. In the Apple IIGS toolbox, the byte value $00, the null character, is used as the EOL character for a C string.

"Hello",0

The above C string is the five-letter word *Hello*. Because the byte value $00 follows the *o*, it is considered the end of the string.

The C string "Four score and seven years ago",0,"our fathers brought forth..." only consists of the first six words. All words after the zero are not considered part of the string.

The biggest advantage of C strings is that they can be any length. Because the EOL byte $00, is used as the terminator, C strings are not limited to 255 characters as are Pascal strings. The only requirement is that you remember to terminate the string with a zero. Otherwise, the toolbox will keep reading characters until it stumbles upon a stray $00.

Text blocks. Characters and strings are read from text blocks at a specific offset and length within the text block. Consider the following block of text: ABCDEFGHIJKLMNOPQRSTUVWXYZ. This is a block of 26 characters. To read the characters JKL, you would specify an offset of nine and a length of three. The letter *A* is considered offset 0. *J* is the tenth letter of the alphabet, yet it is positioned at the ninth offset.

When the toolbox deals with a block of text, you pass three parameters:

- A pointer to the text
- The offset within the text to start reading characters
- The number of characters to read

Any specific character or group of characters can be read anywhere within the text block. Where this method of dealing with strings comes in handy is with long lists of items. Suppose a text block contains a list of 150 filenames, each one 15 characters long. To read the filename number 40, you need to point to the list of filenames, start reading at offset 600 (40 × 15), and read 15 characters (the length).

Refer to the program GREETINGS in Chapter 6 for an example of reading characters and using a text block function to display those characters.

Summary

The following is a brief summary of how to deal with pushing and pulling pointers and handles.

Pushing a pointer (memory address) to the stack:

```
PEA    TEXT|-16       ;PUSH THE HOW
PEA    TEXT           ;THE LOW
```

A pointer may also be pushed to the stack in the following way:

```
PHB                 ;PUSH AN 8 BIT VALUE
PHB                 ;PUSH THE DATA BANK
PEA    TEXT         ;AND NOW THE MEMORY OFFSET
```

Pulling a pointer from the stack:

```
PLA                 ;PULL LOW FIRST
STA    POINTER      ;STORE IT IN THIS 2 WORD LOCATION
PLA                 ;PULL HOW
STA    POINTER+2
```

Pulling a pointer to take advantage of indirect addressing using the zero page:

```
PLA                 ;PULL LOW FIRST
STA    POINTER      ;STORE IT HERE
STA    0            ;AND IN THE ZERO PAGE
PLA                 ;PULL HOW
STA    POINTER+2
STA    2            ;AND HERE IN THE ZERO PAGE
```

Pushing a handle to the stack:

```
LDA    HANDLE+2     ;PUSH HOW FIRST (THIS IS THE
PHA                 ;OPPOSITE OF HOW IT WAS PULLED)
LDA    HANDLE       ;PUSH LOW LAST
PHA
```

Pulling a handle from the stack:

```
PLA                 ;PULL LOW OF HANDLE
STA    HANDLE       ;PUT IT INTO STORAGE
PLA                 ;PULL HOW OF HANDLE
STA    HANDLE+2     ;AND PUT IT INTO STORAGE
```

Chapter 11

Error Handling Routines

Only certain toolbox calls return errors. When they do the error is often fatal. It usually means the program failed to do something early on, such as allocate memory or start up a particular tool set, or it may mean that an invalid parameter was passed to a routine. In

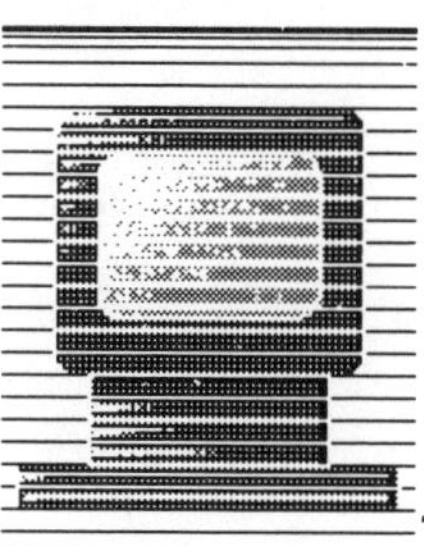

either case, when most tool sets return with an error, there's little a program can do.

In some instances, your program could react to the error by displaying a dialog box warning of some action. For example, if a certain tool set such as the Print Manager is not found on disk, your program could shut off all printing functions, then inform the user that printing has been disabled.

However, if your program can't deal with the error (or you just don't want to do that much programming), an error handler can be written to take care of the situation. This chapter covers three types of error handlers: *specific, general,* and *failsafe.* In the cases of specific and general error handlers, it's assumed the error situation is not recoverable. Failsafe error handlers attempt to recover from certain types of errors. Otherwise, all potential errors are considered fatal.

Specific Error Handlers

A specific error handler is called immediately after a toolbox call. This eats up more code than writing a general error handler, but for eliminating bugs, specific error handlers are hard to beat. (A general error handler which can locate specific bugs is demonstrated later in this chapter.)

You may recall from Chapter 4 that an error is detected after a toolbox call is made. If the A register contains zero and if the C (carry) flag in the status register is reset to zero, no error occurs. However, if the C flag is set to one after making a toolbox call, then the A register contains a 16-bit error code.

Specific error handlers should be called immediately after a potential error can occur, as should all error handling routines. Remember, not all toolbox calls can produce errors. Some will return with the carry flag set and a nonzero value in the A register even when no error has occurred. Only if the toolbox index states that an error is possible should error checking be performed.

```
JSL     $E10000         ;call to potential error-riddled function
```

After the above call, a number of errors could occur. The carry flag in the processor status register is tested to check for an error.

```
     JSL   $E10000      ;CALL TO POTENTIAL ERROR-RIDDLED FUNCTION
     BCC   OK1          ;CARRY CLEAR, GO ON
     ...                ;SPECIFIC ERROR HANDLER GOES HERE
OK1  ANOP               ;PROGRAM CONTINUES HERE
```

If no error occurred, then the flag is clear and the *BCC (Branch if Carry flag is Clear)* opcode branches to a point just past the specific error handler and continues executing code. This is why specific error handlers take up more memory than general error handlers. Each toolbox call with the potential for error must have its own error handler.

Because most of these errors are fatal, the "System Death" toolbox call can be used to shut down the computer. The SysFailMgr function in the Miscellaneous tool set is always available—even after some very fatal errors. It displays an error code and a message.

Function: $1503
Name: SysFailMgr
Halts program and displays an error message.
Push: Error Code (W); String Address (L)
Pull: nothing
Errors: none
Comments: String starts with a count byte. If String Address is 0, the standard message is used.

The simplest specific error handler can contain only a call to this function.

Because a toolbox error places the error number in the A register, A can be pushed on the stack for use by the SysFailMgr. If $00000000 is pushed for the String Address, the standard fatal error message is displayed. To stop a program and display a fatal error, you need to use a routine similar to the following.

```
     JSL   $E10000      ;CALL TO POTENTIAL ERROR-RIDDLED FUNCTION
     BCC   OK1          ;CARRY CLEAR, GO ON
     PHA                ;PUSH ERROR CODE IN A
     PEA   $0000        ;USE STANDARD ERROR
     PEA   $0000
     LDX   #$1503       ;SYSFAILMGR
     JSL   $E10000      ;BOMB OUT HERE
OK1  ANOP               ;PROGRAM CONTINUES HERE
```

If an error occurs, the system stops and "Fatal System Error" is displayed followed by the error number in hexadecimal.

To make the error handler more specific, suppose this particular error might occur after calling the Mythical ShortCircuit function.

```
        JSL   $E10000        ;CALL TO POTENTIAL ERROR-RIDDLED FUNCTION
        BCC   OK1            ;CARRY CLEAR, GO ON
        PHA                  ;PUSH ERROR CODE IN A
        PEA   ER1|-16        ;THIS MEMORY BANK NUMBER
        PEA   ER1            ;THE ERROR MESSAGE BELOW
        LDX   #$1503         ;SYSFAILMGR
        JSL   $E10000        ;BOMB OUT HERE
ER1     DC    I1'ER1E-ER1S'
ER1S    DC    C'ERROR IN SHORT CIRCUIT ROUTINE $'
ER1E    ANOP
OK1     ANOP                 ;PROGRAM CONTINUES HERE
```

This variation displays the message "Error in Short Circuit routine $" followed by the value in register A. The message is a bit more specific than the standard fatal error message. Writing a routine such as this after each potential toolbox error would make tracking errors easy.

Many programmers use assembly language macros to define all that information for them. For example, the above error code could be replaced with

```
    JSL    $E10000      ;CALL TO POTENTIAL ERROR-RIDDLED FUNCTION
    ERROR  'ERROR IN SHORT CIRCUIT ROUTINE $'
                        ;PROGRAM CONTINUES HERE
```

The SysFailMgr call, the BCC instruction and OK1 label, would all be part of the macro command *Error.* Error contains a routine which tests the carry flag and, if set, displays the message listed after the Error macro. (Refer to your assembler's manual for more information on macros.)

General Error Handlers

A general error handler is a single routine capable of dealing with all errors in the system. Its advantage over the specific error handler is that it doesn't take up as much code. Once it is written, you're done. The disadvantage with a general error handler is that it is more difficult to determine the cause of some errors.

Any general error handler is going to look sort of *kludgy.* A kludge is a combination of a clunker and a drudge. It gets the job done, but there is no way to make it look streamlined. General error handlers would work much better if there were a 65816 instruction that jumps to a subroutine based on the condition of the carry flag, such as a JCS instruction, for Jump if Carry is Set. Since there isn't one, an error handler such as the following must be written.

Unlike the specific error handler, which is avoided if the carry flag is clear (the BCC instruction), a general error handler is always called after each toolbox call capable of an error.

```
JSL   $E10000     ;CALL TO ERROR-RIDDLED FUNCTION
JSR   ERRORH      ;CALL TO ERROR-HANDLER
```

Each toolbox call that could err is immediately followed by a call to the general error handler routine, *ErrorH.* (This book uses the label ErrorH for all general error handler routines.)

It's in the ErrorH subroutine where the carry flag is tested. If the carry flag is clear, execution immediately returns to the caller; otherwise, the error handler is invoked.

```
ERRORH  START              ;THIS IS THE ERROR HANDLING SUBROUTINE
        BCS     OOPS       ;BRANCH CARRY SET TO "OOPS"
        RTS                ;OTHERWISE RETURN
OOPS    ANOP               ;ACTUAL ERROR HANDLER FOLLOWS...
```

Once your program transfers control to the error handler, the carry flag is tested. If it's set, execution branches to the *OOPS* routine (in the example) and the error handler takes over. Otherwise it's a quick return back to the caller. This may seem like a lot of overhead, yet it doesn't subtract any noticeable execution time—and it saves space.

Once in the error handler, the error routine can be the same as for the specific routine listed earlier. A call to the SysFailMgr function will handle any fatal errors encountered. Because the A register contains an error code, simply pushing it to the stack, followed by the long address of an error string (or zero if the system default message is used) finishes the routine.

```
ERRORH  START                   ;THIS IS THE ERROR HANDLING SUBROUTINE
        BCS     OOPS            ;BRANCH CARRY SET TO "OOPS"
        RTS                     ;OTHERWISE RETURN
OOPS    ANOP                    ;ACTUAL ERROR HANDLER FOLLOWS...
        PHA                     ;PUSH ERROR CODE IN A
        PEA     ER1|-16         ;THIS MEMORY BANK NUMBER
        PEA     ER1             ;THE ERROR MESSAGE BELOW
        LDX     #$1503          ;SYSFAILMGR
        JSL     $E10000         ;BOMB OUT HERE
ER1     DC      I1'ER1E-ER1S'
ER1S    DC      C'THIS PROGRAM HAS ENCOUNTERED ERROR $'
ER1E    ANOP
```

Keep in mind the string message is displayed on a 40-column screen. If the message appears too long, you might want to insert a carriage return, as in

```
ER1     DC   I1'ER1E-ER1S'
ER1S    DC   C'THIS PROGRAM HAS ENCOUNTERED THE'
        DC   I1'13'
        DC   C'DIABOLICAL ERROR $'
ER1E    ANOP
```

General, Yet Specific, Error Handlers

One method of making general error handlers a bit more specific would be to tag potential trouble spots using the X register (the A register might already contain an error code). For example,

```
JSL   $E10000      ;CALL TO POTENTIAL ERROR-RIDDLED FUNCTION
LDX   #$0001       ;TAG THIS AS POTENTIAL ERROR #1
JSR   ERRORH       ;CALL TO ERROR-HANDLER
```

Each potential error would be sequentially marked. The next call to the error handler would be proceeded by

```
LDX   #$0002       ;TAG THIS ERROR AS #2
```

and so on, marking each potential error with a higher value in the X register.

The actual error handler will then display the error code encountered, as well as the tag number. Using the tag number, the specific error can be tracked and located within the program. The code to do this could be as follows:

```
ERRORH   START            ;THIS IS THE ERROR HANDLING SUBROUTINE
         BCS    OOPS      ;BRANCH IF CARRY SET TO "OOPS"
         RTS              ;OTHERWISE RETURN HERE
OOPS     PHA              ;SAVE A ON THE STACK
         PEA    $0000     ;PUSH LONG RESULT SPACE
         PEA    $0000
         PHX              ;PUSH THE TAG VALUE IN X
         LDX    #$2A0B    ;HEXIT
         JSL    $E10000   ;RETURNS HEX STRING OF TAG VALUE
         PLA              ;GET HEX STRING
         STA    VAL       ;PUT IT IN VAL
         PLA              ;GET HIGH ORDER WORD
         STA    VAL+2     ;PUT IT THERE
;                         ;A IS ALREADY ON THE STACK
         PEA    ER1|-16   ;THIS MEMORY BANK NUMBER
         PEA    ER1       ;THE ERROR MESSAGE BELOW
         LDX    #$1503    ;SYSFAILMGR
         JSL    $E10000   ;BOMB OUT HERE
ER1      DC     I1'ER1E-ER1S'
ER1S     DC     C'ERROR TAG NUMBER $'
VAL      DS     4
         DC     I1'13'
         DC     C'DIABOLICAL ERROR $'
ER1E     ANOP
                END
```

Now, when an error happens and execution branches to the ErrorH routine, the following is displayed on a 40-column screen:

Error tag number $0001
Diabolical error $0101

(This assumes error tag 1 and some error with the Tool Locator tool set.)

Failsafe Error Handlers

Certain errors can be trapped without having to bomb out to the SysFailMgr each time. For example, the Event Manager StartUp function returns an error if the Event Manager has already been started (implying a previous program did not shut it down properly). If this is the case, your program can skip the EMStartUp routine.

The code to test if the Event Manager is already started, based on an error code of $0201, *Event Manager already started,* appears below.

```
        LDX    #$0206        ;EMSTARTUP
        JSL    $E10000
        BCC    OK1           ;NO ERROR, CONTINUE

        CMP    #$0201        ;HAS IT ALREADY BEEN STARTED?
        BEQ    OK1           ;IF SO, BRANCH TO OK1
        JSR    ERRORH        ;OTHERWISE, ASSUME FATAL ERROR
OK1     ANOP                 ;PROGRAM CONTINUES HERE
```

After the EMStartUp function call is made (and this assumes the parameters of EMStartUp have already been pushed to the stack), the carry flag is checked. If the carry is not set, meaning no error occurred, execution continues at the OK1 label.

If the carry flag is set, the value of the A register, the error code, is compared with $0201. If equal, it means the Event Manager has already been started and there is no need to bomb out to the fatal error handler. Program execution continues at the OK1 label. Otherwise, a fatal error is assumed and execution branches to the fatal error handler.

Error $0201 from the Memory Manager is the "unable to allocate block" error. This could also imply that there isn't enough memory for the block. Whatever the circumstances, it's probably not a fatal error and there's no need to bomb the system. Instead, your program could test for this particular error, then skirt around the routines that required the block of memory.

Suppose your program is allocating a temporary block of memory for use as an icon in a dialog box. The icon is not that crucial, so if memory cannot be allocated, your program sets a flag in memory. The following code could be inserted after a call to the Memory Manager's NewHandle function, $0902 to test for error $0201, unable to allocate block.

```
            LDX    #$0902      ;NEWHANDLE FUNCTION FOR ICON
            JSL    $E10000
            BCC    OK1         ;NO ERROR, CONTINUE
            CMP    #$0201      ;IS THE ERROR CODE IN A $0201?
            BEQ    NOICON      ;IF SO, BRANCH TO NOICON
            JSR    ERRORH      ;OTHERWISE, BOMB OUT
NOICON      ANOP               ;UNABLE TO ALLOCATE MEMORY
```

```
          LDA    #$FFFF      ;SET THE ICON-UNAVAILABLE FLAG
          STA    ICONNA      ; INTO THE VARIABLE ICONNA
OK1       ANOP               ;PROGRAM CONTINUES HERE
```

Any time other parts of the program request access to the icon, they first check the IconNA flag to see if the icon is present. If the flag is not equal to zero, that part of your code should skip its reference to the icon.

This technique could be used with any function that has an error potential, and is able to recover from the error.

Another failsafe error handler could be used after certain tool sets are loaded from disk. The only potential toolbox error of the Tool Locator's LoadTools and LoadOneTool functions is $0110, indicating the minimum tool set version was not found.

Suppose the following code is used to load the Print Manager from disk. If the Print Manager is any version earlier than 3.4 (as specified in the tool table), the toolbox returns an error $0110. The following code tests for that error.

```
          LDX    #$0E01      ;LOADTOOLS
          JSL    $E10000
          BCC    OK1         ;NO ERROR, CONTINUE
          CMP    #$0110      ;IS THIS ERROR $0110?
          BEQ    NOTFOUND    ;IF SO, BRANCH TO NOTFOUND
          JSR    ERRORH      ;OTHERWISE, BOMB OUT
NOTFOUND  ANOP               ;SEE BELOW
OK1       ANOP               ;PROGRAM CONTINUES HERE
```

If an error is not returned by the toolbox, execution branches to the OK1 label. Otherwise, the error code is compared with $0110. If that's not the error code, the standard bomb to the ErrorH routine is used. Otherwise, execution branches to NotFound.

The NotFound routine might display a message informing the user that minimum version 3.4 of the Print Manager was not found, then gently return the user to ProDOS. This would be much more polite than printing the relatively harsh message "Fatal System Error -> $0110" on the screen, and then forcing the user to reset the machine.

Chapter 12

The Event Manager

An *event* is anything that happens in the Apple IIGS. Anytime something happens, it's considered an event. Of course, events could be called incidents, occurrences, or even phenomena. But the general idea is that something happened. It might be a key press,

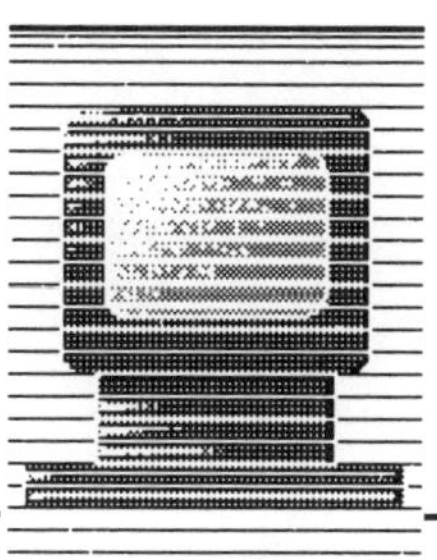

a click of the mouse, activity in a window or pull-down menu, receipt of information from the serial port, or a number of other things.

The Event Manager remains alert for these events at all times without any prompting. When the Event Manager intercepts an event, it places it in a *queue,* another word for a line. Like cars lined up at a garage for service, the events are kept in a queue by the Event Manager until your application (or the system) removes them for examination. Once removed from the queue, your program can act upon the events.

The Event Manager eliminates the necessity to program your own interrupt-driven routines. It takes care of such basic tasks as logging keystrokes and monitoring the mouse, as well as scanning for desktop activity, and controlling windows and pull-down menus.

This chapter covers how the Event Manager works and how to use it in your programs. A majority of your programs will be event-driven, so understanding the Event Manager is important. When you've mastered the Event Manager, graphics, windows, and other applications will be easy.

Types of Events

Unless you're dealing with straight text input/output, the Event Manager will probably be a part of each of your programs. Although the Event Manager is also capable of handling text input and output, there are other tool sets more specific to these tasks. There are four categories of items which are considered events:

- Keyboard events
- Mouse events
- Window events
- Other events

Keyboard events. A keyboard event happens when a key is pressed. There are two types of keyboard events. The first event happens when the key is initially pressed. The Event Manager can tell your program which key was pressed and whether the shift key, control key, option key, or Apple key was also down, or whether or not the key was pressed on the keypad. A second type of keyboard event happens when the key is held down and begins to repeat. This is known as an *auto-key* event.

Mouse events. Mouse events deal with the mouse's button: When the button is pressed, an event occurs; a second event occurs when the button is released. During these two times, the position of the mouse can be obtained. Movement of the mouse is not an event, however; mouse movement can be detected in other ways. This will be illustrated in the next few chapters.

Window events. Window events are the responsibility of the Window Manager tool set. In fact, a specific function of that tool set—the TaskMaster—is designed to look for and add window events to the Event Manager's queue. Any time the mouse is clicked in a window, or activity changes from one window to another, an event is put into the queue.

Other events. Other events include a variety of things—some events your program can define on its own. Switch events occur when the mouse is clicked on a control (button, checkbox, and so on) in a dialog box. When the Classic Desk Accessory menu is accessed by pressing Control-Apple-Esc, an event is generated. If the mouse is clicked inside a window or dialog box, an event occurs. All these miscellaneous events fit into this category.

Using the Event Manager

When working with the Event Manager you will be concerned with three things: the *event queue,* the *event mask,* and the *event record.* These give the Event Manager control and flexibility, allowing your programs to work smoothly.

The event queue. The event queue is a list of all pending events intercepted by the Event Manager. It's maintained and updated by the Event Manager as necessary, so you won't have to deal with it directly. Each time an event occurs, the Event Manager places a code for that event into the queue. A special function of the Event Manager, GetNextEvent, is then used to *poll* (or read) events from the queue.

The event mask. The event mask is a special filter you can apply to the event queue. The event mask directs the Event Manager to only look for certain, specific events. For example, the mask can be set to allow the Event Manager only to place mouse events into the queue. All other types of events would be masked out and ignored.

The event record. The last item (and possibly the most important) is the event record. The event record is a list which contains detailed information about the event. If an event occurs and it's pulled from the queue, your program merely needs to examine the event record to determine what action to take.

To use the Event Manager requires a call to the EMStartUp function. This would be included as part of your program's startup procedure.

The Event Manager does not need to be loaded from disk. However it does require its own direct-page space and your program's User ID. Also, because the Event Manager is responsible for the mouse, you need to tell it where the mouse can and can't go on the screen. The event record and event mask are used when actually reading events from the queue.

Function: $0206
Name: EMStartUp
Starts the Event Manager.
Push: Direct Page (W); Event Queue Size (W); Minimum X (W); Maximum X (W); Minimum Y (W); Maximum Y (W); UserID (W)
Pull: nothing
Errors: $0601, $0606, $0607
Comments: X and Y values refer to mouse clamps.

Obtaining direct-page space was discussed in Chapters 8 and 9. The Event Queue Size determines the size of the queue used to hold events. It can be any value from $0001 through $0E37. If $0000 is specified, the standard queue size of 20 is used.

The X and Y clamping bounds determine where the mouse can move the cursor on the screen. The values are in global coordinates, meaning the upper left corner of the screen is position 0, 0. From that coordinate, the bottom of the screen is position 199 and the right hand side of the screen is position 319 or 639, depending on the screen's resolution.

The User ID is obtained by the Memory Manager when the program was started. Usually, the Event Manager will be the fourth or fifth tool started by your program. Already started should be the Tool Locator, Memory Manager, and Misc tool set. If your program includes the QuickDraw II tool set, it should be started before the Event Manager.

The following code starts the Event Manager. DPage is the address of direct page memory in bank $00. UserID is this program's

User ID. It is assumed that the screen is in the 320 × 200 pixel mode and that QuickDraw II is already started.

```
LDA   DPAGE     ;GET DIRECT PAGE FOR EVENT MANAGER
CLC             ;CLEAR CARRY FLAG FOR ADC
ADC   #$300     ;ALLOW FOR QDII'S DIRECT PAGE
PHA             ;PUSH EM'S DPAGE ON THE STACK
PEA   20        ;EVENT QUEUE SIZE = 20
PEA   0         ;MIN X CLAMP = 0
PEA   320       ;MAX X CLAMP = 320
PEA   0         ;MIN Y CLAMP = 0
PEA   200       ;MAX Y CLAMP = 200
LDA   USERID    ;THIS PROGRAM'S USERID
PHA             ;PUSH ON THE STACK
LDX   #$0206    ;EMSTARTUP
JSL   $E10000
JSR   ERRORH    ;CHECK FOR ERRORS
```

Because QuickDraw II is already started, it has used $300 bytes of direct-page space. The Event Manager's direct page needs to start at DPage + $300. This is why the CLC and ADC #$300 instructions are required.

After the Event Manager is started, it begins looking for tasks and placing them into the queue. Your program can examine the queue for pending events by using the GetNextEvent function.

Acting on Events

The main routine in the Event Manager tool set is GetNextEvent. This function's job is to check on the event queue and report any pending events. If no events are returned, your program can either continue scanning for them or go off and do something else.

If an event is reported by GetNextEvent, it's removed from the queue. Information about the event is placed in the event record. Your program can then examine the event record and act upon the results. For example, if the event record shows a mouse-down event, your program can determine the mouse's position on the screen and then do something at that location.

Function: $0A06
Name: GetNextEvent
Returns the status of the event queue.
Push: Result Space (W); Event Mask (W); Event Record (L)
Pull: Logical Result (W)
Errors: none

Comments: If the Result is a logical true, an event is available. The event is then removed from the queue.

Three values are pushed to the stack: a word of result space, the event mask, and a pointer to the event record.

The event mask is used to filter out certain types of events. By setting specific bits in the event mask, your program can direct GetNextEvent to return only the results of specific events. Table 12-1 shows which bits in the event mask affect which events.

Table 12-1. Event Mask

Bit Set	Events Scanned For
0	Not used
1	Mouse-down events
2	Mouse-up events
3	Keyboard (key down) events
4	Not used
5	Auto-key events
6	Update events
7	Not used
8	Activate events
9	Switch events
10	Desk accessory events
11	Device drive events
12	User defined events
13	User defined events
14	User defined events
15	User defined events

So, for example, if bits 1 and 2 are set, GetNextEvent reports only mouse button events. The value pushed on the stack for the event mask would be $0006. Unless you need to be specific, you should push a value of $FFFF to scan for all types of events.

The event record is a pointer to a structure which contains descriptive information about the event. The structure is 16 bytes long and is described in detail below.

To call GetNextEvent, the following code could be used. This routine is called repeatedly until an event occurs.

```
SCAN    ANOP                    ;SCANNING LOOP
        PHA                     ;PUSH RESULT SPACE
        PEA     $FFFF           ;EVENT MASK (EVERYTHING)
        PEA     EVENTR|-16      ;POINTER TO EVENT RECORD
        PEA     EVENTR
        LDX     #$0A06          ;GETNEXTEVENT
```

```
     JSL     $E10000
     PLA                  ;RETURN LOGICAL RESULT
     BEQ     SCAN         ;KEEP LOOKING IF NO EVENTS PENDING
```

This routine first pushes a word of result space to the stack. The event mask is set to $FFFF, meaning that you are scanning for all types of events. Next, a long pointer to the event record is pushed. And finally, the call to GetNextEvent is made.

GetNextEvent returns a logical result as to whether an event is pending or not. If the result is false, $0000, no event was waiting. Otherwise the type of event and information about the event is found in the event record (see Table 12-2).

Table 12-2. The Structure of the Event Record

Field	Size	Description
What	Word	Code describing event
Message	Long	Value or pointer providing more detail about the event
When	Long	Number of clock "ticks" since the computer was started
Where	Long	Two word values, the Y and X position of the mouse at the time of the event
Modifiers	Word	Describes the state of certain keys, the mouse button, and other information

In the above programming example, EventR would point to the following structure:

```
EVENTR   ANOP            ;EVENT RECORD STRUCTURE
WHAT     DS     2        ;WHAT CODE GOES HERE
MESSAGE  DS     4        ;MESSAGE INFO GOES HERE
WHEN     DS     4        ;WHEN VALUE
WHERE    DS     4        ;Y AND X LOCATION WORD VALUES
MODS     DS     2        ;MODIFIER FLAG
```

When an event is pulled from the event queue, and GetNextEvent returns a nonzero or true value, the Event Manager fills the event record with information about that particular event. Your program can then examine the event record and act upon the event accordingly.

Each field of the event record contains the following information about the event.

What. The value in the What field is called the *event code.* It describes which event took place. The events are numbered 0–15 (these are not bit values). The values in the What field are explained in Table 12-3.

Table 12-3. Value in What Field When the Event Manager Detects an Event

Event Code	Description
0	Null event—nothing has happened
1	The mouse button is down—just pressed
2	The mouse button has been released
3	A key on the keyboard is being pressed
4	Not used
5	Auto-key event—a key is being held down
6	Update event—a window is being changed, redrawn, sized, or its contents updated
7	Not used
8	Activate event generated when a window becomes either active or inactive
9	Switch event activated when one program switches control to another
10	Control-Apple-Esc has been pressed (this event is handled by the Desk Manager)
11	A device driver has generated an event
12	User defined (can be defined by your application)
13	User defined
14	User defined
15	User defined

If an event is pending in the queue, the value of the What field describes the event. For example, if a key is pressed, the What field contains a $3. If the mouse button is pressed, the What field contains a $1. (Note how these values are closely related to their bit positions in the event mask.)

If the previous code detected an event, the following could be used to determine if event code one, a keyboard event, occurred.

```
LDA   EWHAT      ;GET CODE FROM THE EVENT RECORD
CMP   #1         ;WAS IT A KEYPRESS?
BNE   SCAN       ;CONTINUE LOOPING IF NOT
```

The EWhat field of the event record contains a value describing the event. This routine reads the event code into the A register and compares it with one, a keyboard event. If the event is not a keyboard event, the program continues scanning for events. This routine would be followed by the code to act upon a key press.

Message. The message field can be a value or a pointer, depending upon which event was pulled from the queue. For mouse and keyboard events (event codes 1, 2, 3, and 5) the message field contains a value indicating the button number of the mouse or the ASCII value of the key pressed, respectively. (The HOW of the long word is not used.)

For the update and activate events, event codes 6 and 8, the message field is a pointer to the window activated or updated. For the Device Driver and user defined events, codes 11–15, the message field is defined by the device driver or application. And for the switch and desk accessory events, codes 9 and 10, the message field is not defined.

To return the ASCII code of the key typed in the previous example, the following routine can be used.

```
LDA    MESSAGE    ;GET HOW OF MESSAGE
AND    #$00FF     ;CHOP OFF MSB
```

When this routine has been run, register A will contain the ASCII character code of the key pressed. The most significant byte may be reset to zero, but it is recommended that you use the logical AND instruction to be sure. Apple claims that the MSB will be set to zero, but in fact this is the only way to be certain.

The value in register A can be compared with certain key values. For example, suppose the Esc key is being checked. The ASCII code for the Esc key is $1B. The following routine further checks to see if the Esc key was pressed.

```
CMP    #$1B       ;CHECK FOR ESC KEY
BNE    SCAN       ;IF NOT, KEEP SCANNING
```

The routine continues to scan until the Esc key is pressed. Only when that key is pressed does execution fall through to the next program statement.

When. The When field contains the number of ticks since the computer was started. Ticks represent increments of 1/60 second. This field can be monitored to test the time interval between certain events.

For example, to determine if a double click on the mouse took place, your routine would save the When value for the first click, and then compare it to the When value of the second click. If both are a specified number of ticks apart (and the mouse pointer hasn't radically altered position), it is considered a double click.

Where. The Where field gives the location of the mouse at the time of the event. The event doesn't necessarily need to be a mouse event for the position of the mouse to be determined.

The Where field is two words long. The first word contains the Y, or vertical, location of the mouse from the upper right corner of the screen (global coordinates). The second word contains the X, or horizontal, location of the mouse.

Above, the Where field is shown as

```
WHERE DS     4
```

A second way of writing the code would be

```
MOUSEY   DS     2            ;MOUSE'S VERTICAL COORDINATE
MOUSEX   DS     2            ;THE HORIZONTAL COORDINATE
```

If your program were reading the mouse's location after a GetNextEvent call, the following code could be used.

```
      LDA     WHERE+2  ;MOUSE'S X—HORIZONTAL—LOCATION
      ;                ;DO WHATEVER HERE
      LDA     WHERE    ;MOUSE'S Y—VERTICAL—LOCATION
      ;                ;DO WHATEVER HERE
```

The X and Y values can be stored, or pushed directly to the stack for a toolbox call.

Modifiers. The Modifiers' field in the event record allows further description of the event pulled from the queue. Each bit in this long word value further depicts the event (Table 12-4).

Table 12-4. The Meaning of Values in the Modifiers' Field

Bit Set	Description
0	Window pointed to in Message field is being deactivated, otherwise the window is activated
1	Active window is changing from the system window to an application's window, or vice versa
2	Not used
3	Not used
4	Not used
5	Not used
6	Mouse button #1 is down
7	Mouse button #0 is down
8	Apple key is down
9	Shift key is down
10	Caps lock key is down
11	Option (Solid Apple) key is down
12	Control key is down
13	Key on the keypad is down
14	Not used
15	Not used

By examining the Modifier field, for example, your program can tell the difference between a key pressed on the keypad and a key pressed on the main keyboard. It can tell whether an Apple, shift, or control key was down, which button was pressed on the mouse (if it has more than one), and other things.

Program Example

The following is the source code for EVENT.ASM, written for use with the *APW* assembler. It produces the executable file EXAMPLE, which can be run from the *APW* shell. Line numbers have been provided for reference purposes only. You should not type them into your editor.

To assemble and link this program under *APW*, at the *APW* prompt type

#asml event.asm

To run the program, type

#example

You can change the name of the executable program by changing the name listed after the KEEP directive in line 6.

The program starts up the Event Manager and waits for the mouse's button to be pressed. As soon as it's pressed, you're returned to the *APW* shell.

```
1       ****************************************************************************
2       * EVENT MANAGER EXAMPLE
3       ****************************************************************************
4
5               ABSADDR  ON             ;ACTIVATE ABSOLUTE ADDRESSING
6               KEEP     EXAMPLE        ;EXE FILE NAME
7
8       MAIN    START
9
10              PHK                     ;ASSERT CODE BANK ==
        ; DATA BANK
11              PLB                     ;SET ENVIRONMENT
12
13      ;---------------------------------------
14      ; START THE TOOL LOCATOR
15
16              LDX      #$0201         ;TLSTARTUP
```

```
        JSL     $E10000         ;BUMP START THE TOOL LOCATOR

;-----------------------------------------
; START THE MEMORY MANAGER AND RETURN
; A USERID FOR THIS PROGRAM

        PEA     $0000           ;RESULT SPACE
        LDX     #$0202          ;MMSTARTUP
        JSL     $E10000         ;GET A USERID & SOME MEMORY
        JSR     ERRORH          ;CHECK FOR ERRORS
        PLA                     ;GET OUR USERID
        STA     USERID          ;SAVE IT

;-----------------------------------------
; START THE MISC TOOLS TOOL SET

        LDX     #$0203          ;MTSTARTUP
        JSL     $E10000         ;BUMP START MISC. TOOLS
        JSR     ERRORH          ;CHECK FOR ERRORS

;-----------------------------------------
; ESTABLISH AND INITIALIZE A DIRECT PAGE
; FOR THIS PROGRAM

        PEA     $0000           ;LONG RESULT SPACE
        PEA     $0000
        PEA     $0000           ;ONLY ONE PAGE
        PEA     $0100
        LDA     USERID          ;OUR PROGRAM'S ID
        PHA
        PEA     $C005           ;ATTRIBUTES
        PEA     $0000           ;WHERE THE BLOCK BEGINS
        PEA     $0000
        LDX     #$0902          ;NEWHANDLE
        JSL     $E10000
        JSR     ERRORH          ;CHECK FOR ERRORS

        PLA                     ;GET HANDLE OF NEW BLOCK
        STA     0               ;SAVE IN ZERO PAGE AS WELL
        STA     HANDLE          ;AS SAVING IN "HANDLE"
        PLA
        STA     2
        STA     HANDLE+2
```

```
         LDA    [0]            ;NOW GET ACTUAL LOCATION REF.
         STA    DPAGE          ;AND STORE IN DPAGE VARIABLE

;----------------------------------------
; EVENT MANAGER

         LDA    DPAGE          ;GET DPAGE FOR EVENT MANAGER
         PHA
         PEA    20             ;EVENT QUEUE SIZE
         PEA    0              ;MIN X CLAMP
         PEA    320            ;MAX X CLAMP
         PEA    0              ;MIN Y CLAMP
         PEA    200            ;MAX Y CLAMP
         LDA    USERID         ;THE USERID
         PHA
         LDX    #$0206         ;EMSTARTUP
         JSL    $E10000
         JSR    ERRORH

;----------------------------------------
; MAIN PROGRAM EVENT SCANNING LOOP

SCAN     ANOP

         PHA                   ;RESULT SPACE
         PEA    $FFFF          ;EVENT MASK
         PEA    EVENTR|-16
         PEA    EVENTR
         LDX    #$0A06         ;GETNEXTEVENT
         JSL    $E10000
         PLA
         BEQ    SCAN           ;NOTHING

         LDA    EWHAT          ;GET EVENT
         CMP    #1             ;MOUSE DOWN?
         BNE    SCAN           ;IF NOT, KEEP SCANNING

;----------------------------------------
; END OF PROGRAM: SHUTDOWN ALL ROUTINES

DONE     ANOP

         LDX    #$0306         ;EMSHUTDOWN
```

```
        JSL     $E10000
        LDX     #$0303          ;MTSHUTDOWN
        JSL     $E10000         ;SHUTDOWN MISC TOOLS
        LDA     HANDLE+2        ;PUSH HANDLE
        PHA                     ;TO FREE MEMORY TAKEN
        LDA     HANDLE          ;BY THIS PROGRAM
        PHA
        LDX     #$1002          ;DISPOSE HANDLE
        JSL     $E10000
        LDA     USERID          ;SHUT DOWN THIS PROGRAM
        PHA
        LDX     #$0302          ;MMSHUTDOWN
        JSL     $E10000         ;SHUTDOWN MEMORY MANAGER
        LDX     #$0301          ;TLSHUTDOWN
        JSL     $E10000         ;SHUTDOWN TOOL LOCATOR
;----------------------------------------
; EXIT VIA PRODOS 16 MLI CALL $29
        JSL     $E100A8         ;PRODOS 16 CALL
        DC      I2'$29'         ;QUIT FUNCTION
        DC      I4'QPARAMS'     ;QUIT PARAMETERS
*******************************************************************************
* ERROR HANDLER
*******************************************************************************
ERRORH  ANOP
        BCS     UHOH            ;CARRY SET IF ERROR
        RTS                     ;ELSE, RETURN
UHOH    ANOP
        PHA                     ;TOOLBOX RETURNS ERROR IN A
        PEA     $0000           ;USE SYSTEM DEATH MESSAGE
        PEA     $0000
        LDX     #$1503          ;SYSFAILMGR
        JSL     $E10000         ;SHUT THIS DOWN
```

```
146 ****************************************************************************
147 * DATA STORAGE
148 ****************************************************************************
149
150 USERID  DS      2               ;THIS PROGRAM'S USER ID
151 HANDLE  DS      4               ;DIRECT PAGE HANDLE
152 DPAGE   DS      2               ;DIRECT PAGE START
153
154 ;QUIT PARAMETERS:
155
156 QPARAMS ANOP
157         DC      I4'0'           ;RETURN TO PREVIOUS PROGRAM
158         DC      I'0000'         ;THIS PROGRAM NOT RESTARTABLE
159
160 ;EVEN MANAGER EVENT RECORD
161
162 EVENTR  ANOP
163 EWHAT   DS      2               ;EVENT CODE
164 EMSG    DS      4               ;EVENT MESSAGE
165 EWHEN   DS      4               ;EVENT WHEN (TICK COUNT)
166 EWHERE  DS      4               ;EVENT WHERE, MOUSE LOCATION
167 EMODS   DS      2               ;EVENT MODIFYER FLAGS
168
169         END
```

Description of EVENT.ASM

Most of this example program should be familiar by now. Briefly, lines 10 and 11 define this program's environment, causing the program bank to be the same as the data bank.

Lines 16 and 17 start the Tool Locator. Lines 23–28 start the Memory Manager and return a User ID for this program. The User ID is saved in the variable UserID, located at line 150.

The Miscellaneous tool set is started in lines 33–35.

Lines 41–52 establish and set aside a memory block for this program's direct page. Only one block is needed for the Event Manager.

Lines 45–59 store the direct page handle in the variable Handle and in this program's zero page. From the zero page, the actual address of the direct page is obtained and stored in the variable DPage (lines 61 and 62).

The Event Manager is started in lines 67–78. The event queue size is set to 20, and though the mouse is not used by this program, its bounds are set for the 320 × 200 pixel graphics screen.

Lines 83–96 contain the program's main scanning loop. A call is made to GetNextEvent and the result tested in line 92. If no event is pending, execution branches back to line 83 where GetNextEvent is called again.

If an event is pending, line 94 loads the A register with the event code. It's compared against one in line 95 to see if the mouse button is down. If not, line 96 branches back to line 83 where the scanning process continues.

If the button was pressed, execution falls through to the Done routine (line 101) where the program is shut down.

Lines 101–122 shut down the tool sets used by this program. The direct page handle is disposed of in lines 109–114. The Memory Manager is shut down in lines 116–119. And finally, the Tool Locator is shut down in lines 121 and 122.

Lines 127–129 set up a call to ProDOS 16's quit function. The parameters (lines 156–158) instruct this program to return to the previous program in memory—in this case, the *APW* shell.

Lines 134–144 contain a generic error handler routine.

Lines 150–167 contain data and variables used by this program. The event record is stored in lines 162–167. Although this program only takes advantage of the EWhat field, all the fields should be included.

Modifying EVENT.ASM

Different events can be monitored simply by changing the value in line 95. Change the number to

```
CMP #2
```

When the program is modified in this way, the program ends when the mouse button is released. To end the program when a key is pressed, change this line to

```
CMP #3
```

If you make this modification, insert this code at line 97:

```
LDA     EMSG        ;READ KEY VALUE
AND     #$00FF      ;CHOP OFF MSB
CMP     #$1B        ;SEE IF IT'S THE ESC
BNE     SCAN        ;KEEP LOOKING IF NOT
```

After the key is pressed, this code checks the EMSG field to see which key was pressed. The MSB of the value at EMSG is lopped off with the AND instruction, and finally the value is compared with $1B—the Esc key. If there's a match, the execution falls through. Otherwise, the program branches back to the Scan loop to wait for another event.

About the TaskMaster

A second toolbox function which performs duties similar to the Event Manager's GetNextEvent function is the Window Manager's function $1D—the *TaskMaster.* The TaskMaster adds the capabilities of dealing with pull-down menus and windows to the list of things GetNextEvent monitors. By using TaskMaster, detecting window activity and the use of pull-down menus is easy.

The TaskMaster is used in much the same way as the Event Manager. In fact, TaskMaster calls GetNextEvent internally. Like GetNextEvent, TaskMaster sits in a loop and waits for events. Nearly the same items are pushed on the stack before the call, but after the call, TaskMaster returns a special event code. This special event code has the same value as the event code found in the EWhat field of the event record. Additionally, the TaskMaster has special codes of its own for the specific events it monitors.

Most programs that use windows and pull-down menus will probably have the TaskMaster at their core. Only a few modifications are needed to use the TaskMaster rather than GetNextEvent.

First, your program must start the Window Manager. The Window Manager tool set shares direct-page space with the Event Manager, so all that's required for the Window Manager StartUp function is the program's User ID. (Details on starting up and shutting down the Window Manager are covered in Chapter 15.)

The next difference is that the result of the TaskMaster function is not a logical true or false as it is with GetNextEvent. Instead, the TaskMaster returns either zero if no event is pending (which is a logical false anyway), or the event code number. The event code number is the same code found in the EWhat field, with the addition of 12 codes, each representing specific things the TaskMaster looks for (Table 12-5).

Finally, the event record used by the TaskMaster needs to be modified to include a special task mask and an extra descriptive variable, *TaskData*. These allow for the extra duties of the TaskMaster when it comes to handling windows and pull-down menus.

Function: $1D0E
Name: TaskMaster
Returns status of the event queue as well as checks for certain window/menu events.
Push: Result Space (W); Event Mask (W); Event Record (L)
Pull: Extended Event Code (W)
Errors: $0E03
Comments:

The TaskMaster returns a special event code representing a pending event in the queue. If no event is present, $0000 is returned. Otherwise, the Extended Event Code contains the code of the event which took place (Table 12-5).

Table 12-5. TaskMaster Event Codes

Code	Description
0	Null event—nothing has happened
1	Mouse button is down—just pressed
2	Mouse button has been released
3	Key on the keyboard is being pressed
4	Not used
5	Auto-key event—a key is being held down
6	Update event—a window is being changed, redrawn, sized, or its contents updated
7	Not used
8	Activate event generated when a window becomes either active or inactive
9	Switch event activated when one program switches control to another
10	Apple-Control-Esc has been pressed (this event is handled by the Desk Manager)
11	Device driver has generated an event
12	User defined (can be defined by your application)
13	User defined
14	User defined
15	User defined

Extended Event Code	Description
16	Mouse is in desk
17	Menu item was selected
18	Mouse is in the system window

19	Mouse is in the content of a window
20	Mouse is in drag
21	Mouse is in grow
22	Mouse is in goaway
23	Mouse is in zoom
24	Mouse is in info bar
25	Mouse is in vertical scroll
26	Mouse is in horizontal scroll
27	Mouse is in frame
28	Mouse is in drop

The first 16 values are the same as those found in the What field of the event record when GetNextEvent is called. The last 12 values are specific to the TaskMaster. Each of them is tied into an operation involving either a menu or window. For example, the TaskMaster returns an extended event code of 17 if an item from a pull-down menu is selected.

When using TaskMaster, the following two items need to be added to the event record:

TaskData (long)
TaskMask (long)

The event record used by TaskMaster appears as follows:

```
EVENTR    ANOP                  ;EVENT RECORD STRUCTURE
WHAT      DS    2               ;WHAT CODE GOES HERE
MESSAGE   DS    4               ;MESSAGE INFO GOES HERE
WHEN      DS    4               ;WHEN VALUE
WHERE     DS    4               ;Y AND X LOCATION WORD VALUES
MODS      DS    2               ;MODIFIER FLAG
TASKDATA  DS    4               ;ADDITIONAL INFO FROM TASKMASTER
TASKMASK  DC    I4'$3FFF'       ;TASK MASK VALUE
```

TaskData contains additional information about the extended event code. For the standard event codes 0–15, this field will be blank. But for the extended event codes 16–28, the Task Data field contains the values in Table 12-6.

Table 12-6. Task Data Field

Code	Task Data Values
17	Not used
18	Not used
19	Not used
20	HOW = Menu ID, LOW = $0000
21	HOW = Menu ID, LOW = Menu Item

22	Window Pointer
23	Window Pointer
24	Window Pointer
25	Window Pointer
26	Window Pointer
27	Window Pointer
28	Window Pointer

For example, if your program is menu driven, you can take advantage of the value in TaskData to determine which menu item was selected. Items 20 and 21 above deal with menu choices. The other items are handled internally by the Window Manager.

The task mask, like the event mask, is used to filter out certain types of events monitored by the TaskMaster. These events are above and beyond those already filtered by the event mask. (An event mask is still required by the TaskMaster.)

By setting specific bits in the task mask, your program can direct the TaskMaster function to return only the results of specific events. Table 12-7 shows which bits in the task mask affect which events. Note that bits 13–31 must always be set to zero or an error results.

Table 12-7. Events Scanned for by TaskMaster

Bit Set	TaskMaster Scans For
0	MenuKey—Menu item key equivalents
1	Update handling
2	FindWindow—mouse click in a window
3	MenuSelect—choosing a menu item
4	OpenNDA—new desk accessories in the Apple menu
5	System Click
6	Drag Window
7	Select Window
8	Track GoAway button
9	Track Zoom button
10	Grow Window
11	Allow Scrolling
12	Handle special menu items
13–31	Must be set to zero

It's generally a good idea to set all the bits. If the task mask is set to $00003FFF, it will scan for and be able to handle all conceivable events.

Use of the TaskMaster is primarily geared to window- and menu-driven programs. For now, consider it simply an extension of the GetNextEvent call. In later chapters on windowing and using pull-down menus, the full capabilities of the TaskMaster will be explored.

Chapter 13

QuickDraw II—
Pens, Colors, and Patterns

QuickDraw II is the graphics power behind the Apple IIGS (the *G* stands for *Graphics*). This tool set contains over 200 functions, all of which control the high resolution graphics screen.

Even if they do not use

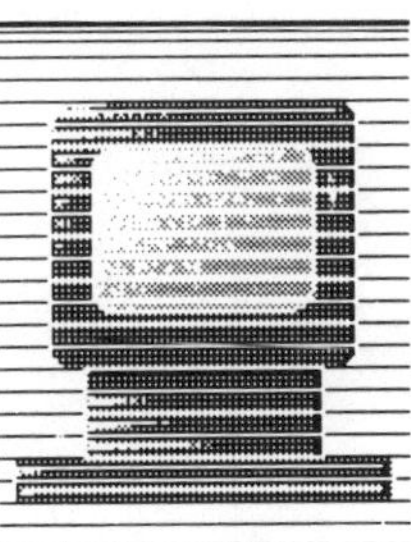

graphics, all programs using the desktop interface require the QuickDraw II tool set to draw menus, windows, dialog boxes, text on the graphics screen, and the mouse cursor. QuickDraw II is an extensive tool set. It could be the subject of a complete book in itself.

In this chapter and in the next, a few of QuickDraw II's graphics capabilities are explored. This chapter provides a fundamental overview of graphics and graphics terms. Chapter 16 covers additional topics in more detail.

Graphics Modes

Unlike some of the other tool sets, QuickDraw II requires some forethought before it's started. For example, because QuickDraw sets the initial resolution of the screen, you should know whether you want your application to run in the 320 or 640 mode (representing high-resolution screens of 320 × 200 or 640 × 200 pixels, respectively). You must make this decision even for programs not using high-resolution graphics.

The graphics mode, or resolution, is closely associated with two terms used in the QuickDraw II toolbox: 320 or 640 Mode and *Chunkiness.*

The *mode* determines the horizontal resolution of the graphics screen. The graphics screen always measures 200 pixels (or dots) from top to bottom, numbered 0–199. The horizontal resolution can be 320 or 640 pixels, depending on the mode. Horizontally, the pixels range 0–319, or 0–639.

In the 320 mode, each pixel represents four bits of color values, ranging from $0 through $F. This means each pixel on the screen can be one of 16 different colors.

In the 640 mode, each pixel represents only two bits of color values. Therefore, any given pixel can be one of four different colors in 640 mode (though more colors can be squeezed out of this mode, which is demonstrated later).

The size of the pixel and, therefore, the screen mode, is also referred to as *chunkiness* by Apple. In the 320 mode, pixels have a chunkiness of four bits. In the 640 mode, pixels have a chunkiness of two bits.

Other than the difference in the number of colors available and the resolution, both screen modes have the same capabilities. For example, you can run a menu-driven program in either mode. The 320 mode will approximate a 40-column screen, and the 640 mode approximates an 80-column screen. This is important to consider if your program has many menus. Or, your decision may be based simply on the fact that one screen is more aesthetically pleasing than the other.

Whatever the basis of your decision may be, you must tell QuickDraw II whether to run in the 320 or 640 mode at startup time. Your program can change graphics modes (there are function calls to do so), but it's uncommon. Generally you should stick with one or the other.

If you do change modes, remember to recalculate the size and positions of your graphics, windows, and dialog boxes. A dialog box that looks fine on the 320 mode screen may appear crunched and off center on the 640-mode screen. (This is covered further in the chapters on windows and dialog boxes.)

The SCB

One term used often in a discussion of QuickDraw II is *SCB*. It stands for *scan line control byte*. It's directly related to the variety of colors you can see on the screen.

Each of the 200 horizontal lines on the screen (the Y-axis) is a scan line. The SCB controls the resolution, graphics interrupts, fill mode, and the colors available to the scan line it's associated with. The structure of the scan line control byte is shown in Table 13-1.

Table 13-1. The Structure of the Scan line Control Byte (SCB)

Bit	Meaning
0	Color Table Reference
1	Color Table Reference
2	Color Table Reference
3	Color Table Reference
4	not used
5	Fill Mode (if set = on)
6	Interrupts (if set = on)
7	Screen Mode (if set = 640 mode)

Bits 0–3, the lower nybble of the byte, indicate which color table the scan line is to use. There can be up to 16 color tables, \$0–\$F, each with 16 different colors in them.

The SCB determines which color table its scan line uses. Because there are 200 scan lines and each has an SCB, each scan line could conceivably be using a different color table. With 16 colors in 16 color tables, it would be possible to have 256 colors on the screen at a time.

Bit five controls the fill mode. When the fill mode is active, the color zero in the color table has no value. Instead, it takes on the color value of the pixel to its left. For example, if the scan line contained the color values 5, 5, 6, 0, 0, E, E, 0, 0, 0, A, and 9, the fill mode would change all the zeros, resulting in the scan line values of 5, 5, 6, 6, 6, E, E, E, E, E, A, and 9.

Bit 6 controls interrupts. An interrupt is generated every 1/60 second as the screen is updated. By turning interrupts on, your program could change color tables as pixels are being drawn. Each color table could be filled with a different set of 16 color values. By manipulating interrupts, color tables, and colors, you could conceivably program all 4096 possible colors on the screen at once.

Bit 7 sets the screen mode. For the 320 mode, this bit is reset to zero. For the 640 mode, this bit is set to one. Normally this bit is only used when setting the Master SCB (which initially sets up the entire screen, as described below). Changing this bit has no effect for individual scan lines.

When QuickDraw II is started, it's given a Master SCB which sets the SCBs for all 200 scan lines. The Master SCB also sets the initial screen mode. For example, the following Master SCB

```
$0000
```

sets the 320 mode. When specifying the 640 mode, the following Master SCB is used:

```
$0080
```

This sets bit 7 of the SCB to the 640 mode and uses color table zero. Color table zero is always used at startup. The reason is simple: You cannot define another color table until QuickDraw II has been started. Therefore, any table value other than zero is still treated as zero.

To change the SCB of a particular scan line after the Master SCB is set, the QuickDraw II function SetSCB is used.

Function: $1204
Name: SetSCB
Sets the scan line Control Byte (SCB) value.
Push: Scan Line (W); New SCB value (W)
Pull: nothing
Errors: $0452
Comments:

This function is covered in the next chapter along with a program that demonstrates its use.

Starting Up QuickDraw II

To start up QuickDraw II and place the IIGS into the graphics mode, simply place a call to QuickDraw II's StartUp function. Four things are required: three pages ($300 bytes) of direct-page space, a Master SCB to set the initial color table and screen mode, the Pixel Map Size, and your program's User ID.

Function: $0204
Name: QDStartUp
Starts QuickDraw II.
Push: Direct Page (W); Master SCB (W); Pixel Map Size (W); UserID (W)
Pull: nothing
Errors: $0401, $0410, Memory Manager Errors
Comments: Clears the Screen as well.

The direct page should already have been obtained by the Memory Manager. The Master SCB value is usually $0080 for the 640 mode or $0000 for the 320 mode. If you want your program to initially use a color table other than the standard ones (covered later in this chapter), it should be done after QuickDraw II is started.

The Pixel Map Size refers to an area in memory QuickDraw II will use for creating images. If you're using the 320 mode, this value should be $0050. For the 640 mode, use $00A0. If you push a value of zero, QuickDraw sets the pixel map to the size of the screen.

Finally, the User ID is the number returned by the Memory Manager when it was started.

The following code could be used to start QuickDraw II in the 320 mode.

```
LDA     DPAGE       ;GRAB DPAGE ADDRESS
PHA                 ;STARTING ADDRESS OF 0 PAGE
PEA     $0000       ;SCREEN MODE 320 ($80 = 640)
PEA     $0000       ;PIXEL MAP SIZE (DEFAULT)
```

```
LDA     USERID      ;OUR PROGRAM'S ID
PHA
LDX     #$0204      ;QDSTARTUP
JSL     $E10000     ;FIRE UP QUICK DRAW II
JSR     ERRORH      ;TEST FOR ERRORS
```

Note the change in the following example for starting QuickDraw II in the 640 mode:

```
LDA     DPAGE       ;GRAB DPAGE ADDRESS
PHA                 ;STARTING ADDRESS OF 0 PAGE
PEA     $0080       ;SCREEN MODE 640
PEA     $0000       ;PIXEL MAP SIZE
LDA     USERID      ;OUR PROGRAM'S ID
PHA
LDX     #$0204      ;QDSTARTUP
JSL     $E10000     ;FIRE UP QUICK DRAW II
JSR     ERRORH
```

The screen mode, which is actually the Master SCB, is changed from $0000 to $0080. This sets bit 7 in the Master SCB, which activates the 640 mode. Also, if you were specifying a pixel map size (not just pushing zero) it would be doubled from $50 to $A0 (80 to 160 decimal). If you forget to alter the pixel map's size, the graphics could look very strange. It's a simple mistake, which is why $0000 is normally used.

Another thing to remember when using either mode is to check the clamping bounds for the mouse as set by the Event Manager's EMStartUp function. The Max X value should be 640 and not 320. If the mouse in your program can't move to the right side of the screen, or it moves off the right edge, you probably forgot to change the clamping bounds.

Shutting down QuickDraw is just a simple call to its ShutDown function.

Function: $0304
Name: QDShutDown
Shuts down QuickDraw II.
Push: nothing
Pull: nothing
Errors: none
Comments:

The code would be

```
LDX     #$0304      ;QDShutDown
JSL     $E10000     ;shutdown Quick Draw II
```

A Graphic Example

The following is source code for GRAPH.ASM, which can be assembled with the *ORCA/M* or *APW* assembler. If you look closely, you may notice a lot of this code also appeared in the EVENT.ASM example from the last chapter. It would only take a few new lines of text to create GRAPH.ASM from the old EVENT.ASM source. (Remember to change the source file's name on disk.)

The executable file this code produces, EXAMPLE, can be run from the *APW* shell. As before, the line numbers are provided for reference purposes only. Don't type them into your editor.

The program starts up QuickDraw II in the 320 mode. The mouse is made visible on the screen and you can move the mouse around. GRAPH.ASM contains a "bullet hole" where various graphics routines will be later tested. Pressing the Esc key ends this program.

```
********************************************************************************
* GRAPH - A GRAPHICS ROUTINE EXAMPLE
********************************************************************************

         ABSADDR  ON            ;ACTIVATE ABSOLUTE ADDRESSING
         KEEP     EXAMPLE       ;EXE FILE NAME

MAIN     START

         PHK                    ;ASSERT CODE BANK ==
; DATA BANK
         PLB                    ;SET ENVIRONMENT

;---------------------------------------
; START THE TOOL LOCATOR

         LDX      #$0201        ;TLSTARTUP
         JSL      $E10000       ;BUMP START THE TOOL LOCATOR

;---------------------------------------
; START THE MEMORY MANAGER AND RETURN
; A USERID FOR THIS PROGRAM

         PEA      $0000         ;RESULT SPACE
         LDX      #$0202        ;MMSTARTUP
         JSL      $E10000       ;GET A USERID & SOME MEMORY
         JSR      ERRORH        ;CHECK FOR ERRORS
```

```
         PLA                        ;GET OUR USERID
         STA      USERID            ;SAVE IT

;----------------------------------------
; START THE MISC TOOLS TOOL SET

         LDX      #$0203            ;MTSTARTUP
         JSL      $E10000           ;BUMP START MISC. TOOLS
         JSR      ERRORH            ;CHECK FOR ERRORS

;----------------------------------------
; ESTABLISH AND INITIALIZE A DIRECT PAGE
; FOR THIS PROGRAM

         PEA      $0000             ;LONG RESULT SPACE
         PEA      $0000
         PEA      $0000             ;$400 - FOUR PAGES
         PEA      $0400
         LDA      USERID            ;THIS PROGRAM'S ID
         PHA
         PEA      $C005             ;ATTRIBUTES
         PEA      $0000             ;WHERE THE BLOCK BEGINS
         PEA      $0000             ; IN MEMORY (DON'T CARE)
         LDX      #$0902            ;NEWHANDLE
         JSL      $E10000
         JSR      ERRORH            ;CHECK FOR ERRORS

         PLA                        ;GET HANDLE OF NEW BLOCK
         STA      0                 ;SAVE IN ZERO PAGE AS WELL
         STA      HANDLE            ;AS SAVING IN "HANDLE"
         PLA
         STA      2
         STA      HANDLE+2

         LDA      [0]               ;NOW GET ACTUAL LOCATION REF.
         STA      DPAGE             ;AND STORE IN DPAGE VARIABLE

;----------------------------------------
; SET UP AND START QUICK DRAW II

         LDA      DPAGE             ;GRAB DPAGE ADDRESS
         PHA                        ;STARTING ADDRESS OF 0 PAGE
         PEA      $0000             ;SCREEN MODE 320 ($80 = 640)
         PEA      $0000             ;PIXEL MAP SIZE
```

```
            LDA     USERID          ;OUR PROGRAM'S ID
            PHA
            LDX     #$0204          ;QDSTARTUP
            JSL     $E10000         ;FIRE UP QUICK DRAW II
            JSR     ERRORH
;----------------------------------------
; EVENT MANAGER
            LDA     DPAGE           ;GET DPAGE FOR EVENT MANAGER
            CLC
            ADC     #$300           ;ALLOW FOR QD2'S DPAGE
            PHA
            PEA     20              ;EVENT QUEUE SIZE
            PEA     0               ;MIN X CLAMP
            PEA     320             ;MAX X CLAMP
            PEA     0               ;MIN Y CLAMP
            PEA     200             ;MAX Y CLAMP
            LDA     USERID          ;THE USERID
            PHA
            LDX     #$0206          ;EMSTARTUP
            JSL     $E10000
            JSR     ERRORH
            LDX     #$CA04          ;INITCURSOR
            JSL     $E10000
;----------------------------------------
; MAIN PROGRAM EVENT SCANNING LOOP
SCAN        ANOP
            JSR     DRAW            ;DRAWING ROUTINE
            PHA                     ;RESULT SPACE
            PEA     $FFFF           ;EVENT MASK
            PEA     EVENTR|-16
            PEA     EVENTR
            LDX     #$0A06          ;GETNEXTEVENT
            JSL     $E10000
            PLA
            BEQ     SCAN            ;NOTHING
GETKEY      LDA     EWHAT           ;GET EVENT
```

```
            CMP       #3              ;KEY PRESS?
            BNE       SCAN            ;IF NOT, KEEP SCANNING
            LDA       EMSG            ;WHICH KEY?
            AND       #$00FF          ;GET RID OF MSB
            CMP       #$1B            ;IS IT ESC?
            BNE       SCAN            ;IF NOT, KEEP LOOPING
;----------------------------------------
; END OF PROGRAM: SHUTDOWN ALL ROUTINES
DONE        ANOP
            LDX       #$0306          ;EMSHUTDOWN
            JSL       $E10000
            LDX       #$0304          ;QDSHUTDOWN
            JSL       $E10000         ;SHUTDOWN QUICK DRAW II
            LDX       #$0303          ;MTSHUTDOWN
            JSL       $E10000         ;SHUTDOWN MISC TOOLS
            LDA       HANDLE+2        ;PUSH HANDLE
            PHA                       ;TO FREE MEMORY TAKEN
            LDA       HANDLE          ;BY THIS PROGRAM
            PHA
            LDX       #$1002          ;DISPOSE HANDLE
            JSL       $E10000
            LDA       USERID          ;SHUT DOWN THIS PROGRAM
            PHA
            LDX       #$0302          ;MMSHUTDOWN
            JSL       $E10000         ;SHUTDOWN MEMORY MANAGER
            LDX       #$0301          ;TLSHUTDOWN
            JSL       $E10000         ;SHUTDOWN TOOL LOCATOR
;----------------------------------------
; EXIT VIA PRODOS 16 MLI CALL $29
            JSL       $E100A8         ;PRODOS 16 CALL
            DC        I2'$29'         ;QUIT FUNCTION
            DC        I4'QPARAMS'     ;QUIT PARAMETERS
```

```
********************************************************************************
* DRAWING ROUTINE
********************************************************************************
DRAW     ANOP

         RTS

********************************************************************************
* ERROR HANDLER
********************************************************************************
ERRORH   ANOP

         BCS      UHOH            ;CARRY SET IF ERROR
         RTS                      ;ELSE, RETURN

UHOH     ANOP
         PHA                      ;TOOLBOX RETURNS ERROR IN A
         PEA      $0000           ;USE SYSTEM DEATH MESSAGE
         PEA      $0000
         LDX      #$1503          ;SYSFAILMGR
         JSL      $E10000         ;SHUT THIS DOWN!

********************************************************************************
* DATA STORAGE
********************************************************************************

USERID   DS       2               ;THIS PROGRAM'S USER ID
HANDLE   DS       4               ;DIRECT PAGE HANDLE
DPAGE    DS       2               ;DIRECT PAGE START

;QUIT PARAMETERS:

QPARAMS ANOP
         DC       I4'$0'          ;RETURN TO PREVIOUS PROGRAM
         DC       I'$0000'        ;THIS PROGRAM NOT RESTARTABLE

;EVEN MANAGER EVENT RECORD

EVENTR   ANOP
EWHAT    DS       2               ;EVENT CODE
EMSG     DS       4               ;EVENT MESSAGE
EWHEN    DS       4               ;EVENT WHEN (TICK COUNT)
EWHERE   DS       4               ;EVENT WHERE, MOUSE LOCATION
```

```
202  EMODS    DS      2                 ;EVENT MODIFIER FLAGS
203
204           END
```

Description of GRAPH.ASM

Most of this program was covered in the description of EVENT.ASM in the last chapter. Here is an explanation of the new material.

Lines 41–52 set up four pages of direct-page space, three for QuickDraw II and one for the Event Manager. The four pages, or size of the block, is established as the long word in lines 43 and 44.

QuickDraw II is started in lines 67–75. First, direct-page space is pushed to the stack; this is followed by the Master SCB, which sets the screen to the 320 mode; next comes the pixel map size; and finally, this program's User ID in lines 71 and 72.

The Event Manager is started in lines 80–93. Because QuickDraw takes up three pages of direct-page space, the Event Manager's direct-page location is calculated in lines 81–83. (This was covered in detail in Chapter 12.)

Lines 95 and 96 call QuickDraw's InitCursor routine. This displays the cursor on the screen.

The main scanning loop of the program is in lines 101–116. First, in line 103, a call is made to the subroutine Draw (found in lines 162–164). Next, lines 105–110 call GetNextEvent. If no event took place, the program branches back to the Scan loop starting at line 101. Otherwise, the type of event is tested in lines 114–116 at the GetKey label. If the event is a keypress, execution falls through to line 118, otherwise the program branches back to Scan.

Line 118 uses the EMsg (message) field of the Event Record to see which key was pressed. The value is masked off in line 119 and then compared with $1B, the Esc key, in line 120. If there is a match, meaning Esc was the key pressed, execution falls through to the Done routine at line 126. Otherwise, execution continues at Scan.

Lines 128–157 shut down the program. The only difference between GRAPH.ASM and EVENT.ASM in the shut down is the QuickDraw II shutdown routine in lines 131 and 132.

The Draw subroutine at line 162 is currently empty. Later, this part of the program will be modified to create graphics on the screen. For now, it contains only an RTS instruction.

Lines 169–179 contain a generic error handling routine. And lines 185–202 contain variables and data storage used by this program.

Drawing with the Pen

There are quite a few ways of creating graphics using QuickDraw II. Two methods discussed in this book are with the graphics pen and using rectangles. This chapter deals with using the pen.

There is a difference between what QuickDraw II calls the *graphics cursor* and the pen. Any QuickDraw II routines which refer to the cursor are talking about the mouse pointer. The pen, on the other hand, is a drawing instrument.

Think of the graphics pen as if it were an electronic felt tip pen. When the pen is *down*, it draws—just as a pen draws when pressed against a sheet of paper. When the pen is *up*, it's still there, but it's not drawing. When the graphics pen is up, it can be moved from one location on the screen to another without drawing.

The graphics pen has color, size, and pattern attributes. This means that you can control the image being drawn by manipulating the attributes of the pen with the toolbox.

By changing the color attribute, the pen can draw in any of the available colors in your screen mode. There are also certain logical manipulations which can be performed using the background pattern of the screen.

The size of the pen can be adjusted using the toolbox call PenSize. You can adjust the size of the pen to as large as the screen if you'd like, or as small as one pixel.

The pattern attributes of the pen are determined by which bits in the pen's shape are set and which are reset. For example, the pen pattern can be changed from a square (the default), to a circle, diagonal line, or a number of odd and interesting configurations simply by rearranging a pixel pattern.

The following program takes advantage of the graphics pen to draw a line on the screen. Later modifications to the program will change the color, size, and pattern of the line. And in the next chapter, a program which uses the mouse to draw a line is demonstrated.

This program builds upon the base of the GRAPH.ASM program listed earlier. It uses the following QuickDraw II toolbox calls.

Function: \$3704
Name: SetSolidPenPat
Changes the pen foreground color.
Push: Color (W)
Pull: nothing
Errors: none
Comments:

Function: \$3C04
Name: LineTo
Draws a line from the current pen position to the given coordinates.
Push: X location (W); Y location (W)
Pull: nothing
Errors: possible Memory Manager errors
Comments:

Function: \$8604
Name: Random
Produces a pseudorandom integer.
Push: Result Space (W)
Pull: Pseudorandom Number (W)
Errors: none
Comments:

Add the following code to the GRAPH.ASM program, just after the subroutine Draw and before line 164 (the RTS instruction).

```
FINDX  PHA                 ;RESULT SPACE
       LDX    #$8604       ;RANDOM
       JSL    $E10000      ;GET A PSEUDO-RANDOM NUMBER
       PLA                 ;NUMBER IS IN A
       AND    #$01FF       ;DESTROY OUT OF RANGE VALUES
       CMP    #319         ;TEST MAX X RANGE
       BCS    FINDX        ;KEEP LOOKING IF OUT OF RANGE
       STA    XPOS         ;OTHERWISE, SAVE IT
FINDY  PHA                 ;RESULT SPACE
       LDX    #$8604       ;RANDOM
       JSL    $E10000
       PLA
       AND    #$01FF       ;DESTROY OUT OF RANGE VALUES
       CMP    #199         ;TEST MAX Y RANGE
       BCS    FINDY        ;KEEP LOOKING IF OUT OF RANGE
       STA    YPOS         ;SAVE IT

       LDA    #$F          ;SET COLOR VALUE = WHITE
       PHA
       LDX    #$3704       ;SETSOLIDPENPAT
       JSL    $E10000

       LDA    XPOS         ;X POSITION OF LINE
       PHA
       LDA    YPOS         ;Y POSITION
       PHA
       LDX    #$3C04       ;LINETO
       JSL    $E10000
```

This is followed by the Draw subroutine's RTS instruction. After the RTS, or in the Data area, add the storage space for the two variables.

```
YPOS   DS    2
XPOS   DS    2
```

Because Draw is called each time the Event Manager's GetNextEvent is called (repeatedly), this program will draw a lot of lines on the screen. The LineTo function draws a line from the pen's current position to the position specified and generated by the Random function call. This program will keep drawing lines until the ESC key is pressed.

Assemble and link the program. You may elect to save the source code to a different name or change the KEEP filename to something other than EXAMPLE. When you run the program, a web of interesting lines will be drawn at random on the screen.

This function can be added to the program to change the pen size.

Function: $2C04
Name: SetPenSize
Changes the dimensions of the drawing pen.
Push: Width (W); Height (W)
Pull: nothing
Errors: none
Comments: Measurements are in Pixels.

The following code should be placed before the Scan label at line 101. Insert the following code at line 100:

```
PEA    $10        ;MAKE IT WIDER
PEA    $5         ;THAN IT IS TALL
LDX    #$2C04     ;SETPENSIZE
JSL    $E10000
```

The reason this code was not inserted into the Draw subroutine is that the pen size does not need to be changed or established each time Draw is called. Therefore, it isn't a good place to put it.

As a prelude to the next section on color, the following code can be added to your program to give it that random-color look. Modify the SetSolidPenPat function call in the Draw subroutine to

```
INC    COLOR      ;CHANGE COLOR VALUE
LDA    COLOR      ;GET COLOR VALUE
AND    #$000F     ;ONLY USE LOW, LOW NIBBLE
```

```
        PHA                 ;PUSH THE COLOR ON THE STACK
        LDX     #$3704      ;SETSOLIDPENPAT
        JSL     $E10000
```

And in the Data area of the program, add the one word storage space.

```
COLOR   DS      2
```

The program now keeps a color value in the variable Color. Color is incremented each time the Draw routine is called. The value is then logically ANDed with $F to produce a color number in the range $0–$F. This value is then passed to the SetSolidPenPat function which changes the color of the random line being drawn.

Save this program's source as RANDOM.LINES, as it will be used again. You may change the KEEP filename to RL or something easy to type, if you wish.

Setting the Colors (320 Mode)

The colors used by QuickDraw II are taken from one of 16 different color tables. Each color table contains 16 colors which are used to draw graphics on the screen. You have a choice of which color table and within that table, which colors are to be used for drawing.

The color tables are numbered 0–15. The values stored in these tables are located in memory bank $E1, starting at location $9E00. Each table is $20 bytes long (see Table 13-2).

Table 13-2. Locations of Color Tables

Color Table	Address
0	$E19E00
1	$E19E20
2	$E19E40
3	$E19E60
4	$E19E80
5	$E19EA0
6	$E19EC0
7	$E19EE0
8	$E19F00
9	$E19F20
10	$E19F40
11	$E19F60
12	$E19F80
13	$E19FA0
14	$E19FC0
15	$E19FE0

Each color table contains 16 color-value words. Each color value represents a color determined by the intensity of the red, green, and blue colors of each pixel on the RGB monitor. Because there can be 16 intensities of each color, and there are three colors, the Apple IIGS is capable of 16 x 16 x 16, or 4096 colors.

Each of the 16 colors is determined by the intensity of its red, green, and blue attributes. Each color attribute ranges from $0, the darkest (black), to $F, the lightest (Table 13-3).

Table 13-3. Color and Intensity Values

Color	Low Intensity Value	High Intensity Value
Blue	$0001	$000F
Green	$0010	$00F0
Red	$0100	$0F00

A color value of $0000 is black: All three colors are turned off. A color value of $0FFF is white: All three colors are at maximum intensity.

The standard color table is used if you haven't designed your own. In the 320 mode, it contains the colors in Table 13-4.

Table 13-4. Default Colors and Intensities

Color Value	Color Number	Setting
Black	0	$0000
Dark Gray	1	$0777
Brown	2	$0841
Purple	3	$07C2
Blue	4	$000F
Dark Green	5	$0080
Orange	6	$0F70
Red	7	$0D00
Beige	8	$0FA9
Yellow	9	$0FF0
Green	10	$00E0
Light Blue	11	$04DF
Lilac	12	$0DAF
Periwinkle	13	$078F
Light Gray	14	$0CCC
White	15	$0FFF

Note how the intensities of the red, green, and blue values are varied to create each individual color. The values can be mixed to add variety to your color tables. For example, if only the red and green values are set, they will make yellow. The following color table contains a variety of yellow colors.

```
YELLOW DC    I2'$0000,$0110,$0220,$0330'
       DC    I2'$0440,$0550,$0660,$0770'
       DC    I2'$0880,$0990,$0AA0,$0BB0'
       DC    I2'$0CC0,$0DD0,$0EE0,$0FF0'
```

The first color in the table is black ($0000). The last color in the table is a very light yellow, $0FF0. Because the Red and Green values are equally incremented, the intensity of the yellow color increases with each value in the table. The third value, color $2, is $0220—a dark greenish yellow. The eleventh value, color $A, is $0AA0—a somewhat lighter yellow.

Each of the 16 color tables can be filled with colors of your choice. Your graphics programs then determine which color table you're going to use and which colors to put into that table.

For example, the random-lines program uses all 16 colors to draw its lines. Each new line is drawn with the next color value in the table, $0–$F, and then it repeats.

You can change color tables in the middle of a program for some interesting effects. This would be similar to an artist changing his or her palette. The QuickDraw II function, SetColorTable, sets the color table you're using.

Function: $0E04
Name: SetColorTable
Sets one of 16 color tables to new values.
Push: Table Number (W); Pointer to new table (L)
Pull: nothing
Errors: $0450
Comments: The new table is a table of 16 word-sized values indicating the new colors for Table Number.

The *Table Number* is the number of the color table you're changing. The new table is a list of the colors for that table. For example, the following code sets color table zero to the colors at label CTable (320 mode is assumed).

```
PEA    $0000        ;SET COLOR TABLE 0
PEA    CTABLE-16    ;THE NEW TABLE'S MEMORY BANK
PEA    CTABLE       ;THE LOCATION OF THE NEW TABLE
LDX    #$0E04       ;SETCOLORTABLE
JSL    $E10000
```

```
CTABLE DC      I2'$0000,$0111,$0005,$000A'
       DC      I2'$000F,$0050,$00A0,$00F0'
       DC      I2'$0500,$0A00,$0F00,$0DA9'
       DC      I2'$0110,$0101,$0011,$09AD'
```

Insert the above code into the RANDOM.LINES program you created earlier. Place the code before the SetPenSize call before the Scan label. Then add the CTable to your program's Data area. Save the resulting source code file as RL.MYCOLOR.

This new routine replaces the standard color table with the colors you've created in CTable. You may alter the colors in the table as you wish. However, remember that the upper nybble of the MSB must always be set to zero.

Setting the Colors (640 Mode)

The 640 mode lacks the variety of colors in the 320 mode. It has the same number of colors and color tables, but the color availability is less. Because there are more dots on the screen, there are fewer colors available for those dots.

To see the 640 mode using the RANDOM.LINES program, modify your code as follows.

To start up QuickDraw in the 640 mode, change the QDStartUp call (line 69) so that $0080 is pushed to the stack. This sets the Master SCB for the 640 mode.

Also, you need to change the X boundaries for the mouse and for the random number generator. Though it's not really used in this program, change the Max X clamp in the Event Manager startup routine from 320 to 640 (line 86).

In the Draw subroutine, change the value of the AND instruction after FindX label from $01FF to $03FF. Then change the value following the CMP instruction from #319 to #639.

Now save, assemble, and link the program. The lines will be a little thinner than before, but the most dramatic difference will be in the variety of colors.

The reason for the smaller variety of colors is that the red, green, and blue attributes in the 640 mode can only be on or off; there is no intensity. If the color attribute is $0, the color is off. When the color attribute is $F, the color is on (Table 13-5).

Table 13-5. 640 Mode Colors and Their Values

Color	Value
Blue	$000F
Green	$00F0
Red	$0F00

The colors can, however, be combined to make other colors. This allows for eight color combinations (Table 13-6).

Table 13-6. Color Value Combinations

Color	Number	Setting
Black	0	$0000
Blue	1	$000F
Green	2	$00F0
Blue/Green	3	$00FF
Red	4	$0F00
Purple	5	$0F0F
Yellow	6	$0FF0
White	7	$0FFF

An interesting thing about the 640 mode is that each color represents only one quarter of the pixel drawn on the screen. Each pixel requires four of the above colors—all mixed together—to make the color of the pixel. So the variety of the colors is the same as for the 320 mode, but you have only four colors to choose from.

For example, the standard color table for the 640 mode contains the colors in Table 13-7.

Table 13-7. Standard Color Table for 640 Mode

Color Value	Color Number	Setting
Black	0	$0000
Red	1	$0F00
Green	2	$00F0
White	3	$0FFF
Black	4	$0000
Blue	5	$000F
Yellow	6	$0FF0
White	7	$0FFF
Black	8	$0000
Red	9	$0F00
Green	10	$00F0
White	11	$0FFF
Black	12	$0000
Blue	13	$000F
Yellow	14	$0FF0
White	15	$0FFF

Blue	13	$000F
Yellow	14	$0FF0
White	15	$0FFF

Notice that black and white alternate with combinations of the other four colors. The four colors might better be viewed as in Table 13-8.

Table 13-8. Colors as They Are Used on the 640 Mode Screen

Color	**1**	**2**	**3**	**4**
Point1	Black	Red	Green	White
Point2	Black	Blue	Yellow	White
Point3	Black	Red	Green	White
Point4	Black	Blue	Yellow	White

Each of the four points are combined to make one color. The four colors used on the screen are actually Black, Purple, Lime, and White (Table 13-9).

Table 13-9. How the Colors Appear on the 640 Mode Screen

Point1	**Point2**	**Point3**	**Point4**	**Result**
Black	+ Black	+ Black	+ Black	= Black
Red	+ Blue	+ Red	+ Blue	= Purple
Green	+ Yellow	+ Green	+ Yellow	= Lime
White	+ White	+ White	+ White	= White

Each color value contains four elements. The four elements describe the colors used to paint the pixel. Hence, Red plus Blue plus Red plus Blue makes Purple—one color. Any of the eight combinations of colors described earlier can be added together to make one of four colors used in the 640 mode.

For example, the following color table for the 640 mode translates into the colors shown in Table 13-10.

```
CTABLE DC      I2'$0F00,$00F0,$000F,$0FFF'
       DC      I2'$0F0F,$00F0,$0FFF,$0FFF'
       DC      I2'$0F00,$00F0,$000F,$0FFF'
       DC      I2'$0F0F,$00F0,$0FFF,$0FFF'
```

Table 13-10. How the Colors in this Example Appear on the 640 Mode Screen

Color	1	2	3	4
	Red	Green	Blue	White
	Violet	Green	White	White
	Red	Green	Blue	White
	Violet	Green	White	White
Result	Pink	Green	Lt. Blue	White

The reason the colors alternate is to avoid striping. For instance, the following color values would produce a black-and-white striped pattern.

$0000	Black
$0FFF	White
$0FFF	White
$0000	Black

However, the following pattern produces a medium gray tone.

$0000	White
$0FFF	Black
$0000	White
$0FFF	Black

Modify the program RL.MYCOLOR to use a color table in 640 mode. First you'll need to change RL.MYCOLOR to come up in the 640 mode. (Change the Master SCB and the X values in EMStartUp and the Draw subroutine.)

Next, modify the color table to contain these values:

```
CTABLE DC       I2'$0F00,$00F0,$0FFF,$0F00'
       DC       I2'$0F0F,$0FF0,$000F,$0000'
       DC       I2'$0F00,$00F0,$0FFF,$0F00'
       DC       I2'$0F0F,$0FF0,$000F,$0000'
```

This will produce random lines in the colors pink, lime, light blue, and dark red.

The complete, modified source listing appears below.

```
**************************************************************************
* RL.MYCOLOR GRAPHICS EXAMPLE
**************************************************************************

            ABSADDR   ON            ;ACTIVATE ABSOLUTE ADDRESSING
            KEEP      EXAMPLE       ;EXE FILE NAME

```

```
MAIN     START

         PHK                        ;ASSERT CODE BANK ==
; DATA BANK
         PLB                        ;SET ENVIRONMENT

;----------------------------------------
; START THE TOOL LOCATOR

         LDX      #$0201            ;TLSTARTUP
         JSL      $E10000           ;BUMP START THE TOOL LOCATOR

;----------------------------------------
; START THE MEMORY MANAGER AND RETURN
; A USERID FOR THIS PROGRAM

         PEA      $0000             ;RESULT SPACE
         LDX      #$0202            ;MMSTARTUP
         JSL      $E10000           ;GET A USERID & SOME MEMORY
         JSR      ERRORH            ;CHECK FOR ERRORS
         PLA                        ;GET OUR USERID
         STA      USERID            ;SAVE IT

;----------------------------------------
; START THE MISC TOOLS TOOL SET

         LDX      #$0203            ;MTSTARTUP
         JSL      $E10000           ;BUMP START MISC. TOOLS
         JSR      ERRORH            ;CHECK FOR ERRORS

;----------------------------------------
; ESTABLISH AND INITIALIZE A DIRECT PAGE
; FOR THIS PROGRAM

         PEA      $0000             ;LONG RESULT SPACE
         PEA      $0000
         PEA      $0000             ;$400 - FOUR PAGES
         PEA      $0400
         LDA      USERID            ;THIS PROGRAM'S ID
         PHA
         PEA      $C005             ;ATTRIBUTES
         PEA      $0000             ;WHERE THE BLOCK BEGINS
         PEA      $0000             ; IN MEMORY (DON'T CARE)
         LDX      #$0902            ;NEWHANDLE
```

```
        JSL     $E10000
        JSR     ERRORH          ;CHECK FOR ERRORS
        PLA                     ;GET HANDLE OF NEW BLOCK
        STA     0               ;SAVE IN ZERO PAGE AS WELL
        STA     HANDLE          ;AS SAVING IN "HANDLE"
        PLA
        STA     2
        STA     HANDLE+2
        LDA     [0]             ;NOW GET ACTUAL LOCATION REF.
        STA     DPAGE           ;AND STORE IN DPAGE VARIABLE
;----------------------------------------
; SET UP AND START QUICK DRAW II
        LDA     DPAGE           ;GRAB DPAGE ADDRESS
        PHA                     ;STARTING ADDRESS OF 0 PAGE
        PEA     $0080           ;SCREEN MODE 360 ($80 = 640)
        PEA     $0000           ;PIXEL MAP SIZE
        LDA     USERID          ;OUR PROGRAM'S ID
        PHA
        LDX     #$0204          ;QDSTARTUP
        JSL     $E10000         ;FIRE UP QUICK DRAW II
        JSR     ERRORH
;----------------------------------------
; EVENT MANAGER
        LDA     DPAGE           ;GET DPAGE FOR EVENT MANAGER
        CLC
        ADC     #$300           ;ALLOW FOR QD2'S DPAGE
        PHA
        PEA     20              ;EVENT QUEUE SIZE
        PEA     0               ;MIN X CLAMP
        PEA     640             ;MAX X CLAMP
        PEA     0               ;MIN Y CLAMP
        PEA     200             ;MAX Y CLAMP
        LDA     USERID          ;THE USERID
        PHA
        LDX     #$0206          ;EMSTARTUP
        JSL     $E10000
        JSR     ERRORH
```

```
            LDX     #$CA04          ;INITCURSOR
            JSL     $E10000

;-----------------------------------------
; MAIN PROGRAM EVENT SCANNING LOOP

            PEA     $0000           ;SET COLOR TABLE 0
            PEA     CTABLE|-16      ;THE NEW TABLE'S MEMORY BANK
            PEA     CTABLE          ;THE LOCATION OF THE NEW TABLE
            LDX     #$0E04          ;SETCOLORTABLE
            JSL     $E10000

            PEA     $10             ;MAKE IT WIDER
            PEA     $5              ;THAN IT IS TALL
            LDX     #$2C04          ;SETPENSIZE
            JSL     $E10000

SCAN        ANOP

            JSR     DRAW            ;DRAWING ROUTINE

            PHA                     ;RESULT SPACE
            PEA     $FFFF           ;EVENT MASK
            PEA     EVENTR|-16
            PEA     EVENTR
            LDX     #$0A06          ;GETNEXTEVENT
            JSL     $E10000
            PLA
            BEQ     SCAN            ;NOTHING

GETKEY      LDA     EWHAT           ;GET EVENT
            CMP     #3              ;KEY PRESS?
            BNE     SCAN            ;IF NOT, KEEP SCANNING

            LDA     EMSG            ;WHICH KEY?
            AND     #$00FF          ;GET RID OF MSB
            CMP     #$1B            ;IS IT ESC?
            BNE     SCAN            ;IF NOT, KEEP LOOPING

;-----------------------------------------
; END OF PROGRAM: SHUTDOWN ALL ROUTINES

DONE        ANOP

```

```
         LDX     #$0306        ;EMSHUTDOWN
         JSL     $E10000

         LDX     #$0304        ;QDSHUTDOWN
         JSL     $E10000       ;SHUTDOWN QUICK DRAW II

         LDX     #$0303        ;MTSHUTDOWN
         JSL     $E10000       ;SHUTDOWN MISC TOOLS

         LDA     HANDLE+2      ;PUSH HANDLE
         PHA                   ;TO FREE MEMORY TAKEN
         LDA     HANDLE        ;BY THIS PROGRAM
         PHA
         LDX     #$1002        ;DISPOSE HANDLE
         JSL     $E10000

         LDA     USERID        ;SHUT DOWN THIS PROGRAM
         PHA
         LDX     #$0302        ;MMSHUTDOWN
         JSL     $E10000       ;SHUTDOWN MEMORY MANAGER

         LDX     #$0301        ;TLSHUTDOWN
         JSL     $E10000       ;SHUTDOWN TOOL LOCATOR

;----------------------------------------
; EXIT VIA PRODOS 16 MLI CALL $29

         JSL     $E100A8       ;PRODOS 16 CALL
         DC      I2'$29'       ;QUIT FUNCTION
         DC      I4'QPARAMS'   ;QUIT PARAMETERS

*****************************************************************************
* DRAWING ROUTINE
*****************************************************************************
DRAW     ANOP

FINDX    PHA                   ;RESULT SPACE
         LDX     #$8604        ;RANDOM
         JSL     $E10000       ;GET A PSUEDORANDOM NUMBER
         PLA                   ;NUMBER IS IN A
         AND     #$03FF        ;DESTROY OUT OF RANGE VALUES
         CMP     #639          ;TEST MAX X RANGE
         BCS     FINDX         ;KEEP LOOKING IF OUT OF RANGE
```

```
         STA     XPOS          ;OTHERWISE, SAVE IT

FINDY    PHA                   ;RESULT SPACE
         LDX     #$8604        ;RANDOM
         JSL     $E10000
         PLA
         AND     #$01FF        ;DESTROY OUT OF RANGE VALUES
         CMP     #199          ;TEST MAX Y RANGE
         BCS     FINDY         ;KEEP LOOKING IF OUT OF RANGE
         STA     YPOS          ;SAVE IT

         INC     COLOR         ;CHANGE COLOR VALUE
         LDA     COLOR         ;GET COLOR VALUE
         AND     #$000F        ;ONLY USE LOW, LOW NIBBLE
         PHA
         LDX     #$3704        ;SETSOLIDPENPAT
         JSL     $E10000

         LDA     XPOS          ;X POSITION OF LINE
         PHA
         LDA     YPOS          ;Y POSITION
         PHA
         LDX     #$3C04        ;LINETO
         JSL     $E10000

         RTS

*****************************************************************************
* ERROR HANDLER
*****************************************************************************
ERRORH   ANOP

         BCS     UHOH          ;CARRY SET IF ERROR
         RTS                   ;ELSE, RETURN

UHOH     ANOP
         PHA                   ;TOOLBOX RETURNS ERROR IN A
         PEA     $0000         ;USE SYSTEM DEATH MESSAGE
         PEA     $0000
         LDX     #$1503        ;SYSFAILMGR
         JSL     $E10000       ;SHUT THIS DOWN!

```

```
*******************************************************************************
* DATA STORAGE
*******************************************************************************
USERID   DS      2                   ;THIS PROGRAM'S USER ID
HANDLE   DS      4                   ;DIRECT PAGE HANDLE
DPAGE    DS      2                   ;DIRECT PAGE START
YPOS     DS      2                   ;RANDOM Y POSITION
XPOS     DS      2                   ;RANDOM X POSITION
COLOR    DS      2                   ;COLOR VALUE
;QUIT PARAMETERS:
QPARAMS  ANOP
         DC      I4'$0'              ;RETURN TO PREVIOUS PROGRAM
         DC      I'$0000'            ;THIS PROGRAM NOT RESTARTABLE
;EVENT MANAGER EVENT RECORD
EVENTR   ANOP
EWHAT    DS      2                   ;EVENT
```

Chapter 14

QuickDraw II and the Mouse

The last chapter covered some things about QuickDraw II, but this tool set is so large, another chapter is necessary to cover all of its aspects. This chapter will discuss rectangles, shapes, patterns, and the cursor. Even though this is an extensive chapter, it only begins to

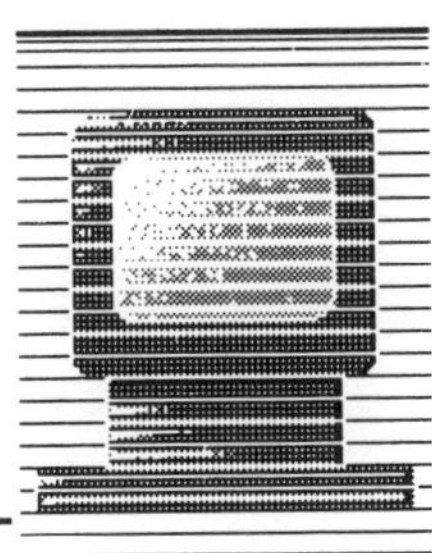

scratch the surface of QuickDraw II's capabilities. However, armed with the information here, you will be able to explore the rest of its functions on your own.

Fun with Rectangles

The last chapter touched upon using the graphics pen to draw shapes. Even though no control was given to the pen in the RANDOM.LINES program, you can see how shapes and figures can be drawn simply by moving the pen from coordinate to coordinate on the screen. In fact, those lines can be saved into polygons which can further be manipulated.

A second way to draw figures on the screen is by using shapes. These shapes are created inside rectangular areas you define on the screen. Though the rectangle is basically a block shape, inside that shape you can place ovals, round rectangles, arcs, and rectangles.

The rectangle in which the shapes are defined can be created in one of two ways. Whichever method you choose, you will plot the coordinates of a rectangle or box, on the screen. The X and Y Min values describe the location of the upper left corner of the rectangle by giving its horizontal and vertical coordinates, respectively. The X and Y Max values describe the location of the lower right corner of the rectangle. The coordinates are measured from the upper left corner of the screen (also known as global coordinates).

The first way to create a rectangle is with the SetRect function.

Function: $4A04
Name: SetRect
Creates a rectangle for drawing shapes.
Push: Rectangle (L); X Min (W); Y Min (W); X Max (W); Y Max (W)
Pull: nothing
Errors: none
Comments: Rectangle points to an eight-byte buffer. This Rectangle buffer is used for subsequent shape-drawing functions.

The Rectangle Pointer points to the memory address of an empty structure. QuickDraw fills the structure with the necessary points as follows.

```
RECTANGLE  DS    0    ;Y MIN
           DS    0    ;X MIN
           DS    0    ;Y MAX
           DS    0    ;X MAX
```

SetRect places the values pushed to the stack into the four-word structure pointed to by Rectangle. All you are doing is placing values in a structure. You can create a rectangle by predefining the X and Y Min and Max values, pushing them on the stack, and letting SetRect deal with them, or by filling the Rectangle structure yourself. If you fill it yourself, be aware that Apple may change the structure at some point in the future. In this case only the SetRect function will be compatible with future versions of the toolbox.

The following two examples show how to create a rectangle for drawing shapes: first, using the SetRect function; and second, by placing the values in the Rectangle structure yourself.

```
PEA    RECTANGLE-16    ;POINTER TO RECTANGLE'S STRUCTURE
PEA    RECTANGLE
PEA    $10             ;MIN X
PEA    $30             ;MIN Y
PEA    $64             ;MAX X
PEA    $A1             ;MAX Y
LDX    #$4A04          ;SETRECT
JSL    $E10000
```

The following code manually fills the Rectangle with the same byte values.

```
LDA    #$30            ;MUST LOAD IMMEDIATE THE VALUES
STA    RECTANGLE       ;MIN Y
LDA    #$10
STA    RECTANGLE+2     ;MIN X
LDA    #$A1
STA    RECTANGLE+4     ;MAX Y
LDA    #$64
STA    RECTANGLE+6     ;MAX X
```

Both routines fill the Rectangle's structure with the these values:

```
RECTANGLE  $0030  ;Y MIN
           $0010  ;X MIN
           $00A1  ;Y MAX
           $0064  ;X MAX
```

However the values got there, the rectangle is now defined. It has width and breadth and a specific location on the screen. Note that nothing is actually drawn yet. Instead, a region has been defined for use by the *shape functions,* which actually draw shapes within the rectangle.

A variety of shapes can be placed inside the rectangle. The shape produced will depend on what you wish to draw and which QuickDraw II functions you use. The shapes are described in Table 14-1.

Table 14-1. Shapes That May Be Drawn Within a Rectangle

Shape	Description
Arc	An arc of a specified length which starts at a given angle within the rectangle. The roundness of the Arc is determined by the dimensions of the rectangle.
Oval	A circle which fits into the rectangle. As with an Arc, the Oval's roundness is determined by the dimensions of the rectangle.
Rectangle	A four-sided rectangle that is the exact size and location of the Rectangle.
Round Rectangle	A rectangle as above, but with rounded corners. The degree to which the corners are rounded is adjustable.

Each shape can be drawn in a specific manner. For example, drawing a rectangle doesn't mean you just create a block on the screen. You have your choice of creating shapes using the techniques in Table 14-2.

Table 14-2. Drawing Methods Available

Method	Description
Erase	Colors the shape using the current background color, rendering the shape invisible.
Fill	Fills the interior of the shape using the specified pattern.
Frame	Draws an outline of the shape using the current pen pattern, size, and color.
Invert	Draws the shape using the opposite of the colors underneath it.
Paint	Fills the shape (solid) with the current pen color.

Patterns are discussed later in this chapter. For now, try the following demonstration program to show each of the shapes and the methods by which they can be created.

Random Shapes Program

This program is built upon the GRAPH.ASM example in the last chapter. It uses the Draw subroutine for the code that creates shapes on the screen. Because Draw is called repeatedly, this program uses QuickDraw II's random number generator to place the shapes at random positions all over the screen. It also uses the color changing routine from the last chapter so that the shapes are drawn in different colors.

This version of the program will simply fill the rectangle with the current pen color. This is done with the PaintRect function:

Function: $5404
Name: PaintRect
Fills the given rectangle with the current pen color.
Push: Rectangle (L)
Pull: nothing
Errors: none
Comments:

The following code should be inserted into the Draw subroutine, before line 164 (the RTS instruction). The line numbers below are relative to line 164. They are used for reference and should not be typed into your source code.

```
1   FINDX   PHA                      ;RESULT SPACE
2           LDX     #$8604           ;RANDOM
3           JSL     $E10000          ;GET A PSUEDORANDOM NUMBER
4           PLA                      ;NUMBER IS IN A
5           AND     #$03FF           ;DESTROY OUT OF RANGE VALUES
6           CMP     #309             ;TEST MAX X RANGE
7           BCS     FINDX            ;KEEP LOOKING IF OUT OF RANGE
8           STA     RECTANGLE+2      ;SAVE MIN X VALUE
9           ADC     #10              ;ADD 10 FOR MAX X VALUE
10          STA     RECTANGLE+6      ;MAX X VALUE
11
12  FINDY   PHA                      ;RESULT SPACE
13          LDX     #$8604           ;RANDOM
14          JSL     $E10000
15          PLA
16          AND     #$01FF           ;DESTROY OUT OF RANGE VALUES
17          CMP     #189             ;TEST MAX Y RANGE
```

```
18          BCS      FINDY          ;KEEP LOOKING IF OUT OF RANGE
19          STA      RECTANGLE      ;SAVE MIN Y VALUE
20          ADC      #10            ;ADD 10 FOR MAX Y
21          STA      RECTANGLE+4    ;SAVE MAX Y
22
23          INC      COLOR          ;CHANGE COLOR VALUE
24          LDA      COLOR          ;GET COLOR VALUE
25          AND      #$000F         ;ONLY USE LOW, LOW NIBBLE
26          PHA
27          LDX      #$3704         ;SETSOLIDPENPAT
28          JSL      $E10000
29
30          PEA      RECTANGLE|-16  ;RECTANGLE POINTER
31          PEA      RECTANGLE
32          LDX      #$5404         ;PAINTRECT
33          JSL      $E10000
```

(Remember to follow this routine with an RTS instruction!)

The following data structures should be placed in the program's Data area.

```
COLOR       DS    2              ;CURRENT PEN COLOR VALUE
RECTANGLE   DS    8              ;RECTANGLE'S STRUCTURE
```

Change the name of your source file to SHAPES.ASM and save it to disk. It would also be a good idea to change the KEEP file name from EXAMPLES to something else.

After assembling and linking the program, run it. You will see a collage of small colored squares randomly appearing on the screen. If you like, you can change the code so that the SetRect function is used instead of stuffing the rectangle's coordinates yourself. The results are the same.

Description of SHAPES.ASM

This description covers only the Draw subroutine in the program, as shown above. Line numbers are references from the Draw label in the original GRAPH.ASM program.

There's little in this listing which hasn't been seen before. The two random–number generating routines for FindX and FindY were covered in the last chapter. In this routine, the random value is stored in the position for X Min in the Rectangle structure (line 8). Next, 10 is added to that value and stored in the position of X Max (lines 9 and 10).

The FindY random routine works much the same way as FindX. The random number returned is first stored in the Min Y position in line 19. Then 10 is added to that value and it's stored in the Max Y position of the Rectangle (lines 20 and 21).

The routine to change the color of the pen in lines 23–28 is from the last chapter. This color is used to fill the rectangle with the PaintRect function in line 32.

Modifying SHAPES.ASM

Here are a dozen or so ways to modify SHAPES.ASM so that you can see the variety of shapes and ways they can be drawn on the screen. Only one line needs to be changed in your program: line 32 (above), which calls the PaintRect function.

The following functions use the same rectangle created by FindX and FindY (you may want to make them bigger by adjusting the values in lines 9 and 20 above). All that changes is the shape drawn in the rectangle and the way the shape is drawn.

Replace line 32 with one of the following:

```
LDX    #$5304    ;FRAMERECT
LDX    #$5504    ;ERASERECT
LDX    #$5604    ;INVERTRECT
```

The Erase function is not as interesting as it might have been in the above example because there's no background. Had this program used a background pattern, the Erase function would perform far more impressive feats.

A fourth variation, Fill, uses a pattern to create the shape on the screen. Patterns and the FillRect function are discussed later in this chapter.

The following four functions draw ovals in the rectangle. They also apply the various methods of drawing: Frame, Paint, Erase, and Invert. To draw ovals, substitute one of these lines for line 32 in the SHAPES.ASM code.

```
LDX    #$5804    ;FRAMEOVAL
LDX    #$5904    ;PAINTOVAL
LDX    #$5A04    ;ERASEOVAL
LDX    #$5B04    ;INVERTOVAL
```

Incidentally, the size of the Frame drawn around the shape is set by the SetPenSize function call. To make a thicker line,

SetPenSize could be added to your program, just before the Scan loop is called.

Function: $2C04
Name: SetPenSize
Changes the dimensions of the drawing pen.
Push: Width (W); Height (W)
Pull: nothing
Errors: none
Comments: Measurements are in Pixels.

Before the Scan loop (about line 101 in your program) you could add the following code:

```
PEA     $5          ;MAKE PEN A LITTLE FATTER
PEA     $5
LDX     #$2C04      ;SETPENSIZE
JSL     $E10000
```

This will make the frames a little more distinct. If the frames become too large for the picture drawn, change the size of the rectangle by changing the values in lines 9 and 20 from 10 to 25 pixels.

Round Rectangles require some additional information before they can be created. The roundness of the rectangle's corners is determined by an oval shape. This oval shape defines the curve of the corner as an X and Y width and height value. The toolbox uses these two values to calculate the curve of the rectangle's corners.

The QuickDraw II function used to Frame a round rectangle is FrameRRect.

Function: $5D04
Name: FrameRRect
Draws a frame around a Round Rectangle.
Push: Rectangle (L); Oval Width (W); Oval Height (W)
Pull: nothing
Errors: Possible Memory Manager errors
Comments: The Oval values define the rounded corners of the Round Rectangle.

To modify the program for round rectangles, change the code at lines 30–33 in the example above to

```
PEA     RECTANGLE-16    ;RECTANGLE POINTER
PEA     RECTANGLE
PEA     10              ;OVAL WIDTH (X VALUE)
PEA     7               ;OVAL HEIGHT (Y VALUE)
LDX     #$5D04          ;FRAMERRECT
JSL     $E10000
```

The variety of round rectangles can be examined by substituting each of the following functions for FrameRRect above.

```
LDX   #$5E04   ;PAINTRRECT
LDX   #$5F04   ;ERASERRECT
LDX   #$6004   ;INVERTRRECT
```

The Arc functions draw a portion of an arc within the rectangle. An arc can be all or part of a circle. When using QuickDraw's arc functions, the angles and lengths are measured in degrees. Zero degrees is straight up, like 12 on the face of a clock. The three o'clock position is 90 degrees, 180 degrees is at six o'clock, and 270 degrees is at nine o'clock.

An arc is specified by giving its starting angle and then the length of the arc. The length is also measured in degrees: a 90-degree arc is one quarter of a circle; a 180-degree arc is half a circle; and a 360-degree arc is a whole circle. By specifying a combination of starting angle and angle length, any part or all of a circle can be drawn using FrameArc.

Function: $6204
Name: FrameArc
Draws a length of an arc.
Push: Rectangle (L); Starting Angle (W); Angle Length (W)
Pull: nothing
Errors: none
Comments: Angles are measured in degrees, with 0 degrees straight up and 90 degrees at the three o'clock position.

The Rectangle defines where the arc is to be drawn and the dimensions of the arc. The Starting Angle directs QuickDraw to start drawing the arc at a specific angle, and the Angle Length defines the length of the arc in degrees. An Angle Length of 360 always draws a full circle no matter where the Starting Angle is placed.

The roundness of the arc, as with the oval shape, is determined by the size of the rectangle. Because the rectangle in SHAPES.ASM is more or less square, the arcs drawn will be proportionally round. If the rectangle is adjusted to long and thin, the arcs (and ovals) will be oblong.

To draw arcs with the SHAPE.ASM program, change the code for creating the shape (altered for round rectangles above) to

```
PEA     RECTANGLE-16        ;RECTANGLE POINTER
PEA     RECTANGLE
PEA     45                  ;STARTING ANGLE, ABOUT 1:30
PEA     270                 ;LENGTH
LDX     #$6204              ;FRAMEARC
JSL     $E10000
```

After saving, assembling, linking, and running the program, you'll see horseshoe shapes all over the screen in different colors. The horseshoe is the arc starting at 45 degrees with a length of 270 degrees. Feel free to change the values in the program to create different arcs.

The following substitutions can be made to view the various methods of creating arcs. The PaintArc routine makes pie shapes when it paints the arc. You may want to change the angles pushed to the stack to 0 and 90 to get a better idea of what's going on.

```
LDX     #$6304       ;PAINTARC (ATTACK OF THE PAC MEN!)
LDX     #$6404       ;ERASEARC
LDX     #$6504       ;INVERTARC
```

Using the Mouse

Using a random-number generator to obtain a screen position is all right for demonstration programs, but in the real world you'll probably want to use the mouse to help plot your graphics.

To do this, a program should generate a graphics shape based on the position of the mouse rather than a random location. The Draw subroutine should be called only when the mouse button is activated—either when it is pressed or when it is released.

From the event record, the position of the mouse can be obtained. The mouse's location is read from the EWhere field of the event record. Those coordinates define the rectangle and draw the shape.

The following modifications should be made to the GRAPH.ASM source code to allow a program to take advantage of the mouse. The biggest change is that the Draw subroutine will only be called when a *mouse up* event occurs. Then the Draw subroutine will obtain coordinates for the rectangle using the mouse's location.

Take the following steps to modify GRAPH.ASM.

Delete the JSR Draw instruction at line 103.

The mouse up event now needs to be tested when GetNextEvent reports an event in the queue. The following code replaces and incorporates the GetKey function between lines 114 and 121. At line 114, insert the following:

```
        LDA   EWHAT      ;GET THE EVENT CODE INTO A
        CMP   #2         ;WAS IT A MOUSE UP EVENT?
        BNE   GETKEY     ;IF NOT, CHECK FOR KEY EVENT
        JSR   DRAW       ;MOUSE IS UP, DRAW THE SHAPE
        BRA   SCAN       ;SCAN FOR MORE EVENTS
GETKEY  CMP   #3         ;WAS IT A KEY PRESS?
        BNE   SCAN       ;IF NOT, KEEP SCANNING
        LDA   EMSG       ;WHICH KEY?
        AND   #$00FF     ;GET RID OF MSB
        CMP   #$1B       ;WAS IT ESC?
        BNE   SCAN       ;IF NOT, KEEP LOOPING
```

This code retrieves the event code number from the EWhat field. Two event codes are checked for: 2 and 3. First the event code is compared with 2, the code for a mouse-up event. If the mouse-up event did not occur, execution branches to the GetKey label. Otherwise, the subroutine at Draw is executed; then, the program continues scanning by branching to the Scan label.

If the event was not a mouse-up event, GetKey checks to see if it was a keyboard event. If not, execution branches back to Scan where it looks for more events. Otherwise, the program checks to see whether the Esc key was pressed. If it was pressed, the program execution falls through to the quit code.

Insert the following code at the Draw subroutine, starting at line 164 (before the RTS instruction). The position of the mouse is first read from the EWhere field of the Event Record; a graphics rectangle is then created using the mouse's position; the color is set using an incrementing color value; and finally, an oval is drawn.

```
        LDA     EWHERE+2        ;GET MOUSE'S X POSITION
        STA     RECTANGLE+2     ;X MIN
        CLC                     ;CLEAR CARRY FOR ADC
        ADC     #$14            ;ADD 20 PIXELS FOR
        STA     RECTANGLE+6     ;X MAX
        LDA     EWHERE          ;GET MOUSE'S Y POS
        STA     RECTANGLE       ;Y MIN
        CLC
        ADC     #$14            ;ADD 20 PIXELS FOR
        STA     RECTANGLE+4     ;Y MAX

        INC     COLOR           ;CHANGE COLOR VALUE
        LDA     COLOR           ;GET COLOR VALUE
        AND     #$000F          ;ONLY USE LOW, LOW NYBBLE
        PHA
        LDX     #$3704          ;SETSOLIDPENPAT
        JSL     $E10000

        PEA     RECTANGLE-16    ;RECTANGLE POINTER
        PEA     RECTANGLE
        LDX     #$5904          ;PAINTOVAL
        JSL     $E10000
```

(Remember to follow this with an RTS instruction!)

The following data structures should be placed into your program's Data area:

```
COLOR       DS    2        ;CURRENT PEN COLOR VALUE
RECTANGLE   DS    8        ;RECTANGLE'S STRUCTURE
```

The last two routines, to change the color and paint the oval, should be familiar to you. The first routine uses the EWhere field of the Event Record to retrieve the position of the mouse. The X and Y coordinates are automatically saved into their corresponding X and Y Min places in the Rectangle structure. The X and Y Max values are calculated by adding $14 to the X and Y values returned from the mouse.

Save your source code under the file name BALLOONS. After assembling and linking the program, run it. Everywhere you click the mouse, a colored circle is drawn. You may wish to experiment with the values returned from the mouse. By adjusting these values, you can cause the circle to be drawn where the mouse is clicked rather than down and to the left. That is achieved with the following code.

```
LDA   EWHERE+2
CLC
SBC   #$A
STA   RECTANGLE+2
CLC
ADC   #$14
STA   RECTANGLE+6
LDA   EWHERE
CLC
SBC   #$A
STA   RECTANGLE
CLC
ADC   #$14
STA   RECTANGLE+4
```

More Information About the SCB

From the last chapter you will recall that an SCB is a scan line control byte. One of the capabilities of the SCB controls is that it can provide a different color table for each scan line. This can be graphically demonstrated by modifying the BALLOONS program.

The following modifications do two things to BALLOONS: First, a second color table is created. Color table one contains colors defined by the SetColorTable function. This new color table is used in addition to the standard color table.

Second, the program changes the color table associated with scan lines 100–199 to the new table. When a balloon is drawn in the bottom half of the screen, it uses the second color table values. Balloons created on the top half of the screen continue to use color table zero. Balloons drawn on the dividing line contain both colors.

These two toolbox functions take care of all the work.

Function: $0E04
Name: SetColorTable
Sets one of 16 color tables to new values.
Push: Table Number (W); Pointer to new table (L)
Pull: nothing
Errors: $0450
Comments: The new table is a table of 16 word-sized values indicating the new colors for Table Number.

Function: $1204
Name: SetSCB
Sets the Scan line Control Byte (SCB) value.
Push: Scan Line (W); New SCB value (W)
Pull: nothing
Errors: $0452
Comments:

Changing the SCBs for the bottom of the screen involves adding only two routines to your code. Before the Scan loop starts at line 101, insert the following code:

```
        PEA     $0001           ;CREATE COLOR TABLE 1
        PEA     CTABLE-16       ;COLOR TABLE'S LOCATION
        PEA     CTABLE
        LDX     #$0E04          ;SETCOLORTABLE
        JSL     $E10000
        JSR     ERRORH          ;CHECK FOR ERRORS
CHGSCB  INC     SCBNUM          ;INCREMENT VARIABLE
        LDA     SCBNUM          ;MOVE INTO A
        CMP     #200            ;199 IS MAX SO
        BEQ     SCAN            ;LEAVE IF DONE
        PHA                     ;PUSH SCANLINE NUMBER
        PEA     $0001           ;SCB - USE TABLE #1
        LDX     #$1204          ;SETSCB
        JSL     $E10000
        JSR     ERRORH          ;CHECK FOR ERRORS
        BRA     CHGSCB
```

Add the following to your program's Data area.

```
SCBNUM  DC      I2'99;          ;START AT SCANLINE 99
CTABLE  DC      I2'$0000,$0D80,$003D,$0F36'
        DC      I2'$01D1,$0888,$0AAF,$013C'
        DC      I2'$0F11,$0C22,$00EE,$0440'
        DC      I2'$0297,$0010,$0011,$09AD'
```

You may change the values in the color table, Ctable, to any values you wish.

These routines first establish new color values for color table 1. Next, the SCBs of the last 99 scan lines on the screen are set to use color table 1; the shapes drawn in that area will take their colors from table 1. Shapes drawn above scan line 100 continue to take their colors from the standard color table.

Assemble, link, and run the program. Now you can have balloons with up to 48 different color schemes on the screen at one time—16 from color table 1, 16 from color table 2, and 16 from both.

DOODLE

Each time GetNextEvent is called, it updates the event record—even if a false result is returned from the toolbox. Specifically, GetNextEvent updates the EWhen and EWhere fields—even when nothing's going on. EWhat will contain zero because no event took place. But if the mouse has moved, its new location is in EWhere. The mouse position is updated regardless of whether an event took place.

Because EWhere is updated, it's easy for a repeatedly called routine to take advantage of the mouse's position. If the Draw routine in GRAPH.ASM were modified to draw a shape at the mouse's position every time it was called, the mouse would continually draw that shape wherever you moved the mouse on the screen.

Better still, the mouse should only draw when its button is pressed. That way the mouse works exactly like a drawing pen: Press the button and the pen is down. Release the button and the pen is up.

Unfortunately, holding the mouse button down does not generate an event. Only when the button is initially pressed does an event occur. To see if the button is still being pressed, you can check the Modifier field of the event record. Or, you can assume the button is down until a mouse up event occurs.

The following is the complete source code for a program called DOODLE. DOODLE draws a line on the screen whenever the mouse's button is pressed, and it continues to draw until the button is released.

DOODLE works by repeatedly calling the Draw subroutine. At the start of this routine is a flag. If the flag is set, it means the mouse button is currently down and the Draw subroutine is executed. If the flag is reset, the mouse button is up and execution returns to the caller.

In the Draw routine, the mouse's current location is obtained from the event record. A line is drawn from the mouse's former location to the current location.

The secret behind DOODLE lies in two new routines. The

MouseUp routine is called each time the mouse button is released. This routine has only one function: to reset the flag used by the Draw routine.

The MouseDown routine sets the flag used by Draw. Because the state of the mouse button is not an event, Draw uses this flag to determine if the button is still down. MouseDown also moves the current pen position to where the mouse button was clicked. The MoveTo function, $3A, moves the pen without drawing. This way the line is drawn from the point where the button is clicked to where it's released.

```
*****************************************************************************
* DOODLE.ASM - MOUSE DRAWING PROGRAM
*****************************************************************************

        ABSADDR  ON           ;ACTIVATE ABSOLUTE ADDRESSING
        KEEP     DOODLE       ;EXE FILE NAME

MAIN    START

        PHK                   ;ASSERT CODE BANK ==
; DATA BANK
        PLB                   ;SET ENVIRONMENT

;-----------------------------------------
; START THE TOOL LOCATOR

        LDX      #$0201       ;TLSTARTUP
        JSL      $E10000      ;BUMP START THE TOOL LOCATOR

;-----------------------------------------
; START THE MEMORY MANAGER AND RETURN
; A USERID FOR THIS PROGRAM


PEA  $0000
;RESULT SPACE
        LDX      #$0202       ;MMSTARTUP
        JSL      $E10000      ;GET A USERID & SOME MEMORY
        JSR      ERRORH       ;CHECK FOR ERRORS
        PLA                   ;GET OUR USERID
        STA      USERID       ;SAVE IT

```

```
;-----------------------------------------
; START THE MISC TOOLS TOOL SET

        LDX     #$0203          ;MTSTARTUP
        JSL     $E10000         ;BUMP START MISC. TOOLS
        JSR     ERRORH          ;CHECK FOR ERRORS

;-----------------------------------------
; ESTABLISH AND INITIALIZE DIRECT PAGE

        PEA     $0000           ;LONG RESULT SPACE
        PEA     $0000
        PEA     $0000           ;FOUR PAGES
        PEA     $0400
        LDA     USERID          ;THIS PROGRAM'S ID
        PHA
        PEA     $E005           ;ATTRIBUTES
        PEA     $0000           ;WHERE OUR BLOCK BEGINS
        PEA     $0000           ; IN MEMORY
        LDX     #$0902          ;NEWHANDLE
        JSL     $E10000
        JSR     ERRORH          ;CHECK FOR ERRORS

        PLA                     ;GET HANDLE OF NEW BLOCK
        STA     0               ;SAVE IN ZERO PAGE AS WELL
        STA     HANDLE          ;AS SAVING IN "HANDLE"
        PLA
        STA     2
        STA     HANDLE+2

        LDA     [0]             ;NOW GET ACTUAL LOCATION REF.
        STA     DPAGE           ;AND STORE IN DPAGE VARIABLE

;-----------------------------------------
; SET UP AND START QUICK DRAW II

        LDA     DPAGE           ;GRAP DPAGE ADDRESS
        PHA                     ;STARTING ADDRESS OF 0 PAGE
        PEA     $0000           ;SCREEN MODE 320
        PEA     $0000           ;PIXEL MAP SIZE
        LDA     USERID
        PHA
```

```
            LDX     #$0204          ;QDSTARTUP
            JSL     $E10000
            JSR     ERRORH

;-----------------------------------------
; EVENT MANAGER

            LDA     DPAGE           ;GET DPAGE FOR EVENT MANAGER
            CLC
            ADC     #$300           ;ALLOW FOR QD2'S DPAGE
            PHA
            PEA     20              ;EVENT QUEUE SIZE
            PEA     0               ;MIN X CLAMP
            PEA     320             ;MAX X CLAMP
            PEA     0               ;MIN Y CLAMP
            PEA     200             ;MAX Y CLAMP
            LDA     USERID          ;THE USERID
            PHA
            LDX     #$0206          ;EMSTARTUP
            JSL     $E10000
            JSR     ERRORH

            LDX     #$CA04          ;INITCURSOR
            JSL     $E10000

;-----------------------------------------
; MAIN PROGRAM EVEN SCANNING LOOP

            PEA     $000F           ;WHITE COLOR
            LDX     #$3704          ;SETSOLIDPENPAT
            JSL     $E10000

SCAN        ANOP

            JSR     DRAW            ;DRAW ROUTINE

            PHA                     ;RESULT SPACE
            PEA     $FFFF           ;EVENT MASK
            PEA     EVENTR|-16
            PEA     EVENTR
            LDX     #$0A06          ;GETNEXTEVENT
            JSL     $E10000
            PLA
```

```
         BEQ    SCAN          ;NOTHING

         LDA    EWHAT         ;GET EVENT
         CMP    #3            ;KEYDOWN?
         BNE    TESTMDN

         LDA    EMSG          ;CHECK INPUT
         AND    #$00FF
         CMP    #$001B        ;ESC?
         BEQ    DONE
         BRA    SCAN

TESTMDN  ANOP
         CMP    #1            ;MOUSE DOWN?
         BNE    TESTMUP       ;IF NOT, KEEP SCANNING
         JSR    MOUSEDOWN
         BRA    SCAN

TESTMUP  ANOP
         CMP    #2
         BNE    SCAN
         JSR    MOUSEUP
         BRA    SCAN

;----------------------------------------
; END OF PROGRAM: SHUTDOWN ALL ROUTINES

DONE     ANOP

         LDX    #$0306        ;EMSHUTDOWN
         JSL    $E10000

         LDX    #$0304        ;QDSHUTDOWN
         JSL    $E10000       ;SHUTDOWN QUICK DRAW II

         LDX    #$0303        ;MTSHUTDOWN
         JSL    $E10000       ;SHUTDOWN MISC TOOLS

         LDA    HANDLE+2      ;PUSH HANDLE
         PHA                  ;TO FREE MEMORY TAKEN
         LDA    HANDLE        ;BY THIS PROGRAM
         PHA
         LDX    #$1002        ;DISPOSE HANDLE
```

```
          JSL     $E10000

          LDA     USERID        ;SHUT DOWN THIS PROGRAM
          PHA
          LDX     #$0302        ;MMSHUTDOWN
          JSL     $E10000       ;SHUTDOWN MEMORY MANAGER

          LDX     #$0301        ;TLSHUTDOWN
          JSL     $E10000       ;SHUTDOWN TOOL LOCATOR

;----------------------------------------
; EXIT VIA PRODOS 16 MLI CALL $29

          JSL     $E100A8       ;PRODOS 16 CALL
          DC      I2'$29'       ;QUIT FUNCTION
          DC      I4'QPARAMS'   ;QUIT PARAMETERS

*****************************************************************************
* ERROR HANDLER
*****************************************************************************
ERRORH    ANOP

          BCS     UHOH          ;CARRY SET IF ERROR
          RTS                   ;ELSE, RETURN

UHOH      ANOP
          PHA                   ;TOOLBOX RETURNS ERROR IN A
          PEA     $0000         ;BANK OF SYSTEM DEATH MESSAGE
          PEA     $0000         ;OFFSET
          LDX     #$1503        ;SYSFAILMGR
          JSL     $E10000       ;SHUT THIS DOWN!

*****************************************************************************
* GRAPHICS DRAWING ROUTINE
*****************************************************************************
DRAW      ANOP
          LDA     DFLAG         ;TEST FLAG
          BNE     ISDOWN
          RTS

ISDOWN    LDA     EWHERE+2      ;X POS
          PHA
          LDA     EWHERE        ;Y POS
          PHA
```

```
            LDX       #$3C04          ;LINETO
            JSL       $E10000
            RTS
MOUSEDOWN       ANOP
            LDA       #$FFFF
            STA       DFLAG
            LDA       EWHERE+2        ;X POS
            PHA
            LDA       EWHERE          ;Y POS
            PHA
            LDX       #$3A04          ;MOVETO
            JSL       $E10000
            RTS
MOUSEUP ANOP
            STZ       DFLAG
            RTS
*******************************************************************************
* DATA STORAGE
*******************************************************************************
USERID  DS        2               ;THIS PROGRAM'S USER ID
HANDLE  DS        4               ;DIRECT PAGE HANDLE
DPAGE   DS        2               ;DIRECT PAGE START
DFLAG   DS        2               ;MOUSE DOWN FLAG
;QUIT PARAMETERS:
QPARAMS ANOP
            DC        I4'$0'          ;RETURN TO PREVIOUS PROGRAM
            DC        I'$0000'        ;THIS PROGRAM NOT RESTARTABLE
;EVENT MANAGER EVENT RECORD
EVENTR  ANOP
EWHAT   DS        2               ;EVENT CODE
```

```
245  EMSG    DS      4                   ;EVENT MESSAGE
246  EWHEN   DS      4                   ;EVENT WHEN (TICK COUNT)
247  EWHERE  DS      4                   ;EVENT WHERE, MOUSE LOCATION
248  EMODS   DS      2                   ;EVENT MODIFYER FLAGS
249
250          END
```

Save this source code as DOODLE.ASM. Assemble, link, and run the program. As usual, press Esc to end the program.

Description of DOODLE.ASM

Most of this code has been used before. The startup and shutdown procedures, error handler, and a few other routines should all be familiar.

The major differences between this program and others is in the Scan loop between lines 104 and 137. Notice that the color of the graphics pen is set to white before the Scan label, at line 100. You might like to set the pen's size here as well.

The Scan loop starts with a call to the Draw subroutine. Next, GetNextEvent is called and if no event is pending, execution branches back to Scan at line 104. Otherwise, three events are tested: mouse up, mouse down, and key press. If a key press is detected, further testing is done to determine if the key pressed was the Esc key. If none of these events occurs, the program keeps scanning—as well as calling—the Draw subroutine.

Depending on which event occurs, three things could happen: If the Esc key is pressed, the program ends; if the mouse button is pressed, the MouseDown routine is called; if the mouse button is released, the MouseUp routine is called.

The Draw routine at line 193 is called repeatedly (in line 106). It checks the status of the DFlag in line 194. (The DFlag is set by MouseUp and reset by MouseDown.) If the DFlag is not zero, the mouse button is currently down and execution branches to the isDown label at line 198. If the mouse button is not down, the subroutine returns with an RTS instruction at line 196.

The isDown routine simply draws a line from the graphic pen's last position to the mouse's current position. The position is read from the EWhere field of the Event Record and the line is drawn with the LineTo function.

The MouseDown routine at line 207 is called each time the mouse's button is pressed. First, the DFlag is set to $FFFF, indicating to the Draw routine that the mouse is down. Next, the pen position is updated by the MoveTo function in line 216. If MoveTo were not called, DOODLE would draw only one continuous line.

MouseUp is called each time the mouse button is released. It has only one duty: to reset the value of the DFlag (line 223).

This program can be modified by adding color and varying pen sizes. In the next section you'll learn how to change the pen's shape by using patterns.

All About Patterns

Patterns can be used for a number of things: There can be background patterns, pen patterns, and patterns used for various shapes. All patterns are defined in the same way. Once you learn how to create patterns, applying them to your graphics is as easy as finding the proper QuickDraw II function call.

All patterns are *repeating*. This means you only need to define one small portion of the pattern. The rest of the graphic image is filled with duplicates of your pattern. This also means the detail of each pattern is limited to the grid in which it's defined.

The way a pattern is made depends on the screen mode. All patterns are a matrix of 8 × 8 pixels. Because the 640-screen mode is less chunky than the 320 mode, it uses the same number of pixels but a smaller grid.

A sample pattern grid for the 320 mode would be

```
PATTERN     ANOP
            DC      H'00000000'
            DC      H'0FFFFFFF'
            DC      H'0FFFFFFF'
            DC      H'0FFFFFFF'
            DC      H'00000000'
            DC      H'FFF0FFFF'
            DC      H'FFF0FFFF'
            DC      H'FFF0FFFF'
```

This creates the classic "brick" pattern (Figure 14-1). The zero pixels take the color black and the F pixels are white. Pixel values are directly associated with the colors in the color table.

Figure 14-1. Graphic of Brick Pattern

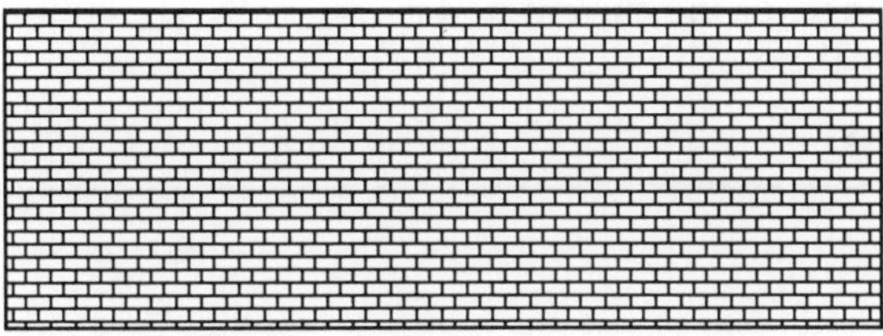

The following creates a similar pattern in the 640 mode. Note how the size of the grid is adjusted for the fewer number of bits per pixel.

```
PATTERN     ANOP
            DC      H'0000'
            DC      H'0FFF'
            DC      H'0FFF'
            DC      H'0FFF'
            DC      H'0000'
            DC      H'F0FF'
            DC      H'F0FF'
            DC      H'F0FF'
```

The following pattern creates a red heart using color 7 from the standard color table, 320 mode.

```
HPATTERN    ANOP
            DC      H'00000000'
            DC      H'00700070'
            DC      H'07770777'
            DC      H'00777770'
            DC      H'00077700'
            DC      H'00007000'
            DC      H'00000000'
            DC      H'00000000'
```

The following two functions change the background pattern for the entire screen. The first, GetPortRect returns the current coordinates for the entire screen (the active port). The second function fills that port, the entire screen, with the indicated pattern.

Function: $2004
Name: GetPortRect
Returns the rectangle of the current port.
Push: Rectangle Pointer (L)
Pull: nothing
Errors: none
Comments:

Function: $5704
Name: FillRect
Fills the interior of the given rectangle with the indicated pattern.
Push: Rectangle (L); Pattern Pointer (L)
Pull: nothing
Errors: none
Comments: The pattern is an 8 × 8 pixel grid.

Add the following code to the DOODLE program to create a background pattern. Insert the following at line 100, before the pen's color is set:

```
PEA    RECTANGLE|-16    ;THE RECTANGLE STRUCTURE
PEA    RECTANGLE
LDX    #$2004           ;GETPORTRECT
JSL    $E10000          ; RETURN THE SCREEN'S PORT
PEA    RECTANGLE|-16    ;USE IT AGAIN
PEA    RECTANGLE
PEA    PATTERN|-16      ;POINTER TO THE PATTERN
PEA    PATTERN
LDX    #$5704           ;FILLRECT
JSL    $E10000
```

You might want to make the pen a little larger when drawing over a background pattern. In order to do that, add the following, right after the above code.

```
PEA    $8               ;MAKE THE PEN A BIT THICKER
PEA    $8
LDX    #$2C04           ;SETPENSIZE
JSL    $E10000
```

And in your program's Data area, add

```
RECTANGLE  DS     8
PATTERN    ANOP
           DC     H'77779999'
           DC     H'77779999'
           DC     H'77779999'
```

```
         DC      H'77779999'
         DC      H'55554444'
         DC      H'55554444'
         DC      H'55554444'
         DC      H'55554444'
```

Assemble, link, and run the program. You'll have a checkerboard pattern on which to DOODLE. If you find this pattern irritating, change it to something else.

The pattern the pen uses can also be changed. Right now, the program uses a solid pattern. To change this, use the following function:

Function: $3004
Name: SetPenPat
Sets the pattern the pen draws.
Push: Pattern Pointer (L)
Pull: nothing
Errors: none
Comments: Don't confuse this with function $32.

After the SetPenPat function, the pen draws using the pattern specified by the Pattern Pointer. Add the following code after the SetSolidPenPat function, originally at line 100 (just before the Scan label). It sets the pen pattern to that found at PenPat.

```
         PEA     PENPAT|-16          ;PEN PATTERN
         PEA     PENPAT
         LDX     #$3004              ;SETPENPAT
         JSL     $E10000
```

Now add the following code to your program's Data area:

```
PENPAT   ANOP
         DC      H'00000000'
         DC      H'00077000'
         DC      H'00766700'
         DC      H'07699670'
         DC      H'07699670'
         DC      H'00766700'
         DC      H'00077000'
         DC      H'00000000'
```

After assembling and linking the file, run it. The graphics pen now draws the diamond pattern specified by Penpat.

If you'd like, you can change any of these programs to the 640 mode to see the effects of a pattern there. Remember to change the Master SCB in QuickDraw's StartUp call, the clamping bounds of the Mouse in the Event Manager's StartUp call, and the size of the pattern table.

The pattern for any shape you create is set by the shape's Fill function. For example, FillRect was used to fill the entire screen earlier in this section. It could also be used to fill a smaller rectangle, for example, the type that was used in the SHAPES.ASM (random rectangles) program. All that's required is a pointer to the pattern and a call to the particular shape's Fill function.

The following functions can be used to fill the various shapes. You may add any of the following, plus the corresponding code and pattern grid, to the SHAPES.ASM source.

Function: $5704
Name: FillRect
Fills the interior of the given rectangle with the indicated pattern.
Push: Rectangle (L); Pattern Pointer (L)
Pull: nothing
Errors: none
Comments: The pattern is an 8 × 8 pixel grid.

Function: $5C04
Name: FillOval
Fills the interior of an oval within a given rectangle using a specific pattern.
Push: Rectangle (L); Pattern Pointer (L)
Pull: nothing
Errors: none
Comments:

Function: $6104
Name: FillRRect
Fills the interior of a Round Rectangle within the given rectangle using a specific pattern.
Push: Rectangle (L); Oval Width (W); Oval Height (W); Pattern Pointer (L)
Pull: nothing
Errors: none
Comments:

Function: $6604
Name: FillArc
Fills the interior of the Arc using a specific pattern.
Push: Rectangle (L); Starting Angle (W); Ending Angle (W) Pattern Pointer (L)
Pull: nothing
Errors: none
Comments:

Changing the Cursor

This chapter has touched upon a number of graphics topics, and yet less than a quarter of QuickDraw II's capabilities have been covered. One final example which is fun and easy to demonstrate is changing the graphics cursor (or *mouse pointer*) to something other than an arrow. This is done with one QuickDraw II function call, SetCursor.

Function: $8E04
Name: SetCursor
Changes the shape and mask of the cursor.
Push: Cursor Record (L)
Pull: nothing
Errors: Possible Memory Manager errors
Comments: See Table 14-3 for details on the record structure.

The cursor record is a structure in memory which contains the size of the cursor, the new cursor shape, the cursor's mask, and the hot spot. Table 14-3 shows the structure of the cursor record.

Table 14-3. Structure of Cursor Record

Item	Size	Description
Rows	Word	The height of the cursor in pixels.
Columns	Word	The width of the cursor in words.
Cursor	Array	Equal to the height and width as defined above.
Mask	Array	Equal in size to the cursor, used to hide the background under the cursor.
YHotspot	Word	The vertical slice of the hot spot.
XHotspot	Word	The horizontal pixel of the hot spot divided by two.

The Rows and Columns determine the size of the cursor. Rows defines the height in pixels, Columns defines the width in pixels. Columns are always word-sized values, meaning the width of the cursor must always be divisible by four. When the array is written to describe the cursor, the last word in each row must be $0000 in order that the cursor will appear correctly on the screen. Take this extra word into account when figuring out the number of columns necessary.

The Cursor itself is defined in an array, very similar to the way a pattern is made. The size of the array is determined by the number of rows and columns. Colors can be used to define the cursor, although it's common to use only black and white.

The Mask is an array which masks out bits under the cursor. It's the same size as the cursor's array. If the mask is set to all zeros, the cursor will appear transparent and take on the opposite color of the background. It's common to set the Mask to the cursor's pattern, but using all white color values. (See below.)

The XHotspot and YHotspot determine where in the cursor is the crucial location for clicking the mouse. For example, if the cursor were an arrow pointing down and to the right, the hot spot might be location 8,8. The Y value for the hotspot is measured by the row. The X value for the hotspot is the number of pixels from the left, divided by two.

It's possible to change the cursor character for any of your programs. As a matter of fact, you can have several cursors and change among them whenever you like. Simply include the SetCursor call with a pointer to the appropriate cursor record.

For example, edit the BALLOONS program source and include the following code. Just after the InitCursor call, which should be around line 94, add

```
PEA    CURSOR|-16        ;PUSH CURSOR RECORD
PEA    CURSOR
LDX    #$8E04            ;SETCURSOR
JSL    $E10000
```

In the Data area of the BALLOONS source, add the following cursor record.

```
CURSOR      DC      I2'11,4'
            DC      H'000F000000000000' ; 1
            DC      H'00F0F00000000000' ; 2
            DC      H'00F0FF0F00000000' ; 3
            DC      H'0FF0F0F0FF000000' ; 4
            DC      H'F0F0F0F0F0F00000' ; 5
            DC      H'F0F0000000F00000' ; 6
            DC      H'F000000000F00000' ; 7
```

```
DC      H'0F00000000F00000' ; 8
DC      H'00F0000000F00000' ; 9
DC      H'000F00000F000000' ;10
DC      H'0000FFFFF0000000' ;11

DC      H'000F000000000000' ; 1
DC      H'00FFF00000000000' ; 2
DC      H'00FFFF0F00000000' ; 3
DC      H'0FFFFFFFFF000000' ; 4
DC      H'FFFFFFFFFFF00000' ; 5
DC      H'FFFFFFFFFFF00000' ; 6
DC      H'FFFFFFFFFFF00000' ; 7
DC      H'0FFFFFFFFFF00000' ; 8
DC      H'00FFFFFFFFF00000' ; 9
DC      H'000FFFFFFF000000' ;10
DC      H'0000FFFFF0000000' ;11
DC      I2'1,3'
```

The size of the new cursor is 11 pixels by 4 words. Note how the fourth word is set to $0000 in each row of both the mask and the cursor. The hotspot is set to the first row and the sixth pixel. This approximates the location of the hand's index finger.

Save the source, assemble, and link the program. Now instead of an arrow pattern, you get the following pattern with the $F values replaced by blanks:

```
DC      H'000 000000000000' ; 1
DC      H'00 0 00000000000' ; 2
DC      H'00 0 0 00000000' ; 3
DC      H'0 0 0 0 000000' ; 4
DC      H' 0 0 0 0 0 00000' ; 5
DC      H' 0 0000000 00000' ; 6
DC      H' 000000000 00000' ; 7
DC      H'0 00000000 00000' ; 8
DC      H'00 0000000 00000' ; 9
DC      H'000 00000 000000' ;10
DC      H'0000 0000000' ;11
```

Chapter 15

Windows

The Apple IIGS has incorporated most of the environment that makes the Macintosh computer successful. Part of this environment is the use of graphics windows to display information, or as work areas.

Creating windows on the screen is done with one function of the Window Manager.

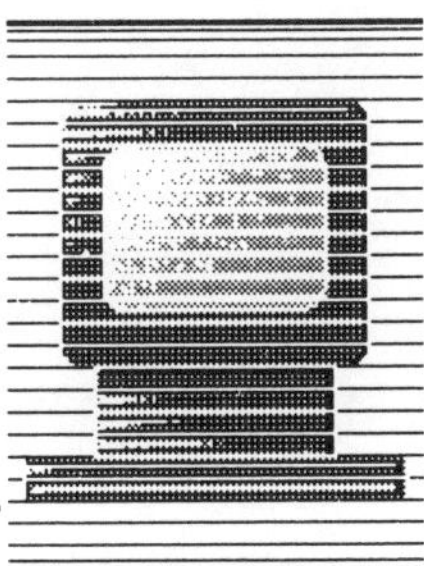

Additional functions control the desktop color and pattern, make the window grow, shrink, move, and put data into the window. All of this is handled via the Window Manager's TaskMaster function. This chapter discusses how to create windows with the toolbox and how to manipulate those windows.

Making and Controlling Windows

Putting a window on the screen and controlling its actions isn't difficult. Most of the complicated work is handled by the *Window Manager*. The Window Manager further calls on the help of the *Control Manager*. The Control Manager deals with buttons, switches, and items called *controls* found in dialog boxes and windows. These two tool sets take care of all the details. You only need to define the window and place something in it.

Before you define the window, you should be familiar with all the window's parts and Apple's terminology for them. Each part has a specific function and is operated in a certain manner. Not every window needs all the controls and parts. Whether you use a given control depends on the window's purpose and how it fits into the rest of your program.

The simplest form of window is a *dialog box*. This uncomplicated window has a place on the screen and a border. It lacks the sophistication and flexibility of the more commonly used windows, yet it's still a window. Incidently, the contents of the dialog box are the responsibility of the Control Manager and *Dialog Manager*. The Window Manager just puts it on the screen and takes it away.

More complex windows can have many things in and around them. Figure 15-1 illustrates the parts of a window and their official names.

In a window you can have any or all of the following:

- Title bar
- Close box (or goaway button)
- Title
- Zoom box (or button)
- Info bar
- Right scroll bar
- Grow box
- Bottom scroll bar

Figure 15-1. Diagram of a Window

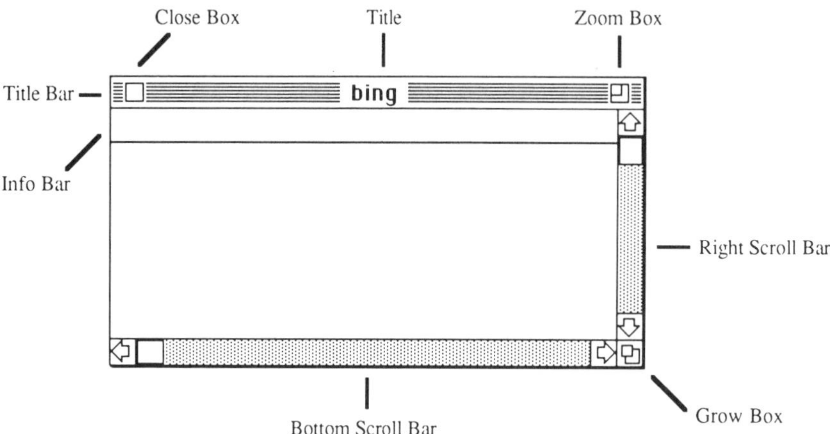

The *title bar* displays an optional title of the window. It can also contain the *goaway* and *zoom* buttons. Also, the title bar is used to drag the window around. If the mouse is clicked and dragged in this region, and if the window is flagged as a moveable window, the window will follow the mouse movement.

The close box, or goaway button, is used to close the window and make it disappear. When the mouse is clicked on the close box, the window goes away.

The title of the window is a string of characters which can be placed into the window's title bar. This can be the name of the document or file in the window, or just a friendly name by which the window is known.

The zoom box is used to instantly make the window a larger size. By setting certain options, you can have your window fill the entire screen when the zoom box is clicked, or you can expand it to a given set of coordinates. When clicked a second time, the zoom box returns the window to its previous size and location on the screen.

The info bar can be used to display additional information about the contents of the window—for example, the size of the document, date, time, and other engrossing information. Or, you can place pull-down menu items into the info bar.

The right scroll bar is used to move the contents of the window up or down. Because the window is technically looking at part of a larger piece of data, the scroll bars are used to move the data past the window, allowing a different piece of it to be viewed.

The bottom scroll bar operates the same as the right scroll bar, only it moves the image under the window right or left.

Finally, the *grow box* is used to resize the window. By grabbing and dragging the grow box, you can change the height and width of the window on the screen.

When creating a window, all the above information is specified in a *window record*. Everything about the window—its size, location, routines, color, and all the above controls—is established by the window record before the window is created.

Although it's a complex structure, the power and detail the window record controls is amazing. Depending on your program, you may elect to use one or all of the above items in your window simply by specifying them in the window record.

Managing the Desktop

The Window Manager takes care of the task of maintaining and updating windows. Almost everything that affects the window is automatically performed by this tool set, whether you grow or shrink the window, zoom it, scroll it, or move it. You have the option of manipulating those events yourself by replacing the toolbox routines with your own, but for everyday programming, the work is done for you by the Window Manager.

Besides windows, the Window Manager also oversees the Desktop function and the TaskMaster.

The Desktop function is used to perform operations dealing with the graphic desktop. For example, setting the current screen color or background pattern is accomplished with the Desktop function. The TaskMaster, covered in Chapter 12, is responsible for most of the work associated with controlling windows.

Function: $0C0E
Name: Desktop
Controls a variety of things dealing with the desktop.
Push: Result Space (L); Command (W); Parameter (L)
Pull: Result (L)
Errors: none
Comments: See chapter 15.

The Desktop function is perhaps the most unusual in the toolbox. Instead of handling only one operation, Desktop has several duties, each performed by one of seven separate commands. To do this, the structure of the Desktop function is a little odd.

For example, the Result Space is not required for all of Desktop's individual operations. Only four of Desktop's seven commands use it. If the command doesn't require the Result Space, then it need not be pushed. Likewise, the Result should not be pulled from the stack after the call.

Desktop works by pushing to the stack a command number, zero through six, followed by a parameter. Occasionally, the parameter might not be used. Still, because it comes after the Command, something does need to be pushed to the stack.

The Desktop function handles these operations:

- Adding or subtracting a region from the desktop
- Setting or returning a handle to the desktop region
- Setting or returning the desktop pattern and colors
- Copying the desktop's region to a memory block

The first two functions and the copy function are rather specific and have interesting uses, but the function you'll probably make the best use of will be to set or change the colors and pattern of the desktop.

In numeric order, the commands available for the Desktop function's Command parameter are

Command: $0000
Name: FromDesk
Removes a region from the desktop, for example, removing a window.
Parameter Region's Handle
Result: Not Used—don't even push the Result Space to the stack.

Command: $0001
Name: ToDesk
Adds a region to the desktop.
Parameter Region's Handle
Result: Not Used—don't even push the Result Space to the stack.

Command: $0002
Name: GetDesktop
Returns a handle to the desktop region.
Parameter Not Used—set to $00000000
Result: Desktop region's handle.

Command: $0003
Name: SetDesktop
Sets the handle of the desktop region.
Parameter Desktop region's handle
Result: Desktop region's handle.

Command: $0004
Name: GetDeskPat
Returns the current pattern and colors of the desktop.
Parameter Not Used—set to $00000000
Result: Desktop Pattern (see settings below).

Command: $0005
Name: SetDeskPat
Redraws the desktop using the given pattern and color.
Parameter Desktop Pattern (see below)
Result: Not Used—don't even push the Result Space to the stack.

Command: $0006
Name: GetVisDesktop
Copies the desktop region to a memory block minus any windows.
Parameter Block's Handle
Result: Not Used—don't even push the Result Space to the stack.

In all cases, the Parameter is a long word as specified, or the value $00000000 (two words of zero). If the Result and the Result Space are not used, do not push or pull them from the stack.

The long word that represents the desktop pattern in functions 4 and 5 is divided into several parts. Each byte in the long word is significant and stands for something. By examining this value you can determine the current desktop pattern and color. Conversely, you can set the colors and pattern by using function 5.

The Parameter for either function is divided into four parts. Each part is one byte of the long word (Table 15-1).

Table 15-1. Parameters for Passing Desktop Pattern and Color

Word	**Meaning**
MSB, HOW	Determines whether your routine or the system draws the desktop.
LSB, HOW	Always set to $00.
MSB, LOW	Used for the system drawing routine to set the pattern.
LSB, LOW	Used for the system drawing routine to set the foreground and background colors.

If your routine is responsible for the desktop, as determined by the MSB, HOW, the other values represent the address of your routine or pattern (a Bank number, followed by the address—three bytes). So, if your routine is responsible, the value returned by function 4 will represent the address of either your pattern or your drawing routine—exactly as you set it.

The MSB of the high order word determines whether you or

the Window Manager will draw the desktop, and which pattern to use. There are three options: $00, $80, and $40.

$00 $00 indicates that your routine will be responsible for drawing the desktop. This byte is followed by the long address of your drawing routine. For example, $00026550 is the value used when the routine in memory bank $02 at address $6550 will be responsible for drawing the desktop.

$80 $80 indicates that the Window Manager will draw the desktop in a pattern you specify. The pattern is located at the address following $80. For example, $80020912 means the Window Manager will use the pattern in bank $02 at address $0912 to draw the desktop.

$40 $40 indicates the default routine for drawing the desktop and setting the pattern. In other words, you are turning the task over to the Window Manager. You will need to specify a few additional options, such as the pattern, foreground and background colors.

For the pattern you have three choices: solid, dithered, and striped. A *solid* pattern uses only the foreground color. A *dithered* pattern alternates the foreground and background color, creating a third color on the screen. A *striped* pattern alternates the foreground and background colors in a pinstripe pattern.

The patterns are set as follows. The foreground color is indicated by *f*, and the background color is indicated by *b*. Both colors are color numbers taken from the current color table.

$400000fb solid
$400001fb dithered
$400002fb striped

When command 4, GetDeskPat, is called, it returns the above values as they were set. You could use command 4 to determine the current desktop pattern or colors and then change them using command 5, SetDeskPat.

The following code shows how you could set the desktop to a specific pattern located at the address Pattern. Patterns were covered in Chapter 14 and the same rules apply here. Remember to adjust the size of your pattern grid for the 640 mode.

```
PEA    $0005         ;SETDESKPAT COMMAND
LDA    #PATTERN|-16  ;BANK OF PATTERN INTO A
ORA    $8000         ;$80 - SET PATTERN
PHA                  ;AND PUSH TO THE STACK
PEA    PATTERN       ;PUSH ADDRESS OF PATTERN
LDX    #$0C0E        ;DESKTOP
JSL    $E10000
```

Pattern is loaded into the A register above so that the bank number of the pattern can be logically ORed with $8000. Otherwise, $00 would be used and the Desktop function would assume location Pattern contains a drawing routine.

To set the color of the desktop, the following code can be used. This sets the desktop to an interesting dithered pattern using the colors 7 and 4 (creating a salmon color on the 640 mode screen).

```
PEA    $0005         ;SETDESKPAT COMMAND
PEA    $4000         ;USE SYSTEM DRAWING AND PATTERN
PEA    $0174         ;DITHERED
LDX    #$0C0E        ;DESKTOP
JSL    $E10000
```

The TaskMaster is a second vital function in the Window Manager tool set. The TaskMaster was introduced in Chapter 12. The most important thing about this function—and the reason why it's in the Window Manager tool set and not the Event Manager—is that it handles all the window-related duties for you. The TaskMaster automatically operates all the controls you put into a window. You needn't lift a finger.

As stated in Chapter 12, the TaskMaster incorporates the Event Manager's GetNextEvent function. Any program which uses windows or pull-down menus should have TaskMaster at its core rather than GetNextEvent. Without the TaskMaster, the routines that monitor window activity would each have to be rewritten.

Function: $1D0E
Name: TaskMaster
Returns status of the event queue as well as checks for certain window/menu events.
Push: Result Space (W); Event Mask (W); Event Record (L)
Pull: Extended Event Code (W)
Errors: $0E03
Comments:

The extended event code returned by the TaskMaster is particular to windows, menus, and the rest of the desktop. Most of the events are handled internally by the Window Manager. However a few of them can be used for your own manipulations.

Table 15-2 lists the Extended Event Codes returned by TaskMaster. The Event Code value in the first column is relative to those events already returned by GetNextEvent. The Extended Code are those events unique to the TaskMaster. When examining the result returned from the TaskMaster function, use the value in the first column.

Table 15-2. Extended Event Codes Returned by the TaskMaster

Event Code	Extended Code	Description
16	0	Mouse is in desk
17	1	A Menu item was selected
18	2	Mouse is in the system window
19	3	Mouse is in the content of a window
20	4	Mouse is in drag
21	5	Mouse is in grow
22	6	Mouse is in goaway
23	7	Mouse is in zoom
24	8	Mouse is in info bar
25	9	Mouse is in vertical scroll
26	10	Mouse is in horizontal scroll
27	11	Mouse is in frame
28	12	Mouse is in drop

For example, when the TaskMaster returns an Extended Event code of 22, the mouse has just been clicked in a window's close box. Your program could intercept and handle this event by closing and erasing the window (which is done by a call to the CloseWindow function, described below).

The Window Manager

The Window Manager manages the desktop, controls windows, and monitors user interaction with windows. If your program uses windows, you need to call the Window Manager's StartUp function. Because the Window Manager shares the Event Manager's direct-page space, only your program's User ID needs to be pushed to the stack when WindStartUp is called.

Also, the Window Manager is a disk-based tool. Before you call WindStartUp, you must first load the Window Manager from disk with the LoadTools function of the Tool Locator. The Window Manager is tool set 14, ($0E). The version of the Window Manager at this writing is 1.3.

Function: $020E
Name: WindStartUp
Starts the Window Manager.
Push: UserID (W)
Pull: nothing
Errors: none
Comments:

To start the Window Manager, the following code could be used.

```
LDA    USERID     ;PUSH YOUR USER ID TO THE STACK
PHA
LDX    #$020E     ;WINDSTARTUP
JSL    $E10000
```

Shutting down the Window Manager is as easy as shutting down any other tool. Don't forget to shut it down if you've started it.

Function: $030E
Name: WindShutDown
Shuts down the Window Manager.
Push: nothing
Pull: nothing
Errors: none
Comments: This call must be made before the Control Manager is shutdown.

If you're using windows in your program, you'll also need the Control Manager. All the items inside the window—scroll bars, buttons, and boxes—are controls. You can't use them in your windows if your program hasn't started the Control Manager.

The Control Manager is one of the fussier tool sets. It insists the Window Manager be started before you call CtlStartUp (when using both). Likewise, you should call the Control Manager's shutdown routine before the Window Manager's shutdown.

Function: $0210
Name: CtlStartUp
Starts the Control Manager.
Push: UserID (W); Direct Page (W)
Pull: nothing
Errors: none
Comments: The Window Manager must be started before making this call.

Function: $0310
Name: CtlShutDown
Shuts down the Control Manager.
Push: nothing
Pull: nothing
Errors: none
Comments: The Window Manager must be shutdown before making this call.

The Control Manager requires its own direct page and the program's User ID when it's started. Because of the direct page requirement, remember to adjust the size of the memory block allocated for direct-page space to include $100 extra bytes.

For example, if the Control Manager, Event Manager, and QuickDraw II were all used in one program, $500 bytes of direct-page space are required ($300 + $100 + $100). Assuming QuickDraw and the Event Manager have already been started, the following code could be used to start the Control Manager.

```
LDA     USERID      ;FIRST, PUSH THE USER ID
PHA
LDA     DPAGE       ;DPAGE = DIRECT PAGE START
CLC
ADC     #$400       ;ACCOUNT FOR QD II AND EM
PHA                 ;PUSH DIRECT PAGE TO USED
LDX     #$0210      ;CTLSTARTUP
JSL     $E10000
```

Incidentally, when using the Window and Control Managers, you should start these tool sets in the following order:

Tool Locator
Memory Manager
Misc tool set
QuickDraw II
Event Manager
Window Manager
Control Manager

That will get the job done for you. Now you're ready to start working with windows.

Making a Window

To create a *window* you need to call only one function in the Window Manager: NewWindow. If you're creating two windows, call it twice; to create three windows, call it three times.

Making a call to NewWindow is fairly easy. In fact, it's a simple function call. Defining the complex window record is the hard part. As stated before, a window can have many things associated with it. The window record is a complete, detailed list of those things.

Function: $090E
Name: NewWindow
Creates and displays (if specified) a new window on the screen.
Push: Result Space (L); Window Record (L)
Pull: Window Pointer (L)
Errors: $0E01, $0E02
Comments: See chapter 15.

First, a long word of result space is pushed to the stack. This is followed by a pointer to the window record. The window record is what actually defines the window.

After the NewWindow call, the toolbox returns a pointer to a window record it uses. You'll need to keep this pointer for further reference to the window. (It's not a handle. Instead, it points to an extended copy of the window record you passed to the toolbox.) There will be one unique window pointer for each window on your screen. You should keep track of each of them.

The following code creates a window on the screen. The window record is located at the label WindRec. The pointer returned by the toolbox is stored at WindPtr.

```
PHA                  ;LONG RESULT SPACE
PHA
PEA     WINDREC|-16  ;BANK OF WINDOW RECORD
PEA     WINDREC
LDX     #$090E       ;NEWWINDOW
JSL     $E10000
PLA                  ;GET WINDOW POINTER
STA     WINDPTR
PLA                  ;GET HIGH ORDER WORD
STA     WINDPTR+2
```

Table 15-3 describes the structure of the window record. The Parameter Name in the following table is used by Apple to describe each item in the window record.

Table 15-3. Structure of the Window Record

Parameter Name	Type	Description
paramlength	Word	Size of this table
wFrame	Word	See below
wTitle	Long	Window's title
wRefCon	Long	User-Defined value
wZoom	Rectangle	Size of window when zoomed
wColor	Long	Window's color table
wYOrigin	Word	Window content's Y origin
wXOrigin	Word	Window content's X origin
wDataH	Word	Height of document
wDataW	Word	Width of document
wMaxH	Word	Max height for grow window
wMaxW	Word	Max width for grow window
wScrollV	Word	Number of Y pixels to scroll
wScrollH	Word	Number of X pixels to scroll
wPageVer	Word	Number of Y pixels to page
wPageHor	Word	Number of X pixels to page
wInfoRefCon	Long	Used by info-bar draw routine
wInfoHeight	Word	Height of info-bar
wFrameDefProc	Long	Window definition procedure
wInfoDefProc	Long	Info-bar drawing routine
wContDefProc	Long	Content drawing procedure
wPosition	Rectangle	Window's starting coordinates
wPlane	Long	Position, front to back
wStorage	Long	Memory for window record

Fortunately, it's possible to set most of these parameters to zero, which causes the Window Manager to substitute defaults. However, if you want to use them, you will have near total control over the window created.

Before getting into the descriptions, and to avoid some confusion, the following is a sample window record. It's used in the WINDOW program at the end of this chapter, where it's further described.

```
WINDOWR  ANOP
         DC     I'WREND-WINDOWR'        ;SIZE OF PARAMETER LIST
         DC     I'%1101111110100000'    ;FRAME TYPE
         DC     I4'WTITLE'              ;TITLE STRING POINTER
         DC     I4'0'                   ;RESERVED
         DC     I2'0,0,0,0'             ;POSITION WHEN ZOOMED 0=DEF
         DC     I4'0'                   ;POINTER TO COLOR TABLE
         DC     I2'0,0'                 ;CONTENTS VERT/HORZ ORIGIN
         DC     I2'200,640'             ;HEIGHT/WIDTH OF DOCUMENT
         DC     I2'200,640'             ;HEIGHT WIDTH FOR GROW WINDOW
         DC     I2'4,16'                ;VERT/HORZ PIXELS FOR SCROLL
         DC     I2'40,160'              ;VERT/HORZ PIXELS SCROLL PAGE
         DC     I4'0'                   ;VALUE PASSED TO INFORMATION
         DC     I2'0'                   ;HEIGHT OF INFO BAR
         DC     I4'0'                   ;WINDOW DEFINITION
         DC     I4'0'                   ;DRAW INFO BAR ROUTINE
         DC     I4'0'                   ;DRAW INTERIOR
         DC     I2'40,100,159,540'      ;STARTING POSITION AND SIZE
         DC     I4'$FFFFFFFF'           ;STARTING PLANE
         DC     I4'0'                   ;WINDOW RECORD
WREND    ANOP
```

The first value in the window record is the total number of bytes in the window record. This is kind of a perversion on the Pascal type of string. It's actually used by the Memory Manager when it moves this record into the internal window record managed by the Window Manager.

The second value in the window record informs the Window Manager of the things to put in the window and how to draw the window's frame. The bits in this word control each individual aspect of the window. If you want a standard window that has everything, the bit pattern will appear as follows.

```
;              - - - - = = = = - - - - = = = =
DC      I2'%  1 1 0 1 1 1 1 1 1 0 1 0 0 0 0 0' ;WINDOW WITH
                                                ;EVERYTHING
```

or

```
DC      I2'$DFA0'                               ;SAME THING,
                                                ;IN HEX
```

In the documentation of the window structure in this book, a series of *dashes* and *equals* are used to help identify the bit structure of the window frame word. This makes it easy to identify which bits are active and which items are placed into the window.

Individually, the bits can be set or reset to control the parameters listed in Table 15-4. The bits set above are highlighted with an asterisk (*).

Table 15-4. Bit Record and Parameters Set

Bit Set	Parameter
0	The window is highlighted (set by NewWindow)
1	Window is zoomed
2	Internal use (determines window record allocation)
3	Window's controls can be active when the window is inactive (normally reset to zero)
4	The window has an info bar
5*	The window is visible
6	An inactive window will be made active if the mouse is clicked inside of it
7*	The window can be moved (dragged around by its title bar)
8*	The window has a zoom box
9*	The size of the window is flexible
10*	The window has a grow box
11*	The window has an up and down scroll bar (right side)
12*	The window has a left and right scroll bar (bottom)
13	The window has a double frame, like an Alert dialog box
14*	The window has a goaway button
15*	The window has a title bar

Bit 0. Controls whether the window is highlighted or not. When the window is created, the NewWindow function resets this bit to zero, so whatever you initially place here is not crucial.

Bit 1. Determines whether or not the window is zoomed when it first appears. When the window is zoomed, it usually fills the entire screen, so it's a good idea to keep this bit reset to zero.

Bit 2. Defines how the window was allocated. If set, the NewWindow call allocated the window record. This bit is used internally by the Window Manager, so how you set it has no effect.

Bit 3. Determines how the window's controls operate. When this bit is reset to zero, its controls become inactive when the window is deactivated. When this bit is set, the controls can still be manipulated. However, by setting this bit, your program is responsible for the actions taken by the active controls in an inactive window.

Bit 4. If set, puts an information bar into the window. If the window has an information bar further action needs to be taken to place information into the bar. See the rest of the window record below.

Bit 5. Determines if the window is visible or invisible. If set, the window created will be visible on the screen.

Bit 6. Used to activate an inactive window if the mouse clicks anywhere on the window. If this bit is reset, it's up to your program to determine when a window can become active.

Bit 7. Controls the mobility of the window. If set, the window can be moved around the screen by dragging the mouse on the window's title bar. The window should have a title bar if this bit is set.

Bit 8. If set, puts a zoom box into the window's title bar. The zoom box, when clicked, enlarges the window up to the size of the full screen. The window should have a title bar if this bit is set.

Bit 9. Defines the flexibility of the window. If set, the zoom and grow aspects of the window will not change the origin of the window's data.

Bit 10. If set, places a grow box in the lower right corner of the window. The window should have either a left and right or up and down (or both) scroll bar.

Bit 11. Determines if the window has a left and right scroll bar on its bottom.

Bit 12. Determines if the window has an up and down scroll bar on its right side.

Bit 13. Controls the window frame. If this bit is set, the window will have a double frame like an alert window. This bit is used by the Dialog Manager when it creates a window. Bits 4, 8, 9, 10, 11, 12, 14, and 15 must be reset to zero if this bit is set.

Bit 14. Determines if the window has a goaway, or close box, on the left side of its title. The window should have a title bar if this bit is set.

Bit 15. Places a title bar into the window. If set, the window will have a title bar across its top, in which a goaway button, title string, and zoom button can be placed. The window can also be moved when the mouse is dragged in this region.

Besides the frame type, and all its many bits, there are still two dozen more items in the window record. In order, they are

wTitle. A pointer to a Pascal string which will be centered in the window's title bar. The window should have a title bar if a string is specified. Use a long word of zero if the window doesn't have a title.

wRefCon. A long-word value which can be used by your programs. It has no significance and is reserved for your use. Normally, it's set to zero.

wZoom. A rectangle that indicates the size of the window when it's zoomed. If four words of zero are specified, the zoomed size is the entire screen. The window should have a zoom button to make use of this parameter.

wColor. A long-word pointer to the address of a color table used to draw the window's frame. If zero is specified, the standard color table is used.

wOrigin. Sets the Y and X coordinates of the window's data origin in global coordinates. The Y value is first, followed by X.

wDataH. A word that determines the height (the number of Y pixels) of your data.

wDataW. A word that determines the width (X pixels) of your data.

wMaxH. Determines the maximum height allowed by the window's grow box. This value should be tied to the value for wDataH above.

wMaxW. Sets the maximum width allowed by the window's grow box. As with wMaxH, this value should be tied to the value for wDataW above.

wScrollV. Sets the number of pixels to scroll in the window's content region when the user clicks on an up or down arrow button.

wScrollH. Sets the number of pixels to scroll in the window's content region when the user clicks on a left or right arrow button.

wPageVer. Determines the number of pixels to scroll when the user clicks in the right (up and down) scroll bar (the paging effect).

wPageHor. Determines the number of pixels to scroll when the user clicks in the bottom (left and right) scroll bar.

wInfoRefCon. A long-word string pointer or a value passed to the window drawing routine. If a string pointer is used, that string appears in the window's information bar. This value can be set to zero if your window lacks an information bar.

wInfoHeight. A value that sets the height, in pixels, of the information bar.

wFrameDefProc. Points to a routine that defines the window. Specify zero to use the standard routine.

wInfoDefProc. Points to a routine that puts information into the information bar. A routine must be specified if wInfoRefCon and wInfoHeight are used. Use zero if your window lacks an information bar.

wContDefProc. Points to a routine that draws the window's contents. Use zero if your window comes up empty.

wPosition. A rectangle giving the window's starting location on the screen, and its size. The values are in global coordinates in this order: Y Min, X Min, Y Max, X Max.

wPlane. Instructs the Window Manager where to place the new window. If a long word of zero is specified, the window will be behind every other window on the screen. If a long word of $FFFFFFFF is specified, the window will be the first and topmost window on the display.

wStorage. A pointer to a memory location where the window record can be stored. Zero is normally used, allowing the Window Manager to take care of this job.

Closing a Window

Compared to the window record and all that's involved with creating a window, getting rid of a window is easy. Simply call the CloseWindow function.

Function: $0B0E
Name: CloseWindow
Removes a window from the display releasing all memory, controls, and other items associated with the window.
Push: Window Pointer (L)
Pull: nothing
Errors: none
Comments:

All that's required to make this call is the Window Pointer returned by *New Window*. The Window Manager will carefully remove the window from the screen, redrawing whatever was underneath it.

Incidentally, windows do not need to be closed as part of a shutdown procedure. The Window Manager's ShutDown function will take care of any open windows when it is shutdown. So, while CloseWindow is not a requirement, it is proper procedure. Nothing bad will happen if you forget to do it.

A Window Program

The following is the source code for a program WINDOW. This code creates a sample window with all the options on the 640-mode screen. Feel free to manipulate the values in the window record as you please. No code has been included to place information in the window.

Enter the following code into your editor. You might notice bits and pieces that are familiar to you. If possible, you can cut and paste some of the standard routines from other source code, and as usual, don't type in the line numbers.

```
******************************************************************************
* WINDOW DEMONSTRATION PROGRAM
******************************************************************************

         ABSADDR  ON               ;ACTIVATE ABSOLUTE ADDRESSING
         KEEP     WINDOW           ;EXE FILE

MAIN     START

         PHK                       ;ASSERT CODE BANK ==
; DATA BANK
         PLB

;----------------------------------------
; START THE TOOL LOCATOR

         LDX      #$0201           ;TLSTARTUP
         JSL      $E10000

;----------------------------------------
; START THE MEMORY MANAGER AND GET USER ID

         PEA      $0000            ;RESULT SPACE
         LDX      #$0202           ;MMSTARTUP
         JSL      $E10000          ;GET A USERID & SOME MEMORY
         JSR      ERRORH
         PLA                       ;SAVE USERID
         STA      USERID

;----------------------------------------
; START THE MISC TOOLS TOOL SET

         LDX      #$0203           ;MTSTARTUP
         JSL      $E10000
         JSR      ERRORH

;----------------------------------------
; GET DIRECT PAGE SPACE

```

```
            PEA     $0000           ;LONG RESULT SPACE
            PEA     $0000
            PEA     $0000           ;FIVE PAGES
            PEA     $0500
            LDA     USERID          ;PROGRAM'S ID
            PHA
            PEA     $C005           ;ATTRIBUTES
            PEA     $0000           ;WHERE BLOCK BEGINS
            PEA     $0000           ; IN MEMORY
            LDX     #$0902          ;NEWHANDLE
            JSL     $E10000
            JSR     ERRORH

            PLA                     ;GET HANDLE OF NEW BLOCK
            STA     0               ;INTO ZERO PAGE
            STA     HANDLE

            PLA
            STA     2
            STA     HANDLE+2

            LDA     [0]
            STA     DPAGE           ;SAVE START IN DPAGE

;-----------------------------------------
; SET UP AND START QUICK DRAW II

            LDA     DPAGE
            PHA                     ;STARTING ADDRESS OF 0 PAGE
            PEA     $0080           ;SCREEN MODE 640
            PEA     $0000           ;MASTER SCB
            LDA     USERID          ;OUR PROGRAM'S ID
            PHA
            LDX     #$0204          ;QDSTARTUP
            JSL     $E10000
            JSR     ERRORH

;-----------------------------------------
; EVENT MANAGER

            LDA     DPAGE
            CLC
            ADC     #$300
            PHA
```

```
        PEA     $0014           ;EVENT QUEUE
        PEA     $0000
        PEA     $280            ;MAX X CLAMP
        PEA     $0000
        PEA     $C8             ;MAX Y CLAMP
        LDA     USERID
        PHA
        LDX     #$0206          ;EMSTARTUP
        JSL     $E10000
        JSR     ERRORH
        LDX     #$CA04          ;INITCURSOR
        JSL     $E10000
;----------------------------------------
; LOAD DISK-BASED TOOLBOX ROUTINES
        PEA     TOOLIST|-16     ;BANK OF TOOL LIST
        PEA     TOOLIST
        LDX     #$0E01          ;LOADTOOLS
        JSL     $E10000
        JSR     ERRORH
;----------------------------------------
; SET UP AND START WINDOW MANAGER
        LDA     USERID          ;THIS PROGRAM'S ID
        PHA
        LDX     #$020E          ;WINDSTART
        JSL     $E10000
;----------------------------------------
; SET UP CONTROL MANAGER
        LDA     USERID
        PHA
        LDA     DPAGE
        CLC
        ADC     #$400           ;ACCOUNT FOR QD II AND EM
        PHA
        LDX     #$0210          ;CTRSTARTUP
        JSL     $E10000
        JSR     ERRORH
```

```
;----------------------------------------
; REDRAW THE ENTIRE DESKTOP

          PEA       $5              ;SETDESKPAT
          PEA       $4000           ;DEFAULT
          PEA       $0070
          LDX       #$0C0E          ;SET DESKTOP
          JSL       $E10000

;----------------------------------------
; DRAW THE WINDOW

          PEA       $0000           ;LONG RESULT SPACE
          PEA       $0000
          PEA       WINDOWR|-16
          PEA       WINDOWR
          LDX       #$090E          ;NEWWINDOW
          JSL       $E10000
          JSR       ERRORH

          PLA                       ;GET WINDOW POINTER
          STA       WINDPTR
          PLA
          STA       WINDPTR+2

;----------------------------------------

SCAN      ANOP

          PHA                       ;RESULT SPACE
          PEA       $FFF7           ;EVENT MASK
          PEA       EVENTR|-16
          PEA       EVENTR
          LDX       #$1D0E          ;TASKMASTER
          JSL       $E10000
          PLA
          BEQ       SCAN            ;NOTHING

          CMP       #22             ;IN GOAWAY
          BNE       SCAN

          LDA       WINDPTR+2       ;REMOVE THE WINDOW
          PHA
```

```
        LDA     WINDPTR
        PHA
        LDX     #$0B0E          ;CLOSEWINDOW
        JSL     $E10000

;---------------------------------------
; END OF PROGRAM: SHUTDOWN ALL ROUTINES

        LDX     #$0310          ;CTRLSHUTDOWN
        JSL     $E10000

        LDX     #$0306          ;EMSHUTDOWN
        JSL     $E10000

        LDX     #$030E          ;WINDSHUTDOWN
        JSL     $E10000         ;SHUTDOWN WINDOW MNGR

        LDX     #$0304          ;QDSHUTDOWN
        JSL     $E10000         ;SHUTDOWN QUICK DRAW II

        LDX     #$0303          ;MTSHUTDOWN
        JSL     $E10000         ;SHUTDOWN MISC TOOLS

        LDA     HANDLE+2        ;PUSH HANDLE
        PHA                     ;TO FREE MEMORY TAKEN
        LDA     HANDLE          ;BY THIS PROGRAM
        PHA
        LDX     #$1002          ;DISPOSE HANDLE
        JSL     $E10000

        LDA     USERID          ;SHUT DOWN THIS PROGRAM
        PHA
        LDX     #$0302          ;MMSHUTDOWN
        JSL     $E10000         ;SHUTDOWN MEMORY MANAGER

        LDX     #$0301          ;TLSHUTDOWN
        JSL     $E10000         ;SHUTDOWN TOOL LOCATOR

;---------------------------------------
; EXIT VIA PRODOS 16 MLI CALL $29

        JSL     $E100A8         ;PRODOS 16 CALL
        DC      I2'$29'         ;QUIT FUNCTION
        DC      I4'QPARAMS'     ;QUIT PARAMETERS
```

```
**************************************************************************
* ERROR HANDLER
**************************************************************************
ERRORH   ANOP

         BCS       UHOH           ;CARRY SET IF ERROR
         RTS                      ;ELSE, RETURN

UHOH     ANOP
         PHA                      ;TOOLBOX RETURNS ERROR IN A
         PEA       $0000          ;BANK OF SYSTEM DEATH MESSAGE
         PEA       $0000          ;OFFSET
         LDX       #$1503         ;SYSFAILMGR
         JSL       $E10000        ;SHUT THIS DOWN!

*
* DATA STORAGE
*

OLDDP    DS        2              ;DIRECT PAGE STORED HERE
USERID   DS        2              ;THIS PROGRAM'S USER ID
HANDLE   DS        4              ;ZERO PAGE HANDLE
DPAGE    DS        2              ;DIRECT PAGE STARTING LOCATION
WINDPTR  DS        4              ;WINDOW POINTER

TOOLIST  DC        I'2'           ;TOTAL NUMBER OF TOOLS
         DC        I'$0E,$0000'   ;WINDOW MANAGER
         DC        I'$10,$0000'   ;CONTROL MANAGER

;QUIT PARAMETERS:

QPARAMS  ANOP
         DC        I4'$0'         ;RETURN TO PREVIOUS PROGRAM
         DC        I'$0000'       ;THIS PROGRAM NOT RESTARTABLE

;EVENT MANAGER AND TASKMASTER

EVENTR   ANOP
EWHAT    DS        2
EMSG     DS        4
EWHEN    DS        4
```

```
EWHERE  DS      4
EMODS   DS      2
TDATA   DS      4                  ;TASK DATA
TMASK   DC      I4'$1FFF'          ;TASK MASK

;WINDOW PARAMETERS:
WTITLE  DC      I1'10'
        DC      C'TWEEDLEDEE'

WINDOWR ANOP
        DC      I'WREND-WINDOWR'      ;SIZE OF PARAMETER LIST

;FRAME TYPE
;                    - - - - ====- - - - ====
        DC    I'%    1 1 0 1 1 1 1 1 1 0 1 0 0 0 0 0'
        DC      I4'WTITLE'         ;TITLE
        DC      I4'0'              ;RESERVED
        DC      I2'0,0,0,0'        ;POSITION WHEN ZOOMED 0=DEF
        DC      I4'0'              ;POINTER TO COLOR TABLE
        DC      I2'0,0'            ;CONTENTS VERT/HORZ ORIGIN
        DC      I2'200,640'        ;HEIGHT/WIDTH OF DOCUMENT
        DC      I2'200,640'        ;HEIGHT WIDTH FOR GROW WINDOW
        DC      I2'4,16'           ;VERT/HORZ PIXELS FOR SCROLL
        DC      I2'40,160'         ;VERT/HORZ PIXELS SCROLL PAGE
        DC      I4'0'              ;VALUE PASSED TO INFORMATION
                                   DRAW
        DC      I2'0'              ;HEIGHT OF INFO BAR
        DC      I4'0'              ;WINDOW DEFINITION
        DC      I4'0'              ;DRAW INFO BAR ROUTINE
        DC      I4'0'              ;DRAW INTERIOR
        DC      I'40,100,159,540'  ;STARTING POSITION AND SIZE
        DC      I4'$FFFFFFFF'      ;STARTING PLANE
        DC      I4'0'              ;WINDOW RECORD
WREND   ANOP

        END
```

After typing in the code, save it as WINDOW.ASM. Assemble, link, and run the program. You will see a window titled *Tweedledee*. You can move the window, size it, zoom it, and manipulate with its scroll bars.

Description of WINDOW.ASM

A lot of the code should be fairly obvious by now. The crucial parts pertaining to this chapter are as follows.

Because five pages of direct-page space are needed by the tool sets in this program, lines 41 and 42 push a long word of $500 to the stack for the NewHandle call. This creates five pages of direct space for use by this program.

QuickDraw II is started in lines 66–74. The 640 mode is established by setting the Master SCB to $80 in line 68.

Lines 100–104 load two disk-based tools, the Window and Control Managers, into memory with the LoadTools function.

After being loaded from disk, the Window Manager is started in lines 109–112. The Control Manager is started at lines 117–125. The Control Manager's direct page is set at an offset of $400 bytes (line 121). This accounts for the one page taken by the Event Manager and the three pages taken by QuickDraw II.

Lines 130–134 set the desk pattern using the Desktop function. Command five is used at line 130 to set the desktop pattern. The system default pattern is used, and the foreground color is set to pink by lines 131 and 132. A pattern is not used.

This program's window is created in lines 139–150. Result space is first pushed to the stack, followed by the window record's address. The window pointer returned from the toolbox is stuffed into the memory location at WindPtr.

This program's main scanning loop is at lines 154–166. The TaskMaster function at line 160 requires the same information pushed to the stack as GetNextEvent. If no event took place, nothing is returned from the stack, and execution branches back to Scan. If an event did occur, it's compared with 22 in line 165. Extended Event Code 22 means the mouse was clicked in the goaway box. If so, execution falls through to line 168. You should note that while the program is spinning between lines 154 and 166, the window on the screen is continually updated. There's no need to test for standard window events as they are handled by the Window Manager.

If a click did occur in the goaway box, execution falls through to line 168. The window is closed via the CloseWindow call. After this, the program is shutdown.

New items in the program's Data area include Line 238, storage for the program's window pointer (returned by the toolbox in lines 147 and 150).

Lines 240–242 contain the tool list used by the LoadTools function in lines 100–104.

The event record in lines 252–259 has been extended to add the TaskMaster's two items—task data and the task mask.

Lines 262 and 263 contain a Pascal string to be used as the title of the window. This title is automatically centered in the title bar by the Window Manager.

Finally, the window record is listed in lines 265–286. Almost all items in the window are included. For detail on each parameter, refer back to the descriptive section earlier in this chapter.

Two Windows Program

Putting a second window into the program is as easy as copying two blocks of code and renaming some labels. The Window Manager takes care of the labor involved in operating a number of windows on the screen at once. You create the second window's window record and call NewWindow a second time.

To do this, you could copy two blocks of code and change the labels in the second block to prevent some assembly errors. Do this by changing the word *Window*, used in the labels, to *W2ndow.*

First, make a duplicate of the block of text from lines 139–150. This causes a second NewWindow call to be made. In the duplicate text, change *WindowP* to *W2ndowP,* and *WindPtr* to *W2ndPtr.* Place the new block right after the old. The two NewWindow functions will create two windows on the screen. Of course to do this, you'll need to add another window record.

To create the new window record, copy the original record and place the duplicate at the end of the source code. Change all the Window references to W2ndow. Rename the title of the window (which should be at pointer Wt2tle) to *Tweedledum.* Change the starting location of the window by adding 10 to each value. None of the other parameters in the window record need to be changed.

Before saving, make a duplicate of WindPtr. Call it *W2ndPtr.* Double check to be sure none of the new labels duplicate old labels, which would cause the assembler to err.

Rename the source code W2NDOW.ASM (to be consistent). Assemble and run the new program. Now you have two windows.

Because the window record of each window directs the Window Manager to make that window active if the mouse is clicked in it, you can switch between these windows. However, because the CloseWindow routine was not modified, only window Tweedledee disappears before the program quits, regardless of which window's close button you press.

Chapter 16

Pull-Down Menus

The main reason the Apple IIGS has a toolbox, windows, graphics, and so on, is to write menu-driven programs. Menu-driven programs provide a list of menus, or item categories across the top of the screen. When the mouse is clicked on a menu title, a whole list of options is

displayed. Making a choice is as easy as dragging the mouse down through the menu and releasing it on the desired menu item. This is the pull-down menu interface.

This chapter deals with placing pull-down menus into your Apple IIGS applications. Programming a menu driven application is a breeze with the toolbox. The pull-down menu environment Apple has provided for the IIGS means half the design work involved in creating a program has already been done. This frees your mind to think more about what an application does and how to use it.

All About Menus

Menus, the way they work, and the items they contain are all covered in a book published by Apple called *Apple's Human Interface Guidelines.* It's also called "the Tognazzini guide" after its principle author, Bruce Tognazzini.

Apple's Human Interface Guidelines describes how a menu-driven program operates, which menus should contain which items, how an item should appear in a pull-down menu, and other interesting tidbits—all of which provide a degree of consistency among Apple's menu-driven programs.

This book is about programming the Apple IIGS toolbox and not a reference guide like the *Human Interface Guidelines.* However, a few important general issues should be discussed as part of an introduction to programming pull-down menus.

The pull-down menus are placed across the top of the screen, starting at the left with the Apple menu. Each menu has menu items underneath it which are displayed when the mouse is clicked on the menu title. The number of menus and menu items can vary, although it really depends on the screen size and the name of each menu. The 640-mode screen can hold twice as many menu items as the 320-mode screen.

Apple. The Apple menu, denoted by the colored, copyrighted, company logo, is reserved for special purposes. Although not required by every program, if you do include the Apple menu it should have an *About. . .* menu item, followed by utilities, called New Desk Accessories.

The About. . . item is the first item in the Apple menu and it's used to display a dialog box on the screen. The dialog box tells about the program or programmers, or contains other interesting information about the program.

Under the About. . . item can be utility items for the program. More commonly, though, there will be special menu items called *New Desk Accessories.* These items are placed into the Apple menu by a special function of the Menu Manager and they are located in the /SYSTEM/DESK.ACCS/ prefix of your system disk. New desk accessories can include, for example, a clock, calculator, notepad, or any of a number of interesting items.

File. After the Apple menu, two other common menus are File and Edit. File contains a list of disk-related functions. For example, Open, Close, Save, Save As, Revert, and so on. All these deal with files saved and loaded from disk. Their precise use is covered by the *Human Interface Guidelines.* The File menu also optionally contains a Help menu item, and the Quit item.

Edit. After the File menu comes another common menu, Edit. The Edit menu contains the standard desktop editing commands, Cut, Paste, Copy, Clear, and, optionally, the Show Clipboard item. Again, the uses of these are covered in the Human Interface Guidelines. Also, many of these functions are already handled by specific tool sets within the toolbox.

Any menus which are necessary to your program can be placed on the menu bar. The menu titles should pertain to the items within the menu, and all the items should somehow be related. For example, the Fish menu should contain Halibut, Salmon, Trout, Catfish, Sea Bass, and Shark, but not Candy. You could also group the fish by type—say fresh water over deep sea fish.

Another convention with pull-down menus is having a key equivalent. This means, pressing the Apple key along with the letter key shown in the menu is the same as choosing that menu item with the mouse. For some operations, especially text-based applications, pressing a key equivalent is much faster than using the mouse.

Certain key equivalents are reserved for use with special menu items. Apple-C, Apple-X and Apple-V are reserved for Copy, Cut and Paste, respectively. Apple-O and Apple-S are reserved for Open and Save. And Apple-Q is reserved for Quit. These are specified in the *Human Interface Guidelines.* So to be consistent, your programs should limit the use of these key equivalents.

Inside the Menu

Pull-down menus are put on the screen by passing a menu record to the toolbox. This works in much the same way as the window record works to create a window. Menu records, however, are much easier to deal with.

Everything you see in the pull-down menu, the names of the menu items, the type style they're in, the key equivalents, check marks, whether the item is dimmed (disabled)—all of this is specified in the menu record.

The menu record is a structure that contains text strings. The text strings describe each of the menu items and the attributes of the menu items, and they assign each item a unique ID number. It's the ID number which is used to determine which item was selected from a pull-down menu. (This is handled by the TaskMaster and is demonstrated later in this chapter.)

Before going into detail with the menu record, Figure 16-1 shows all the parts of a pull-down menu and their official references.

Figure 16-1. The Menu Bar

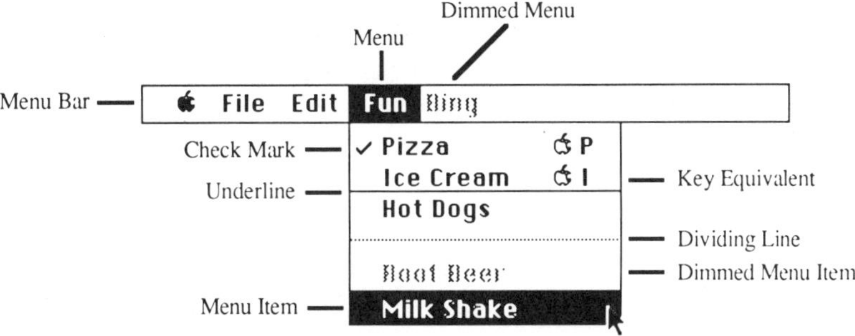

The menu bar. A graphic area on top of the screen which contains menus. Menus are referred to by their names in the menu bar. *File* represents the File menu. *Edit* represents the Edit menu, and so on.

Menu items. The individual items under each menu. They are grouped into areas that contain similar items. Separating these areas are dividing lines. A dividing line can be on a line by itself, or an underline separating two menu items.

Key equivalents. These are shown to the right side of a menu item. Pressing the Apple key and the key listed by the menu item is the same as choosing that menu item with the mouse.

Checkmarks. Used to indicate a menu item that turns something on or off. If the checkmark is present, the item is currently on. Selecting the item again turns the checkmark—as well as the item's function—off.

Dimmed menus and menu items. Show that the menu or item is present, but its function is not currently available. Only after certain operations will the menu or menu item be activated. (The state of each menu item can be changed using functions of the Menu Manager.)

The Menu Record

The *menu record* is what provides the information required to create pull-down menus. Its structure is rather simple, as it is composed entirely of strings. The menu record is passed to the Menu Manager function NewMenu. From there, the Menu Manager takes the text and places it into a menu handle.

Aside from creating the text of menus, a number of optional items can be specified: whether or not the menu item is dimmed, checked, has a key equivalent, or is displayed in a unique text style. Most important, a menu item identification number is assigned to the menu item. It is this number which is later used by your program to carry out the function of each menu item.

The menu record follows this type of structure:

- First menu title
- Menu item
- End

- Second menu title
- Menu item
- Menu item
- Menu item
- End

- Third menu title
- Menu item
- Menu item
- Dividing line
- Menu item
- End

Each line in the menu record is a string of characters, containing the following items:

- Title or Item character
- Title/Item name
- Special characters
- Carriage return character ($0D)

Title or Item character. Each string starts with a Title or Item character. Menu titles use the Title character, while menu items under that title use the Item character. This is followed by a string describing the menu item's name. And finally, special characters are included to set the menu item's attributes and give it an ID number. After each string is the carriage return character, $0D.

Each menu ends with a special End of Menu marker. This text character appears after each separate menu.

Title characters. Title characters are two identical text characters that identify a menu title. Punctuation and math symbols can be used, as well as text characters. The characters must be identical, and these characters must be the same for each menu title in the menu record.

Item character. Item characters are two identical text characters that identify a menu item. The Item characters must be identical. They cannot be the same characters used as the Title characters above.

The Title and Item characters must be the same for each menu title and every menu item in the menu record. If any one of them is different, the menus will not be displayed properly and their contents might be confused.

Title/Item name. The Title/Item name is a text string which describes the menu title or item name. For example, "File" or "Change Colors." It's a good idea to place a few spaces on either side of the title string; otherwise, the menu titles will butt against each other.

The only exception to the Title/Item name is the Apple menu. For that menu, the commercial *at* (@) character is used as the Apple logo. This only applies to the first menu on the screen. The @ may be included in any other menu title as the Apple logo, but only the Apple logo (not any text) can appear in the menu's title.

When a single hyphen (-) is specified as an item string, it places a dividing line in the menu. This type of menu item should be dimmed (see below), so that it cannot be chosen as a legal menu item. It's purpose is to divide the contents of a menu.

Special characters. Special Characters are used to describe each menu title and menu item, and to assign important menu items an item ID. The special characters must follow the backslash (\ ) character. (Some other documentation may suggest using the vertical bar (|) character instead. *Do not do this!* The computer will crash.)

Special characters following \ are explained in Table 16-1.

Table 16-1. Special Characters and Their Functions

Character	Function
*	Specifies the following characters are to be used as a key equivalent.
B	Makes the menu item bold.
C	Places a character in front of the menu item.
D	Dims and disables the menu or menu item.
H	Used instead of N to specify the ID number as a value.
I	Italicize the menu item's text.
N	Is followed by the menu item's ID number.
U	Underlines the menu item's text.
V	Places an dividing line between this item and the next.
X	Activates color replace for highlighting the menu.

The letter may be upper- or lowercase. These characters must follow the \ or they will be considered part of the menu title or menu item text string.

* The asterisk (*) specifies the next two characters as keyboard equivalents for choosing that menu item. The Menu Manager places the first of these characters into the menu, right-justified after the menu's item name and following an Apple character graphic. The following allows both Apple-M and Shift-Apple-M to be used as key equivalents.

```
DC C'—MENU ITEM\*MM'
```

If you use the following code, only Shift-Apple-M is accepted as the key equivalent.

```
DC C'—MENU ITEM\*M '
```

Incidentally, when you put an Apple key equivalent in a menu, the TaskMaster traps it for you. You don't have to scan for this key; it will be interpreted by the TaskMaster as if the menu item had been chosen by the mouse.

B The letter *B* makes the menu item bold. This will work only if the system font, or the font you have chosen as the system font, is capable of boldface. Otherwise, the menu item appears in normal text.

C The letter *C* places the character following it in front of the item in the menu. For example,

```
DC C'—HOT ITEM\C!'
```

The above menu item is named *Hot Item.* When this menu item is created and displayed in the pull-down menu, there will be an exclamation point, !, *in front* of the word Hot.

D The letter *D* dims the menu or menu item, disabling it. If it is used in menu titles, the entire menu is disabled and dimmed. For individual items, only that item is dimmed. This means the item cannot be chosen and its item ID will not be returned by the TaskMaster. The state of a menu item, disabled or active, can be set or reset using the Menu Manager functions EnableMItem and DisableMItem.

H The letter *H* is used instead of *N* to set the menu item's ID to a value rather than a text string. When N is used, it's followed by a decimal text string. When H is used, it's followed by a two-byte hexadecimal number, or word value, and not a text string. See N below.

I The letter *I* is used to italicize the text of the menu item or title. This special character only applies if the system font is able to be italicized. Otherwise, the text shown is the standard font.

N The letter *N* specifies the menu item's ID number. N is followed by a decimal string of characters specifying the ID. Not every menu item needs an ID and only certain IDs can be used. Table 16-2 describes how the Menu Manager has allocated various menu item ID values.

Table 16-2. How Menu Item ID Values Are Allocated

Values	Description
0	Used internally
1–249	Used by New Desk Accessory Items and Menu Titles
250	Reserved for the Edit menu's Undo item
251	Reserved for the Edit menu's Cut item
252	Reserved for the Edit menu's Copy item
253	Reserved for the Edit menu's Paste item
254	Reserved for the Edit menu's Clear item
255	Reserved for the File menu's Close item
256–65534	Can be used by your menu items
65535	Internal use to flag last menu item

For example, the first menu item in your program, the About. . . item, could have an ID of 256 ($100).

```
DC C'—ABOUT...\N256'
```

Or, you could use the special character H to show this value in hex:

```
DC C'—ABOUT...\H',H'0100'
```

Another way to present this would be

```
DC C'—ABOUT..\H',I2'256'
```

For the H character, a value and not a text string follows the H. With either method, the menu item's ID number is set to 256. When the TaskMaster detects that a menu item has been chosen, or its key equivalent pressed, the Task Data field will contain the menu item's ID number.

Menu Titles should be given an ID number starting with one for the first menu and increasing sequentially through as many menus as you have. The ID number is used by the Task Data field to determine from which menu an item was selected.

U The letter *U* underlines the text of the menu item or title. As with B and I, this happens only if the current system font supports underline.

V The letter *V* is used to put a dividing line between the current menu item and the next. The line is not an underline, but rather a straight line from one side of the menu to the other. The next menu item still appears directly below this one. (To have a little more space, use the hyphen character, described earlier.)

X The letter *X* changes the way a menu is chosen. It causes the item to be chosen using color replace to highlight the menu, rather than inverse characters. When using color menus, such as the Apple menu, this keeps the colors active when the menu or menu item is chosen, rather than inversing them.

Carriage return. After each menu item or title string is the carriage return character, $0D. This notifies the Menu Manager that the current menu title or item definition has ended and a new one follows.

End of menu marker. At the end of each menu is an End of menu marker. This is a single character, and it is not followed by a carriage return. The single character must be different from the Item and Title Characters which start each menu item or title string. Also, this character's use must be consistent after each menu.

The following is an example of a menu record. Use the comments in the listing and refer back to the definitions above to decipher what's going on.

Attention

If some programs crash, especially with a Fatal Error $0045 or $0110, don't panic. Most likely, the problem is that you have a one-drive system. The program is telling you that it can't find certain tool sets that need to be loaded from disk.

To run a program that accesses a tool set on disk, your system or boot disk must be online. This means that the program, or more specifically, the Tool Locator tool set, must be able to find tool sets in the \SYSTEM\TOOLS prefix of your system or boot disk. Error $0045 indicates that a volume is not online, and error $0110 tells you that a tool set has not been found.

If this is your situation, you should copy your executable file from your development disk (the one used to assemble your program) to your boot disk. Once this is done, running the program should cause no errors.

You might also consider a RAM upgrade, or if you already have extra RAM in your system (over 512K), designate a portion of that memory as a ramdisk. You can then copy the executable file from your development disk to the ramdisk and run it from there.

```
MENU1    DC C'>>@\XN1',I1'13'                    ;APPLE MENU, X HIGHLIGHTING
         DC C'—ABOUT...\N256V',I1'13'            ;ABOUT ITEM, UNDERLINED
         DC C'X'                                 ;END OF MENU 1

MENU2    DC C'>> BREAD \N2',I1'13'               ;BREAD MENU
         DC C'—PUMPERNICKLE\N257*PP',I1'13'      ;USES APPLE P AND SHIFT APPLE P
                                                 ;KEYS
         DC C'—RYE\N258',I1'13'
         DC C'—WHEAT\IN259',I1'13'               ;ITALICIZED
         DC C'—WHITE\DN260',I1'13'               ;DIMMED
         DC C'---\D',I1'13'                      ;DIMMED DIVIDING LINE, NO ID
         DC C'—TOAST\C|BN261',I1'13'             ;|TOAST, BOLD ITEM
         DC C'X'                                 ;END OF MENU 2

MENU3    DC C'>> WINE \N3',I1'13'                ;WINE MENU
         DC C'—RED\N262',I1'13'
         DC C'—WHITE\N263',I1'13'
         DC C'—BLUE\N264*B ',I1'13'              ;APPLE B ONLY
         DC C'X'                                 ;END OF MENU 3 AND MENU RECORD
```

The Menu Manager

To use menus in your program you'll need to start the Menu Manager. All the functions that create, control, and manipulate menus on the screen are put into the Menu Manager. Some of the functions are used internally. The majority of them are easily understood by anyone familiar with a pull-down menu program. (A few of the common functions are illustrated in the next section.)

The Menu Manager, like the Window and Control Managers, is a disk-based tool. Before you call MMStartUp, you must first load the Menu Manager—and any other disk-based tools the program uses—into memory. The Menu Manager is tool set 15, $0F. The version of the Menu Manager at this writing is 1.3.

To start the Menu Manager, you should already have the Tool Locator, Memory Manager, Miscellaneous Tools, QuickDraw II, Event Manager, and Window Manager started.

Function: $020F
Name: MMStartUp
Starts the Menu Manager.
Push: UserID (W); Direct Page (W)
Pull: nothing
Errors: none
Comments:

The following code could be used to start the Menu Manager. This assumes that QuickDraw II and the Event Manager have already been started. Because those tool sets together require $400 bytes of direct-page space, the Menu Manager's direct page starts at an offset of $400 from the start of the DPage memory block:

```
LDA   USERID    ;PUSH YOUR USER ID TO THE STACK
PHA
LDA   DPAGE     ;DIRECT PAGE START
CLC
ADC   #$400     ;ALLOW FOR QD II AND EM'S D PAGE
PHA
LDX   #$020F    ;MMSTARTUP
JSL   $E10000
```

After MMStartUp is called, the toolbox draws the menu bar on the top of the screen. Of course, it's empty at this point. It's up to you to place your menus on the screen (covered in the next section).

Shutting down the Menu Manager involves calling its shutdown function, $03.

Function: $030F
Name: MMShutDown
Shuts down the Menu Manager.
Push: nothing
Pull: nothing
Errors: none
Comments:

As always, it's a good idea to shut the Menu Manager and other tool sets down in the reverse order of their startup. If the Menu Manager was the last tool your program started, it should be the first one shut down.

When you're writing a program that requires the Menu Manager, you'll need the following tool sets, started in this order:

- Tool Locator
- Memory Manager
- Miscellaneous tool set
- QuickDraw II
- Event Manager
- Window Manager
- Menu Manager

The Window and Menu Managers must be loaded from disk with the LoadTools function before they can be started. Optional tool sets you may wish to include are the Control, Dialog, and Font Manager—all depending on the complexity of your program.

Creating Menus and Menu Items

Creating the menus your program uses is done using the menu record. Each menu record is given a menu handle by the NewMenu function. You can then use the menu handle to actually place the menu into your application's menu bar.

No error checking is done by NewMenu. If your menu record contains some bad information, the NewMenu function will still create a menu handle, but that menu will be unusable on the screen.

Function: $2D0F
Name: NewMenu
Creates a menu handle from a menu record.
Push: Result Space (L); menu record (L)
Pull: Menu Handle (L)
Errors: none
Comments:

Almost immediately after calling the NewMenu function to create a menu handle, the InsertMenu function should be called. InsertMenu takes the menu handle and places that menu at a specific position on the menu bar (it still isn't drawn, only its position is plotted). The menu's location on the menu bar is specified by the position parameter of the InsertMenu function.

Function: $0D0F
Name: InsertMenu
Places a menu into the menu bar.
Push: Menu Handle (L); Position (W)
Pull: nothing
Errors: none
Comments: If Position is $0000, the menu is inserted at the start (left) of the menu bar, otherwise menu is inserted at the end.

When using InsertMenu, the menu handle is the first parameter pushed to the stack. If InsertMenu is called immediately after NewMenu, there's no need to pull and then push the menu handle—just leave it on the stack (see below).

The position parameter determines where the menu is placed on the menu bar. If $0000 is specified, the menu is inserted as the first menu on the left. Otherwise, it's placed at the position specified.

The following code shows how a menu's handle is created with NewHandle, then how the menu is inserted as the first menu item on the menu bar.

```
        PHA                  ;LONG WORD RESULT SPACE
        PHA
        PEA    MENU1|-16     ;FIRST MENU'S MENU RECORD
        PEA    MENU1
        LDX    #$2D0F        ;NEWMENU - CREATE HANDLE
        JSL    $E10000
;                            ;THE MENU HANDLE IS NOW ON THE
;                            ;STACK. KEEP IT THERE FOR THE
;                            ;NEXT TOOLBOX CALL, INSERTMENU...
        PEA    $0000         ;INSERT IT ON THE LEFT
        LDX    #$0D0F        ;INSERTMENU
        JSL    $E10000
```

If more menus need to be placed on the menu bar, their code would follow and look similar to the above example. Remember that when $0000 is used by the InsertMenu call, the menus are inserted "backward." To insert them in order, push a value other than $0000 for the InsertMenu function.

After the menus have all been inserted, you need to call the FixMenuBar function.

Function: $130F
Name: FixMenuBar
Calculates the size of the menu bar's menus and items.
Push: Result Space (W)
Pull: Size (W)
Errors: none
Comments: Size is the height in pixels.

The FixMenuBar function, as stated in the reference, returns the height of the menu bar in pixels. However, it also serves the important function of calculating and adjusting the size of all the menus on the screen. If this function is not called before the menu bar is displayed, all the menu items will appear on top of each other and the program will be worthless.

The result space is used to return the size of the menu bar after the toolbox call. Normally, this value is discarded, but it still must be pulled from the stack. However, the height of the menu should be taken into account when plotting the location of windows and dialog boxes. The value returned from the FixMenuBar function can be used to assist you. Unless your menus use a font other than the system font, the menu bar is usually 13 pixels in height for either the 320 or 640 mode.

Note that NewMenu and InsertMenu do not actually display

the menus on the screen. Instead, they're building the internal structure of the menu bar. Only after the menus are created, inserted and fixed, can you display them in the menu bar. This is done with the function DrawMenuBar.

Function: $2A0F
Name: DrawMenuBar
Displays the menu bar and menus on the screen.
Push: nothing
Pull: nothing
Errors: none
Comments:

This function simply displays all the work you've done so far. Each menu is displayed in its proper position and is ready for action. However, in order to use the pull-down menus, your program must activate the TaskMaster function in the Window Manager. Otherwise, the menus just sit there. TaskMaster is at the heart of all menu-driven programs.

Acting on Menu Selections

Any time a menu item is selected either with the mouse or with the key equivalent, it generates an event. To intercept and act upon these events, the Window Manager's TaskMaster function is used.

Choosing a menu item generates an extended event code $11 (17, decimal). If, after calling the TaskMaster, $0011 is returned from the stack, the user has chosen a menu item. The menu number and item ID can be obtained by examining the task data field in the extended event record.

From this long word, you can determine which menu item and from which menu it was selected: the high order word reflects the menu number and the low order word is the menu item ID number. Your program can examine the task data field and then act upon the result. For example, the following assembler statement assumes the TaskMaster returned an extended result code of $11—a menu selection. This examines the task data field to determine which menu item was selected.

```
LDA    TDATA       ;GET MENU ID NUMBER
```

Now the menu ID number is in the A register. If your ID numbers are sequential, and they start at $100, you could take advantage of a table structure to execute the menu's various functions.

For example, the menu record described earlier in this chapter contained a list of breads and wines. The ID numbers of all these items started at 256 ($100) and moved sequentially up through 265. For each one of these menu items, there is a corresponding routine in the program. The following table contains a list of long word pointers, each containing the address of a routine used by the bread and wine program.

```
TABLE         ANOP                        ;TABLE OF ROUTINES
;FIRST MENU:
              DC   I'ABOUT'               ;ITEM 256, ABOUT...
;SECOND MENU:
              DC   I'PUMPERNICKEL'        ;ITEM 257
              DC   I'RYE'                 ;ITEM 258
              DC   I'WHEAT'               ;ITEM 259
              DC   I'WHITE'               ;ITEM 260
              DC   I'TOAST'               ;ITEM 261
;THIRD MENU:
              DC   I'RED'                 ;ITEM 262
              DC   I'WHITE'               ;ITEM 263
              DC   I'BLUE'                ;ITEM 264
```

Each name defined above is the label of a routine in the program. If the user selects the Pumpernickel menu item, you want the program to execute the Pumpernickel routine. This can be done using the X index register to jump to the routine in the above table.

```
              LDA  TDATA                  ;GET MENU ID NUMBER
              AND  #$00FF                 ;ONLY USE LSB (MSB = $01)
              ASL  A                      ;DOUBLE THE VALUE
              TAX                         ;PUT INTO INDEX REGISTER
              JSR  (TABLE,X)              ;CALL TO THAT ROUTINE
```

Each routine is at an offset from the start of Table. This offset is equal to the menu ID number, minus $100, multiplied by two. The third routine, is Rye, which is menu ID number 258, $102. If this item is chosen, it's loaded into the A register. The AND #$00FF gets rid of the MSB, leaving $0002.

Next, the ASL instruction rotates the number left, multiplying it by two. The A register now contains $0004. This is put into the X register and used as an offset within Table to jump to the Rye routine. Because each pointer to a routine takes up two bytes, the Rye routine pointer is actually at an offset of four bytes from the start of the table. If this sounds confusing, refer to an assembly language book on indexed-indirect addressing.

Using a table like this makes executing routines associated with specific menu items a lot easier than a list of CMP instructions. Tables are the preferred way of programming among the elite assembly language programmers. And as long as you have a complete, sequential list, it takes up less memory.

After the menu item's function is called and execution returns, you'll need to unhighlight the menu in the menu bar. The Menu Manager doesn't do this automatically.

When a pull-down menu is selected, its title appears in inverse type. After an item is choosen, the item flashes briefly, and then the menu disappears. As long as the function you've selected is operating, the menu title remains in inverse type (highlighted).

Because the TaskMaster has no way of knowing when your function is complete, it keeps the menu title highlighted. Your routine must make the title normal again. This is done with the HiliteMenu function.

Function: $2C0F
Name: HiliteMenu
Highlights a menu title as either inversed or normal.
Push: Hilight (W); Menu ID (W)
Pull: nothing
Errors: none
Comments: If Hilight is $0000, the menu is changed to normal; otherwise, the menu is changed to inversed.

The menu number is kept in the high order word of the task data field. After your function is complete, the following code can be used to change the menu title back to its normal state.

```
PEA   $0000        ;CHANGE TO NORMAL
LDA   TDATA        ;GET HOW, MENU NUMBER
PHA                ;PUSH IT
LDX   #$2C0F       ;HILITEMENU
JSL   $E10000
```

The value $0000 tells the HiliteMenu function to draw the menu as normal. If this routine is called after a menu item's function is complete, the menu will be returned to normal.

The Menu Program

The following is the source code for MENU.ASM, written with the ORCA/M assembler. After typing it in, save it as MENU.ASM.

```
****************************************************************************
* MENU.ASM MENU INTERFACE PROGRAM
****************************************************************************

         ABSADDR ON
         KEEP MENU                    ;EXE FILE IS MENU

MAIN     START

         PHK                          ;ASSERT CODE BANK ==
; DATA BANK
         PLB

;----------------------------------------
; START THE TOOL LOCATOR

         LDX    #$0201                ;TLSTARTUP
         JSL    $E10000               ;BUMP START THE TOOL LOCATOR

;----------------------------------------
; START THE MEMORY MANAGER AND RETURN
; A USERID FOR THIS PROGRAM

         PEA    $0000                 ;RESULT SPACE
         LDX    #$0202                ;MMSTARTUP
         JSL    $E10000               ;GET A USERID & SOME MEMORY
         JSR    ERRORH
         PLA                          ;GET OUR USERID
         STA    USERID                ;SAVE IT

;----------------------------------------
; START THE MISC TOOLS TOOL SET

         LDX    #$0203                ;MTSTARTUP
         JSL    $E10000               ;BUMP START MISC. TOOLS
         JSR    ERRORH

;----------------------------------------
; ESTABLISH A DIRECT PAGE

```

```
        PEA   $0000                 ;LONG RESULT SPACE
        PEA   $0000
        PEA   $0000                 ;CREATE A FIVE-PAGE BLOCK
        PEA   $0500
        LDA   USERID
        PHA
        PEA   $C005                 ;ATTRIBUTES
        PEA   $0000
        PEA   $0000
        LDX   #$0902                ;NEWHANDLE
        JSL   $E10000
        JSR   ERRORH

        PLA                         ;GET HANDLE OF NEW BLOCK
        STA   0
        STA   HANDLE                ;AND COPY THE RESULT TO HANDLE

        PLA
        STA   2
        STA   HANDLE+2              ;THE HIGH ORDER WORD

        LDA   [0]
        STA   DPAGE

;----------------------------------------
; SET UP AND START QUICK DRAW II

        LDA   DPAGE
        PHA                         ;STARTING ADDRESS OF 0 PAGE
        PEA   $0000                 ;MASTER SCB, 320 MODE
        PEA   $0000
        LDA   USERID                ;OUR PROGRAM'S ID
        PHA
        LDX   #$0204                ;QDSTARTUP
        JSL   $E10000
        JSR   ERRORH

;----------------------------------------
; SET UP AND START THE EVENT MANAGER

        LDA   DPAGE
        CLC
        ADC   #$300                 ;ALLOW FOR QD II
        PHA
```

```
         PEA   $0014
         PEA   $0000
         PEA   $0140
         PEA   $0000
         PEA   $00C8
         LDA   USERID
         PHA
         LDX   #$0206              ;EMSTARTUP
         JSL   $E10000
         JSR   ERRORH

         LDX   #$CA04              ;INITCURSOR
         JSL   $E10000             ;DISPLAY THE MOUSE

;-----------------------------------------
; LOAD DISK BASED TOOLS INTO RAM

         PEA   TOOLIST|-16         ;POINT AT LIST
         PEA   TOOLIST
         LDX   #$0E01              ;LOADTOOLS
         JSL   $E10000
         JSR   ERRORH

;-----------------------------------------
; START UP THE WINDOW MANAGER

         LDA   USERID
         PHA
         LDX   #$020E              ;WINDSTART
         JSL   $E10000
         JSR   ERRORH

;-----------------------------------------
; START THE MENU MANAGER

         LDA   USERID
         PHA
         LDA   DPAGE               ;GET A DIRECT PAGE FOR
         CLC                       ;THE MENU MANAGER
         ADC   #$400               ;ALLOW FOR EM AND QD
         PHA
         LDX   #$020F              ;MENUSTARTUP
         JSL   $E10000
```

```
        JSR     ERRORH
;---------------------------------------
; SET UP MENUS ON THE SCREEN
        PEA     $0000           ;RESULT SPACE (L) FOR
        PEA     $0000           ;THE MENU'S HANDLE
        PEA     MENU4|-16       ;BANK OF LAST MENU
        PEA     MENU4
        LDX     #$2D0F          ;NEWMENU
        JSL     $E10000
        PEA     $0000           ;INSERT WINDOW AT LEFT
        LDX     #$0D0F          ;INSERTMENU
        JSL     $E10000
;MENU3...
        PEA     $0000           ;RESULT SPACE (L) FOR
        PEA     $0000           ;MENU 3'S HANDLE
        PEA     MENU3|-16       ;BANK
        PEA     MENU3           ;OFFSET
        LDX     #$2D0F          ;NEWMENU
        JSL     $E10000
        PEA     $0000           ;INSERT WINDOW AT LEFT
        LDX     #$0D0F          ;INSERTMENU
        JSL     $E10000
;MENU2...
        PEA     $0000           ;RESULT SPACE FOR
        PEA     $0000           ;MENU 2'S HANDLE
        PEA     MENU2|-16       ;BANK
        PEA     MENU2           ;OFFSET
        LDX     #$2D0F          ;NEWMENU
        JSL     $E10000
        PEA     $0000           ;INSERT WINDOW AT LEFT
        LDX     #$0D0F          ;INSERTMENU
        JSL     $E10000
;MENU1 (APPLE MENU)
        PEA     $0000           ;RESULT SPACE FOR
        PEA     $0000           ;APPLE MENU'S HANDLE
        PEA     MENU1|-16       ;BANK
```

```
        PEA     MENU1               ;OFFSET
        LDX     #$2D0F              ;NEWMENU
        JSL     $E10000
        PEA     $0000               ;INSERT WINDOW AT LEFT
        LDX     #$0D0F              ;INSERTMENU
        JSL     $E10000

;----------------------------------------
; CALCULATE THE HEIGHT AND DISPLAY THE MENU BAR

        PEA     $0000               ;RESULT SPACE
        LDX     #$130F              ;FIXMENUBAR
        JSL     $E10000
        PLA                         ;DISCARD HEIGHT VALUE

        LDX     #$2A0F              ;DRAWMENUBAR
        JSL     $E10000

        PEA     $0005               ;SETDESKPAT
        PEA     $4000               ;DEFAULT
        PEA     $0050               ;COLOR IT GREEN
        LDX     #$0C0E              ;DESKTOP
        JSL     $E10000

;----------------------------------------
; MAIN SCAN LOOP

        STZ     QUITF               ;INIT QUIT FLAG

SCAN    ANOP                        ;MAIN LOOP
        LDA     QUITF               ;TEST QUIT CONDITION
        BNE     DONE                ;QUITE IF NOT=0

        PEA     $0000               ;RESULT SPACE
        PEA     $FFFF               ;EVENT MASK
        PEA     EVENTR-16           ;EVENT RECORD
        PEA     EVENTR
        LDX     #$1D0E              ;TASKMASTER
        JSL     $E10000
        PLA                         ;GET TASK CODE
        BEQ     SCAN                ;IF NOTHING, CONTINUE LOOPING

        CMP     #17                 ;MENU ITEM CODE
```

```
         BNE    SCAN                 ;AND THEN KEEP SCANNING

;---------------------------------------
; A MENU ITEM HAS BEEN CHOSEN


DOMENU   LDA    TDATA                ;GET MENU ITEM #
         AND    #$00FF
         ASL    A                    ;DOUBLE THE VALUE
         TAX
         JSR    (MTABLE,X)           ;DO THE ROUTINE

         PEA    $0000                ;BOOLEAN FALSE
         LDA    TDATA+2              ;THE MENU#
         PHA
         LDX    #$2C0F               ;HILITEMENU
         JSL    $E10000

         BRA    SCAN

;---------------------------------------
; END OF PROGRAM: SHUTDOWN ALL ROUTINES

DONE     ANOP

         LDX    #$030F               ;MENUSHUTDOWN
         JSL    $E10000

         LDX    #$030E               ;WINDSHUTDOWN
         JSL    $E10000

         LDX    #$0306               ;EMSHUTDOWN
         JSL    $E10000

         LDX    #$0304               ;QDSHUTDOWN
         JSL    $E10000

         LDX    #$0303               ;MTSHUTDOWN
         JSL    $E10000

         LDA    HANDLE+2
         PHA
         LDA    HANDLE
         PHA
```

```
        LDX   #$1002                ;DISPOSE HANDLE
        JSL   $E10000

        LDA   USERID
        PHA
        LDX   #$0302                ;MMSHUTDOWN
        JSL   $E10000

        LDX   #$0301                ;TLSHUTDOWN
        JSL   $E10000

;----------------------------------------
; EXIT VIA PRODOS 16 MLI CALL $29

        JSL   $E100A8               ;PRODOS 16 CALL
        DC    I2'$29'               ;QUIT FUNCTION
        DC    I4'QPARAMS'           ;QUIT PARAMETERS

******************************************************************************
* QUIT MENU ITEM'S ROUTINE...
******************************************************************************

QUIT    LDA   #$FFFF                ;SET QUIT FLAG
        STA   QUITF

NOTHING ANOP                        ;NOTHING FLAG
        RTS

******************************************************************************
* ERROR HANDLER
******************************************************************************
ERRORH  BCS   UHOH                  ;CARRY SET IF ERROR
        RTS                         ;ELSE, RETURN

UHOH    ANOP
        PHA                         ;TOOLBOX RETURNS ERROR IN A
        PEA   0000                  ;BANK OF SYSTEM DEATH MESSAGE
        PEA   0000                  ;OFFSET
        LDX   #$1503                ;SYSFAILMGR
        JSL   $E10000               ;SHUT THIS DOWN!

******************************************************************************
* DATA STORAGE
******************************************************************************

```

```
USERID  DS     2                        ;THIS PROGRAM'S USER ID
HANDLE  DS     4                        ;DIRECT PAGE HANDLE
DPAGE   DS     2                        ;DIRECT PAGE
QUITF   DS     2                        ;QUIT FLAG (<>0 FOR QUIT)

TOOLIST DC     I'2'                     ;LOAD TWO TOOLS:
        DC     I'$0E,$0103'             ;THE WINDOW MANAGER AND
        DC     I'$0F,$0103'             ;THE MENU MANAGER

;---------------------------------------—
; MENU DEFINITION TABLES

MENU1   DC     C'>>@\XN1',I1'13'
        DC     C'—ABOUT MENU...\N256V',I1'13'
        DC     C'.'

MENU2   DC     C'>> FILE \N2',I1'13'
        DC     C'—OPEN\N257*OO',I1'13'
        DC     C'—CLOSE\N258',I1'13'
        DC     C'—NEW\N259V',I1'13'
        DC     C'—DESTROY RAM\N260DV',I1'13'
        DC     C'—QUIT\N261',I1'13'
        DC     C'.'

MENU3   DC     C'>> BREAKFAST \N3',I1'13'
        DC     C'—EGGS\N262',I1'13'
        DC     C'—TOAST\N263',I1'13'
        DC     C'—SPAM\N264*SS',I1'13'
        DC     C'.'

MENU4   DC     C'>> ODD \N4',I1'13'
        DC     C'—CHOOSE ME!\N265B',I1'13'
        DC     C'—CHOOSE ME!\N266I',I1'13'
        DC     C'—CHOOSE ME!\N267U',I1'13'
        DC     C'—CHOOSE ME!\N268X',I1'13'
        DC     C'---\D',I1'13'
        DC     C'—ODD...\N269',I1'13'
        DC     C'.'

;EVENT RECORD

EVENTR  ANOP
EWHAT   DS     2
EMSG    DS     4
```

```
EWHEN  DS     4
EWHERE DS     4
EMODS  DS     2
TDATA  DS     4
TMASK  DC     I4'$3FFF'

;-----------------------------------------
; TABLE OF MENU ITEMS AND ROUTINES

MTABLE ANOP                             ;ROUTINES
       DC     I'NOTHING'                ;ABOUT MENU/257
;FILE MENU #2
       DC     I'NOTHING'                ;OPEN/258
       DC     I'NOTHING'                ;CLOSE/259
       DC     I'NOTHING'                ;NEW/260
       DC     I'NOTHING'                ;DESTROY RAM/261
       DC     I'QUIT'                   ;EXIT/262
;BREAKFAST MENU #3
       DC     I'NOTHING'                ;EGGS/263
       DC     I'NOTHING'                ;TOAST/264
       DC     I'NOTHING'                ;SPAM/265
;ODD MENU #4
       DC     I'NOTHING'                ;CHOOSE ME/266
       DC     I'NOTHING'                ;CM/267
       DC     I'NOTHING'                ;CM/268
       DC     I'NOTHING'                ;CM/269
       DC     I'NOTHING'                ;ODD/270

;QUIT PARAMETERS:

QPARAMSANOP
       DC     I4'$0'                    ;RETURN TO PREVIOUS PROGRAM
       DC     I'$0000'

       END
```

Assemble, link and run this program to experiment with the pull-down menus. As this program is written, only one menu item—Quit—has any effect. Feel free to change the menu items or manipulate the menu record to see what effect it has.

Description of MENU.ASM

This description covers only the parts of MENU.ASM pertaining to this chapter. The MENU program starts the following tools, in order: Tool Locator, Memory Manager, Miscellaneous tool set, QuickDraw II, Event Manager, Window Manager, and Menu Manager.

There are four menus in this program. They are defined with the menu record in lines 356–373. Each menu is inserted into the menu bar in lines 132–176. Notice how the menu handle is left on the stack between the NewMenu and InsertMenu calls. InsertMenu inserts each menu on the left, which is why the menus are started up "backward."

Lines 181–184 fix the menu bar. The menu bar height is discarded. The menus are then displayed using the DrawMenuBar call in lines 186 and 187. A desktop pattern is set by the routines in lines 189–193.

The main scanning loop is between lines 200 and 214. First, zero is stored in a special Quit Flag. This flag's status is set when the Quit menu item is selected. Each pass through the scan loop tests this flag (lines 201 and 202) to see if Quit has been selected. Otherwise, the TaskMaster is called.

Lines 210 and 211 check for an event. If no event occurred, the Scan loop is repeated. Otherwise, event code 17, which means an item was selected from a pull-down menu, is tested in line 213. If an item has not been selected, execution continues through the Scan loop.

If a pull-down menu item was selected, lines 220–232 act upon it. Line 220 loads the A register with the LOW of the task data field. This contains the menu ID number of the menu item selected. The routines in lines 221–224 branch to the appropriate subroutine using indexed indirect addressing on the routine table, MTable.

After the menu item's function is executed, the menu title is to be unhighlighted. Line 226 pushes zero to the stack to get rid of the highlight. Line 227 gets the menu number from the task data field and line 228 pushes it to the stack. A call is then made to the HiliteMenu function, and execution branches back to the Scan label.

Lines 237–274 shutdown the program.

The function called when the Quit menu item is selected is in lines 280–284. This simply stores $FFFF into the Quit flag. A second routine, *nothing*, is also included at line 283. This is the routine called when other menu items are selected. True to its name, it does nothing. But that doesn't mean you can't make it do something.

Lines 289–297 contain a standard error handler, and line 303 starts this program's Data area. The list of tool sets loaded from disk is at lines 308–310. Lines 315–340 contain the menu record, defining each of the menus on the screen, and the extended event record used by TaskMaster is in lines 344–351.

Lines 356–373 contain the table of routines executed as each menu item is chosen. The menu item's name is in the comment field along with the item's ID number. The only real routine is the Quit item at line 363. The other menu items simply branch to the nothing routine, which contains a simple RTS instruction (at lines 283 and 284).

Chapter 17

Dialog Boxes

One way a program communicates with the user on the Apple IIGS is through *dialog boxes.* Dialog boxes are graphic windows on the screen that can display information, or allow the user to make choices, or input information. Along with windows and pull-down menus, dialog boxes are a

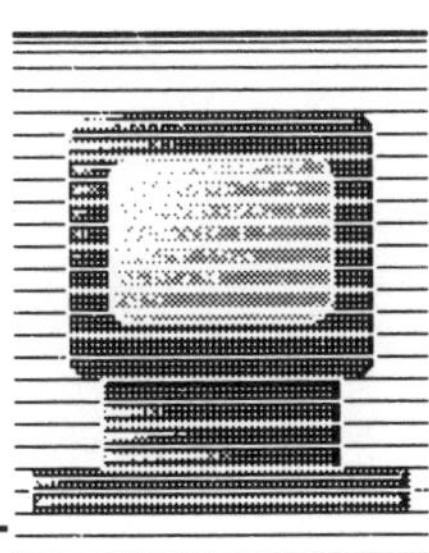

standard convention of the Apple desktop.

This chapter explains the various types of dialog boxes, how they are created, and how controls are placed inside them. Dialog boxes come in several types, each with many potential arrangements of items inside.

The Duties of the Dialog Box

A dialog box is put on the screen to receive input from the user, display a message, or offer advice. There are basically two types of dialog boxes: *modeless* and *modal.*

Modeless dialog boxes. A modeless dialog box is more like a window than a dialog box. It has a frame like a window, and in some cases can be moved like a window. Unlike a modal dialog box, a modeless dialog box can be manipulated at the same time as other items in the program. It's like a panel that can always be accessed. You can still manipulate other items on the desktop while the modeless dialog box is displayed.

Modal dialog boxes. A modal dialog box is a nonmoveable window—simply a frame. Inside the frame are *buttons, radio buttons, check boxes, text, input boxes,* or other items the user can manipulate. Nothing else in the program can be done until the operations of the modal dialog box have been completed. Usually this is signaled by the user clicking on a button labeled *OK* or *Cancel.* After the manipulations are completed, the dialog box disappears and the program continues.

Alert. The alert is a special type of modal dialog box that notifies the user of some potentially hazardous situation, or it can be used to signal the user to proceed with caution.

There are three types of alerts, each corresponding to a different level of attention. Each Alert has its own unique icon, or graphic picture, which the Dialog Manager places in the upper left corner of the box.

The icon is put into the alert automatically. It's up to you to furnish messages and buttons for your alerts.

Figure 17-1. Note Alert

Figure 17-2. Caution Alert

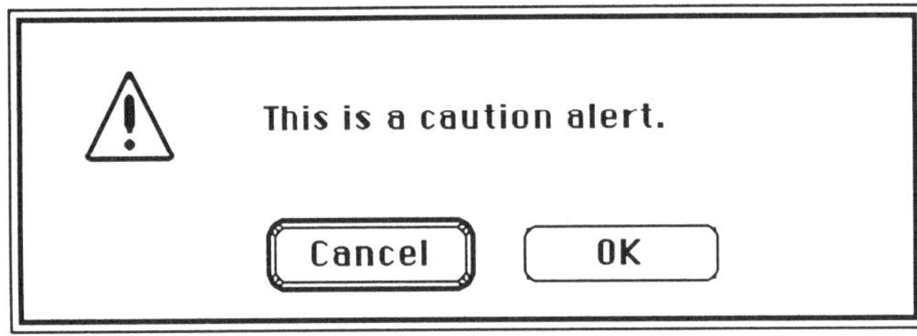

Figure 17-3. Stop Alert

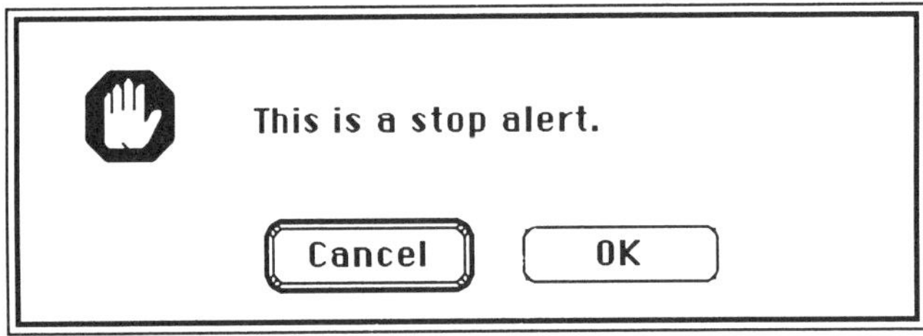

Buttons, Check Boxes, and Switches

The things placed inside dialog boxes are called *items.* There can be many items in a dialog box, or only one. It depends on the function of the dialog. You might be able to shoehorn dozens of items in a large box, but making them overly complicated would defeat the purpose of the friendly IIGS interface.

Items fall into two types: Those that can be manipulated by the user and those that can't. An example of those that can't is text.

Manipulable items. Items that can be manipulated are referred to as *controls.* Controls include switches such as buttons, radio buttons, and check boxes; and other items that can be moved with the mouse. Suggested use of these items is covered in the Apple Human Interface Guidelines, but their use will be explained briefly here.

Buttons. A push button is used to directly communicate with the program. For example, a button labeled OK signifies that the information in the dialog is okay, and the program should continue. Cancel means to ignore the changes and continue. A button labeled Help would activate a help screen. Buttons are always named as action words and pressing the button immediately performs the action.

Radio buttons. Radio buttons are like the station selection buttons on a car radio. Only one button can be down at a time. Pressing another button unhighlights the first one. Radio buttons should be used with a list of options, only one of which can be chosen. An example might be a selection of screen colors: press one button for blue, another for red. The screen can't be both blue and red, so the second selection would deselect the first.

Check boxes. Check boxes simply show if an option, or toggle, is currently on or off. A check, or X, in the box indicates the option is currently on. No check means the option is off. Clicking in the check box changes it from its present state, toggling the selection on or off.

Text. A special type of text used in dialog boxes is called LongStatText. LongStatText refers to characters in the dialog box that can be edited with the mouse. Text that can't be edited with the mouse is called StatText.

User item. Can be of two types. The first would be a *graphic control,* such as a dial, thermometer, gauge, or other graphic image that represents something. This image is created and updated by the program.

A second type of user item is called the *user control* item. This is a user defined control. Unlike the user item which could be just an image, the user control item could be a uniquely designed switch. For example, a knife switch like those featured in the Frankenstein movies of the 1930s could be used to begin a routine.

Placing these switches into a dialog box is as easy as putting them into a record or template and calling the proper Dialog Manager function. You specify the type of control item, it's location, and a few other options, and the toolbox does the rest.

Other items. Other items in a dialog box, not necessarily controls, include input boxes where text can be entered, icons, graphic images and pictures, and even user-designed controls. These involve a little more preparation than the controls above.

Table 17-1 shows a list of items you can place in a dialog box, followed by its type.

Table 17-1. Items and Their Types

Item	Type
Button	Switch
Check box	Switch
Edit line	Input box
Icon	Graphic image
Picture	Graphic image
Radio buttons	Switch
Scroll bar	Special dialog control
Text	Characters
User item	User-defined

Using the Dialog Manager

To use dialog boxes in your program, you'll need to start up the Dialog Manager. The Dialog Manager controls everything dealing with dialog boxes on the screen. It uses QuickDraw II and the Window Manager to draw the boxes, and the Control Manager to set up the controls and switches inside the dialog boxes. Further, if your dialog box contains a text input box, you'll need to start the LineEdit tool set. The Dialog Manager is the most dependent tool set covered in this book.

The Dialog Manager is a disk-based tool, so it needs to be loaded into RAM before it's started. Also, the Dialog Manager shares direct-page space with the Control Manager. There are a lot of intricacies involved in starting the Dialog Manager.

- The Dialog Manager requires the Control Manager
- The Control Manager requires the Window Manager be started before the Control Manager
- The Window Manager requires the Event Manager because it shares direct-page space with the Event Manager

If you're going to use the Dialog Manager, start the tools in this order:

Tool Locator
Memory Manager
Miscellaneous tool set
QuickDraw II
Event Manager
Window Manager
Control Manager
Dialog Manager

The last three tool sets are loaded from disk. Also remember that if you intend to use the Menu Manager, it must be started after the Window Manager. Remember, it needs to be loaded from disk.

The Dialog Manager StartUp function is as follows:

Function: $0215
Name: DialogStartUp
Starts the Dialog Manager.
Push: UserID (W)
Pull: nothing
Errors: none
Comments: The Control Manager must be started before making this call.

The code to accomplish a DialogStartUp is relatively simple. There are no structures to define, no strings to pull.

```
LDA    USERID        ;PUSH THIS PROGRAM'S USER ID
PHA
LDX    #$0215        ;DIALOGSTARTUP
JSL    $E10000
```

And now you're ready to program some dialog boxes. Although DialogStartUp does not return any errors, you must have already started the Control Manager before making the above call. This holds true even if your dialog boxes contain no controls.

The Dialog Manager's ShutDown function should be included in your program's quit code.

Function: $0315
Name: DialogShutDown
Shuts down the Dialog Manager.
Push: nothing
Pull: nothing
Errors: none
Comments:

This is a simple call, as are most of the other tool sets' Shut-Down functions.

```
LDX    #$0315         ;SHUTDOWN THE DIALOG MANAGER
JSL    $E10000
```

Building a Dialog Box

The first part of creating a dialog box involves putting a window (actually just a rectangle) on the screen. The location and size of the box are given in global coordinates, referenced from the upper left corner of the screen.

If your program has a menu bar, it will take up space on the top of the screen. Apple recommends no dialog box be placed closer than 25 pixels to the top of the screen. If it is any higher, part of it will be hidden by the menu bar.

Also, it's possible to draw a dialog box so that part of it extends beyond the screen's edge. This will not result in an error, but it looks unprofessional. Remember the differences between the 320 and 640 modes when plotting the position and size of dialog boxes.

Function: $0A15
Name: NewModalDialog
Creates a modal dialog box on the screen.
Push: Result Space (L); Rectangle (L); Visible Flag (W) Window Reference (L)
Pull: Dialog Port (L)
Errors: Possible Memory Manager errors
Comments: See chapter 17.

First, a long word of result space is pushed to the stack. The next item pushed is a pointer to the dialog box's rectangle. This location holds four word values, the Min Y and Min X locations, and the Max Y and Max X locations.

The visible flag is either $0000 to make the dialog box invisible or $8000 (a logical "true") to make it visible. Dialog boxes can be created and placed invisibly on the screen. However, visible dialog boxes are more common.

The window reference is a long word value your application may use for any purpose. Typcially, a long word of zero is specified.

The following code would place a dialog box on the screen:

```
PHA                     ;LONG WORD RESULT SPACE
PHA
PEA     DIALOGR|-16     ;POINTER TO RECTANGLE
PEA     DIALOGR
PEA     $8000           ;MAKE IT VISIBLE
PEA     $0000           ;WINDOW REFERENCE = 0
PEA     $0000
LDX     #$0A15          ;NEWMODALDIALOG
JSL     $E10000
```

After the above call, the dialog box is displayed on the screen and the toolbox returns a long word pointer to the dialog box. The pointer can be obtained with the following code:

```
PLA                     ;GET POINTER TO DIALOG
STA     DLGPTR
PLA                     ;GET HIGH ORDER WORD
STA     DLGPTR+2
```

You need to save the pointer returned from the NewModal-Dialog call. This value is used in later functions when placing items into the dialog box.

The following rectangle is used by the above code to place the dialog box in the center of a 320-mode screen.

```
DIALOGR  ANOP
         DC      I2‘40’        ;Y MIN
         DC      I2‘70’        ;X MIN
         DC      I2‘160’       ;Y MAX
         DC      I2‘240’       ;X MAX
```

The box is 40 pixels from the top and bottom of the screen, and 70 pixels from both sides. This centers it on the display.

Once the location is plotted and a pointer is returned and stored, you can start placing items into the dialog box. Each item is positioned in its own rectangle inside the dialog box. The item's rectangle is expressed relative to the upper left corner of the dialog box, which is location 0,0.

To place an item in the dialog box, begin by telling the Dialog Manager which dialog box the item is associated with. Give the item a reference number, tell the Dialog Manager what the item is and where to place it inside the dialog box, and pass along any other parameters needed.

The format for these items is used by several Dialog Manager functions. Whichever function you choose to place the item's information into the dialog box, you will need to specify the information in Table 17-2.

Table 17-2. Information Passed to Dialog Manager

Description	Value
Dialog port pointer	Long pointer (optional)
Item reference number	Word value
Item's location/rectangle	Rectangle
Item type	Word value
Item description	Long pointer/handle
Item value	Word value
Visible flag	Word value
Color table pointer	Long pointer

Dialog port pointer. Necessary when using the NewDItem function. The pointer serves as a reference to the dialog box the item is placed into. This is why the dialog port pointer is retained when it is returned by the NewModalDialog function.

Item reference number. Used to identify the item placed into the dialog. Its value can be anything you dream up. The assigned value is returned when that item is selected in the dialog box.

For example, suppose a dialog box has two buttons: LEFT and RIGHT. LEFT's reference number is $0006 and RIGHT's is $0007. When RIGHT is pushed, $0007 is returned from the Dialog Manager. When LEFT is pushed, $0006 is returned.

A good method of assigning reference numbers is to give the dialog box a value in the MSB of the reference number, and then give each item a sequential value starting with, say, $01. For example, suppose the dialog box with the RIGHT/LEFT buttons is given a value of $50. Then LEFT's Reference Number would be $5006, and RIGHT's would be $5007. Another dialog box would have item reference numbers of $4503, $4504, $4505, and so on. (This convention is recommended by the authors, but it is not mandatory.)

Two special item reference numbers are $0001 and $0002. The item assigned an ID value of $0001 is considered the default item. Pressing the Return key is the same as choosing that item. If the item is a button, that button will have a double border on it. Most often, Reference Number $0001 is used for the OK button. Reference Number $0002 is for the cancel button. It has no key equivalent.

Item's location/rectangle. The item's location/rectangle determines where in the dialog box the item will be located. These are not global coordinates. The coordinates of the rectangle are relative to the dialog box and not to the entire screen.

Each item (even text items) must have a specified position in order that the Dialog Manager can place it in the dialog box.

The following example shows a rectangle, given in local coordinates, used for placing text into a dialog box.

```
TEXTRECT     DC    I2'102,16,117,246'
TEXTSTR      DC    C'CHOOSE A NEW COLOR PATTERN:'
```

The only exceptions are control items such as buttons and check boxes. They require only a Min Y and Min X argument. The Dialog Manager calculates the size of the button based on the length of the text inside. The Max Y and Max X arguments can be set to zero.

The following example shows how an OK button's position is defined, again in relative coordinates.

```
OKBUTPOS     DC    I2'120,146,0,0'
OKTEXT       DC    C'OK'
```

The Max Y and Max X values are set to zero. The Dialog Manager determines the size of the button and the location of its lower right corner by examining the length of the string (in this case "OK") in the current font.

Every item in the dialog box needs a location. You must be careful when plotting these locations. It's possible to have one area overlay another. This happens often with text rectangles. If a text rectangle covers up a button or check box, you won't be able to see or access it.

Most of your time spent creating dialog boxes will be in adjusting the values of the item rectangles. After a while, you will get used to the size of certain items and it will become easier.

Item type. A word value that describes the kind of item you're adding to the dialog box. Every control and item has a specific identification number (see Table 17-3).

Table 17-3. Item Type Identification Numbers

Item Name	Item Type
Button	$000A
Check box	$000B
Edit line	$0011
Icon	$0012
Picture	$0001
Radio buttons	$000C
Scroll bar	$000D
Text	$000F
Text (longstat)	$0010
User item	$0014
User control	$0015

When placing a button into a dialog box, $000A is used. Text items have a type of $000F. The item type identification is how the Dialog Manager tells the Control Manager to deal with the item.

To disable any of the above items, logically OR its value with $8000. For example, to display a check box, yet have it appear dimmed in the dialog box, use an item type of $800B. The status of an item can be changed using specific Dialog Manager functions. Text items are almost always expressed as $800F.

Item description. A long pointer or handle depending on the item (Table 17-4).

Item	Item Description
Button	Pointer to text inside the button
Check box	Pointer to text beside the Check box
Edit line	Pointer to text which will appear in the input box
Icon	Handle to a memory block containing the icon's image
Picture	Handle to a memory block containing the picture's image

Radio buttons	Pointer to text beside the button
Scroll bar	Not used, set to zero
Text	Pointer to the text
Text (LongStatText)	Pointer to the text
User item	Could be a text pointer
User control	Could be a text pointer

In all the cases where a text pointer is required, the text is a Pascal-type string (Pascal strings start with a count byte which gives the length of the text). This holds true whether the text is a paragraph, a page, or just two letters.

The handle to the icon or picture image is allocated by the Memory Manager. It's up to your program to transfer the icon or picture's image into the memory block.

Item value. Contains an initial value, or in the case of input boxes, contains the maximum number of characters allowed. For most of the dialog box items, this word is simply set to zero.

Visible flag. Determines whether the item is to be made visible. Setting this word to $0000 makes the item visible, $8000 makes it invisible. Note that this is opposite of the visible flag used by NewModalDialog. The status of whether or not an item is visible can be changed by additional Dialog Manager functions.

There is a difference between making an item invisible and disabling it. A *disabled* menu item appears dimmed on the screen. You cannot choose the item, but you can see it. Supposedly, later activities or conditions of the program would change the item to a visible state.

Invisible items could be used to hide an option when it wasn't available. For example, a dialog box could offer the user a choice of reusing a file or appending to its end. The dialog box would probably have four buttons labeled Reuse, Append, OK, and Cancel.

If the Append option was not available (the file was binary or a nontext file ill suited for appending), the Append button should be made invisible and disabled. The user should not be able to choose Append. However, other implementations of the dialog box may make the Append button visible.

Another example is when a large amount of text is displayed. Certain pages of the text could be made invisible. Displaying the next page would be as easy as changing the visibility status of two pages.

Color table pointer. A long pointer to a color table used for creating the dialog box. Normally this pointer is set to zero (to use the standard color table).

Placing a Button in a Dialog Box

The following is an example record used to put an OK button item in a dialog box.

```
        DC  I2'1'                ;ITEM REFERENCE NUMBER = $0001
        DC  I2'100,56,0,0'       ;ITEM'S LOCATION/RECTANGLE
        DC  I2'$000A             ;ITEM TYPE = BUTTON
        DC  I4'BTNTXT'           ;ITEM DESCRIPTION STRING POINTER
        DC  I2'0'                ;ITEM VALUE, 0—NOT USED
        DC  I2'0'                ;VISIBLE FLAG, MAKE VISIBLE
        DC  I4'0'                ;COLOR TABLE POINTER, 0 = DEFAULT
BTNTXT      DC I1'2'             ;LENGTH OF STRING
            DC C'OK'
```

The NewDItem function can be used to place this item into the dialog box after it is created with a NewModalDialog function.

Function: $0D15
Name: NewDItem
Places an item into a dialog box.
Push: Dialog Pointer (L); Item Reference (W); Rectangle (L); Item Type (W); Item Pointer (L); Item Value (W); Visible Flag (W); Color Table (L)
Pull: nothing
Errors: $150A, $150B
Comments:

Using the above values, and assuming the pointer returned by NewModalDialog is stored at memory location DlgPtr, the code would be

```
        LDA   DLGPTR+2       ;PUSH HIGH ORDER WORD FIRST
        PHA
        LDA   DLGPTR         ;THEN LOW ORDER WORD
        PHA
        PEA   $0001          ;DEFAULT OK BUTTON
        PEA   BUTLOC|-16     ;LOCATION OF BUTTON'S RECTANGLE
        PEA   BUTLOC
        PEA   $000A          ;ITEM TYPE = BUTTON
        PEA   BTNTXT|-16     ;LOCATION OF STRING
        PEA   BTNTXT
        PEA   $0000          ;ITEM VALUE DEFAULT
```

```
        PEA   $0000              ;VISIBLE FLAG, MAKE VISIBLE
        PEA   $0000              ;COLOR TABLE POINTER
        PEA   $0000
        LDX   #$0D15             ;NEWDITEM
        JSL   $E10000
        JSR   ERRORH             ;CHECK FOR ERRORS
BUTLOC  DC    I2'100,56,0,0'     ;ITEM'S LOCATION/RECTANGLE
BTNTXT  DC    I1'2'              ;LENGTH OF STRING
        DC    C'OK'
```

The example may seem a little complex. Imagine having a dialog box with 20 items in it. Each item would require similar instructions for it to be placed into the dialog box. Fortunately, there's a faster way using GetNewDItem.

Function: $3315
Name: GetNewDItem
Adds an item to a dialog using a template.
Push: Dialog Port (L); Template (L)
Pull: nothing
Errors: $150A, $150C
Comments: Also see NewDItem.

GetNewDItem does the same thing as NewDItem, except a pointer to a template containing all the item's descriptions is used and not the item's descriptions themselves. This saves a lot of processor time and code space. The above long routine can now be replaced with

```
        LDA   DLGPTR+2           ;PUSH DIALOG POINTER, HOW
        PHA
        LDA   DLGPTR             ;THEN LOW ORDER WORD
        PHA
        PEA   ITEM1|-16          ;POINTER TO ITEM'S TEMPLATE
        PEA   ITEM1
        LDX   #$3315             ;GETNEWDITEM
        JSL   $E10000
        JSR   ERRORH             ;CHECK FOR ERRORS
```

And the item template would be

```
ITEM1   DC    I2'1'              ;ITEM REFERENCE NUMBER = $0001
        DC    I2'100,56,0,0'     ;ITEM'S LOCATION/RECTANGLE
        DC    I2'$000A           ;ITEM TYPE = BUTTON
        DC    I4'BTNTXT'         ;BUTTON'S STRING
        DC    I2'0'              ;ITEM VALUE
        DC    I2'0'              ;VISIBLE FLAG
```

```
        DC      I4'0'           ;COLOR TABLE POINTER
BTNTXT  DC      I1'2'           ;LENGTH OF STRING
        DC      C'OK'
```

The items created are not placed in the dialog box immediately. Before they are displayed, you must call the Modal Dialog function (covered later in this chapter). Then the items are displayed. Remember that items are placed into the dialog box in the opposite order of how they are defined.

An Example of a Dialog Box

The following is not stand-alone code. Instead, it's provided so you can see all the steps involved in creating a dialog box. It goes only as far as putting the dialog box up and defining the items. Displaying those items and acting upon dialog box events is covered in the next section.

```
;DIALOG BOX EXAMPLE STARTUP

        PEA     $0000           ;RESULT SPACE
        PEA     $0000
        PEA     DLGRECT|-16     ;POINTER TO THE LOCATION OF
                                ;THE
        PEA     DLGRECT         ;WINDOW SIZE
        PEA     $8000           ;TRUE VALUE, MAKE VISIBLE
        PEA     $0000           ;WINDOW REFERENCE—
        PEA     $0000           ;NOT USED BY THIS PROGRAM
        LDX     #$0A15          ;NEWMODALDIALOG
        JSL     $E10000
        PLA                     ;GET POINTER TO DIALOG PORT
        STA     DLGPTR          ;AND PUT HERE
        PLA
        STA     DLGPTR+2        ;(IT'S A LONG WORD)

;PUT AN [OK] BUTTON INSIDE THE BOX:

        LDA     DLGPTR+2        ;PUSH DIALOG PORT POINTER
        PHA                     ;AGAIN
        LDA     DLGPTR
        PHA
        PEA     ITEM1|-16       ;TEMPLATE
        PEA     ITEM1
        LDX     #$3315          ;GETNEWDITEM
        JSL     $E10000         ;ADD ITEM TO THE DIALOG BOX
```

```
                JSR     ERRORH

;PUT A [CANCEL] BUTTON INSIDE THE BOX:

                LDA     DLGPTR+2            ;PUSH DIALOG PORT POINTER
                PHA                         ;AGAIN
                LDA     DLGPTR
                PHA
                PEA     ITEM2|-16           ;TEMPLATE
                PEA     ITEM2
                LDX     #$3315              ;GETNEWDITEM
                JSL     $E10000             ;ADD ITEM TO THE DIALOG BOX
                JSR     ERRORH

;PUT THE TEXT IN THE DIALOG BOX:

                LDA     DLGPTR+2            ;PUSH DIALOG PORT POINTER
                PHA                         ;AGAIN
                LDA     DLGPTR
                PHA
                PEA     ITEM3|-16           ;THIRD ITEM'S TEMPLATE
                PEA     ITEM3
                LDX     #$3315              ;GETNEWDITEM
                JSL     $E10000
                JSR     ERRORH

;DIALOG BOX INFORMATION

DLGRECT         DC      I2'30,70,85,250'    ;LOCATION,SIZE OF DIALOG BOX

ITEM1           DC      I2'1'               ;ITEM REFERENCE
                DC      I2'33,110,0,0'      ;LOCATION OF OK BUTTON
                DC      I2'$000A'           ;IS BUTTON
                DC      I4'B1TXT'           ;BUTTON'S TEXT
                DC      I2'0'               ;ITEM VALUE
                DC      I2'0'               ;VISIBLE
                DC      I4'0'               ;COLOR TABLE

B1TXT           DC      I1'2'               ;TEXT OF OK BUTTON
                DC      C"OK"

ITEM2           DC      I2'2'               ;ITEM REFERENCE
                DC      I2'33,15,0,0'       ;LOCATION OF OK BUTTON
                DC      I2'$000A'           ;IS BUTTON
```

```
                DC      I4'B2TXT'               ;BUTTON'S TEXT
                DC      I2'0'                   ;ITEM VALUE
                DC      I2'0'                   ;VISIBLE
                DC      I4'0'                   ;COLOR TABLE

     B2TXT      DC      I1'6'                   ;TEXT OF OK BUTTON
                DC      C'CANCEL'

     ITEM3      DC      I2'$0040'               ;ITEM REFERENCE
                DC      I2'10,10,30,150'        ;LOCATION TEXT RECTANGLE
                DC      I2'$800F'               ;IS TEXT, DISABLED
                DC      I4'TEXTPTR'             ;TEXT
                DC      I2'0'                   ;ITEM VALUE
                DC      I2'0'                   ;VISIBLE
                DC      I4'0'                   ;COLOR TABLE

     TEXTPTR    DC      I1'ENDTEXT-STEXT'
     STEXT      DC      C'BEAM ME OUTTA HERE!'
     ENDTEXT    ANOP

                END
```

This code creates a dialog box in roughly the top center of the screen. Three items are placed into the dialog: an OK button (which is set as the default button), a Cancel button, and a string of text.

Modifying the Subroutine

The following code is the same as above, except the NewModalDialog function is replaced by GetNewModalDialog.

Function: $3215
Name: GetNewModalDialog
Creates a modal dialog using a template.
Push: Result Space (L); Template (L)
Pull: Dialog Port (L)
Errors: none
Comments: Also see NewModalDialog.

Study the code to see how this new function uses templates almost exclusively to define the dialog box.

```
     ;DIALOG EXAMPLE STARTUP

                PEA     $0000                   ;RESULT SPACE
                PEA     $0000
                PEA     DLGTEMP|-16             ;DIALOG TEMPLATE
```

```
                PEA     DLGTEMP
                LDX     #$3215              ;GETNEWMODALDIALOG
                JSL     $E10000
                PLA                         ;GET POINTER TO DIALOG PORT
                STA     DLGPTR              ;AND PUT HERE
                PLA
                STA     DLGPTR+2

;DIALOG BOX INFORMATION

DLGTEMP         ANOP
                DC      I2'30,70,85,250'    ;LOCATION,SIZE OF DIALOG BOX
                DC      I2'$8000'           ;VISIBLE
                DC      I4'0'               ;WINDOW REFERENCE
                DC      I4'ITEM1'           ;ITEM POINTER
                DC      I4'ITEM2'
                DC      I4'ITEM3'
                DC      I4'0'               ;END OF TABLE

ITEM1           DC      I2'1'               ;ITEM REFERENCE
                DC      I2'33,110,0,0'      ;LOCATION OF OK BUTTON
                DC      I2'$000A'           ;IS BUTTON
                DC      I4'B1TXT'           ;BUTTON'S TEXT
                DC      I2'0'               ;ITEM VALUE
                DC      I2'0'               ;VISIBLE
                DC      I4'0'               ;COLOR TABLE

B1TXT           DC      I1'2'               ;TEXT OF OK BUTTON
                DC      C"OK"

ITEM2           DC      I2'2'               ;ITEM REFERENCE
                DC      I2'33,15,0,0'       ;LOCATION OF OK BUTTON
                DC      I2'$000A'           ;IS BUTTON
                DC      I4'B2TXT'           ;BUTTON'S TEXT
                DC      I2'0'               ;ITEM VALUE
                DC      I2'0'               ;VISIBLE
                DC      I4'0'               ;COLOR TABLE

B2TXT           DC      I1'6'               ;TEXT OF OK BUTTON
                DC      C'CANCEL'

ITEM3           DC      I2'$0040'           ;ITEM REFERENCE
                DC      I2'10,10,30,150'    ;LOCATION TEXT RECTANGLE
                DC      I2'$800F'           ;IS TEXT, DISABLED
```

```
             DC     I4'TEXTPTR'           ;TEXT
             DC     I2'0'                 ;ITEM VALUE
             DC     I2'0'                 ;VISIBLE
             DC     I4'0'                 ;COLOR TABLE
    TEXTPTR  DC     I1'ENDTEXT-STEXT'
    STEXT    DC     C'BEAM ME OUTTA HERE!'
    ENDTEXT  ANOP
             END
```

GetNewModalDialog uses one big template for everything inside the dialog box. This saves overhead and complications. The format of the template is shown in Table 17-5.

Table 17-5. Format of Template

Item	Description
Dialog's rectangle	Rectangle
Visible flag	$8000 for visible, $0000 if not
Window reference	Long word, any value
Item template	Long pointer
Item template (and so on)	Long pointer
End of record	Long word with value of zero

Acting on Dialog Events

Dialog boxes are usually displayed after some form of action. Either the user selects a menu item to determine the direction of program flow, or a certain condition arises and the dialog box pops up to allow the user to choose a course of action to cope with the situation.

Controlling a dialog box is not done directly by the TaskMaster. Instead, the same routine responsible for displaying the dialog box also returns a *hit item ID.* This is the item reference number of an item which the user has selected with the mouse or manipulated in some way.

Function: $0F15
Name: ModalDialog
Handles events in the front-most dialog window.
Push: Result Space (W); Filter Procedure (L)
Pull: Item Hit (W)
Errors: $150D
Comments: A long word of zero is used for the standard filter procedure.

The ModalDialog function places all the items into the dialog's window. Then it waits for an item to be selected with the mouse. When an item is chosen, its reference number is returned from the toolbox.

The following code detects activity in a dialog box:

```
PHA                    ;RESULT SPACE
PEA     $0000          ;FILTER PROCEDURE—
PEA     $0000          ; USE 0 FOR DEFAULT
LDX     #$0F15         ;MODALDIALOG
JSL     $E10000
PLA
```

After the above routine, the item reference number of the selected item is pulled into the A register. This value can be examined further to determine what actions to take.

Internally, ModalDialog calls the Event Manager's GetNextEvent function. When a true result is returned from GetNextEvent, the Dialog Manager translates it into the item reference number of the item manipulated in the dialog box. ModalDialog returns only when an item in the dialog is selected.

The following code completes the program example above. This time, the ModalDialog function has been added. The routine waits for an item to be selected. Only the OK button (reference number $0001) is scanned for. If pressed, the dialog box is removed from the screen with the CloseDialog function.

```
*******************************************************************************
* DIALOG EXAMPLE
*******************************************************************************
MEMORY   START
         USING GLOBAL

;SET UP THE DIALOG BOX:

         PEA     $0000              ;RESULT SPACE
         PEA     $0000
         PEA     DLGTEMP|-16        ;DIALOG TEMPLATE
         PEA     DLGTEMP
         LDX     #$3215             ;GETNEWMODALDIALOG
         JSL     $E10000
         PLA                        ;GET POINTER TO DIALOG PORT
         STA     DLGPTR             ;AND PUT HERE
         PLA
```

```
                STA     DLGPTR+2

;NOW WAIT UNTIL THE BUTTON IS CLICKED
;THE DIALOG MANAGER TAKES CARE OF EVERYTHING ELSE

WAIT            ANOP
                PEA     $0000                   ;RESULT SPACE
                PEA     $0000                   ;LONG SPACE— USE DEFAULT
                PEA     $0000                   ; VALUES
                LDX     #$0F15                  ;MODALDIALOG
                JSL     $E10000

                PLA                             ;GET ANY RESULTS
                CMP     #$1                     ;IF WE GET ONE, BUTTON
                                                ;PRESSED
                BNE     WAIT

DONE            LDA     DLGPTR+2                ;PUSH DIALOG PORT POINTER
                PHA
                LDA     DLGPTR
                PHA
                LDX     #$0C15                  ;CLOSEDIALOG
                JSL     $E10000                 ;REMOVE IT FROM THE SCREEN

                RTS                             ;ALL DONE

;DIALOG BOX INFORMATION

DLGTEMP         ANOP
                DC      I2'30,70,85,250'        ;LOCATION,SIZE OF DIALOG BOX
                DC      I2'$8000'               ;VISIBLE
                DC      I4'0'                   ;WINDOW REFERENCE
                DC      I4'ITEM1'               ;ITEM POINTER
                DC      I4'ITEM2'
                DC      I4'ITEM3'
                DC      I4'0'                   ;END OF TABLE

ITEM1           DC      I2'1'                   ;ITEM REFERENCE
                DC      I2'33,110,0,0'          ;LOCATION OF OK BUTTON
                DC      I2'$000A'               ;IS BUTTON
                DC      I4'B1TXT'               ;BUTTON'S TEXT
                DC      I2'0'                   ;ITEM VALUE
                DC      I2'0'                   ;VISIBLE
```

```
             DC      I4'0'                   ;COLOR TABLE
    B1TXT    DC      I1'2'                   ;TEXT OF OK BUTTON
             DC      C"OK"
    ITEM2    DC      I2'2'                   ;ITEM REFERENCE
             DC      I2'33,15,0,0'           ;LOCATION OF OK BUTTON
             DC      I2'$000A'               ;IS BUTTON
             DC      I4'B2TXT'               ;BUTTON'S TEXT
             DC      I2'0'                   ;ITEM VALUE
             DC      I2'0'                   ;VISIBLE
             DC      I4'0'                   ;COLOR TABLE
    B2TXT    DC      I1'6'                   ;TEXT OF OK BUTTON
             DC      C'CANCEL'
    ITEM3    DC      I2'$0040'               ;ITEM REFERENCE
             DC      I2'10,10,30,150'        ;LOCATION TEXT RECTANGLE
             DC      I2'$800F'               ;IS TEXT, DISABLED
             DC      I4'TEXTPTR'             ;TEXT
             DC      I2'0'                   ;ITEM VALUE
             DC      I2'0'                   ;VISIBLE
             DC      I4'0'                   ;COLOR TABLE
    TEXTPTR  DC      I1'ENDTEXT-STEXT'
    STEXT    DC      C'BEAM ME OUTTA HERE!'
    ENDTEXT  ANOP
             END
```

If you decide to include this as part of another program, remember to start up and shut down the Control Manager and Dialog Manager as part of the program's code. Also check for the appropriate direct-page space and the size of the screen. The above code was written for a 320-mode screen.

Alerts

Alerts are special types of dialog boxes. They're easier to define than the modal dialog boxes (although technically, an alert is a type of modal dialog box). Most of the work involved in using alerts is done for you by the Dialog Manager. This includes creating and placing an optional alert icon into the dialog box.

Alerts are displayed using templates. The type of alert, Note, caution, or stop is determined by the function called. A fourth type of alert, just called *alert,* does not display an icon in the upper left corner of the box.

Function: $1715
Name: Alert
Brings up an alert dialog.
Push: Result Space (W); Alert Template (L); Filter Procedure (L)
Pull: Item Hit (W)
Errors: none
Comments: The number of the selected item in the alert dialog is returned after the call. If its value is -1 the dialog box was not drawn.

Function: $1815
Name: StopAlert
Brings up an alert dialog with the stop icon
Push: Result Space (W); Alert Template (L); Filter Procedure (L)
Pull: Item Hit (W)
Errors: none
Comments: (Same as alert call). The stop icon is a stop-sign shape containing the image of an opened hand, and is placed in the upper left corner of the dialog box.

Function: $1915
Name: NoteAlert
Brings up an alert dialog with the note icon.
Push: Result Space (W); Alert Template (L); Filter Procedure (L)
Pull: Item Hit (W)
Errors: none
Comments: (Same as alert call). The note icon contains a face with an exclamation point inside a cartoon-like bubble, and is placed in the upper left corner of the dialog box.

Function: $1A15
Name: CautionAlert
Brings up an alert dialog with the caution icon.
Push: Result Space (W); Alert Template (L); Filter Procedure (L)
Pull: Item Hit (W)
Errors: none
Comments: (Same as alert call). The caution icon is a triangle with an exclamation point inside, and is placed in the upper left corner of the dialog box.

Not only does each alert function display the information in the dialog box, but it also works like ModalDialog to trap events. The value returned from each function, the item hit, is the reference number of an item selected inside the alert. Your program can then act upon this selection.

The filter template is normally set to zero to use the system default. The *alert template* points to a list which describes the location of the alert dialog box, special values called alert stages, and the items inside the alert.

The alert template is shown in Tabe 17-6.

Table 17-6. The Alert Template

Item	Description
Location	Rectangle
ID number	Word value
First stage alert	Byte value
Second stage alert	Byte value
Third stage alert	Byte value
Fourth stage alert	Byte value
Item template	Long pointer
Item template	Long pointer
(and so on)	
Table end	Long zero

Location. A rectangle indicating the position and size of the alert box on the screen.

ID number. A unique value identifying the alert dialog box, like a reference number.

Alert stages. The different alert stages are used each time the alert is called. For example, the first time an alert appears, it's a first-stage alert. If the user makes the same error twice, it's a second stage and so on. By manipulating the bits in the different stage values, you can adjust the way the alert box is presented. Table 17-7 explains the effect of the bits in the alert stage byte.

Table 17-7. Effect of Bits in Alert Stage Byte

Bit	Meaning
0	Number of beeps
1	Number of beeps (see below)
2	Not used
3	Not used
4	Not used
5	Not used
6	Default button, one or two
7	Draw alert dialog box

Bits 0 and 1 set the number of times the speaker beeps before the alert is drawn (Table 17-8).

Table 17-8. Number of Beeps

Bit 1	0	Beeps
0	1	One
1	0	Two
1	1	Three

Bits 2–5 are not used and should be reset to zero.

Bit 6 determines which button, or item ID number, is to be the default choice—the button with a double frame which can also be selected by pressing Return. If this bit is reset to zero, item ID $0001 is the default. If bit 6 is set to one, item ID $0002 is the default.

Bit 7 determines if the alert dialog is to be drawn or not. Setting this bit to one draws and displays the dialog. Resetting the bit to zero does not.

Each time the alert function is called, it uses the next highest alert stage level. Each stage could, for example, increase the number of times the speaker beeps. Stage 4 is the highest level and any further appearance of the alert dialog will use stage 4's bit settings.

```
DC   H'01'          ;FIRST STAGE
DC   H'81'          ;SECOND STAGE
DC   H'82'          ;THIRD STAGE
DC   H'83'          ;FOURTH STAGE
```

In the above example, four alert stages are set. The first simply beeps the speaker. An alert dialog is not displayed. The second alert stage displays the dialog box (bit 7 is set), and beeps once. The third stage displays the dialog and beeps twice. The fourth, and all following stages, displays the dialog box and beeps the speaker three times.

Item templates. The item templates are pointers to items placed into the alert dialog box. Any number of items can be included in the list. A long word of zero indicates the end of the list.

Item templates take on the structure shown in Table 17-9. The values are the same for the dialog box item template described earlier.

Table 17-9. Item Template Structure

Item	Description
Item reference number	Word value
Item's location/rectangle	Rectangle
Item type	Word value
Item description	Long pointer/handle
Item value	Word value
Bit value	Word value
Color table pointer	Long pointer

Most of these items are the same for an alert as they are for a dialog box. In fact, the last three items can all be set to zero to use the defaults.

The following is not stand-alone code. It is an example to show how an alert is placed on the screen. To include this as part of another program, remember to start the Control and Dialog Managers, and make sure enough direct-page space is set aside. This code assumes a 320-mode screen.

```
;ALERT EXAMPLE

          PHA                          ;RESULT SPACE
          PEA     WARNING|-16          ;ALERT TEMPLATE POINTER
          PEA     WARNING
          PEA     $0000                ;FILTER POINTER (USE DEFAULT)
          PEA     $0000
          LDX     #$1815               ;CAUTIONALERT
          JSL     $E10000

          PLA                          ;GET HIT ITEM ID
          CMP     #0001                ;IS IT OKAY?
          BEQ     OVER1

          RTS

OVER1     PHA     ;RESULT SPACE
          PEA     WARNING2|-16         ;ALERT TEMPLATE POINTER
          PEA     WARNING2
          PEA     $0000                ;FILTER POINTER
          PEA     $0000
          LDX     #$1915               ;CAUTIONALERT
          JSL     $E10000

```

```
            PLA                              ;GET HIT ITEM ID
            RTS
;FIRST ALERT'S TEMPLATE
WARNING     DC      I'40,30,100,290'         ;DIALOG'S RECTANGLE
            DC      I'2374'                  ;ID NUMBER
            DC      H'02'                    ;FIRST STAGE ALERT
            DC      H'81'                    ;SECOND STAGE
            DC      H'81'                    ;THIRD
            DC      H'81'                    ;FOURTH
            DC      I4'ITEM01'               ;FIRST ITEM TEMPLATE
            DC      I4'ITEM02'               ;SECOND ITEM TEMPLATE
            DC      I4'ITEM03'               ;THIRD ITEM
            DC      I4'0'                    ;NULL TERMINATOR
;ITEMS IN FIRST ALERT:
ITEM01      DC      I2'0001'                 ;ITEM ID
            DC      I2'35,150,00,00'         ;DISPLAY RECTANGLE
            DC      I2'10'                   ;TYPE = BUTTON
            DC      I4'BUT10'                ;ITEM DESCRIPTOR
            DC      I2'0'                    ;VALUE OF ITEM
            DC      I2'0'                    ;DEFAULT BIT VECTOR
            DC      I4'0'                    ;DEFAULT COLOR TABLE
ITEM02      DC      I2'1348'                 ;ITEM ID
            DC      I2'10,60,30,240'         ;DISPLAY RECTANGLE
            DC      I2'15'                   ;TYPE = TEXT
            DC      I4'MSG1'                 ;ITEM DESCRIPTOR
            DC      I2'0'                    ;VALUE
            DC      I2'0'                    ;BIT VECTOR
            DC      I4'0'                    ;COLOR TABLE
ITEM03      DC      I2'0002'                 ;ITEM ID
            DC      I2'35,40,00,00'          ;DISPLAY RECTANGLE
            DC      I2'10'                   ;TYPE = BUTTON
            DC      I4'BUT20'                ;ITEM DESCRIPTOR
            DC      I2'0'                    ;VALUE OF ITEM
            DC      I2'0'                    ;DEFAULT BIT VECTOR
            DC      I4'0'                    ;DEFAULT COLOR TABLE
BUT10       DC      I1'2'                    ;TEXT OF FIRST BUTTON
```

```
            DC      C'OK'

BUT20       DC      I1'6'                  ;SECOND BUTTON
            DC      C'CANCEL'

MSG1        DC      I1'STR010-STR009'      ;TEXT IN RECTANGLE
STR009      DC      C"BE CAREFUL! DANGER HERE!"
STR010      ANOP

;SECOND ALERT BOX'S TEMPLATE:

WARNING2    DC      I'50,30,110,290'       ;DIALOG'S RECTANGLE
            DC      I'6374'                ;ID NUMBER (UNIQUE)
            DC      H'81'                  ;FIRST STAGE ALERT
            DC      H'81'                  ;SECOND STAGE
            DC      H'81'                  ;THIRD
            DC      H'81'                  ;FOURTH
            DC      I4'ITEM11'             ;FIRST ITEM TEMPLATE
            DC      I4'ITEM12'             ;SECOND ITEM TEMPLATE
            DC      I4'0'                  ;NULL TERMINATOR

;ITEMS IN SECOND ALERT:

ITEM11      DC      I2'6345'               ;ITEM ID
            DC      I2'35,150,00,00'       ;DISPLAY RECTANGLE
            DC      I2'10'                 ;TYPE = BUTTON
            DC      I4'BUT11'              ;ITEM DESCRIPTOR
            DC      I2'0'                  ;VALUE OF ITEM
            DC      I2'0'                  ;DEFAULT BIT VECTOR
            DC      I4'0'                  ;DEFAULT COLOR TABLE

ITEM12      DC      I2'6348'               ;ITEM ID
            DC      I2'10,60,30,240'       ;DISPLAY RECTANGLE
            DC      I2'15'                 ;TYPE = TEXT
            DC      I4'MSG2'               ;ITEM DESCRIPTOR
            DC      I2'0'                  ;VALUE
            DC      I2'0'                  ;BIT VECTOR
            DC      I4'0'                  ;COLOR TABLE

BUT11       DC      I1'6'                  ;BUTTON'S TEXT
            DC      C'I KNOW'

MSG2        DC      I1'STR012-STR011'
STR011      DC      C"YOU'RE MAKING A LOT OF ERRORS"
STR012      ANOP
```

The first alert is a caution alert. It's first stage is set to $02, meaning no alert is displayed and the speaker beeps twice.

The next time this subroutine is called, a second stage alert takes place. The speaker beeps, then displays two buttons, OK and Cancel, and the message, "Be careful! Danger here!" If the user selects Cancel, the subroutine returns to the caller. Otherwise, a second alert is displayed.

The second alert is a note alert. It displays two items: a text string informing the user that, "You're making a lot of errors," and a button that says, "I know."

Chapter 18

Sound

The Sound and Note Synthesizer tool sets provide the sound and music for the Apple IIGS (where the S stands for Sound) and Apple has supplied the IIGS with some of the best sound capabilities of any computer. The powerful Ensoniq sound chip is capable of 15 different sound voices for

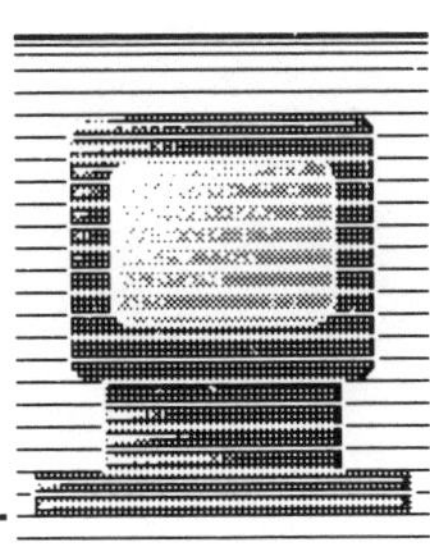

multiphonic music as well as interesting sounds and voice synthesis.

Unfortunately, the sound tools are not complete at this writing. This does not imply that the IIGS is incapable of sound, or that the toolbox routines don't work; instead, it means the documentation in this chapter is not as comprehensive as the documentation on the other tool sets. Although the programs function properly and the examples are accurate, quite a bit of information is lacking.

As far as programming sound using the toolbox goes, it can be done. However, most developers are programming the sound capabilities of the Apple IIGS directly on the low hardware level. Programs such as *Music Construction Set* from Electronic Arts, and *The Music Studio* from Activision both program the computer's sound chip directly, bypassing the toolbox routines.

The Sound Manager and Note Synthesizer

The Ensoniq sound chip is also referred to as the 5503 Digital Oscillator Chip, or "DOC." The DOC provides the IIGS with 15 voices by using 32 pairs of oscillators. Two of the oscillators are reserved: (32 - 2)/2 = 15.

An entire 64K bank of memory is dedicated to the DOC for creating sound, music, and voice synthesis. The DOC also works with a General Logic Unit (GLU) which allows sound to be generated without much assistance from the 65816 microprocessor.

Creating sound using the toolbox is done with three tool sets, the Sound Manager, Note Synthesizer, and Note Sequencer. Only the Sound Manager and Note Synthesizer are available as this book goes to press. Both of these tool sets control different aspects of the DOC. Programming the computer's sound capabilities using these tool sets is preferred over direct hardware access.

The Sound Manager is a ROM-based tool set, number $08. It controls sound waveforms (discussed below), the DOC's RAM, and sound generators. The Note Synthesizer plays individual notes.

To start the Sound Manager and ready the IIGS to produce sounds, a call is placed to the Sound Manager's StartUp function. One page of direct-page space is needed.

Function: $0208
Name: SoundStartUp
Starts the Sound Manager.
Push: Direct Page (W)
Pull: nothing
Errors: $0810, $0818
Comments:

To shutdown the Sound Manager, a call is made to function $03, SoundShutDown.

Function: $0308
Name: SoundShutDown
Shuts down the Sound Manager.
Push: nothing
Pull: nothing
Errors: none
Comments:

The Note Synthesizer is a disk-based tool set, number $19. Its primary responsibility is playing individual notes using one of the DOC's sound generators. To start the Note Synthesizer, a call is made to the NSStartUp function.

Function: $0219
Name: NSStartUp
Starts the Note Synthesizer.
Push: Update Rate (W); User Update Routine (L)
Pull: nothing
Errors: none
Comments: Starts up the Note Synthesizer, Update Rate is in hertz, #70 ($46) = 60 Hz updates.

The update rate determines the number of times the User Update Routine is called and the number of times a sound envelope is generated. For 60 Hertz updates, a value of $0046 is used. The higher the update rate value, the smoother the sound.

The User Update Routine is a music-playing routine called during a timer interrupt. This routine is used when playing a sequence of notes, and it's automatically called by the Note Synthesizer, depending on the update rate. Normally, a long word of zero (meaning no User Update Routine) is used.

To start the Note Synthesizer, the following code could be used. It's assumed the Sound Manager has already been started and that the Note Synthesizer has been loaded from disk.

```
PEA   $0046       ;VALUE FOR 60 HZ UPDATES
PEA   $0000       ;USE DEFAULT (NO) UPDATE ROUTINE
PEA   $0000
LDX   #$0219      ;NSSTARTUP
JSL   $E10000
```

To shut down the Note Synthesizer, a call is made to its ShutDown function.

Function: $0319
Name: NSShutDown
Shuts down the Note Synthesizer.
Push: nothing
Pull: nothing
Errors: none
Comments:

When creating sound and music with the Sound Manager and Note Synthesizer tool sets, you'll be dealing with two items, the *sound wave* and an *instrument.* The sound wave is handled by the Sound Manager. The instrument is used to create variety (accent, volume, pitch, duration, and so on) in the sounds, and is handled by the Note Synthesizer.

The Sound Wave

The sound wave describes the sound's wave form. It has two aspects, frequency and amplitude. The shape of a sound wave determines whether the sound produced is either smooth or choppy. A smooth wave, such as a *sine wave,* produces a smooth sound. A choppy wave, such as a *square wave,* makes a choppy, sometimes tinny sound.

To the DOC, the sound wave is a series of byte values, each of which defines an amplitude of the wave. The wave length can be from one to 65535, the full size of the DOC's sound RAM. Most sound waves are 256 bytes long.

All values in the wave representing amplitude are byte-sized integers. The lowest value possible is $FF, the highest is $01, and $80 is considered zero. The values are in *twos compliment* form, a means of representing positive and negative numbers within the span of one byte's range. In this case, $FF would be thought of as −1 and $01 as +1. A byte value of $00 should be avoided as it stops the sound oscillator.

The sound wave is under the control of the Sound Manager. The WriteRAMBlock and ReadRAMBlock functions are used to put and get a sound wave pattern to and from sound RAM. The only way to access sound RAM using the toolbox is with these two functions.

Function: $0908
Name: WriteRAMBlock
Copies a block of memory from standard RAM into the DOC.
Push: Source Block (L); DOS Address (W); Length (W)
Pull: nothing
Errors: $0810, $0811
Comments:

Because sound RAM in the computer is separate from main memory, this function is used to transfer sound wave patterns to sound memory. The ReadRAMBlock function is used to read information from sound RAM and copy it to regular memory.

Function: $0A08
Name: ReadRAMBlock
Copies a block of memory from the DOC to the location you specify.
Push: Destination Block (L); DOC Address (W); Length (W)
Pull: nothing
Errors: $0810, $0811
Comments:

The sound wave must be established in sound memory before the sound can be created. A sound wave can be a series of byte values in your assembly source, or it can be created using a program, or it can be loaded from disk. Once in memory, WriteRAMBlock is used to transfer the sound wave values into sound RAM.

The following BASIC program creates a portion of a sine wave using the BASIC SIN function. This is a smooth sound wave pattern with values ranging from 1 to 99. This BASIC program divides the curve from zero to pi (3.14159, or one radian) into 256 slices.

```
10 FOR X = 0 TO 3.14159 STEP .012318
20 PRINT INT (100 * SIN (X)),
30 NEXT X
```

Each of the slices is multiplied by 100 in line 20. This creates the integer values needed for the sine wave. The STEPping rate is set to .012318, which is 3.14159 divided by 255. Two zero values are produced by this example. They should be changed to one when used in a sound wave.

The byte values created by the above BASIC code are used in both examples at the end of this chapter. They were copied straight from the BASIC output into the assembly source code. They could have, instead, been created by the assembly program, or saved on disk and loaded into memory.

The following assembly code creates a triangle wave pattern at the address WaveF.

```
         SEP     #$30          ;FOR USING EIGHT-BIT REGISTERS
         LONGA   OFF
         LONGI   OFF
         LDX     #$00
         LDA     #$C0
LOOP1    STA     WAVEF,X
         DEC     A
         INX
         CPX     #$80          ;HALFWAY THERE YET?
         BNE     LOOP1         ;KEEP GOING IF NOT
LOOP2    STA     WAVEF,X
         INC     A
         INX
         CPX     #$FF
         BNE     LOOP2
         REP     #$30          ;RETURN TO 16-BIT REGS.
         LONGA   ON
         LONGI   ON
```

This routine builds a simple triangle wave. The wave pattern starts at $C0, then ramps down to $40, then ramps up again to $C0. The SEP #$30 and REP #$30 instructions set and reset the width of the accumulator and index registers. LONGA and LONGI are directives which instruct the APW assembler to generate eight-bit code.

A triangle wave is somewhat sharper than a sine wave. The sounds it produces are smooth, but not as smooth as a sine wave, and it's relatively simple to create using assembly source as above.

Once the wave pattern is in memory, WriteRAMBlock is used to move it into sound RAM. If the sound wave is $100 bytes long and it sits at the memory location labeled WaveF, the following code could be used to move the wave into sound RAM.

```
PEA   WAVEF|-16    ;PUSH LONG ADDRESS OF SOUND WAVE
PEA   WAVEF
PEA   $0000        ;START AT $0000 IN SOUND RAM
PEA   $0100        ;LENGTH IS $100 BYTES
LDX   #$0908       ;WRITERAMBLOCK
JSL   $E10000
JSR   ERRORH       ;TEST FOR ERRORS
```

Several sound waves could be loaded into the DOC, each starting at a different location in sound RAM. To use a different sound wave, its starting location is specified as part of an instrument record, discussed in the next section.

The Instrument

The Note Synthesizer uses a structure called an instrument to define the sounds it makes. The structure is part of an instrument record which controls a number of details about the sound processed. By altering items in the instrument record, you can change the sound produced. One instrument record may mimic the sound of a violin, while another can create the sound of a pipe organ.

Unfortunately, this is the section where most of the good, detailed information is missing. Not enough material was obtained in time to finish work on the instrument record. While it does function properly, this book contains no details on how individual parts of the record are used to create different sounds. At a future date, books and materials for fully using the toolbox to create sound will be available (check with COMPUTE! Books for a catalog of upcoming publications). Until then, the following is as complete as possible under the conditions given. Table 18-1 describes an instrument record.

Table 18-1. The Instrument Record

Description	Value
Envelope	(see below)
Release segment	Byte
Priority increment	Byte
Pitch bend range	Byte
Vibrato depth	Byte
Vibrato speed	Byte
Not used	Byte
A wave count	Byte
B wave count	Byte
A wave	Six bytes * A wave count
B wave	Six bytes * B wave count

The following assembly source is an example of how an instrument would look in assembly.

```
INSTREC   DC   I1'$40'              ;FIRST SEGMENT
          DC   I2'$7F00'
          DC   I1'$00'              ;SECOND SEGMENT
          DC   I2'$0000'
          DC   I1'$00'              ;THIRD SEGMENT
          DC   I2'$0000'
          DC   I1'$00'              ;FOURTH SEGMENT
          DC   I2'$0000'
          DC   I1'$00'              ;FIFTH SEGMENT
          DC   I2'$0000'
          DC   I1'$00'              ;SIXTH SEGMENT
          DC   I2'$0000'
          DC   I1'$00'              ;SEVENTH SEGMENT
          DC   I2'$0000'
          DC   I1'$00'              ;EIGHTH SEGMENT
          DC   I2'$0000'
          DC   I1'1'                ;RELEASE SEGMENT
          DC   I1'32'               ;PRIORITY INCREMENT
          DC   I1'2'                ;PITCH BEND RANGE
          DC   I1'75'               ;VIBRATO DEPTH
          DC   I1'85'               ;VIBRATO SPEED
          DC   I1'0'                ;NOT USED
          DC   I1'1'                ;A WAVE COUNT
          DC   I1'1'                ;B WAVE COUNT
          DC   I1'127,0,0,0,0,0'    ;THE A WAVE
          DC   I1'127,0,0,0,0,0'    ;THE B WAVE
```

Envelope. The envelope controls four parts of the sound: *attack, decay, sustain,* and *release.* The attack and decay happen quickly, when the sound is first made. For example, pressing a key on a piano produces an attack as the sound is first made, then a slight decay. Sustain happens as the key is held down and the sound continues to resonate. Release is the fade of the sound once the key is released. Each of these aspects of an envelope can be altered to control how the sound is made. A staccato note would have a tiny sustain, while a legato note would have a long sustain.

Attack, decay, and sustain are part of the instrument record. When the Note Synthesizer's NoteOn function is called, the sound produced follows the envelope pattern as specified in the instrument record. The release part of the envelope is triggered when the

NoteOff function is called. NoteOff instructs the DOC to halt the sound started by NoteOn.

The envelope consists of a one-byte breakpoint followed by a word-sized increment. There must be eight sets of breakpoints and increments. If the instrument record uses only a few of them, the rest are filled with zeros.

The format is

Breakpoint (byte), Increment (word)

The breakpoint is a sound level that measures a change in amplitude. The increment is a fixed value. The MSB of the increment word is an integer ranging from 0 to 255. The LSB is a fraction, depending on which bits are set (Table 18-2).

Table 18-2. LSB of Increment Word

Bit	Fraction
0	1/256
1	1/128
2	1/64
3	1/32
4	1/16
5	1/8
6	1/4
7	1/2

An increment of $0000 indicates sustain.

Release segment. Determines where the release portion of the envelope takes place, minus one. A release segment value of 3 would indicate the release takes place on the fourth segment. (See the programs below for examples.)

Priority increment. Deals with the sound generators. This will be discussed in detail below.

Pitch bend range. The pitch bend range is either 1, 2, or 4. It deals with the number of semitones the pitch is raised.

Vibrato depth. Controls the vibrato. Its value ranges from 0 (for vibrato off) to 127 (for a very high vibrato).

Vibrato speed. A value indicating the frequency of the vibrato.

Wave count. Used to describe a wavelist. There are two wavelists: A and B. The wave count is a value that describes the number of waveforms in each wavelist.

The wavelist is a record structure that contains individual waveforms. Each wavelist is six bytes long and there can be from 1 to 255 of them, as specified by the wave count value.

The meaning of the six bytes in the wavelist are explained in Table 18-3.

Table 18-3. Meaning of Wavelist Bytes

Description	Size	Meaning
TopKey	Byte	The highest MIDI semitone in the waveform
WaveAddress	Byte	MSB of the waveform address
WaveSize	Byte	The size of the wave table and frequency resolution
DOC mode	Byte	A mode byte for the DOC
RelPitch	Word	A fixed word value, similar to increment for the envelope, used to tune the waveform

Additional information on the priority increment, pitch bend range, vibrato depth and speed, wave count, and wavelists is not yet available. These are all the details available on the instrument record. At this point, only experimentation will tell what each of the pieces does in relation to the sound produced.

To make the notes, the NoteOn function of the Note Synthesizer is used. But first, a sound generator must be allocated using the AllocGen function, $09.

Function: $0919
Name: AllocGen
Returns a generator to be used for playing notes.
Push: Result Space (W); Request Priority (W)
Pull: Generator (W)
Errors: $1921
Comments:

The request priority is a value ranging from $00 to $7F, with $00 a low priority and $7F high. After this function is called, a generator number is returned from the stack. This number is then used by NoteOn to generate the note.

Function: $0B19
Name: NoteOn
Starts playing a note on a specified generator.
Push: Generator (W); Semitone (W); Volume (W); Instrument (L)
Pull: nothing
Errors: $1924
Comments:

First, the generator number is pushed to the stack. This is followed by the semitone, or value of the note played. $FF indicates a high-pitched note, $00 is a low-pitched note. The actual note value as related to a musical scale depends on the instrument record.

The volume is a byte value from $00 to $FF with $FF being very loud. $0080 is a good medium volume to use. Instrument is a long-word pointer to the instrument record, as briefly described above.

After the note is played, NoteOff is called and the DOC stops generating the sound.

Function: $0C19
Name: NoteOff
Stops playing a note on a specified generator.
Push: Generator (W); Semitone (W)
Pull: nothing
Errors: none
Comments: Generator and Semitone must be the same as when NoteOn was called.

The generator number and the semitone (the note being played) must be the same as used by NoteOn. While it won't produce an error if the values are different, the note will continue to play.

The following code could be used to play one note. It's assumed the tool sets have all been started, and that an instrument record exists at the label Instr.

```
PEA    $0000        ;RESULT SPACE
PEA    $0040        ;MEDIUM PRIORITY
LDX    #$0919       ;ALLOCGEN
JSL    $E10000
JSR    ERRORH       ;TEST FOR ERRORS

PLA                 ;GET GENERATOR NUMBER
STA    GENNUM       ; AND SAVE IT
PHA                 ; AND PUSH IT TO THE STACK
PEA    $0055        ;PLAY THE NOTE $55
PEA    $0080        ;VOLUME VALUE
PEA    INSTR|-16    ;INSTRUMENT RECORD POINTER
PEA    INSTR
LDX    #$0B19       ;NOTEON
JSL    $E10000
JSR    ERRORH       ;TEST FOR ERRORS
```

```
;THE SOUND IS NOW PLAYING. TIME TO TURN IT OFF:
        LDA     GENNUM          ;GET GENERATOR NUMBER
        PHA                     ;PUSH IT
        PEA     $0055           ;NOTE $55
        LDX     #$0C19          ;NOTEOFF
        JSL     $E10000
```

This routine only plays one note, semitone $55. Other routines could read the note from a list, or react to user input to produce the sounds.

PHONE

The following is the source code for a sound program, PHONE. This program will simulate the sound of a ringing telephone using the Sound Manager and Note Synthesizer tool sets.

```
*********************************************************************************
* PHONE RINGING PROGRAM
*********************************************************************************

            ABSADDR ON
            KEEP PHONE                  ;EXE FILE

MAIN        START

            PHK                         ;ENVIRONMENT
            PLB

;-----------------------------------------
; START SOME BASIC TOOLSETS

            LDX     #$0201              ;TLSTARTUP
            JSL     $E10000

            PEA     $0000
            LDX     #$0202              ;MMSTARTUP
            JSL     $E10000
            JSR     ERRORH
            PLA
            STA     USERID

            LDX     #$0203              ;MISC TOOLS STARTUP
            JSL     $E10000
            JSR     ERRORH

```

```
;-----------------------------------------
; GRAB ONE DIRECT PAGE FOR THE SOUND MGR.

         PEA    $0000           ;LONG RESULT SPACE
         PEA    $0000
         PEA    $0000           ;ONE PAGE
         PEA    $0100
         LDA    USERID          ;PROGRAM'S ID
         PHA
         PEA    $C005           ;ATTRIBUTES
         PEA    $0000           ;BLOCK'S START
         PEA    $0000           ;(DON'T CARE)
         LDX    #$0902          ;NEWHANDLE
         JSL    $E10000
         JSR    ERRORH

         PLA                    ;GET HANDLE OF NEW BLOCK
         STA    0               ; INTO ZERO PAGE
         PLA
         STA    2
         LDA    [0]             ;GET START ADD. IN A

;-----------------------------------------
; START THE SOUND TOOLS

         PHA                    ;PASS THE DPAGE START
         LDX    #$0208          ;SOUNDSTARTUP
         JSL    $E10000
         JSR    ERRORH

;-----------------------------------------
; COPY THE WAVEFORM INTO THE DOC

         PEA    WAVE|-16        ;WAVE FORM'S ADDRESS
         PEA    WAVE
         PEA    $0              ;STARTING ADDRESS IN DOC
         PEA    $100            ;LENGTH
         LDX    #$0908          ;WRITERAMBLOCK
         JSL    $E10000
         JSR    ERRORH

;-----------------------------------------
; LOAD AND START THE NOTE SYNTHESIZER

```

```
            PEA     $0019           ;TOOL $19, NOTE SYNTH.
            PEA     $0000           ;VERSION NUMBER
            LDX     #$0F01          ;LOADONETOOL
            JSL     $E10000
            JSR     ERRORH

            PEA     $0046           ;60 HZ UPDATES
            PEA     $0000           ;ZERO = NO INTERRUPT ROUTINE
            PEA     $0000
            LDX     #$0219          ;NSSTARTUP
            JSL     $E10000
            JSR     ERRORH

;---------------------------------------
; NOW, FAKE THE PHONE RINGING

            LDA     #6              ;SIX RINGS
            STA     RINGS           ;INTO RING COUNTER

DORING      ANOP

            LDY     #33             ;DING THE BELL 33 TIMES
LOOP        PHY                     ;SAVE THE COUNT ON THE STACK
            JSR     PLAY            ;RING THE BELL (SOUND)

            LDX     #$4000          ;DELAY BETWEEN EACH BELL
                                    ;SOUND
DELAY       DEX
            BNE     DELAY

            PLY                     ;GET BELL COUNT BACK
            DEY                     ;33 TIMES YET?
            BNE     LOOP            ;IF NO, KEEP LOOPING

            DEC     RINGS           ;SIX RINGS YET?
            BEQ     EXIT            ;KEEP RINGING UNTIL SOMEONE
                                    ;ANSWERS

            LDA     #9              ;A DELAY BETWEEN RINGS
            TAY                     ;PUT A INTO Y
WAIT1       DEY
            BNE     WAIT1
            DEC     A
```

```
         BNE     WAIT1
         BRA     DORING
;---------------------------------------
; END OF PROGRAM, SHUTDOWN ALL TOOLS
EXIT     ANOP
         LDX     #$0319             ;NSSHUTDOWN
         JSL     $E10000
         LDX     #$0308             ;SOUNDSHUTDOWN
         JSL     $E10000
         LDX     #$0303             ;MTSHUTDOWN
         JSL     $E10000
         LDA     USERID             ;FOR CLOSING ALL HANDLES
         PHA
         LDX     #$1102             ;DISPOSEALL
         JSL     $E10000
         LDA     USERID
         PHA
         LDX     #$0302             ;MMSHUTDOWN
         JSL     $E10000
         LDX     #$0301             ;TLSHUTDOWN
         JSL     $E10000
         JSL     $E100A8            ;PRODOS 16 CALL
         DC      I2'$29'            ;QUIT
         DC      I2'QPARAMS         ' ;QUIT PARAMETERS
************************************************************************
* PLAY A SOUND USING THE NOTE SYNTH
************************************************************************
PLAY     ANOP
         PEA     $0000              ;RESULT SPACE
         PEA     $0040              ;PRIORITY
         LDX     #$0919             ;ALLOCGEN
         JSL     $E10000
```

```
            JSR     ERRORH
            PLA                             ;GET GENERATOR NUMBER
            STA     GENNUM
            LDA     GENNUM
            PHA
            PEA     $006E                   ;SEMITONE VALUE
            PEA     112                     ;VOLUME
            PEA     INSTRUM|-16             ;LONG PTR TO INSTRUMENT DEF
            PEA     INSTRUM
            LDX     #$0B19                  ;NOTEON
            JSL     $E10000
            JSR     ERRORH
            LDA     GENNUM
            PHA
            PEA     $006E                   ;SEMITONE
            LDX     #$0C19                  ;NOTEOFF
            JSL     $E10000
            JSR     ERRORH
            RTS
*********************************************************************************
* ERROR HANDLER
*********************************************************************************
ERRORH      ANOP
            BCS     UHOH                    ;CARRY SET IF ERROR
            RTS                             ;ELSE, RETURN
UHOH        ANOP
            PHA                             ;ERROR NUMBER ON STACK
            PEA     $0000                   ;USE DEFAULT MSG.
            PEA     $0000
            LDX     #$1503                  ;SYSFAILMGR
            JSL     $E10000
*********************************************************************************
* DATA AREA
*********************************************************************************
USERID      DS      2
```

```
RINGS      DS      2
GENNUM     DS      2
QPARAMS    ANOP
           DC      I4'0'
           DC      I2'0'
;----------------------------------------
; THIS DATA APPROXIMATES A SINE WAVE
WAVE       DC      I1'1,1,2,3,4,6,7,8,9,11,12,13'
           DC      I1'14,15,17,18,19,20,21,23,24,25,26,27'
           DC      I1'29,30,31,32,33,34,36,37,38,39,40,41'
           DC      I1'42,44,45,46,47,48,49,50,51,52,53,54'
           DC      I1'55,56,57,58,59,60,61,62,63,64,65,66'
           DC      I1'67,68,69,70,70,71,72,73,74,75,75,76'
           DC      I1'77,78,79,79,80,81,81,82,83,84,84,85'
           DC      I1'85,86,87,87,88,88,89,90,90,91,91,92'
           DC      I1'92,93,93,93,94,94,95,95,95,96,96,96'
           DC      I1'97,97,97,97,98,98,98,98,98,99,99,99'
           DC      I1'99,99,99,99,99,99,99,99,99,99,99,99'
           DC      I1'99,99,99,99,99,99,99,99,98,98,98,98'
           DC      I1'97,97,97,97,96,96,96,95,95,95,94,94'
           DC      I1'93,93,93,92,92,91,91,90,90,89,88,88'
           DC      I1'87,87,86,85,85,84,84,83,82,81,81,80'
           DC      I1'79,79,78,77,76,75,75,74,73,72,71,70'
           DC      I1'70,69,68,67,66,65,64,63,62,61,60,59'
           DC      I1'58,57,56,55,54,53,52,51,50,49,48,47'
           DC      I1'46,45,44,42,41,40,39,38,37,36,35,33'
           DC      I1'32,31,30,29,28,26,25,24,23,22,20,19'
           DC      I1'18,17,15,14,13,12,11,9,8,7,6,4'
           DC      I1'3,2,1,1'
;----------------------------------------
; THE INSTRUMENT RECORD:
INSTRUM    DC      I1'$7F'                 ;FIRST SEGMENT
           DC      I2'$7F00'
           DC      I1'$70'                 ;SECOND
           DC      I2'$0114'
           DC      I1'$30'                 ;THIRD
           DC      I2'$0030'
           DC      I1'0'                   ;FOURTH
           DC      I2'$0514'
```

```
247         DC      I1'0'                   ;FILL OUT TO 8 W/ZERO
248         DC      I2'00'
249         DC      I1'0'                   ;SIX
250         DC      I2'00'
251         DC      I1'0'                   ;SEVEN
252         DC      I2'00'
253         DC      I1'0'                   ;EIGHT
254         DC      I2'00'
255         DC      I1'3'                   ;RELEASE SEGMENT - 1
256         DC      I1'32'                  ;PRIORITY INCREMENT
257         DC      I1'2'                   ;PITCH BEND RANGE
258         DC      I1'40'                  ;VIBRATO DEPTH
259         DC      I1'40'                  ;VIBRATO SPEED
260         DC      I1'0'                   ;NOT USED
261         DC      I1'1'                   ;NUMBER OF WAVEPTRS FOR OSC A
262         DC      I1'1'                   ;NUMBER OF WAVEPTRS FOR OSC B
263         DC      I1'112,0,0,0,0,16' ;
264         DC      I1'112,0,0,0,0,16' ;
265
266         END
```

After typing in the code, save it as PHONE.ASM. Assemble, link, and run the program. The phone will ring for six durations, after which you'll return to the *APW* shell.

Description of PHONE.ASM

The following comments pertain only to the sound portion of the code.

The Sound Manager is started in lines 55–58. Note how the address of the direct page is not saved in memory, but immediately pushed to the stack in line 55. Because this is the only tool set using a direct page, this trick can be used.

Lines 63–69 copy the sound wave into sound RAM. First, the wave's address is pushed, followed by the starting value in the DOC (zero is fine), and the length of the wave.

The Note Synthesizer is loaded and started in lines 74–85. First, it's loaded from disk using the LoadOneTool function of the Tool Locator in lines 74–77, and then NSStartUp is called with an update range of 60 Hz and no user routine.

Lines 90–117 simulate the ringing phone. The key is the JSR to the subroutine Play in line 97. This routine is called 33 times, with a delay between each time, in lines 95–105. The delay prevents the sounds from running into each other and distorting the ringing noise. Lines 107–115 create a delay between the rings, just as a real phone pauses between rings.

Once the phone has finished ringing, all tool sets are shut down and the program's memory is released in the Quit Code, lines 122–148.

The Play subroutine in lines 153–181 contains the sound generation code. First, a sound generator is allocated in lines 155–159. The generator number is retrieved and saved in line 161 and 162. Next, the NoteOn function is called to play the semitone $006E in lines 164–172. Finally, the semitone is stopped by the NoteOff function in lines 174–179.

The sound wave used by this program is defined in lines 213–234. These values were produced by the BASIC program listed earlier in this chapter. The only difference is that the value zero generated by the BASIC program was changed to one for use in the sound wave (zero shuts off the sound generator).

The instrument record is listed in lines 239–264. Because very little is known about the values in the record, the numbers listed were experimented with until a bell-ringing sound was produced. Other than that, nothing is known about the individual values beyond what was earlier described.

PIANO

This program uses the keyboard like a piano. For each key pressed, a different sound is produced. It's a slight modification on the PHONE program, but there are enough changes that it warrants having its own listing.

```
*********************************************************************************
* PIANO PROGRAM
*********************************************************************************

           ABSADDR ON
           KEEP PIANO                    ;EXE FILE

MAIN       START

           PHK                           ;ENVIRONMENT
           PLB

;----------------------------------------
; START SOME BASIC TOOLSETS

```

```
         LDX    #$0201          ;TLSTARTUP
         JSL    $E10000
         PEA    $0000
         LDX    #$0202          ;MMSTARTUP
         JSL    $E10000
         JSR    ERRORH
         PLA
         STA    USERID
         LDX    #$0203          ;MISC TOOLS STARTUP
         JSL    $E10000
         JSR    ERRORH
;-----------------------------------------
; GRAB ONE DIRECT PAGE FOR THE SOUND MGR.
         PEA    $0000           ;LONG RESULT SPACE
         PEA    $0000
         PEA    $0000           ;ONE PAGE
         PEA    $0100
         LDA    USERID          ;PROGRAM'S ID
         PHA
         PEA    $C005           ;ATTRIBUTES
         PEA    $0000           ;BLOCK'S START
         PEA    $0000           ; (DON'T CARE)
         LDX    #$0902          ;NEWHANDLE
         JSL    $E10000
         JSR    ERRORH
         PLA                    ;GET HANDLE OF NEW BLOCK
         STA    0               ; INTO ZERO PAGE
         PLA
         STA    2
         LDA    [0]             ;GET START ADD. IN A
;-----------------------------------------
; START THE SOUND TOOLS
         PHA                    ;PASS THE DPAGE START
         LDX    #$0208          ;SOUNDSTARTUP
         JSL    $E10000
         JSR    ERRORH
```

```
;----------------------------------------
; COPY THE WAVEFORM INTO THE DOC
           PEA    WAVE|-16          ;WAVE FORM'S ADDRESS
           PEA    WAVE
           PEA    $0                ;STARTING ADDRESS IN DOC
           PEA    $100              ;LENGTH
           LDX    #$0908            ;WRITERAMBLOCK
           JSL    $E10000
           JSR    ERRORH
;----------------------------------------
; LOAD AND START THE NOTE SYNTHESIZER
           PEA    $0019             ;TOOL $19, NOTE SYNTH.
           PEA    $0000             ;VERSION NUMBER
           LDX    #$0F01            ;LOADONETOOL
           JSL    $E10000
           JSR    ERRORH
           PEA    $0046             ;60 HZ UPDATES
           PEA    $0000             ;ZERO = NO INTERRUPT ROUTINE
           PEA    $0000
           LDX    #$0219            ;NSSTARTUP
           JSL    $E10000
           JSR    ERRORH
;----------------------------------------
; NOW, MAESTRO...
           PEA    MESSAGE|-16       ;A TITLE MESSAGE
           PEA    MESSAGE
           LDX    #$200C            ;WRITECSTRING
           JSL    $E10000
GETKEY     PHA                      ;RESULT SPACE
           PEA    $0000             ;DON'T ECHO CHAR.
           LDX    #$220C            ;READCHAR
           JSL    $E10000
           PLA
           AND    #$007F            ;GET RID OF JUNK
           CMP    #$1B              ;WAS ESC PRESSED?
```

```
            BEQ     EXIT                ;LEAVE IF SO
            STA     NOTE                ;SAVE THE CHARACTER
            JSR     PLAY                ;RING THE BELL (SOUND)
            BRA     GETKEY
;----------------------------------------
; END OF PROGRAM, SHUTDOWN ALL TOOLS
EXIT        ANOP
            LDX     #$0319              ;NSSHUTDOWN
            JSL     $E10000
            LDX     #$0308              ;SOUNDSHUTDOWN
            JSL     $E10000
            LDX     #$0303              ;MTSHUTDOWN
            JSL     $E10000
            LDA     USERID              ;FOR CLOSING ALL HANDLES
            PHA
            LDX     #$1102              ;DISPOSEALL
            JSL     $E10000
            LDA     USERID
            PHA
            LDX     #$0302              ;MMSHUTDOWN
            JSL     $E10000
            LDX     #$0301              ;TLSHUTDOWN
            JSL     $E10000
            JSL     $E100A8             ;PRODOS 16 CALL
            DC      I2'$29'             ;QUIT
            DC      I2'QPARAMS'         ;QUIT PARAMETERS
*******************************************************************************
* PLAY A SOUND USING THE NOTE SYNTH
*******************************************************************************
PLAY        ANOP
```

```
           PEA    $0000                ;RESULT SPACE
           PEA    $0040                ;PRIORITY
           LDX    #$0919               ;ALLOCGEN
           JSL    $E10000
           JSR    ERRORH
           PLA                         ;GET GENERATOR NUMBER
           STA    GENNUM
           LDA    GENNUM
           PHA
           LDA    NOTE                 ;NOTE ENTERED
           PHA
           PEA    $0080                ;VOLUME
           PEA    INSTRUM|-16          ;LONG PTR TO INSTRUMENT DEF
           PEA    INSTRUM
           LDX    #$0B19               ;NOTEON
           JSL    $E10000
           JSR    ERRORH
           LDA    GENNUM
           PHA
           LDA    NOTE
           PHA
           LDX    #$0C19               ;NOTEOFF
           JSL    $E10000
           JSR    ERRORH
           RTS
******************************************************************************
* ERROR HANDLER
******************************************************************************
ERRORH     ANOP
           BCS    UHOH                 ;CARRY SET IF ERROR
           RTS                         ;ELSE, RETURN
UHOH       ANOP
           PHA                         ;ERROR NUMBER ON STACK
           PEA    $0000                ;USE DEFAULT MSG.
           PEA    $0000
           LDX    #$1503               ;SYSFAILMGR
```

```
         JSL    $E10000
*********************************************************************************
* DATA AREA
*********************************************************************************
USERID   DS     2
RINGS    DS     2
GENNUM   DS     2
NOTE     DS     2
QPARAMS  ANOP
         DC     I4'0'
         DC     I2'0'
MESSAGE  DC     "PLAY THE KEYBOARD LIKE A PIANO."
         DC     I1'13,10'
         DC     C"SOME LETTERS MAY BE TOO HIGH PITCHED TO HEAR (USE CAPS LOCK)."
         DC     I1'13,10'
         DC     C"PRESS ESC TO QUIT."
         DC     I1'0'
;-----------------------------------------
; THIS DATA APPROXIMATES A SINE WAVE
WAVE     DC     I1'1,1,2,3,4,6,7,8,9,11,12,13'
         DC     I1'14,15,17,18,19,20,21,23,24,25,26,27'
         DC     I1'29,30,31,32,33,34,36,37,38,39,40,41'
         DC     I1'42,44,45,46,47,48,49,50,51,52,53,54'
         DC     I1'55,56,57,58,59,60,61,62,63,64,65,66'
         DC     I1'67,68,69,70,70,71,72,73,74,75,75,76'
         DC     I1'77,78,79,79,80,81,81,82,83,84,84,85'
         DC     I1'85,86,87,87,88,88,89,90,90,91,91,92'
         DC     I1'92,93,93,93,94,94,95,95,95,96,96,96'
         DC     I1'97,97,97,97,98,98,98,98,98,99,99,99'
         DC     I1'99,99,99,99,99,99,99,99,99,99,99,99'
         DC     I1'99,99,99,99,99,99,99,99,98,98,98,98'
         DC     I1'97,97,97,97,96,96,96,95,95,95,94,94'
         DC     I1'93,93,93,92,92,91,91,90,90,89,88,88'
         DC     I1'87,87,86,85,85,84,84,83,82,81,81,80'
         DC     I1'79,79,78,77,76,75,75,74,73,72,71,70'
         DC     I1'70,69,68,67,66,65,64,63,62,61,60,59'
         DC     I1'58,57,56,55,54,53,52,51,50,49,48,47'
```

```
         DC      I1'46,45,44,42,41,40,39,38,37,36,35,33'
         DC      I1'32,31,30,29,28,26,25,24,23,22,20,19'
         DC      I1'18,17,15,14,13,12,11,9,8,7,6,4'
         DC      I1'3,2,1,1'

;---------------------------------------
; THE INSTRUMENT RECORD:

INSTRUM  DC      I1'$7F'                ;FIRST SEGMENT
         DC      I2'$7F00'
         DC      I1'$70'                ;SECOND
         DC      I2'$0114'
         DC      I1'$20'                ;THIRD
         DC      I2'$0030'
         DC      I1'0'                  ;FOURTH
         DC      I2'$0514'
         DC      I1'0'                  ;FILL OUT TO 8 W/ZERO
         DC      I2'00'
         DC      I1'0'                  ;SIX
         DC      I2'00'
         DC      I1'0'                  ;SEVEN
         DC      I2'00'
         DC      I1'0'                  ;EIGHT
         DC      I2'00'
         DC      I1'3'                  ;RELEASE SEGMENT - 1
         DC      I1'32'                 ;PRIORITY INCREMENT
         DC      I1'2'                  ;PITCH BEND RANGE
         DC      I1'40'                 ;VIBRATO DEPTH
         DC      I1'40'                 ;VIBRATO SPEED
         DC      I1'0'                  ;NOT USED
         DC      I1'4'                  ;NUMBER OF WAVEPTRS FOR OSC A
         DC      I1'4'                  ;NUMBER OF WAVEPTRS FOR OSC B

         DC      I1'59,0,0,0,0,16'
         DC      I1'71,0,0,0,0,0'
         DC      I1'59,0,0,0,0,16'
         DC      I1'59,0,0,0,0,0'

         DC      I1'112,0,0,0,0,16'
         DC      I1'59,0,0,0,0,0'
         DC      I1'71,0,0,0,0,16'
         DC      I1'127,0,0,0,0,12'

         END
```

After typing this program in, save it as PIANO.ASM. Assemble, link, and run the program. Then, type a few keys on the keyboard. Some keys, especially those with high ASCII values, will produce high pitched sounds. Capital-letter keys can be better heard. The sound produced is very close to that of a piano.

Description of PIANO.ASM

The following items are notably different from PHONE.ASM with regard to sound.

The value of the notes generated by the Play subroutine are produced by the ASCII code of the key pressed on the keyboard. The key is returned by the ReadChar function in lines 95–100. The value is further manipulated to make sure it's an ASCII code and that the Esc key, which ends the program, was not pressed. The value of the key is stored in Note and then execution jumps to the subroutine Play.

The Play subroutine in lines 144–174 is very similar to the Play subroutine in the PHONE program. The exception is that the value for the semitone produced by NoteOn is obtained from the memory location Note, the value of the key pressed. This value is used with NoteOn in line 157 and with NoteOff in line 168.

The sound wave is the same sine wave as used by PHONE; however, the instrument record in lines 240–173 is altered. The most apparent difference is in the multiple wavelists used in lines 265–268 and 270–273. Again, little is known about what these mean other than that they produced a better sound than when only one wavelist was specified.

Chapter 19

Short Cuts

Much of the code encountered in this book is very inefficient. Its primary purpose is to illustrate toolbox programming in machine language. While it gets the job done and is easy to understand and follow, there are better and faster ways to accomplish the same things.

This chapter shows how

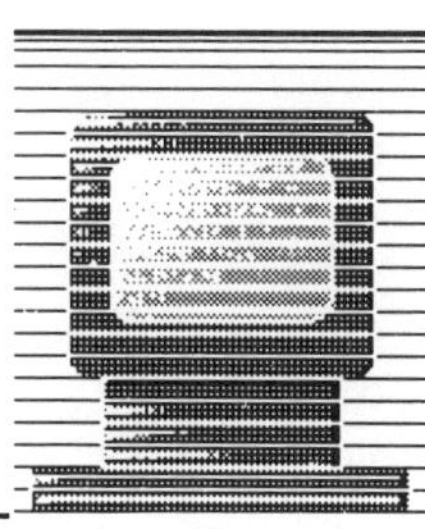

to optimize your code. Your toolbox applications can be streamlined by using the subroutines presented here. These techniques can be considered more advanced than what has been used so far.

Eliminating Redundancy

These special routines were designed and written to eliminate the redundancy of certain toolbox functions. By taking advantage of them and using them in your programming, you will be able to

- Reduce the amount of code produced by the assembler
- Conserve memory, which implies that your programs will launch and run faster
- Modify and update your program more effectively
- Make your code more readable through the use of the special utility subroutines

Please note that the following examples are only snippets from larger programs. They do not represent completed code. You can apply them to any of your existing code or feel free to use them in any future programs. These examples are all of common toolbox routines, most of which are required by every program you write.

Managing Direct Page Buffers

One of the first things an application does is consult the Memory Manager. Your program will want two things: A User ID for the program, and direct-page space for the various tool sets. For example, QuickDraw II, the Event Manager, Dialog Manager, Window Manager, and others all need direct-page space.

Before, while, or during the writing of your program, you must determine the amount of direct-page space needed for each of your tool sets. And, if you add a tool set later, you'll need to adjust this value.

As an example, suppose your program needs ten pages, or $A00 bytes, of direct-page space. A typical call to the Memory Manager's NewHandle function would be

```
DPMEM  EQU   $00000A00       ;AMOUNT OF MEMORY NEEDED
       PHA                   ;MAKE ROOM FOR A LONG RESULT
       PHA
```

```
PEA    DPMEM-16         ;SPECIFY SIZE OF THE BLOCK
PEA    DPMEM
LDA    USERID           ;GET OUR USER ID
PHA                     ; AND PUSH IT ON STACK
PEA    $C005            ;MEMORY ATTRIBUTES FOR DPAGE
PEA    $0000            ;USE ZERO
PEA    $0000
LDX    #$0902           ;NEWHANDLE
JSL    $E10000          ;CALL THE TOOLBOX
```

After making this call, the handle to the direct page's memory block is pulled from the stack and safely stored elsewhere in your program. So far, the values have been stored in a memory location "Handle" and in the program's zero page.

```
PLA                     ;A = LOW BYTE OF HANDLE
PLX                     ;X = HIGH BYTE OF HANDLE
STA    HANDLE           ;SAVE THE HANDLE FOR DISPOSAL
STX    HANDLE+2         ;WHEN SHUTTING DOWN
STA    0                ;CREATE A LONG POINTER TO
STX    2                ;THE ADDRESS VALUE WE NEED
LDA    [0]              ;NOW GET THE MEMORY BLOCK'S ADDRESS
STA    DPAGE            ;AND SAVE A COPY OF IT IN DPAGE
```

From the zero page, the actual location of the memory block in bank $00 is obtained. This value is quickly stuffed into the memory location DPage.

Every time a tool set requiring its own direct page is started, you need to perform some arithmetic. So far, it's been common to handle this operation as follows:

```
LDA    DPAGE            ;GET ADDRESS OF MEMORY BLOCK
CLC                     ;CLEAR CARRY FOR ADDITION
ADC    #$300            ;ADD IN THE NEXT BUFFER'S OFFSET
PHA                     ;PUSH IT ON THE STACK FOR THE CALL
```

There are some problems with this approach. Just to be mean, they're placed in the following list:

- It's repetitious. You'll do this many times before calling a tool set's Startup function.
- You are responsible for remembering what the offset will be. If you remove or insert a new tool set, you'll have to adjust all your offset calculations.
- If you start up many tool sets, it can be a mess.

The following subroutine calculates the address of the next available direct page buffer and returns it in both the accumulator and Y registers.

```
GETDP   LDA   #$100           ;ASK FOR ONE 256 BYTE DP BLOCK
GETDPS  CLC                   ;ALTERNATE ENTRY POINT
        LDY   DPAGE           ;GET CURRENT BASE ADDRESS IN Y
        ADC   DPAGE           ;ADD TO LAST DP BUFFER ADDRESS
        STA   DPAGE           ;UPDATE BASE ADDRESS
        TYA                   ;RETURN ENTRY VALUE IN A
        RTS
```

The value of the direct page's starting location is saved in DPage. This is first loaded into the Y register for storage. Next, the value of DPage is added to the value in the A register, $100. This is saved in the DPage variable as the start of the next direct page. The current value, saved in Y, is then transferred to the A register and returned from the subroutine.

Now, when you need to get the address of the next $100-byte direct page buffer, perform a JSR to GetDP. Upon return, the accumulator contains the desired address. The DPage variable will contain a starting address for the next tool set's direct page.

By using the above subroutine, the following code could be used to start the Menu Manager:

```
        LDA   USERID          ;PREPARE TO STARTUP MENU MANAGER
        PHA                   ;PUSH OUR USER ID FIRST
        JSR   GETDP           ;GET NEXT DIRECT PAGE ADDRESS
        PHA                   ;AND PUSH IT ONTO THE STACK
        LDX   #$020F          ;MENUSTARTUP
        JSL   $E10000         ;STARTUP THE MENU MANAGER
```

If your program needs to allocate more than one page of memory (starting up the Print Manager, for example), first load the accumulator with the amount of space you require, then JSR to the subroutine's alternate entry point, GetDPs.

```
        LDA   USERID          ;PREPARE TO STARTUP PRINT MANAGER
        PHA                   ;PUSH USER ID FIRST
        LDA   #$200           ;REQUIRES 2 DIRECT PAGES
        JSR   GETDPS          ;GET NEXT DIRECT PAGE ADDRESS
        PHA                   ;AND PUSH IT ONTO THE STACK
        LDX   #$0213          ;PMSTARTUP
        JSL   $E10000         ;STARTUP THE PRINT MANAGER
```

For this example, $200 bytes of direct-page space will be allocated. The next direct page location will be calculated as DPage + $200.

The GetDP subroutine continues to maintain the DPage variable for subsequent calls to GetDP. The value for the next direct page location is updated automatically. You still have to initially calculate the total space needed for the direct page's memory block.

Automatic Shutdown

Most applications, especially those using windows and pull-down menus, will use the Tool Locator's LoadTools function to read tool sets from disk into memory. For example, the following tool list might be used in a fairly complex program.

```
TOOLIST  DC    I'3'                     ;COUNT WORD
         DC    I'$0E,0'                 ;WINDOW MANAGER
         DC    I'$0F,0'                 ;MENU MANAGER
         DC    I'$10,0'                 ;CONTROL MANAGER
```

One way to optimize the tool list would be to make the assembler do the work of calculating the number of items in the list. In this way, you could add and subtract items without needing to update the count word.

The following code borrows its logic from the Pascal strings used by the toolbox. The first word in the list contains a calculation to figure out the exact count of tool sets in the list. The number is divided by four because each item in the list takes two words—or four bytes—of space.

```
TOOLIST  DC    I'(ENDLIST-TOOLIST-1)/4' ;COUNT WORD CALCULATION
         DC    I'$0E,0'                 ;WINDOW MANAGER
         DC    I'$0F,0'                 ;MENU MANAGER
         DC    I'$10,0'                 ;CONTROL MANAGER
         :
         :
ENDLIST  ANOP                           ;END OF TOOL LIST
```

Items can now be freely added to or subtracted from the list. As the list telescopes, the assembler will always calculate its proper size.

When LoadTools function is called, it looks into your boot disk's SYSTEM/TOOLS subdirectory. LoadTools searches for files named TOOLxxx, where xxx matches the tool set's number in decimal. If the TOOLxxx file is found, its version number is compared with that in your tool list. If the number is greater than the number you specified, the tool set is loaded from disk into memory. Otherwise, an error occurs.

Incidentally, the LoadTools function will not load a tool set which already resides in memory. If a program prior to yours has loaded a few tool sets, they will still be in memory—even after the previous program has shut them down.

Consider the following tool list.

```
TOOLIST  DC    I'(ENDLIST-TOOLIST-1)/4'   ;COUNT WORD
         DC    I'$01,0'                   ;TOOL LOCATOR
         DC    I'$02,0'                   ;MEMORY MANAGER
         DC    I'$03,0'                   ;MISCELLANEOUS TOOLS
         DC    I'$04,0'                   ;QUICKDRAW II
         DC    I'$06,0'                   ;EVENT MANAGER
         DC    I'$0E,0'                   ;WINDOW MANAGER
         DC    I'$0F,0'                   ;MENU MANAGER
         DC    I'$10,0'                   ;CONTROL MANAGER
         DC    I'$12,0'                   ;QUICKDRAW AUX.
         DC    I'$14,0'                   ;LINEEDIT
         DC    I'$15,0'                   ;DIALOG MANAGER
         DC    I'$05,0'                   ;DESK MANAGER
         DC    I'$17,0'                   ;STANDARD FILES
ENDLIST  ANOP                             ;END OF TOOL LIST
```

LoadTools will skip over those tool sets already available in memory. Only those tool sets in the list which are not already resident are loaded. The ROM tool sets have been included in the above list to further illustrate the point. Even though they are already in memory, having the LoadTools call attempt to load them from disk will not crash the program.

Besides being used by LoadTools, the tool list also provides a resource for keeping track of which tool sets need to be shut down before your program quits. By taking advantage of the tool set's number in the list, your program could automatically shut down every tool set that was started up.

The following code could be used as a general shut down procedure. This eliminates the repetitive series of LDX #$03xx and JSL $E10000 calls commonly used to shut down the tool sets.

```
SHUTDOWN LDA   TOOLIST          ;GET NUMBER OF TOOL SETS IN LIST
         ASL   A                ;...TIMES 2
         ASL   A                ;...TIMES 2 AGAIN (OR TIMES 4)
         TAX                    ;MAKE X AN INDEX OVER LONG WORDS
         LDA   TOOLIST-2,X      ;GET A TOOL SET ID FROM THE LIST
         CMP   #2+1             ;IS IT MEMORY MANAGER (#2)
;                               ;OR TOOL LOCATOR (#1) ?
         BCC   SHUT0            ;NO, SKIP IF LESS THAN
         ORA   #$0300           ;TURN IT INTO THE SHUTDOWN FUNCTION
         TAX                    ;PLACE IN X FOR THE FUNCTION CALL
         JSL   $E10000          ;PERFORM THE TOOL SHUTDOWN
SHUT0    DEC   TOOLIST          ;TOOLIST = TOOLIST - 1
         BNE   SHUTDOWN         ;IF NOT THE LAST ONE, DO THE NEXT
         LDA   USERID           ;PUSH USER ID
         PHA
         LDX   #$1102           ;DISPOSEALL
         JSL   $E10000          ;FREE ALL MEMORY USED
         LDA   USERID           ;SHUT DOWN MEMORY MANAGER TOOL
         PHA
         LDX   #$0302           ;MMSHUTDOWN
         JSL   $E10000
         LDX   #$0301           ;SHUT DOWN TOOL LOCATOR LAST
         JSL   $E10000
         RTS
```

This subroutine works its way through the tool list. The same list of tool sets used by LoadTools now serves as a reference for your program's shutdown procedure.

The loop between ShutDown and Shut0 reads each tool set number from the tool list. That number is logically ORed with $0300 to create the tool set's ShutDown function. When the value is transferred to the X register and a JSL is made to the toolbox, the tool set is shut down.

The variable Toolist, which contains the number of tools in the list, serves as an index into the list. As each tool is shutdown, the Toolist variable is decremented. This continues until all tools are shut down.

Two special cases are the Memory Manager and Tool Locator. These tool sets must be shut down last and in that order. Their tool set numbers are checked for in the above subroutine with the CMP #2 + 1 instruction. If found in the list, either tool set is skipped using the BCC (Branch if Carry Clear). (Both 2 and 1 are less than 3, and the BCC instruction branches if the value in A is less than 3.)

Once the the program has completely cycled through the tool list, the Memory Manager disposes of all handles used by the program, then the Memory Manager and Tool Locator tool sets are shut down.

If you add an additional tool set in your program, you need only update your tool list. No longer is it necessary to change the count word value at the start of the list, nor do you need to add the tool set's ShutDown function to your program's quit code. (You still need to start up the tool.)

Installing Pull-Down Menus

Installing pull-down menus is another potential space-waster in your applications. For example, the following code is used to place just one menu structure into the system's menu bar.

```
            PHA                     ;LONG RESULT SPACE
            PHA
            PEA    FILEMENU|-16     ;POINT TO OUR FILE MENU STRUCTURE
            PEA    FILEMENU
            LDX    #$2D0F           ;NEWMENU
            JSL    $E10000          ;CREATE THE NEW MENU
;                                   ;(HANDLE IS ON THE STACK)
            PEA    $0000            ;INSERT MENU BEFORE ALL OTHERS
            LDX    #$0D0F           ;INSERTMENU
            JSL    $E10000
```

This creates and inserts one pull-down menu. Simply repeat the above steps for each menu in your program.

Imagine if you have nine menus to install. It would take up quite a bit of code and be very repetitive. In fact, the only thing that would differ from one menu insertion to the next would be the address of the menu's data structure.

By building a loop around the basic creation and insertion routines for one menu, you can cut down on a lot of extra work, space, and time.

```
NEXTMENU    PHA                     ;LONG RESULT SPACE
            PHA
            PHB                     ;PUSH DATA BANK REGISTER TWICE
            PHB                     ;(BECAUSE PHB PUSHES ONLY A BYTE)
            LDA    MENUTABLE        ;GET MENU COUNT
            ASL    A                ;MULTIPLY BY 2
            TAX                     ;TO MAKE IT AN INDEX
            LDA    MENUTABLE,X      ;GET ADDRESS OF NEXT MENU STRUCTURE
```

```
        PHA                     ;AND PUSH IT ON THE STACK
        LDX     #$2D0F          ;NEWMENU
        JSL     $E10000         ;CREATE THE NEW MENU
                                ;(HANDLE IS ON THE STACK)
        PEA     $0000           ;INSERT MENU BEFORE ALL OTHERS
        LDX     #$0D0F          ;INSERTMENU
        JSL     $E10000
        DEC     MENUTABLE       ;DECREMENT COUNTER
        BNE     NEXTMENU        ;AND LOOP UNTIL NO MORE MENUS
        RTS
```

By adding just seven instructions to the basic menu creation procedure, the above routine installs any number of pull-down menus.

The only major change is that the address of the menu's record structure is kept in a table and referenced using a variable at the table's start, just like the tool list. The two PHB instructions put the program's data bank on the stack (covered in Chapter 10). The location of the menu's record is kept in the list and read in the same way the tool sets were read for the shutdown code.

The list of menus would appear as follows. Remember, each menu is actually a pointer to a menu record.

```
MENUTABLE DC    I'(TABLEEND-MENUTABLE-1)/2'    ;COUNT WORD
          DC    I'APPLEMENU'
          DC    I'FILEMENU'
          DC    I'EDITMENU'
          DC    I'OPTIONSMENU'
          DC    I'WINDOWSMENU'
          DC    I'FONTSMENU'
          DC    I'STYLEMENU'
          DC    I'BINGMENU'
TABLEEND  ANOP
```

Not only will this program save memory, but for programs with many menus, it makes it easier to add or remove a menu. Just place another pointer to the menu's structure into MenuTable and the menu will appear on the screen.

Conclusions

The tricks discussed above are typical among Apple programmers weaned on computer systems with only 48K of RAM. On those machines, programmers attempted to squeeze every last byte of free memory out of the computer, trying to make their jobs easier at the same time.

Just because the Apple IIGS has many hundreds of kilobytes in RAM doesn't mean that sloppy code is allowable. It doesn't take an expert to spot short cuts provided in the toolbox. A good example is the use of templates when defining items in a dialog box (see the chapter on dialog boxes).

You may notice that those routines which use the templates appear quite late in the Dialog Manager reference. Perhaps they were added as an afterthought by those members of the Toolbox Design team who saw inefficiencies with the other method of doing things.

You should find it easy to eliminate redundancies in your own toolbox applications. Optimizing code and making it efficient should be a part of any programmer's repertoire.

Tool Sets

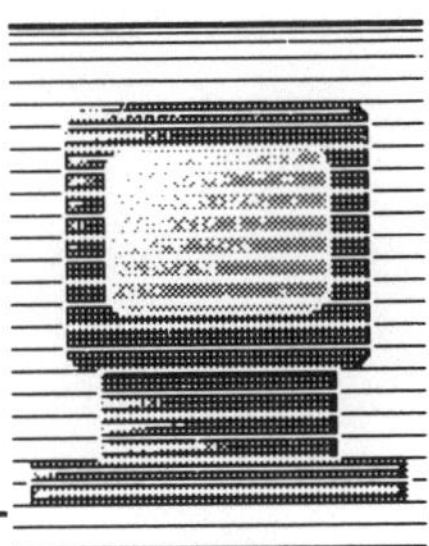

Toolbox Call Index

All known toolbox calls are documented in the following indices. Each of the 835 calls was extensively researched to insure that it performed as documented.

The tool sets are listed numerically, starting with $01 (the Tool Locator), through $1C (the List Manager). Within each index, the tool set functions are presented in numerical order.

At the end of this section is an indexed alphabetical list of all the tool sets' function names.

The Apple IIGS Toolbox Tool Sets

Hex	Dec	Tool Set
$01	1	Tool Locator
$02	2	Memory Manager
$03	3	Misc. Tool Set
$04	4	QuickDraw II
$05	5	Desk Manager
$06	6	Event Manager
$07	7	Scheduler
$08	8	Sound Manager
$09	9	Apple Desktop Bus
$0A	10	SANE
$0B	11	Integer Math
$0C	12	Text Tool Set
$0D	13	(Internal Use)
$0E	14	Window Manager
$0F	15	Menu Manager
$10	16	Control Manager
$11	17	Loader
$12	18	QuickDraw II Aux.
$13	19	Print Manager
$14	20	Line Edit
$15	21	Dialog Manager
$16	22	Scrap Manager
$17	23	Standard File
$18	24	Disk Utilities
$19	25	Note Synthesizer
$1A	26	Note Sequencer
$1B	27	Font Manager
$1C	28	List Manager

Tool Sets

About the Tool Sets and Functions

Each entry starts out with the tool set's number, name, and release version (as this book goes to press).

Tool Set: $01
Tool Set Name: Tool Locator
Version Number: 1.2

This is followed by the tool set's functions in numeric order. For example,

Function: $0101
Name: TLBootInit
Initializes the Tool Locator.
Push: nothing
Pull: nothing
Errors: none
Comments: Do not make this call.

Function: After the word *Function,* the function number in hexadecimal, followed by the tool set number appears .

Name: Represents the name of the function as defined by Apple. This is followed by a brief description of what the function does.

Push: Shows the values to push on the stack before making the toolbox call. Values are listed in the order they are pushed. After each value is its size, either (B) for byte, (W) for word, or (L) for long word. If the value is an address, or memory location, it is a (L) long word composed of a bank number and memory offset within that bank. Unless otherwise specified, all (L) values are considered to be addresses or pointers to memory locations. Other (L) values are Handles and Values, and they are presented as such.

Pull: Shows the values to be pulled from the stack. The first value listed is the first value pulled from the stack. Values marked with the symbol (L) follow the same rules as for Push (above).

Errors: Indicates whether errors are possible. The error code appears in the A register after making the call. All error codes are listed at the end of each tool set. $0000 is returned if no error occurred.

Comments: Comments about the function, its values and results, possible cautions, or a combination of each. Two common comments are *This is an internal call* and *Do not make this call*. Both imply that your applications should not meddle with that particular function. The first comment refers to functions which are used by other toolbox functions. These functions are not designed for use by your applications and, instead, are called using other toolbox routines. The second comment is a warning that the call should not be made and might cause your computer to crash. These routines are also used internally by the toolbox and there's no good reason to call them.

The following example is from the Text tool set, number $0C function $22.

Function: $220C
Name: ReadChar
Reads one character from the input device.
Push: Result Space (W); Echo flag (W)
Pull: ASCII Character (W)
Errors: Possible Pascal errors
Comments: Echo flag is $0001 to echo, $0000 no echo. The character returned is the LSB of the word; its high bit is clear. The character is affected by the AND and OR masks of function $09.

This function reads a character from the input device (usually the keyboard). The Result Space first pushed on the stack can be $0000 or any other "throw-away" value. The toolbox returns the character from the keyboard in this space. For the Echo flag, as described in the Comments section, either $0001 or $0000 is pushed to echo, or not, respectively, the character typed to the screen.

$0101

The character input is pulled from the stack. Because it is a word value (W), the MSB is insignificant. The character typed will be in the LSB of the word.

Tool Set $01: Tool Locator

Tool Set: $01
Tool Set Name: Tool Locator
Version Number: 1.2

Function: $0101
Name: TLBootInit
Initialize Tool Locator.
Push: nothing
Pull: nothing
Errors: none
Comments: Do not make this call.

Function: $0201
Name: TLStartUp
Starts the Tool Locator.
Push: nothing
Pull: nothing
Errors: none
Comments: This call must be made before any other tools are used. TLStartUp is the first function called in any application.

Function: $0301
Name: TLShutDown
Shuts down the Tool Locator.
Push: nothing
Pull: nothing
Errors: none
Comments: As with function $02, this must be the last function called just before a program quits.

Function: $0401
Name: TLVersion
Returns version number of the Tool Locator.
Push: Result Space (W)
Pull: Version Number (W)
Errors: none
Comments: LSB is major release, MSB minor release.

Function: $0501
Name: TLReset
Called when the computer is reset.
Push: nothing
Pull: nothing
Errors: none
Comments: Do not make this call.

Function: $0601
Name: TLStatus
Returns activity status of the Tool Locator.
Push: Result Space (W)
Pull: Status (W)
Errors: none
Comments: The Tool Locator is always active.

Function: $0901
Name: GetTSPtr
Returns a pointer to the tool set's Function Pointer Table (FPT).
Push: Result Space (L); Tool Type (W); Tool Set (W)
Pull: FPT Pointer (L)
Errors: none
Comments: Tool Type is $0000 for system tools, $8000 for user-defined tools.

Function: $0A01
Name: SetTSPtr
Sets a tool set's FPT to the indicated address.
Push: Tool Type (W); Tool Set (W); FPT Pointer (L)
Pull: nothing
Errors: none
Comments:

Function: $0B01
Name: GetFuncPtr
Returns a pointer to a specific function number, minus one.
Push: Result Space (L); Tool Type (W); Function number (B); Tool Set (B)
Pull: Function Pointer (L)
Errors: none
Comments:

Function: $0C01
Name: GetWAP
Returns the Work Area Pointer (WAP) for a tool set.
Push: Result Space (L); Tool Type (W); Tool Set (W)
Pull: WAP (L)
Errors: none
Comments:

Function: $0D01
Name: SetWAP
Sets the WAP for a tool set.
Push: Tool Type (W); Tool Set (W); New Work Area Pointer (L)
Pull: nothing
Errors: none
Comments:

Function: $0E01
Name: LoadTools
Loads a list of tool sets into memory.
Push: Pointer to tool table (L)
Pull: nothing
Errors: $0110
Comments: See Chapter 9 for an example.

Function: $0F01
Name: LoadOneTool
Loads a single tool set into memory.
Push: Tool Set (W); Version number (W)
Pull: nothing
Errors: $0110
Comments: Version number if the minimum, $0000 loads all versions.

Function: $1001
Name: UnloadOneTool
Unloads the specified tool set.
Push: Tool Set (W)
Pull: nothing
Errors: none
Comments:

Function: $1101
Name: TLMountVolume
Displays a dialog box prompting the user to enter the System Disk.
Push: Result Space (W); Min X (W); Min Y (W); Title String Pointer (L); 2nd String Pointer (L); Button 1 Text Pointer (L); Button 2 Text Pointer (L)
Pull: Button number (W)
Errors: none
Comments: If your application is not using the graphics mode, use function $12 instead. Strings are Pascal and should be less than around 40 characters long.

Function: $1201
Name: TLTextMountVolume
Displays a dialog box on the text screen.
Push: Result Space (W); Title String Pointer (L); 2nd String Pointer (L); Button 1 Text Pointer (L); Button 2 Text Pointer (L)
Pull: Button number (W)
Errors: none
Comments: Return key = $0001, ESC = $0002.

Summary of Tool Set $01 Error Codes

$0100 Unable to mount system startup volume
$0110 Bad tool set version number

Tool Set $02: Memory Manager

Tool Set: $02
Tool Set Name: Memory Manager
Version Number: 1.2

Function: $0102
Name: MMBootInit
Initialize the Memory Manager.
Push: nothing
Pull: nothing
Errors: none
Comments: Do not make this call.

Function: $0202
Name: MMStartUp
Starts the Memory Manager.
Push: Result Space (W)
Pull: UserID (W)
Errors: $0207
Comments: One of the first calls made by an application.

Function: $0302
Name: MMShutDown
Shuts down the Memory Manager.
Push: UserID (W)
Pull: nothing
Errors: none
Comments: Make this call when your application is finished.

Function: $0402
Name: MMVersion
Returns version number of the Memory Manager.
Push: Result Space (W)
Pull: Version Number (W)
Errors: none
Comments: LSB is major release, MSB minor release.

Function: $0502
Name: MMReset
Called when the computer is reset.
Push: nothing
Pull: nothing
Errors: $0201
Comments: Do not make this call.

Function: $0602
Name: MMStatus
Returns activity status of the Memory Manager.
Push: Result Space (W)
Pull: Status (W)
Errors: none
Comments: This call returns $FFFF for active, $0000 for inactive.

Function: $0902
Name: NewHandle
Makes a block of memory available to your program.
Push: Result Space (L); Block Size (L); UserID (W); Attributes (W); Address of Block (L)
Pull: Block's Handle (L)
Errors: $0201, $0204, $0207
Comments: See Chapter 8 for Attributes and other information.

Function: $0A02
Name: ReAllocHandle
Reallocates a purged block.
Push: Block Size (L); UserID (W); Attributes (W); Address of Block (L); Old Block's Handle (L)
Pull: nothing
Errors: $0201, $0203, $0204, $0206, $0207
Comments:

Function: $0B02
Name: RestoreHandle
Reallocates a purged block.
Push: Old Block's Handle (L)
Pull: nothing
Errors: $0201, $0203, $0206, $0208
Comments: Uses same parameters of original block (unlike function $0A which allows the parameters to be reset).

Function: $1002
Name: DisposeHandle
Deallocates a block and releases its memory.
Push: Block's Handle (L)
Pull: nothing
Errors: $0206
Comments: The block is deleted regardless of its locked status or purge level.

Function: $1102
Name: DisposeAll
Releases all blocks associated with a UserID.
Push: UserID (W)
Pull: nothing
Errors: $0207
Comments: Ruthless.

Function: $1202.
Name: PurgeHandle
Purges a block of memory.
Push: Block's Handle (L)
Pull: nothing
Errors: $0204, $0205, $0206
Comments: The block must be purgeable and unlocked. The block's handle is not deallocated by this call.

Function: $1302
Name: PurgeAll
Purges all blocks associated with a UserID.
Push: UserID (W)
Pull: nothing
Errors: $0204, $0205, $0207
Comments: The blocks must all be purgeable and unlocked.

Function: $1802
Name: GetHandleSize
Returns the size of a block associated with a given handle.
Push: Result Space (L); Handle (L)
Pull: Block's Size (L)
Errors: $0206
Comments:

Function: $1902
Name: SetHandleSize
Resets the size, larger or smaller, of a given block.
Push: New size of block (L); Handle (L)
Pull: nothing
Errors: $0201, $0202, $0204, $0206
Comments:

Function: $1A02
Name: FindHandle
Returns handle in which an address is located.
Push: Result Space (L); Address (L)
Pull: Handle (L)
Errors: none
Comments:

Function: $1B02
Name: FreeMem
Returns memory available for programs.
Push: Result Space (L)
Pull: Integer Value (L)
Errors: none
Comments: Returns the total number of bytes in memory, not counting RAM disks or other allocated blocks.

Function: $1C02
Name: MaxBlock
Returns memory available to programs.
Push: Result Space (L)
Pull: Integer Value (L)
Errors: none
Comments: Returns the largest free block in memory.

Function: $1D02
Name: TotalMem
Returns total RAM in the System.
Push: Result Space (L)
Pull: Integer Value (L)
Errors: none
Comments: Returns all RAM in your IIGS, including the basic 256K, any RAM disks, and so on.

Function: $1E02
Name: CheckHandle
Tests a memory handle for validity.
Push: Handle (L)
Pull: nothing
Errors: $0206
Comments: The error is returned if the handle is invalid.

Function: $1F02
Name: CompactMem
Compacts Memory.
Push: nothing
Pull: nothing
Errors: none
Comments: Performs memory "garbage collection," purging purgeable blocks and reorganizing memory. Don't do this during an interrupt.

Function: $2002
Name: HLock
Locks and sets a specific handle to a purge level of zero.
Push: Handle (L)
Pull: nothing
Errors: $0206
Comments:

Function: $2102
Name: HLockAll
Locks and sets all handles associated with a specific UserID to a purge level of zero.
Push: UserID (W)
Pull: nothing
Errors: $0207
Comments:

Function: $2202
Name: HUnLock
Unlocks a block of memory.
Push: Handle (L)
Pull: nothing
Errors: $0206
Comments:

Function: $2302
Name: HUnLockAll
Unlocks all blocks of memory associated with a specific UserID.
Push: UserID (W)
Pull: nothing
Errors: $0207
Comments:

Function: $2402
Name: SetPurge
Resets the purge level of a given block.
Push: New Purge Level (W); Handle (L)
Pull: nothing
Errors: $0206
Comments: Only the lower two bits of the word pushed are significant.

Function: $2502
Name: SetPurgeAll
Resets the purge level for all blocks associated with a given UserID.
Push: New Purge Level (W); UserID (W)
Pull: nothing
Errors: $0207
Comments:

Function: $2802
Name: PtrToHand
Copies a number of bytes from a specific memory address to a handle.
Push: Source address (L); Destination handle (L); Length (L)
Pull: nothing
Errors: $0202, $0206
Comments:

Function: $2902
Name: HandToPtr
Copies a number of bytes from a handle to a specific memory address.
Push: Source handle (L); Destination address (L); Length (L)
Pull: nothing
Errors: $0202, $0206
Comments:

Function: $2A02
Name: HandToHand
Copies a number of bytes from one block to another.
Push: Source handle (L); Destination handle (L); Length (L)
Pull: nothing
Errors: $0202, $0206
Comments:

$2B02

Function: $2B02
Name: BlockMove
Copies a block of memory from one address to another.
Push: Source Address (L); Destination Address (L); Length (L)
Pull: nothing
Errors: none
Comments:

Summary of Tool Set $02 Error Codes

$0201 Unable to allocate block
$0202 Illegal operation on an empty handle
$0203 Empty handle expected for this operation
$0204 Illegal operation on a lock or immovable block
$0205 Attempt to purge an unpurgeable block
$0206 Invalid handle given
$0207 Invalid User ID given
$0208 Operation illegal on block specified attributes

Tool Set $03: Miscellaneous Tool Set

Tool Set: $03
Tool Set Name: Miscellaneous tool set
Version Number: 1.2

Function: $0103
Name: MTBootInit
Initialize the Miscellaneous tool set environment.
Push: nothing
Pull: nothing
Errors: none
Comments: Clears Heartbeat task pointer, tick counter, mouse flag. Don't make this call.

Function: $0203
Name: MTStartup
Starts up the Miscellaneous tool set.
Push: nothing
Pull: nothing
Errors: none
Comments:

Function: $0303
Name: MTShutDown
Shuts down the Miscellaneous tool set.
Push: nothing
Pull: nothing
Errors: none
Comments:

Function: $0403
Name: MTVersion
Returns the version number of the Miscellaneous tool set.
Push: Result Space (W)
Pull: Version number (W)
Errors: none
Comments:

Function: $0503
Name: MTReset
Called when the system is reset.
Push: nothing
Pull: nothing
Errors: none
Comments: Don't make this call.

Function: $0603
Name: MTStatus
Returns the activity status of the Miscellaneous tool set.
Push: Result Space (W)
Pull: Status flag (W)
Errors: none
Comments: $FFFF is always returned indicating an active state.

Function: $0903
Name: WriteBRAM
Write 256 bytes to the Apple IIGS's battery RAM.
Push: Address of 256 bytes of data (L)
Pull: nothing
Errors: none
Comments: Changes to battery RAM are not effected until after a reboot.

Function: $0A03
Name: ReadBRAM
Read battery RAM (256 bytes) to a specified address.
Push: Address of 256 byte buffer (L)
Pull: nothing
Errors: none
Comments: The first 252 bytes are battery RAM bytes, the last four bytes are checksum values.

Function: $0B03
Name: WriteBParam
Write a specific value into battery RAM.
Push: Value (W), Parameter Reference Number (W)
Pull: nothing
Errors: none
Comments: Changes to battery RAM are not effected until after a reboot.

Function: $0C03
Name: ReadBParam
Reads a specific value from battery RAM.
Push: Result Space (W), Parameter Reference Number (W)
Pull: Value (W)
Errors: none
Comments: Yes/Fast values are $0001 while No/Normal values are $0000.

Function: $0D03
Name: ReadTimeHex
Reads the time from the clock and return it in hex format.
Push: Result Space (W); (W); (W); (W)
Pull: Min/Sec (W); Year/Hour (W); Month/Day (W); Weekday/Null (W)
Errors: none
Comments: 00 = Sun, 00 = Jan, 00 = first day of month.

Function: $0E03
Name: WriteTimeHex
Sets the clock.
Push: Month/Day (W); Year/Hour (W); Minute/Second (W)
Pull: nothing
Errors: none
Comments: See function $0D.

Function: $0F03
Name: ReadASCIITime
Creates a 20-character string indicating the date and time.
Push: Buffer Address (L)
Pull: nothing
Errors: none
Comments: Text returned has the high bit set.

Function: $1003
Name: SetVector
Installs an interrupt vector address.
Push: Vector reference number (W); Address of the routine (L)
Pull: nothing
Errors: none
Comments: This installs the vector, not the interrupt service routine.

Function: $1103
Name: GetVector
Returns the address of an interrupt vector.
Push: Result Space (L); Vector reference number (W)
Pull: Vector's Address (L)
Errors: none
Comments:

Function: $1203
Name: SetHeartBeat
Places a task into the HeartBeat task manager queue.
Push: Pointer to task header (L)
Pull: nothing
Errors: $0303, $0304, $0305
Comments:

Function: $1303
Name: DelHeartBeat
Removes a task from the HeartBeat task queue.
Push: Pointer to task header (L)
Pull: nothing
Errors: $0304, $0306
Comments:

Function: $1403
Name: ClrHeartBeat
Clears all queued HeatBeat tasks.
Push: nothing
Pull: nothing
Errors: none
Comments:

Function: $1503
Name: SysFailMgr
Halts program and displays an error message.
Push: Error Code (W); String Address (L)
Pull: nothing
Errors: none
Comments: String starts with a count byte. If String Address is zero, the standard message is used.

Function: $1603
Name: GetAddr
Return the address of a firmware value.
Push: Result Space (L); Parameter Reference Number (W)
Pull: Address of parameter (L)
Errors: none
Comments:

Function: $1703
Name: ReadMouse
Get the current status, position, and mode of the mouse.
Push: Result Space (W); (W); (W)
Pull: Mouse Mode (B); Mouse Status (B); Y Position (W); X Position (W)
Errors: none
Comments: Positions are screen relative.

$1803

Function: $1803
Name: InitMouse
Initializes clamping bounds ($0–$3FF), resets mouse mode and status.
Push: Mouse slot (W)
Pull: nothing
Errors: none
Comments: If the value for Mouse slot is zero, the slots are searched.

Function: $1903
Name: SetMouse
Assigns a mouse mode.
Push: Mouse mode value (W)
Pull: nothing
Errors: none
Comments: The mode value is in the low byte of the word pushed.

Function: $1A03
Name: HomeMouse
Set the mouse X and Y coordinates to the minimum clamp position.
Push: nothing
Pull: nothing
Errors: none
Comments:

Function: $1B03
Name: ClearMouse
Set the mouse's X and Y postions to zero.
Push: nothing
Pull: nothing
Errors: none
Comments: The Button status and Mouse mode remains unchanged.

Function: $1C03
Name: ClampMouse
Assign new minimum and maximum X and Y clamping bounds.
Push: Minimum X (W); Maximum X (W); Minimum Y (W); Maximum Y (W)
Pull: nothing
Errors: none
Comments: This call also calls HomeMouse after setting the new bounds.

Function: $1D03
Name: GetMouseClamp
Gets the current minimum and maximum clamping bounds.
Push: Space for results (W); (W); (W); (W)
Pull: Maximum Y (W); Minimum Y (W); Maximum X (W); Minimum X (W)
Errors: none
Comments:

Function: $1E03
Name: PosMouse
Positions the mouse to the specified X and Y locations.
Push: X position (W); Y position (W)
Pull: nothing
Errors: none
Comments:

Function: $1F03
Name: ServeMouse
Get mouse interrupt status.
Push: Result Space (W)
Pull: Interrupt Status (W)
Errors: none
Comments: The status is in the low byte of the word returned.

Function: $2003
Name: GetNewID
Install a new User ID.
Push: Result Space (W); Type/Aux ID fields (W)
Pull: New User ID (W)
Errors: $030B
Comments: Type and AUX ID values are discussed in Chapter 8.

Function: $2103
Name: DeleteID
Remove User IDs from the current User ID list.
Push: Type/Main ID fields (W)
Pull: nothing
Errors: none
Comments: Any IDs which match the Type and Main ID fields are removed.

Function: $2203
Name: StatusID
Determines if a User ID is active.
Push: Type/Main ID fields (W)
Pull: nothing
Error: $030B
Comments: On return, if carry is set, the specified User ID is NOT active.

Function: $2303
Name: IntSource
Activates or deactivates an interrupt source.
Push: Source reference number (W)
Pull: nothing
Errors: none
Comments:

Function: $2403
Name: FWEntry
Call an Apple II firmware routine.
Push: Result Space (W); (W); (W); (W); A Reg (W); X Reg (W); Y Reg (W); Address (W)
Pull: Y Reg (W); X Reg (W); A Reg (W); Processor Status (W)
Errors: none.
Comments:

Function: $2503
Name: GetTick
Gets the tick counter's current setting.
Push: Result Space (L)
Pull: Tick count (L)
Errors: none
Comments:

Function: $2603
Name: PackBytes
Compress a block of memory.
Push: Result Space (W); Data Address (L); Address of size WORD (L); Output buffer address (L); Output buffer size (W)
Pull: Pack Bytes produced (W)
Errors: none
Comments:

Function: $2703
Name: UnpackBytes
Decompress a block of memory which was packed with function $26, PackBytes.
Push: Result Space (W); Address of packed data (L); Size of data (W); Handle to buffer's address (L); Address of output buffer size WORD (L)
Pull: Number of bytes unpacked (W)
Errors: none
Comments:

Function: $2803
Name: Munger
Manipulate characters within a string.
Push: Result Space (W); Handle of String (L); Address of count WORD (L); Target string address (L); Target string length (W); Replacement String Address (L); Replacement String Length (W); Address of Padding Character (L)
Pull: Target string found flag (W)
Errors: none
Comments: Found flag will be zero if the target string was found.

Function: $2903
Name: GetIRQ Enable
Get the hardware interrupt status.
Push: Result Space (W)
Pull: Status (W)
Errors: none
Comments: A bit set to 1 means the corresponding interrupt is enabled.

Function: $2A03
Name: SetAbsClamp
Sets new minimum and maximum X and Y absolute clamping bounds.
Push: Minimum X (W); Maximum X (W); Minimum Y (W); Maximum (Y)
Pull: nothing
Errors: none
Comments:

Function: $2B03
Name: GetAbsClamp
Returns absolute clamping values.
Push: Result Space (W); (W); (W); (W)
Pull: Maximum Y (W); Minimum Y (W); Maximum X (W); Minimum X (W)
Errors: none
Comments:

Function: $2C03
Name: SysBeep
Beep!
Push: nothing
Pull: nothing
Errors: none
Comments: Makes a call to the system's bell vector.

Summary of Tool Set $03 Error Codes

$0301	Bad Input Parameter
$0302	No device for input parameter
$0303	Task is already in the Heartbeat queue
$0304	No signature in Task Header was detected
$0305	Damaged Queue was detected during insert or delete
$0306	Task was not found during delete
$0307	Firmware task was unsuccessful
$0308	Detected damaged Heartbeat queue
$0309	Attempted dispatch to a device that is disconnected
$030B	ID tag not available

Tool Set $04: QuickDraw II

Tool Set: $04
Tool Set Name: QuickDraw II
Version Number: 1.2

Function:
$0104
Name: QDBootInit
Initialize QuickDraw II.
Push: nothing
Pull: nothing
Errors: none
Comments: Do not make this call.

Function: $0204
Name: QDStartUp
Starts QuickDraw II.
Push: Direct Page (W); Master SCB (W); Pixel Map Size (W); UserID (W)
Pull: nothing
Errors: $0401, $0410, Memory Manager errors
Comments: Clears the Screen as well.

Function: $0304
Name: QDShutDown
Shuts down QuickDraw II.
Push: nothing
Pull: nothing
Errors: none
Comments:

Function: $0404
Name: QDVersion
Returns version number of QuickDraw II.
Push: Result Space (W)
Pull: Version Number (W)
Errors: none
Comments: LSB is major release, MSB minor release.

Function: $0504
Name: QDReset
Called when the computer is reset.
Push: nothing
Pull: nothing
Errors: none
Comments: Do not make this call.

Function: $0604
Name: QDStatus
Returns activity status of the QuickDraw II.
Push: Result Space (W)
Pull: Status (W)
Errors: none
Comments: Returns $0000 if QuickDraw II is not installed.

Function: $0904
Name: GetAddress
Returns a pointer to one of QuickDraw's internal tables.
Push: Result Space (L); Table ID (W)
Pull: Table's Address (L)
Errors: none
Comments:

Function: $0A04
Name: GrafOn
Activates the super hi-res graphics screen.
Push: nothing
Pull: nothing
Errors: none
Comments:

Function: $0B04
Name: GrafOff
Shuts off the super hi-res graphics screen.
Push: nothing
Pull: nothing
Errors: none
Comments:

Function: $0C04
Name: GetStandardSCB
Returns the current SCB.
Push: Result Space (W)
Pull: Standard SCB (W)
Errors: none
Comments: The SCB is in the low byte of the word pulled.

Function: $0D04
Name: InitColorTable
Returns the color table used with the current mode.
Push: Color Table Pointer (L)
Pull: nothing
Errors: none
Comments: The pointer points at an empty $20-byte structure to be filled with the current color table's values.

Function: $0E04
Name: SetColorTable
Sets one of 16 color tables to new values.
Push: Table Number (W); Pointer to new table (L)
Pull: nothing
Errors: $0450
Comments: The new table is a table of 16, word-sized values indicating the new colors for Table Number.

Function: $0F04
Name: GetColorTable
Duplicates the contents of one color table to another.
Push: Table Number (W); Destination table pointer (L)
Pull: nothing
Errors: $0450
Comments: Refer to Chapter 12 for a list of table locations in memory.

Function: $1004
Name: SetColorEntry
Changes a specific color in a color table.
Push: Table Number (W); Color Number (W); New Color (W)
Pull: nothing
Errors: $0450, $0451
Comments:

Function: $1104
Name: GetColorEntry
Returns the color of a specific color table entry.
Push: Result Space (W); Table Number (W); Color Number (W)
Pull: Color (W)
Errors: $0450, $0451
Comments:

Function: $1204
Name: SetSCB
Sets the Scan line Control Byte (SCB) value.
Push: Scan Line (W); New SCB value (W)
Pull: nothing
Errors: $0452
Comments:

Function: $1304
Name: GetSCB
Returns the SCB value for a given scan line.
Push: Result Space (W); Scan Line (W)
Pull: SCB value (W)
Errors: $0452
Comments:

Function: $1404
Name: SetAllSCBs
Sets the SCB value for all scan lines.
Push: New SCB Value (W)
Pull: nothing
Errors: none
Comments:

Function: $1504
Name: ClearScreen
Clears the screen using the specified color.
Push: Color (W)
Pull: nothing
Errors: none
Comments:

Function: $1604
Name: SetMasterSCB
Sets the Master SCB to the value indicated.
Push: Master SCB value (W)
Pull: nothing
Errors: none
Comments: The SCB values is in the low byte of the word pushed.

Function: $1704
Name: GetMasterSCB
Returns the Master SCB.
Push: Result Space (W)
Pull: Master SCB value (W)
Errors: none
Comments:

Function: $1804
Name: OpenPort
Opens a standard port using the memory locations given.
Push: Port Pointer (L)
Pull: nothing
Errors: Possible Memory Manager errors
Comments:

Function: $1904
Name: InitPort
Initializes a standard port using the memory locations given.
Push: Port Pointer (L)
Pull: nothing
Errors: Possible Memory Manager errors
Comments:

Function: $1A04
Name: ClosePort
Closes a port and releases the memory used.
Push: Port Pointer (L)
Pull: nothing
Errors: Possible Memory Manager errors
Comments:

Function: $1B04
Name: SetPort
Sets the current port.
Push: Port Pointer (L)
Pull: nothing
Errors: none
Comments: The port associated with the pointer pushed becomes the current port.

Function: $1C04
Name: GetPort
Returns the current port.
Push: Result Space (L)
Pull: Pointer to Current Port (L)
Errors: none
Comments:

Function: $1D04
Name: SetPortLoc
Sets the map information structure of the current port.
Push: Information Structure Pointer (L)
Pull: nothing
Errors: none
Comments:

Function: $1E04
Name: GetPortLoc
Returns the map information structure of the current port.
Push: Information Structure Pointer (L)
Pull: nothing
Errors: none
Comments:

Function: $1F04
Name: SetPortRect
Resets the rectangle of the current port.
Push: Rectangle Pointer (L)
Pull: nothing
Errors: none
Comments:

Function: $2004
Name: GetPortRect
Returns the rectangle of the current port.
Push: Rectangle Pointer (L)
Pull: nothing
Errors: none
Comments:

Function: $2104
Name: SetPortSize
Changes the active area of the GrafPort and the GrafPort's size.
Push: Width (W); Height (W)
Pull: nothing
Errors: none
Comments: This call is used by the Window Manager.

Function: $2204
Name: MovePortTo
Changes the screen location of the current GrafPort.
Push: Min X (W); Min Y (W)
Pull: nothing
Errors: none
Comments: The location is relative to the upper-left hand corner of the screen. This call is used by the Window Manager.

Function: $2304
Name: SetOrigin
Resets the upper left corner of the Port rect to the specified point.
Push: Min X (W); Min Y (W)
Pull: nothing
Errors: Possible Memory Manager errors
Comments:

Function: $2404
Name: SetClip
Copies a region into the Clip Region.
Push: Region's Handle (L)
Pull: nothing
Errors: Possible Memory Manager errors
Comments:

Function: $2504
Name: GetClip
Copies the Clip Region to the handle specified.
Push: Region's Handle (L)
Pull: nothing
Errors: Possible Memory Manager errors
Comments:

Function: $2604
Name: ClipRect
Changes the clip region to the specified rectangle.
Push: Rectangle (L)
Pull: nothing
Errors: Possible Memory Manager errors
Comments:

Function: $2704
Name: HidePen
Turns the pen off, meaning no drawing occurs.
Push: nothing
Pull: nothing
Errors: none
Comments:

Function: $2804
Name: ShowPen
Turns the pen on, allowing it to draw.
Push: nothing
Pull: nothing
Errors: none
Comments:

Function: $2904
Name: GetPen
Returns the pen location relative to the current port.
Push: Point Pointer (L)
Pull: nothing
Errors: none
Comments: The pen location is returned to the memory location pointed at by Point Pointer.

Function: $2A04
Name: SetPenState
Sets the Pen's State to the items in the PenState Record Pointer.
Push: PenState Record Pointer (L)
Pull: nothing
Errors: none
Comments:

Function: $2B04
Name: GetPenState
Returns a copy of the PenState Record at the specified address.
Push: PenState Pointer (L)
Pull: nothing
Errors: none
Comments:

Function: $2C04
Name: SetPenSize
Changes the dimensions of the drawing pen.
Push: Width (W); Height (W)
Pull: nothing
Errors: none
Comments: Measurements are in Pixels.

Function: $2D04
Name: GetPenSize
Returns the pen size at the specified address.
Push: Point (L)
Pull: nothing
Errors: none
Comments:

Function: $2E04
Name: SetPenMode
Changes the way the graphics pen draws and how the background pattern affects drawing.
Push: Pen Mode (W)
Pull: nothing
Errors: none
Comments:

Function: $2F04
Name: GetPenMode
Returns the current Pen Mode.
Push: Result Space (W)
Pull: Pen Mode (W)
Errors: none
Comments:

Function: $3004
Name: SetPenPat
Sets the pattern the pen draws.
Push: Pattern Pointer (L)
Pull: nothing
Errors: none
Comments: Don't confuse this with function $32.

Function: $3104
Name: GetPenPat
Places a copy of the current pen pattern at the specified address.
Push: Pattern Pointer (L)
Pull: nothing
Errors: none
Comments:

Function: $3204
Name: SetPenMask
Sets the Pen Mask to the pattern at location Mask Pointer.
Push: Mask Pointer (L)
Pull: nothing
Errors: none
Comments:

Function: $3304
Name: GetPenMask
Returns a copy of the pen mask at the specified address.
Push: Mask Pointer (L)
Pull: nothing
Errors: none
Comments:

Function: $3404
Name: SetBackPat
Changes the background pattern to the one at address Pattern.
Push: Pattern (L)
Pull: nothing
Errors: none
Comments:

Function: $3504
Name: GetBackPat
Returns a copy of the current background pattern to the structure at Pattern Pointer.
Push: Pattern Pointer (L)
Pull: nothing
Errors: none
Comments:

Function: $3604
Name: PenNormal
Returns the graphics pen to its normal state.
Push: nothing
Pull: nothing
Errors: none
Comments:

Function: $3704
Name: SetSolidPenPat
Changes the pen foreground color.
Push: Color (W)
Pull: nothing
Errors: none
Comments:

Function: $3804
Name: SetSolidBackPat
Sets the background pattern to solid and the color given.
Push: Color (W)
Pull: nothing
Errors: none
Comments:

Function: $3904
Name: SolidPattern
Sets the pattern at Pattern Pointer to solid using the specified color.
Push: Pattern Pointer (L); Color (W)
Pull: nothing
Errors:
Comments:

Function: $3A04
Name: MoveTo
Moves the pen to the given horizontal and vertical coordinates.
Push: X location (W); Y location (W)
Pull: nothing
Errors: none
Comments:

Function: $3B04
Name: Move
Moves the pen relative to its current location.
Push: X pixels (W); Y pixels (W)
Pull: nothing
Errors: none
Comments: Negative integer values do not move the pen left and up, respectively.

Function: $3C04
Name: LineTo
Draws a line from the current pen position to the given coordinates.
Push: X location (W); Y location (W)
Pull: nothing
Errors: Possible Memory Manager errors
Comments:

Function: $3D04
Name: Line
Draws a line relative to the current pen position.
Push: X pixels (W); Y pixels (W)
Pull: nothing
Errors: Possible Memory Manager errors
Comments: See function $3B.

Function: $3E04
Name: SetPicSave
Resets picture save field to a new value.
Push: New PicSave Value (L)
Pull: nothing
Errors: none
Comments: This is an internal call.

Function: $3F04
Name: GetPicSave
Returns the current picture save field.
Push: Result Space (L)
Pull: PicSave value (L)
Errors: none
Comments:

Function: $4004
Name: SetRgnSave
Resets the region save field to a new value.
Push: Region Save Value (L)
Pull: nothing
Errors: none
Comments: This is an internal call.

Function: $4104
Name: GetRgnSave
Returns a copy of the Region Save field.
Push: Result Space (L)
Pull: Region Save Value (L)
Errors: none
Comments:

Function: $4204
Name: SetPolySave
Sets or changes the Polygon Save Value.
Push: Poly Save Value (L)
Pull: nothing
Errors: none
Comments: This is an internal call.

Function: $4304
Name: GetPolySave
Returns the current PolySave value.
Push: Result Space (L)
Pull: PolySave (L)
Errors: none
Comments:

Function: $4404
Name: SetGrafProcs
Sets or changes the GrafProcs of the current GrafPort.
Push: GrafProcs Record (L)
Pull: nothing
Errors: none
Comments:

Function: $4504
Name: GetGrafProcs
Returns the address of the GrafProcs Record used with the current GrafPort.
Push: Result Space (L)
Pull: GrafProcs Record (L)
Errors: none
Comments:

Function: $4604
Name: SetUserField
Sets or changes the UserField value of a GrafPort.
Push: UserField Value (L)
Pull: nothing
Errors: none
Comments:

Function: $4704
Name: GetUserField
Returns the GrafPort's UserField value.
Push: Result Space (L)
Pull: UserField Value (L)
Errors: none
Comments:

Function: $4804
Name: SetSysField
Sets the SysField value for the GrafPort.
Push: SysField Value (L)
Pull: nothing
Errors: none
Comments: This is an internal call.

Function: $4904
Name: GetSysField
Returns the SysField value from the current GrafPort.
Push: Result Space (L)
Pull: SysField Value (L)
Errors: none
Comments:

Function: $4A04
Name: SetRect
Creates a rectangle for drawing shapes.
Push: Rectangle (L); X Min (W); Y Min (W); X Max (W); Y Max (W)
Pull: nothing
Errors: none
Comments: Rectangle points to an 8-byte buffer. This Rectangle buffer is used for subsequent shape-drawing functions.

Function: $4B04
Name: OffsetRect
Moves a rectangle the given number of pixels right and down.
Push: Rectangle (L); X pixels (W); Y pixels (W)
Pull: nothing
Errors: none
Comments:

Function: $4C04
Name: InsetRect
Moves a rectangle the given number of pixels left and up.
Push: Rectangle (L); X pixels (W); Y pixels (W)
Pull: nothing
Errors: none
Comments:

Function: $4D04
Name: SectRect
Copies the intersection of two rectangles and places it into a third, destination rectangle.
Push: Result Space (W); First Rectangle (L); Second Rectangle (L); Destination Rectangle (L)
Pull: Logical Result (W)
Errors: none
Comments: The Result is a logical True if an intersection exists.

Function: $4E04
Name: UnionRect
Copies the union of two rectangles to a destination rectangle.
Push: First Rectangle (L); Second Rectangle (L); Destination Rectangle (L)
Pull: nothing
Errors: none
Comments:

Function: $4F04
Name: PtInRect
Determines if a given pixel coordinate is within a certain rectangle.
Push: Result Space (W); Point (L); Rectangle (L)
Pull: Logical Result (W)
Errors: none
Comments: The Result is a logical True if the Point is within the Rectangle.

Function: $5004
Name: Pt2Rect
Copies the first point to the upper left corner of a rectangle and the second point to the lower right corner.
Push: First Point (L); Second Point (L); Rectangle (L)
Pull: nothing
Errors: none
Comments:

Function: $5104
Name: EqualRect
Compares two Rectangles.
Push: Result Space (W); First Rectangle (L); Second Rectangle (L)
Pull: Logical Result (W)
Errors: none
Comments: The Result is a logical True if the two rectangles are the same.

Function: $5204
Name: EmptyRect
Checks to see if a rectangle is empty.
Push: Result Space (W); Rectangle (L)
Pull: Logical Result (W)
Errors: none
Comments: If Result is a logical True, the Rectangle is empty.

Function: $5304
Name: FrameRect
Draws a frame around the given rectangle.
Push: Rectangle (L)
Pull: nothing
Errors: Possible Memory Manager errors
Comments: The frame uses the current pen pattern, mode, and size.

Function: $5404
Name: PaintRect
Fills the given rectangle with the current pen color.
Push: Rectangle (L)
Pull: nothing
Errors: none
Comments:

Function: $5504
Name: EraseRect
Fills the given rectangle with the current background color, rendering it invisible.
Push: Rectangle (L)
Pull: nothing
Errors: none
Comments:

Function: $5604
Name: InvertRect
Inverts, or exclusive ORs, pixels in the given rectangle with the background pattern.
Push: Rectangle (L)
Pull: nothing
Errors: none
Comments:

Function: $5704
Name: FillRect
Fills the interior of the given rectangle with the indicated pattern.
Push: Rectangle (L); Pattern Pointer (L)
Pull: nothing
Errors: none.
Comments: The pattern is an 8 x 8 pixel grid.

Function: $5804
Name: FrameOval
Draws an oval frame in the given rectangle.
Push: Rectangle (L)
Pull: nothing
Errors: Possible Memory Manager errors
Comments: See function $53.

Function: $5904
Name: PaintOval
Fills an oval region within a given rectangle.
Push: Rectangle (L)
Pull: nothing
Errors: none
Comments: The color and pattern are set by the pen functions .

Function: $5A04
Name: EraseOval
Fills an oval region within a given rectangle using the background color.
Push: Rectangle (L)
Pull: nothing
Errors: none
Comments:

Function: $5B04
Name: InvertOval
Inverts, or exclusive ORs, an oval within a given rectangle using the background pattern.
Push: Rectangle (L)
Pull: nothing
Errors: none
Comments:

Function: $5C04
Name: FillOval
Fills the interior of an oval within a given rectangle using a specific pattern.
Push: Rectangle (L); Pattern Pointer (L)
Pull: nothing
Errors: none
Comments:

Function: $5D04
Name: FrameRRect
Draws a frame around a Round Rectangle.
Push: Rectangle (L); Oval Width (W); Oval Height (W)
Pull: nothing
Errors: Possible Memory Manager errors
Comments: The Oval values define the rounded corners of the Round Rectangle.

Function: $5E04
Name: PaintRRect
Fills a round rectangle within the given rectangle using the current pen color and pattern.
Push: Rectangle (L); Oval Width (W); Oval Height (W)
Pull: nothing
Errors: none
Comments:

Function: $5F04
Name: EraseRRect
Fills a round rectangle with the current background color, rendering it invisible.
Push: Rectangle (L); Oval Width (W); Oval Height (W)
Pull: nothing
Errors: none
Comments:

Function: $6004
Name: InvertRRect
Inverts, or exclusive ORs, a round rectangle within the given rectangle with the background pattern.
Push: Rectangle (L); Oval Width (W); Oval Height (W)
Pull: nothing
Errors: none
Comments:

Function: $6104
Name: FillRRect
Fills the interior of a Round Rectangle within the given rectangle using a specific pattern.
Push: Rectangle (L); Oval Width (W); Oval Height (W); Pattern Pointer (L)
Pull: nothing.
Errors: none
Comments:

Function: $6204
Name: FrameArc
Draws a length of an arc.
Push: Rectangle (L); Starting Angle (W); Angle Length (W)
Pull: nothing
Errors: none
Comments: Angles are measured in degrees, with zero straight up and 90 at the three o'clock position.

Function: $6304
Name: PaintArc
Fills the given arc with the current pen color.
Push: Rectangle (L); Starting Angle (W); Ending Angle (W)
Pull: nothing
Errors: none
Comments: The color and pattern are set by the pen functions.

Function: $6404
Name: EraseArc
Fills an arc with the current background color, rendering it invisible.
Push: Rectangle (L); Starting Angle (W); Ending Angle (W)
Pull: nothing
Errors: none
Comments:

Function: $6504
Name: InvertArc
Inverts, or exclusive ORs, an arc within a given rectangle using the background pattern.
Push: Rectangle (L); Starting Angle (W); Ending Angle (W)
Pull: nothing
Errors: none
Comments:

Function: $6604
Name: FillArc
Fills the interior of the arc using a specific pattern.
Push: Rectangle (L); Starting Angle (W); Ending Angle (W); Pattern Pointer (L)
Pull: nothing
Errors: none
Comments:

Function: $6704
Name: NewRgn
Creates a new region.
Push: Result Space (L)
Pull: New Region Handle (L)
Errors: Possible Memory Manager errors
Comments:

Function: $6804
Name: DisposeRgn
Disposes the given region.
Push: Region's Handle (L)
Pull: nothing
Errors: Possible Memory Manager errors
Comments:

Function: $6904
Name: CopyRgn
Copies one region to another.
Push: Source Region's Handle (L); Destination Region's Handle (L)
Pull: nothing
Errors: Possible Memory Manager errors
Comments:

Function: $6A04
Name: SetEmptyRgn
Empties a given region.
Push: Region's Handle (L)
Pull: nothing
Errors: Possible Memory Manager errors
Comments:

Function: $6B04
Name: SetRectRgn
Resets a region to the rectangle pushed on the stack.
Push: Region's Handle (L); Min X (W); Min Y (W); Max X (W); Max Y (W)
Pull: nothing
Errors: Possible Memory Manager errors
Comments:

Function: $6C04
Name: RectRgn
Resets a region to the rectangle specified.
Push: Region's Handle (L); Rectangle (L)
Pull: nothing
Errors: Possible Memory Manager errors
Comments:

Function: $6D04
Name: OpenRgn
Begins the definition of a region.
Push: nothing
Pull: nothing
Errors: $0430, possible Memory Manager errors
Comments:

Function: $6E04
Name: CloseRgn
Finishes and returns a handle to the region created using OpenRgn.
Push: Region's Handle (L)
Pull: nothing
Errors: $0431, possible Memory Manager errors
Comments:

Function: $6F04
Name: OffsetRgn
Moves a region the given number of pixels right and down.
Push: Region's Handle (L); X pixels (W); Y pixels (W)
Pull: nothing
Errors: Possible Memory Manager errors
Comments:

Function: $7004
Name: InsetRgn
Moves a region the given number of pixels left and up.
Push: Region's Handle (L); X pixels (W); Y pixels (W)
Pull: nothing
Errors: Possible Memory Manager errors
Comments:

Function: $7104
Name: SectRgn
Takes the intersection of two regions and places it into a destination region.
Push: First Region's Handle (L); Second Region's Handle (L); Destination Region's Handle (L)
Pull: nothing
Errors: Possible Memory Manager errors
Comments:

Function: $7204
Name: UnionRgn
Places the union of two regions into a third, destination region.
Push: First Region's Handle (L); Second Region's Handle (L); Destination Region's Handle (L)
Pull: nothing
Errors: Possible Memory Manager errors
Comments:

Function: $7304
Name: DiffRgn
Returns to a third region the differences between a first and second region.
Push: First Region's Handle (L); Second Region's Handle (L); Third Region's Handle (L)
Pull: nothing.
Errors: Possible Memory Manager errors
Comments:

Function: $7404
Name: XorRgn
Returns the difference of the union and intersection of two regions into a destination region.
Push: First Region's Handle (L); Second Region's Handle (L); Destination Region's Handle (L)
Pull: nothing
Errors: Possible Memory Manager errors
Comments:

Function: $7504
Name: PtInRgn
Determines if a point is within a specified region.
Push: Result Space (W); Point (L); Region's Handle (L)
Pull: Logical Result (W)
Errors: Possible Memory Manager errors
Comments: The Result is a logical True if the point is within the given region.

Function: $7604
Name: RectInRgn
Checks to see if a Rectangle intersects a region.
Push: Result Space (W); Rectangle (L); Region's Handle (L)
Pull: Logical Result (W)
Errors: Possible Memory Manager errors
Comments: The Result is a logical True if the Rectangle intersects any part of the given region.

Function: $7704
Name: EqualRgn
Checks to see if two regions are equal.
Push: Result Space (W); First Region's Handle (L); Second Region's Handle (L)
Pull: Logical Result (W)
Errors: Possible Memory Manager errors
Comments: The Result is a logical True if both regions are equal.

Function: $7804
Name: EmptyRgn
Checks to see if a given region is empty.
Push: Result Space (W); Region's Handle (L)
Pull: Logical Result (W)
Errors: Possible Memory Manager errors
Comments: The Result is a logical True if the region is empty.

Function: $7904
Name: FrameRgn
Draws a frame around the given region.
Push: Region's Handle (L)
Pull: nothing
Errors: Possible Memory Manager errors
Comments:

Function: $7A04
Name: PaintRgn
Fills the given region with the current pen color.
Push: Region's Handle (L)
Pull: nothing
Errors: none
Comments:

Function: $7B04
Name: EraseRgn
Fills the given region with the current background color, rendering it invisible.
Push: Region's Handle (L)
Pull: nothing
Errors: none
Comments:

Function: $7C04
Name: InvertRgn
Inverts, or exclusive ORs, a region using the background pattern.
Push: Region's Handle (L)
Pull: nothing
Errors: none
Comments:

Function: $7D04
Name: FillRgn
Fills the interior of the region using a specific pattern.
Push: Region's Handle (L); Pattern Pointer (L)
Pull: nothing
Errors: none
Comments:

Function: $7E04
Name: ScrollRect
Scrolls a rectangle the given number of pixels.
Push: Rectangle (L); Scroll X (W); Scroll Y (W); Region's Handle (L)
Pull: nothing
Errors: Possible Memory Manager errors
Comments:

Function: $7F04
Name: PaintPixels
Moves pixels from one place to another.
Push: Pixel Parameter Block Pointer (L)
Pull: nothing
Errors: $0420
Comments:

Function: $8004
Name: AddPt
Adds two points and puts the result in the Destination Pointer.
Push: Source Point (L); Destination Point (L)
Pull: nothing
Errors: none
Comments:

Function: $8104
Name: SubPt
Subtracts the source point from the destination point and places the result at the destination point.
Push: Source Point (L); Destination Point (L)
Pull: nothing
Errors: none
Comments:

Function: $8204
Name: SetPt
Sets a point to a specific location.
Push: Point (L); X (W); Y (W)
Pull: nothing
Errors: none
Comments: You can also fill the values yourself. See Chapter 14.

Function: $8304
Name: EqualPt
Checks to see if two points are equal.
Push: Result Space (W); First Point (L); Second Point (L)
Pull: Logical Result (W)
Errors: none
Comments: The Result is a logical True if they are equal.

Function: $8404
Name: LocalToGlobal
Converts the coordinates of a Point from Local to Global.
Push: Point (L)
Pull: nothing
Errors: none
Comments:

Function: $8504
Name: GlobalToLocal
Converts the coordinates at Point from Global to Local values.
Push: Point (L)
Pull: nothing
Errors: none
Comments:

Function: $8604
Name: Random
Produces a pseudorandom integer.
Push: Result Space (W)
Pull: Pseudorandom Number (W)
Errors: none
Comments:

Function: $8704
Name: SetRandSeed
Sets the random number seed for function $86.
Push: Seed Value (L)
Pull: nothing
Errors: none
Comments: The Seed Value is a 32-bit integer.

Function: $8804
Name: GetPixel
Returns the pixel at the given location.
Push: Result Space (W); X (W); Y (W)
Pull: Pixel (W)
Errors: none
Comments: X and Y are in global coordinates.

Function: $8904
Name: ScalePt
Scales a point from one rectangle to another.
Push: Point (L); Source Rectangle (L); Destination Rectangle (L)
Pull: nothing
Errors: none
Comments:

Function: $8A04
Name: MapPt
Maps a point from one rectangle to another.
Push: Point (L); Source Rectangle (L); Destination Rectangle (L)
Pull: nothing
Errors: none
Comments:

Function: $8B04
Name: MapRect
Maps a rectangle from one rectangle to another.
Push: Rectangle (L); Source Rectangle (L); Destination Rectangle (L)
Pull: nothing
Errors: none
Comments:

Function: $8C04
Name: MapRgn
Maps a region from one rectangle to another.
Push: Region's Handle (L); Source Rectangle (L); Destination Rectangle (L)
Pull: nothing
Errors: Possible Memory Manager errors
Comments:

Function: $8E04
Name: SetCursor
Changes the shape and mask of the cursor.
Push: Cursor Record (L)
Pull: nothing
Errors: Possible Memory Manager errors
Comments: See Chapter 14 for details on the record structure.

Function: $8F04
Name: GetCursorAdr
Returns the address of the Cursor Record.
Push: Result Space (L)
Pull: Cursor Record Pointer (L)
Errors: none
Comments:

Function: $9004
Name: HideCursor
Makes the mouse pointer invisible.
Push: nothing
Pull: nothing
Errors: none
Comments:

Function: $9104
Name: ShowCursor
Displays the cursor if the cursor was hidden with function $90.
Push: nothing
Pull: nothing
Errors: none
Comments:

Function: $9204
Name: ObscureCursor
Hides the cursor until the mouse is moved.
Push: nothing
Pull: nothing
Errors: none
Comments:

Function: $9404
Name: SetFont
Changes the current font to the one specified.
Push: Font Handle (L)
Pull: nothing
Errors: none
Comments: Normally this is done using the Font Manager.

Function: $9504
Name: GetFont
Returns the current font's handle.
Push: Result Space (L)
Pull: Font Handle (L)
Errors: none
Comments:

Function: $9604
Name: GetFontInfo
Returns a copy of the Font Record at the indicated address.
Push: Record Pointer (L)
Pull: nothing
Errors: none
Comments:

Function: $9704
Name: GetFontGlobals
Returns a pointer to the Font Globals Record.
Push: Font Globals Record Pointer (L)
Pull: nothing
Errors: none
Comments:

Function: $9804
Name: SetFontFlags
Sets or changes the Font Flags to the value given.
Push: Flag value (W)
Pull: nothing
Errors: none
Comments: $0000 sets a proportional font.

Function: $9904
Name: GetFontFlags
Returns a copy of the current Font Flags word.
Push: Result Space (W)
Pull: Flags (W)
Errors: none
Comments: See function $98.

Function: $9A04
Name: SetTextFace
Sets the style of the text face.
Push: Face Value (W)
Pull: nothing
Errors: none
Comments: Values are: $0000 plain, $0001 Bold, $0002 Italic, $0004 Underline, $0008 Outline, $0010 Shadow.

Function: $9B04
Name: GetTextFace
Returns the Text Face Value.
Push: Result Space (W)
Pull: Face Value (W)
Errors: none
Comments: See function $9A04.

Function: $9C04
Name: SetTextMode
Sets or changes the way text is drawn on the screen in relation to the background pattern.
Push: Text Mode (W)
Pull: nothing
Errors: none
Comments:

Function: $9D04
Name: GetTextMode
Returns the text mode.
Push: Result Space (W)
Pull: Text Mode (W)
Errors: none
Comments:

Function: $9E04
Name: SetSpaceExtra
Sets the Space Width value used when justifying text.
Push: Space Width (L)
Pull: nothing
Errors: none
Comments: The number pushed is a Fixed Point value.

Function: $9F04
Name: GetSpaceExtra
Returns the Space Width value from the current GrafPort.
Push: Result Space (L)
Pull: Space Width (L)
Errors: none
Comments: The value returned is Fixed Point.

Function: $A004
Name: SetForeColor
Sets the foreground color for writing text.
Push: Color (W)
Pull: nothing
Errors: none
Comments:

Function: $A104
Name: GetForeColor
Returns the foreground color used for writing text.
Push: Result Space (W)
Pull: Color (W)
Errors: none
Comments:

Function: $A204
Name: SetBackColor
Sets the background color for writing text.
Push: Color (W)
Pull: nothing
Errors: none
Comments:

Function: $A304
Name: GetBackColor
Returns the background color used for writing text.
Push: Result Space (W)
Pull: Color (W)
Errors: none
Comments:

Function: $A404
Name: DrawChar
Displays a single character using the current font.
Push: Character (W)
Pull: nothing
Errors: none
Comments: Character is in low byte of word pushed; character is drawn at the current pen position.

Function: $A504
Name: DrawString
Draws a Pascal-type string of characters using the current font.
Push: String Address (L)
Pull: nothing
Errors: none
Comments: The string at String Address starts with a count byte.

$A604

Function: $A604
Name: DrawCString
Draws a "C" string of characters using the current font.
Push: String Address (L)
Pull: nothing
Errors: none
Comments: The string ends with the byte $00.

Function: $A704
Name: DrawText
Draws a number of characters in a string using the current font.
Push: String Address (L); Length (W)
Pull: nothing
Errors: none
Comments: All or part of the string can be drawn by varying the Length.

Function: $A804
Name: CharWidth
Returns the pixel width of a character.
Push: Result Space (W); Character (W)
Pull: Character's Pixel Width (W)
Errors: none
Comments:

Function: $A904
Name: StringWidth
Returns the total width of all pixels in a string of text.
Push: Result Space (W); String Address (L)
Pull: String Width (W)
Errors: none
Comments: The String is a Pascal-type string.

Function: $AA04
Name: CStringWidth
Returns the total width of all pixels in a C string.
Push: Result Space (W); String Address (L)
Pull: String Width (W)
Errors: none
Comments: The String ends with the byte $00.

Function: $AB04
Name: TextWidth
Returns the total width of all pixels in a section of text.
Push: Result Space (W); String Address (L); Length (W)
Pull: String Width (W)
Errors: none
Comments:

Function: $AC04
Name: CharBounds
Sets the rectangle (size) for a specific character.
Push: Character (W); Rectangle (L)
Pull: nothing
Errors: none
Comments:

Function: $AD04
Name: StringBounds
Sets the rectangle according to the length and size of the text string.
Push: String Address (L); Rectangle (L)
Pull: nothing
Errors: none
Comments:

Function: $AE04
Name: CStringBounds
Returns a rectangle based on the size of a string of characters.
Push: String Address (L); Rectangle (L)
Pull: nothing
Errors: none
Comments: The string is a C string.

Function: $AF04
Name: TextBounds
Sets the rectangle based on the size and length of the text string.
Push: String Address (L); Length (W); Rectangle (L)
Pull: nothing
Errors: none
Comments:

Function: $B204
Name: SetSysFont
Changes the system font.
Push: New Font's Handle (L)
Pull: nothing
Errors: none
Comments:

Function: $B304
Name: GetSysFont
Returns the current system font.
Push: Result Space (L)
Pull: System Font's Handle (L)
Errors: none
Comments:

Function: $B404
Name: SetVisRgn
Copies the Visible Region to a memory block.
Push: Block's Handle (L)
Pull: nothing
Errors: none
Comments:

Function: $B504
Name: GetVisRgn
Duplicates the contents of the VisRgn to the region's handle specified.
Push: Region's Handle (L)
Pull: nothing
Errors: none
Comments:

Function: $BC04
Name: FramePoly
Draws a frame around a polygon.
Push: Poly's Handle (L)
Pull: nothing
Errors: Possible Memory Manager errors
Comments:

Function: $BD04
Name: PaintPoly
Fills the given polygon with the current pen color.
Push: Poly's Handle (L)
Pull: nothing
Errors: Possible Memory Manager errors
Comments:

Function: $BE04
Name: ErasePoly
Fills the given polygon with the current background color, rendering it invisible.
Push: Poly's Handle (L)
Pull: nothing
Errors: Possible Memory Manager errors
Comments:

Function: $BF04
Name: InvertPoly
Inverts, or exclusive ORs, an polygon using the background pattern.
Push: Poly's Handle (L)
Pull: nothing
Errors: Possible Memory Manager errors
Comments:

Function: $C004
Name: FillPoly
Fills the interior of a polygon with the specified pattern.
Push: Poly's Handle (L); Pattern Pointer (L)
Pull: nothing
Errors: Possible Memory Manager errors
Comments:

Function: $C104
Name: OpenPoly
Begins defining a polygon by opening a handle to the polygon.
Push: Result Space (L)
Pull: Poly's Handle (L)
Errors: $0440, possible Memory Manager errors.
Comments:

Function: $C204
Name: ClosePoly
Completes the definition of a polygon.
Push: nothing
Pull: nothing
Errors: $0441, possible Memory Manager errors
Comments:

Function: $C304
Name: KillPoly
Removes a specific polygon.
Push: Poly's Handle (L)
Pull: nothing
Errors: Possible Memory Manager errors
Comments:

Function: $C404
Name: OffsetPoly
Moves a polygon the given number of pixels right and down.
Push: Poly's Handle (L); X pixels (W); Y pixels (W)
Pull: nothing
Errors: Possible Memory Manager errors
Comments:

Function: $C504
Name: MapPoly
Maps a polygon from one rectangle to another.
Push: Poly's Pointer (L); Source Rectangle (L); Destination Rectangle (L)
Pull: nothing
Errors: none
Comments:

Function: $C604
Name: SetClipHandle
Resets the Clip Region to the handle specified.
Push: Clip Region Handle (L)
Pull: nothing
Errors: none
Comments:

Function: $C704
Name: GetClipHandle
Returns the handle to the current Clip Region.
Push: Result Space (L)
Pull: Clip Region Handle (L)
Errors: none
Comments:

Function: $C804
Name: SetVisHandle
Sets or Changes the VisRgn handle in the GrafPort.
Push: Visible Region Handle (L)
Pull: nothing
Errors: none
Comments:

Function: $C904
Name: GetVisHandle
Returns a handle to the Visible Region.
Push: Result Space (L)
Pull: Visible Region Handle (L)
Errors: none
Comments:

Function: $CA04
Name: InitCursor
Initializes, or resets, the mouse pointer on the screen.
Push: nothing
Pull: nothing
Errors: none
Comments: This call will make the cursor visible.

Function: $CB04
Name: SetBufDims
Resets the clipping and text buffers set by the QDStartUp function.
Push: Width of pixel map (W); Tallest font height (W); Max Font Bounds Rectangle (FBR) Extent (W)
Pull: nothing
Errors: Possible Memory Manager errors
Comments:

Function: $CC04
Name: ForceBufDims
Resets the clipping and text buffers as function $CB does, but does not pad the FBR extent.
Push: Width of pixel map (W); Tallest font height (W); Max FBR Extent (W)
Pull: nothing.
Errors: Possible Memory Manager errors
Comments:

Function: $CD04
Name: SaveBufDims
Saves the current buffer dimensions.
Push: Record Pointer (L)
Pull: nothing
Errors: none
Comments: The record is eight bytes long.

Function: $CE04
Name: RestoreBufDims
Restores the buffer dimensions previously saved with function $CD.
Push: Record Pointer (L)
Pull: nothing
Errors: Possible Memory Manager errors
Comments:

Function: $CF04
Name: GetFGSize
Returns the Font Global Records Size.
Push: Result Space (W)
Pull: Font Global Records Size (W)
Errors: none
Comments:

Function: $D004
Name: SetFontID
Sets the FontID field for a GrafPort.
Push: Pointer to FontID value (L)
Pull: nothing
Errors: none
Comments: This call does not change the current font.

Function: $D104
Name: GetFontID
Returns the current Font ID.
Push: Result Space (L)
Pull: FontID (L)
Errors: none
Comments:

Function: $D404
Name: SetCharExtra
Changes the character width of each character in the current font.
Push: Width Value (L)
Pull: nothing
Errors: none
Comments: Width Value is a fixed-point number.

Function: $D504
Name: GetCharExtra
Returns the width of the CharExtra field.
Push: Result Space (L)
Pull: Width Value (L)
Errors: none
Comments: The value returned is a fixed-point number.

Function: $D604
Name: PPToPort
Copies pixels from a rectangle into the current port.
Push: Parameter Block Pointer (L); Source Rectangle (L); Destination Min X (W); Destination Min Y (W); Pen Mode (W)
Pull: nothing.
Errors: $0420
Comments:

Function: $D704
Name: InflateTextBuffer
Resets the width and height of the text buffer.
Push: Width (W); Height (W)
Pull: nothing
Errors: none
Comments:

$D804

Function: $D804
Name: GetRomFont
Places information about the ROM font at the specified address.
Push: Result Space (W); Address (L)
Pull: Length of record (W)
Errors: none
Comments:

Function: $D904
Name: GetFontLore
Returns information about the current Font.
Push: Result Space (W); Record Pointer (L); Length (L)
Pull: Bytes transferred (W)
Errors: none
Comments:

Summary of Tool Set $04 Error Codes

$0401 QuickDraw already initialized
$0402 Cannot Reset
$0403 QuickDraw is not initialized
$0410 Screen is reserved
$0411 Bad Rectangle
$0420 Chunkiness is not equal
$0430 Region is already open
$0431 Region is not open
$0432 Region scan overflow
$0433 Region is full
$0440 Poly is already open
$0441 Poly is not open
$0442 Poly is too big
$0450 Bad table number
$0451 Bad color number
$0452 Bad scan line

Tool Set $05: Desk Manager

Tool Set: $05
Tool Set Name: Desk Manager
Version Number: 1.2

Function: $0105
Name: DeskBootInit
Initialize Desk Manager.
Push: nothing
Pull: nothing
Errors: none
Comments: Do not make this call.

Function: $0205
Name: DeskStartUp
Starts the Desk Manager.
Push: nothing
Pull: nothing
Errors: none
Comments: The tools used by your New Desk Accessories (NDA) should be started.

Function: $0305
Name: DeskShutDown
Shuts down the Desk Manager.
Push: nothing
Pull: nothing
Errors: none
Comments:

Function: $0405
Name: DeskVersion
Returns version number of the Desk Manager.
Push: Result Space (W)
Pull: Version Number (W)
Errors: none
Comments: LSB is major release, MSB minor release.

Function: $0505
Name: DeskReset
Called when the computer is reset.
Push: nothing
Pull: nothing
Errors: none
Comments: Do not make this call.

Function: $0605
Name: DeskStatus
Returns activity status of the Desk Manager.
Push: Result Space (W)
Pull: Status (W)
Errors: none
Comments: $0000 is returned if the Desk Manager is inactive.

Function: $0905
Name: SaveScrn
Saves the screen before a CDA is called.
Push: nothing
Pull: nothing
Errors: none
Comments: This is an internal call.

Function: $0A05
Name: RestScrn
Restores the screen after a CDA is called.
Push: nothing
Pull: nothing
Errors: none
Comments: This is an internal call.

Function: $0B05
Name: SaveAll
Saves variables before a CDA is called.
Push: nothing
Pull: nothing
Errors: none
Comments: This is an internal call.

Function: $0C05
Name: RestAll
Restores preserved variables after a CDA is called.
Push: nothing
Pull: nothing
Errors: none
Comments: This is an internal call.

Function: $0E05
Name: InstallNDA
Loads New Desk Accessories from the /SYSTEM/DESK.ACCS/ prefix of the boot disk.
Push: NDA Handle (L)
Pull: nothing
Errors: none
Comments: Called by ProDOS 16 at boot time.

Function: $0F05
Name: InstallCDA
Places a Classic Desk Accessory in the CDA menu.
Push: CDA ID Handle (L)
Pull: nothing
Errors: none
Comments: Called by ProDOS 16 at boot time.

Function: $1105
Name: ChooseCDA
Displays Classic Desk Accessory Menu.
Push: nothing
Pull: nothing
Errors: none
Comments: This has the same effect as pressing Apple-Control-Esc.

Function: $1305
Name: SetDAStrPtr
Changes the names of the computer's built-in Classic Desk Accessories.
Push: Alternate CDA Handle (L); String table (L)
Pull: nothing
Errors: none
Comments:

Function: $1405
Name: GetDAStrPtr
Returns a string pointer for a Classic Desk Accessory.
Push: Result Space (L); CDA ID (W)
Pull: String Pointer (L)
Errors: none
Comments: Can be used by function $13 to change a built-in CDA's name.

Function: $1505
Name: OpenNDA
Opens the NDA after it's chosen from the Apple menu.
Push: Result Space (W); Menu ID (W)
Pull: NDA number (W)
Errors: $0510
Comments:

Function: $1605
Name: CloseNDA
Closes a specific NDA.
Push: NDA number (W)
Pull: nothing
Errors: none
Comments: NDA number is returned by function $15.

Function: $1705
Name: SystemClick
Called by TaskMaster when the mouse is clicked in a system window.
Push: Event Record (L); System Window (L); Find Window Result (W)
Pull: nothing
Errors: none
Comments:

Function: $1805
Name: SystemEdit
Allows editing commands to be used with certain windows.
Push: Result Space (W); Edit Type (W)
Pull: Logical Result (W)
Errors: none
Comments: Edit types values are 1-Undo, 2-Cut, 3-Copy, 4-Paste, and 5-Clear.

Function: $1905
Name: SystemTask
Used by TaskMaster to update a desk accessory.
Push: nothing
Pull: nothing
Errors: none
Comments:

Function: $1A05
Name: SystemEvent
A type of "event manager" for desk accessories.
Push: Result Space (W); Event What (W); Event Msg (L); Event When (L); Event Where (L); Event Mods (W)
Pull: Logical Result (W)
Errors: none
Comments: This is an internal call.

Function: $1B05
Name: GetNumNDAs
Returns a number equal to all the NDAs installed.
Push: Result Space (W)
Pull: Total NDAs (W)
Errors: none
Comments:

Function: $1C05
Name: CloseNDAbyWinPtr
Closes a NDA when Close is chosen from the File menu.
Push: Window Pointer (L)
Pull: nothing
Errors: $0510, $0511
Comments:

Function: $1D05
Name: CloseAllNDAs
Closes all open New Desk Accessories.
Push: nothing
Pull: nothing
Errors: none
Comments:

Function: $1E05
Name: FixAppleMenu
Places NDAs into your application's Apple menu.
Push: Menu ID (W)
Pull: nothing
Errors: none
Comments:

Summary of Tool Set $05 Error Codes

$0510 Desk Accessory is not available
$0511 Window pointer does not belong to the NDA

Tool Set $06: Event Manager

Tool Set: $06
Tool Set Name: Event Manager
Version Number: 1.0

Function: $0106
Name: EMBootInit
Initialize Event Manager.
Push: nothing
Pull: nothing
Errors: none
Comments: Do not make this call.

Function: $0206
Name: EMStartUp
Starts the Event Manager.
Push: Direct Page (W); Event Queue Size (W); Minimum X (W); Maximum X (W); Minimum Y (W); Maximum Y (W); UserID (W).
Pull: nothing
Errors: $0601, $0606, $0607
Comments: X and Y values refer to mouse clamps. See Chapter 12 for detailed information.

Function: $0306
Name: EMShutDown
Shuts down the Event Manager.
Push: nothing
Pull: nothing
Errors: none
Comments:

Function: $0406
Name: EMVersion
Returns version number of the Event Manager.
Push: Result Space (W)
Pull: Version Number (W)
Errors: none
Comments: LSB is major release, MSB minor release.

Function: $0506
Name: EMReset
Called when the computer is reset.
Push: nothing
Pull: nothing
Errors: none
Comments: Do not make this call.

Function: $0606
Name: EMStatus
Returns activity status of the Event Manager.
Push: Result Space (W)
Pull: Status (W)
Errors: none
Comments: Returns $0000 if the Event Manager is inactive.

Function: $0906
Name: DoWindows
Returns the Event Manager's direct page for use by the Window Manager's StartUp routine.
Push: Result Space (W)
Pull: Event Manager's Direct Page (W)
Errors: none
Comments: This is an internal call.

Function: $0A06
Name: GetNextEvent
Returns the status of the event queue.
Push: Result Space (W); Event Mask (W); Event Record (L)
Pull: Logical Result (W)
Errors: none
Comments: If the Result is a logical true, an event is available. The event is then removed from the queue.

Function: $0B06
Name: EventAvail
Examines the event queue for an event, but keeps the event in the queue.
Push: Result Space (W); Event Mask (W); Event Record (L)
Pull: Logical Result (W)
Errors: none
Comments: The Event Mask and Record are covered in Chapter 12.

Function: $0C06
Name: GetMouse
Returns the current position of the mouse.
Push: Point Pointer (L)
Pull: nothing
Errors: none
Comments: The Point Pointer points at a structure which will contain the Y and X (one word each) position of the mouse.

Function: $0D06
Name: Button
Tests to see if a mouse button is down.
Push: Result Space (W); Button number (W)
Pull: Logical Result (W)
Errors: $0605
Comments: Button number is either $0000 or $0001. The result is True if the button is currently down.

Function: $0E06
Name: StillDown
Determines if the mouse button is still down.
Push: Result Space (W); Button Number (W)
Pull: Logical Result (W)
Errors: $0605
Comments: A logical True means the button is still down.

Function: $0F06
Name: WaitMouseUp
Determines if the mouse button has been released.
Push: Result Space (W); Button Number (W)
Pull: Logical Result (W)
Errors: $0605
Comments: The logical result is False if the button is released. The mouse event is then removed from the queue.

Function: $1006
Name: TickCount
Returns the total tick count since the computer was started.
Push: Result Space (L)
Pull: Total Ticks (L)
Errors: none
Comments: Ticks are 1/60 second.

Function: $1106
Name: GetDblTime
Returns the maximum number of ticks (time count) allowed for a double click of the mouse.
Push: Result Space (L)
Pull: Tick value (L)
Errors: none.
Comments:

Function: $1206
Name: GetCaretTime
Returns the number of ticks (time count) between blinks of the insert bar, or insertion point, cursor.
Push: Result Space (L)
Pull: Tick value (L)
Errors: none
Comments:

Function: $1306
Name: SetSwitch
Informs the Event Manager that a switch event is pending.
Push: nothing
Pull: nothing
Errors: none
Comments: This is an internal call.

Function: $1406
Name: PostEvent
Places a specific event and event message into the event queue.
Push: Result Space (W); Event Code (W); Event Msg (L)
Pull: Result (W)
Errors: $0604
Comments:

Function: $1506
Name: FlushEvents
Empties the event queue of all pending events.
Push: Result Space (W); Event Mask (W); Event Types (W)
Pull: Result (W)
Errors: none
Comments: The Event Mask specifies which events to flush. Event Types is a bit mask which allows certain tasks to stop the removal process. If the process is stopped, the Result contains the code of the event which stopped the flushing. Otherwise, the Result is zero.

Function: $1606
Name: GetOSEvent
Returns the status of the Event Queue, minus window and switch events.
Push: Result Space (W); Event Mask (W); Event Record (L)
Pull: Logical Result (W)
Errors: none
Comments: See function $0A.

Function: $1706
Name: OSEventAvail
Tests to see if an event other than a window or switch event is pending in the queue.
Push: Result Space (W); Event Mask (W); Event Record (L)
Pull: Logical Result (W)
Errors: none
Comments: Use function $16 to remove the event from the queue.

Function: $1806
Name: SetEventMask
Changes the event mask used by the system.
Push: System Event Mask (W)
Pull: nothing
Errors: none
Comments: This mask is normally set to allow all events.

Function: $1906
Name: FakeMouse
Used with a pointing device other than the mouse.
Push: Change Flag (W); Mod Latch (B); Padding (B); Max X position (W); Max Y position (W); Button Status (W)
Pull: nothing
Errors: none
Comments:

Summary of Tool Set $06 Error Codes

$0601	The Event Manager has already been started
$0602	Reset error
$0603	The Event Manager is not active
$0604	Bad event code number (greater than 15)
$0605	Bad button number value
$0606	Queue size greater than 3639
$0607	No memory for event queue
$0681	Fatal error: event queue is damaged
$0682	Fatal error: event queue handle damaged

Tool Set $07: Scheduler

Tool Set: $07
Tool Set Name: Scheduler
Version Number: 1.1

Function: $0107
Name: SchBootInit
Initialize the Scheduler.
Push: nothing
Pull: nothing
Errors: none
Comments: Do not make this call.

$0207

Function: $0207
Name: SchStartUp
Starts the Scheduler.
Push: nothing
Pull: nothing
Errors: none
Comments: No need to make this call—the Scheduler is always active.

Function: $0307
Name: SchShutDown
Shuts down the Scheduler.
Push: nothing
Pull: nothing
Errors: none
Comments: No need to make this call.

Function: $0407
Name: SchVersion
Returns version number of the Scheduler.
Push: Result Space (W)
Pull: Version Number (W)
Errors: none
Comments: LSB is major release, MSB minor release.

Function: $0507
Name: SchReset
Called when the computer is reset.
Push: nothing
Pull: nothing
Errors: none
Comments: Do not make this call.

Function: $0607
Name: SchStatus
Returns activity status of the Scheduler.
Push: Result Space (W)
Pull: Status (W)
Errors: none
Comments: The Scheduler is always active.

Function: $0907
Name: SchAddTask
Adds one of four task items to the Scheduler's queue.
Push: Result Space (W); Task Pointer (L)
Pull: Logical Result (W)
Errors: none
Comments: If Result is nonzero, the task was added.

Function: $0A07
Name: SchFlush
Removes all tasks in the Scheduler queue.
Push: nothing
Pull: nothing
Errors: none
Comments: Do not make this call.

Summary of Tool Set $07 Error Codes

None

Tool Set $08: Sound Manager

Tool Set: $08
Tool Set Name: Sound Manager
Version Number: 1.1

Function: $0108
Name: SoundBootInit
Initialize the Sound Manager.
Push: nothing
Pull: nothing
Errors: none
Comments: Do not make this call.

Function: $0208
Name: SoundStartUp
Starts the Sound Manager.
Push: Direct Page (W)
Pull: nothing
Errors: $0810, $0818
Comments:

Function: $0308
Name: SoundShutDown
Shuts down the Sound Manager.
Push: nothing
Pull: nothing
Errors: none
Comments:

Function: $0408
Name: SoundVersion
Returns version number of the Sound Manager.
Push: Result Space (W)
Pull: Version Number (W)
Errors: none
Comments: LSB is major release, MSB minor release.

Function: $0508
Name: SoundReset
Called when the computer is reset.
Push: nothing
Pull: nothing
Errors: none
Comments: Do not make this call.

Function: $0608
Name: SoundToolStatus
Returns activity status of the Sound Manager.
Push: Result Space (W)
Pull: Status (W)
Errors: none
Comments: Returns $0000 if the Sound Manager is inactive.

Function: $0908
Name: WriteRAMBlock
Copies a block of memory from standard RAM into the DOC.
Push: Source Block (L); DOS Address (W); Length (W)
Pull: nothing
Errors: $0810, $0811
Comments:

Function: $0A08
Name: ReadRAMBlock
Copies a block of memory from the DOC to the location you specify.
Push: Destination Block (L); DOC Address (W); Length (W)
Pull: nothing
Errors: $0810, $0811
Comments:

Function: $0B08
Name: GetTableAddress
Returns a table used to access certain low-level routines.
Push: Result Space (L)
Pull: Table Address (L)
Errors: none
Comments:

Function: $0C08
Name: GetSoundVolume
Returns the volume setting for a particular generator.
Push: Result Space (W); Generator Number (W)
Pull: Volume (W)
Errors: none
Comments:

Function: $0D08
Name: SetSoundVolume
Changes the volume setting for a particular generator.
Push: Volume (W); Generator Number (W)
Pull: nothing
Errors: none
Comments:

Function: $0E08
Name: FFStartSound
Starts generating sound on a specific generator.
Push: Channel Generator Mode (W); Parameter Block (L)
Pull: nothing
Errors: $0812, $0813, $0814, $0815, $0817
Comments:

Function: $0F08
Name: FFStopSound
Stops generating sound on a specific generator.
Push: Generator Mask (W)
Pull: nothing
Errors: none
Comments: Each bit of the Mask corresponds to a generator number.

Function: $1008
Name: FFSoundStatus
Returns the status of all sound generators.
Push: Result Space (W)
Pull: Status Word (W)
Errors: none
Comments: Each bit of the Status Word corresponds to a generator number.

Function: $1108
Name: FFGeneratorStatus
Returns the status of a specific generator.
Push: Result Space (W); Generator Number (W)
Pull: Status Word (W)
Errors: none
Comments:

Function: $1208
Name: SetSoundMIRQV
Sets an interrupt vector called each time the DOC generates an interrupt.
Push: IRQ Vector (L)
Pull: nothing
Errors: none
Comments:

Function: $1308
Name: SetUserSoundIRQV
Sets a vector used by a user-defined synthesizer interrupt.
Push: Result Space (L); User IRQ Vector (L)
Pull: Old User IRQ Vector (L)
Errors: none
Comments:

Function: $1408
Name: FFSoundDoneStatus
Determines if a specific generator is done playing.
Push: Result Space (W); Generator Number (W)
Pull: Logical Result (W)
Errors: $0813
Comments: Result is False ($0000) if generator is still playing.

Summary of Tool Set $08 Error Codes

$0810 No DOC chip or RAM found
$0811 DOC address range error
$0812 No SAppInt call made
$8013 Invalid generator number
$0814 Synthesizer mode error
$0815 Generator busy error
$8017 Master IRQ not assigned
$0818 Sound Tools already started
$08FF Fatal Error—Unclaimed sound interrupt

Tool Set $09: Apple Desktop Bus

Tool Set: $09
Tool Set Name: Apple Desktop Bus
Version Number: 1.0

Function: $0109
Name: ADBBootInit
Initialize the Apple Desktop Bus.
Push: nothing
Pull: nothing
Errors: none
Comments: Do not make this call.

Function: $0209
Name: ADBStartUp
Starts the Apple Desktop Bus.
Push: nothing
Pull: nothing
Errors: none
Comments:

Function: $0309
Name: ADBShutDown
Shuts down the Apple Desktop Bus.
Push: nothing
Pull: nothing
Errors: none
Comments:

Function: $0409
Name: ADBVersion
Returns version number of the Apple Desktop Bus.
Push: Result Space (W)
Pull: Version Number (W)
Errors: none
Comments: LSB is major release, MSB minor release.

Function: $0509
Name: ADBReset
Called when the computer is reset.
Push: nothing
Pull: nothing
Errors: none
Comments: Do not make this call.

Function: $0609
Name: ADBStatus
Returns activity status of the Apple Desktop Bus.
Push: Result Space (W)
Pull: Status (W)
Errors: none
Comments: Returns $0000 if the Apple Desktop Bus is inactive.

Function: $0909
Name: SEND
Transmits information to the ADB microcontroller.
Push: Data Structure Bytes (W); Data Structure (L); ADB Command (W).
Pull: nothing
Errors: $0910
Comments:

Function: $0A09
Name: RCV
Receives information from the ADB microcontroller.
Push: Data Structure Bytes (W); Data Structure (L); ADB Command (W)
Pull: nothing
Errors: $0910
Comments:

Function: $0B09
Name: RDmem
Reads a value from the ADB microcontroller's memory.
Push: Data Out Structure (L); Data In Structure (L); ADB Command (W)
Pull: nothing
Errors: $0910
Comments:

Function: $0D09
Name: ADBpoll
Reads information from the Apple Desktop Bus.
Push: Completion Vector (L)
Pull: nothing
Errors: $0910, $0982
Comments:

Function: $0E09
Name: ADBrcv
Receives information from the ADB.
Push: ADB Command (W); Completion Vector (L); Input (W)
Pull: nothing
Errors: $0910, $0982
Comments:

Function: $0F09
Name: ABSON
Turns automatic polling on.
Push: nothing
Pull: nothing
Errors: none
Comments:

Function: $1009
Name: ABSOFF
Turns automatic polling off.
Push: nothing
Pull: nothing
Errors: none
Comments: This is an internal call.

Function: $1109
Name: RDABS
Returns the status of automatic polling.
Push: Result Space (W)
Pull: Logical Result (W)
Errors: none
Comments: The Logical Result is True when polling is on.

Function: $1209
Name: Scale
Initiates scaling for use by absolute devices.
Push: Data Structure (L)
Pull: nothing
Errors: none
Comments:

Function: $1309
Name: RDScale
Reads the scaling used by absolute devices.
Push: Data Structure (L)
Pull: nothing
Errors: none
Comments:

Function: $1409
Name: SRQPL
Places a device into the Service Request (SRQ) list.
Push: Completion Vector (L); ADB Register/Address (W)
Pull: nothing
Errors: $0910, $0983, $0984
Comments:

Function: $1509
Name: SRQRMV
Removes the specified device from the SRQ list.
Push: ADB Register/Address (W)
Pull: nothing
Errors: $0910, $0982
Comments:

Function: $1609
Name: CLRSRQTBL
Clears the SRQ list.
Push: nothing
Pull: nothing
Errors: none
Comments:

Summary of Tool Set $09 Error Codes

$0910 Command not completed
$0982 Busy, command pending
$0983 Device not present at address
$0984 List is full

Tool Set $10: Control Manager

Tool Set: $10
Tool Set Name: Control Manager
Version Number: 1.3

Function: $0110
Name: CtlBootInit
Initializes the Control Manager.
Push: nothing
Pull: nothing
Errors: none
Comments: Do not make this call.

Function: $0210
Name: CtlStartUp
Starts the Control Manager.
Push: UserID (W); Direct Page (W)
Pull: nothing
Errors: none
Comments: The Window Manager must be started before making this call.

Function: $0310
Name: CtlShutDown
Shuts down the Control Manager.
Push: nothing
Pull: nothing
Errors: none
Comments: The Window Manager must be shutdown before making this call.

Function: $0410
Name: CtlVersion
Returns the version number of the Control Manager.
Push: Result Space (W)
Pull: Version (W)
Errors: none
Comments: LSB is major release, MSB minor release.

Function: $0510
Name: CtlReset
Resets the Control Manager.
Push: nothing
Pull: nothing
Errors: none
Comments: Do not make this call.

Function: $0610
Name: CtlStatus
Determines if the Control Manager is active.
Push: Result Space (W)
Pull: Active (W)
Errors: none
Comments: A nonzero value is returned if active.

Function: $0910
Name: NewControl
Creates a control.
Push: Result Space (L); Window (L); Bounds Rectangle (L); Title (L); Flag (W); Value (W); Param 1 (W); Param 2 (W); Definition Procedure (L); RefCon (L); Color Table (L).
Pull: Control Handle (L)
Errors: none
Comments:

Function: $0A10
Name: DisposeControl
Removes a control from a window's control list.
Push: Control Handle (L)
Pull: nothing
Errors: none
Comments: The control is not removed from the screen, so use HideControl first if necessary.

$0B10

Function: $0B10
Name: KillControls
Removes all controls in a window.
Push: Window (L)
Pull: nothing
Errors: none
Comments: Repeated calls to DisposeControl are made until all controls are removed.

Function: $0C10
Name: SetCtlTitle
Specifies the title for a control.
Push: Title (L); Control Handle (L)
Pull: nothing
Errors: none
Comments:

Function: $0D10
Name: GetCtlTitle
Returns a control's CtlData value.
Push: Result Space (L); Control Handle (L)
Pull: CtlTitle (L)
Errors: none
Comments: If a control has a title, CtlTitle contains its address.

Function: $0E10
Name: HideControl
Hides a control behind the background pattern.
Push: Control Handle (L)
Pull: nothing
Errors: none
Comments:

Function: $0F10
Name: ShowControl
Reveals a hidden control.
Push: Control Handle (L)
Pull: nothing
Errors: none
Comments:

Function: $1010
Name: DrawControls
Draws each visible control in the window.
Push: Window (L)
Pull: nothing
Errors: none
Comments: The controls are drawn in reverse order.

Function: $1110
Name: HiliteControl
Specifies the highlighting of a control.
Push: State (W); Control Handle (L)
Pull: nothing
Errors: none
Comments: State values are: 0 = No highlighting, 1–253 = Part Code, 255 = Inactive. 254 is reserved.

Function: $1310
Name: FindControl
Determines which control was selected by the user.
Push: Result Space (W); Found Control Handle Storage (L); X Point (W); Y Point (W); Window (L).
Pull: Found (W)
Errors: none
Comments:

$1410

Function: $1410
Name: TestControl
Determines the visible and active portion of a control.
Push: Result Space (W); X Point (W); Y Point (W); Control Handle (L).
Pull: Part Code (W)
Errors: none
Comments:

Function: $1510
Name: TrackControl
Tracks the mouse during a drag, performing appropriate functions.
Push: Result Space (W); Start X (W); Start Y (W); Action Procedure (L); Control Handle (L).
Pull: Part Code (W).
Errors: none
Comments:

Function: $1610
Name: MoveControl
Specifies a control's location.
Push: X Location (W); Y Location (W); Control Handle (L)
Pull: nothing
Errors: none
Comments:

Function: $1710
Name: DragControl
Draws an outline of the control item during a drag event.
Push: Start X (W); Start Y (W); Limit Rectangle (L); Slop Rectangle (L); Axis (W); Control Handle (L)
Pull: nothing
Errors: none
Comments: Axis controls the movement according to the following values: 0 = No constraint, 1 = Horizontal, 2 = Vertical. After the drag, MoveControl is called to change the control's location.

Function: $1810
Name: SetCtlIcons
Specifies the handle to a new icon font.
Push: Result Space (L); New Font Handle (L)
Pull: Old Font Handle (L)
Errors: none
Comments:

Function: $1910
Name: SetCtlValue
Specifies the value of a control.
Push: Value (W); Control Handle (L)
Pull: nothing
Errors: none
Comments:

Function: $1A10
Name: GetCtlValue
Return the value of a control.
Push: Result Space (W); Control Handle (L)
Pull: Value (W)
Errors: none
Comments:

Function: $1B10
Name: SetCtlParams
Sets the values for a control's parameters.
Push: Param 2 (W); Param 1 (W); Control Handle (L)
Pull: nothing
Errors: none
Comments: The control is redrawn if necessary.

Function: $1C10
Name: GetCtlParams
Returns a control's parameters.
Push: Result Space (L); Control Handle (L)
Pull: Param 2 (W); Param 1 (W)
Errors: none
Comments:

Function: $1D10
Name: DragRect
Drags a rectangle outline around the screen during a drag event.
Push: Result Space (L); Action Procedure (L); Drag Pattern (L); Start X (W); Start Y (W); Drag Rectangle (L); Limit Rectangle (L); Slop Rectangle (L); Axis (W); Drag Flag (W)
Pull: Move Delta (L)
Errors: $1001
Comments: Axis controls the movement according to the following values: 0 = No constraint, 1 = Horizontal, 2 = Vertical. Move Delta returns the distance the control has moved with the X amount in the high order word and the Y amount in the low order word.

Function: $1E10
Name: GrowSize
Return the size of the grow box control.
Push: Result Space (L)
Pull: Height (W); Width (W)
Errors: none
Comments: This is helpful in determining the size of a scroll bar.

Function: $1F10
Name: GetCtlDpage
Returns the address of the Control Manager's direct page.
Push: Result Space (W)
Pull: Direct Page (W)
Errors: none
Comments: Normally, this call is made by the Dialog Manager.

Function: $2010
Name: SetCtlAction
Specifies a new action procedure for a control.
Push: Action Procedure (L); Control Handle (L)
Pull: nothing
Errors: none
Comments:

Function: $2110
Name: GetCtlAction
Returns the CtlAction value of a control.
Push: Result Space (L); Control Handle (L)
Pull: CtlAction (L)
Errors: none
Comments:

Function: $2210
Name: SetCtlRefCon
Specifies a control's RefCon value.
Push: RefCon (L); Control Handle (L)
Pull: nothing
Errors: none
Comments:

Function: $2310
Name: GetCtlRefCon
Returns a control's CtlRefCon value.
Push: Result Space (L); Control Handle (L)
Pull: CtlRefCon (L)
Errors: none
Comments:

Function: $2410
Name: EraseControl
Erases a control with the background pattern.
Push: Control Handle (L)
Pull: nothing
Errors: none
Comments:

Function: $2510
Name: DrawOneCtl
Draws one control in the window.
Push: Control Handle (L)
Pull: nothing
Errors: none
Comments:

Summary of Tool Set $10 Error Codes

none

Tool Set $11: Loader

Tool Set: $11
Tool Set Name: Loader
Version Number: 1.1

Function: $0111
Name: LoaderInit
Initialize System Loader.
Push: nothing
Pull: nothing
Errors: none
Comments: Do not make this call.

Function: $0211
Name: LoaderStartUp
Starts the Loader.
Push: nothing
Pull: nothing
Errors: none
Comments: Do not make this call.

Function: $0311
Name: LoaderShutDown
Shuts down the Loader.
Push: nothing
Pull: nothing
Errors: none
Comments: Do not make this call.

Function: $0411
Name: LoaderVersion
Returns version number of the Loader.
Push: Result Space (W)
Pull: Version Number (W)
Errors: none
Comments: LSB is major release, MSB minor release.

Function: $0511
Name: LoaderReset
Called when the computer is reset.
Push: nothing
Pull: nothing
Errors: none
Comments: Do not make this call.

Function: $0611
Name: LoaderStatus
Returns activity status of the Loader.
Push: Result Space (W)
Pull: Status (W)
Errors: none
Comments: This call always returns $FFFF for active.

Function: $0711
Name: InitialLoad
Loads a program into memory.
Push: Result Space (W); Result Space (W); Result Space (L); Result Space (W); UserID (W); Filename Address (L); Memory Flag (W)
Pull: UserID (W); Starting Address (L); Stack Address (W); Stack Size (W)
Errors: $1104, $1105, $1109, $110A, $110B; Also possible ProDOS and Memory Manager Errors
Comments: The file must be a load file type.

Function: $0A11
Name: Restart
Restarts a dormant program in memory.
Push: Result Space (W); Result Space (W); Result Space (L); Result Space (W); UserID (W)
Pull: UserID (W); Starting Address (L); Stack Address (W); Stack Size (W)
Errors: $1101, $1105, $1108; Also possible ProDOS and Memory Manager Errors.
Comments: See function $12.

Function: $0B11
Name: LoadSegNum
Transfers a Load Segment from disk to memory.
Push: Result Space (L); UserID (W); Load-file number (W); Load-segment number (W)
Pull: Segment Address (L)
Errors: $1101, $1102, $1104, $1105, $1107, $1109, $110A, $110B; Also possible ProDOS and Memory Manager Errors
Comments:

Function: $0C11
Name: UnLoadSegNum
Removes a load segment from memory.
Push: UserID (W); Load-file number (W); Load-segment number (W)
Pull: nothing
Errors: $1101, $1105; also possible ProDOS and Memory Manager errors
Comments:

Function: $0D11
Name: LoadSegName
Transfers a named Load Segment from disk to memory.
Push: Result Space (W); Result Space (W); Result Space (L); UserID (W); Address of load-file name (L); Address of load-segment name (L)
Pull: Address of segment (L) load-file number (W); load-segment number (W)
Errors: $1101, $1104, $1105, $1107, $1109, $110A, $110B; also possible ProDOS and Memory Manager errors
Comments:

Function: $0E11
Name: UnloadSeg
Unloads a segment without knowing various parameters.
Push: Result Space (W); Result Space (W); Result Space (W); Address in segment (L)
Pull: UserID (W); load-file number (W); load-segment number (W);
Errors: $1101, $1105, also possible ProDOS and Memory Manager errors
Comments:

Function: $0F11
Name: GetLoadSegInfo
Returns Memory Segment Table entry for a segment.
Push: UserID (W); load-file number (W); load-segment number (W); Address of buffer (L)
Pull: nothing
Errors: $1101, $1105, also possible ProDOS and Memory Manager errors
Comments:

Function: $1011
Name: GetUserID
Returns a UserID matching the specified pathname.
Push: Result Space (W); Address of pathname (L)
Pull: UserID (W)
Errors: $1101, $1105, also possible ProDOS and Memory Manager errors
Comments:

Function: $1111
Name: GetPathname
Returns address of pathname associated with a UserID.
Push: Result Space (L); UserID (W); load-file number (W)
Pull: Address of pathname (L)
Errors: $1101, $1105, also possible ProDOS and Memory Manager errors
Comments:

Function: $1211
Name: UserShutdown
Closes down completed applications.
Push: Result Space (W); UserID (W); quit flag (W)
Pull: UserID (W)
Errors: $1105, also possible ProDOS and Memory Manager errors
Comments:

Summary of Tool Set $11 Error Codes

$0000 No error
$1101 Segment or Entry not found
$1102 Incompatible object module format (OMF) version
$1103
$1104 File is not a load file
$1105 System Loader is busy
$1106
$1107 File version error
$1108 UserID error
$1109 Segment number is out of sequence
$110A Illegal load record found
$110B Load segment is foreign

Tool Set $12: QuickDraw Auxiliary

Tool Set: $12
Tool Set Name: QuickDraw Auxiliary
Version Number: 1.0

Function: $0112
Name: QDAuxBootInit
Initializes the QuickDraw Auxiliary tool set.
Push: nothing
Pull: nothing
Errors: none
Comments: Do not make this call.

Function: $0212
Name: QDAuxStartUp
Starts the QuickDraw Auxiliary tool set.
Push: nothing
Pull: nothing
Errors: none
Comments: QuickDraw II must already be started.

Function: $0312
Name: QDAuxShutDown
Shuts down the QuickDraw Auxiliary tool set.
Push: nothing
Pull: nothing
Errors: none
Comments: Make this call when your application is finished.

Function: $0412
Name: QDAuxVersion
Returns the version number of the QuickDraw Auxiliary tool set.
Push: Result Space (W)
Pull: Version (W)
Errors: none
Comments: LSB is major release, MSB minor release.

Function: $0512
Name: QDAuxReset
Resets the QuickDraw Auxiliary tool set.
Push: nothing
Pull: nothing
Errors: none
Comments: Do not make this call.

Function: $0612
Name: QDAuxStatus
Determines if the QuickDraw Auxiliary tool set is active.
Push: Result Space (W)
Pull: Active (W)
Errors: none
Comments: A nonzero value is returned if active.

Function: $0912
Name: CopyPixels
Causes a region of pixels to conform to a specified rectangle size by stretching or compressing.
Push: Source (L); Destination (L); Source Rectangle (L); Destination Rectangle (L); Pen Transfer Mode (W); Mask Region Handle (L)
Pull: nothing
Errors: none
Comments:

Function: $0A12
Name: WaitCursor
Change the mouse cursor to the watch cursor.
Push: nothing
Pull: nothing
Errors: none
Comments: Restore the arrow cursor with InitCursor.

Summary of Tool Set $12 Error Codes

none

Tool Set $13: Print Manager

Tool Set: $13
Tool Set Name: Print Manager
Version Number: 0.1

Function: $0113
Name: PMBootInit
Initializes the Print Manager.
Push: nothing
Pull: nothing
Errors: none
Comments: Do not make this call.

Function: $0213
Name: PMStartUp
Starts the Print Manager.
Push: User ID (W); Direct Page (W)
Pull: nothing
Errors: none
Comments:

Function: $0313
Name: PMShutDown
Shuts down the Print Manager.
Push: nothing
Pull: nothing
Errors: none
Comments: Make this call when your application is finished.

Function: $0413
Name: PMVersion
Returns the version number of the Print Manager.
Push: Result Space (W)
Pull: Version (W)
Errors: none
Comments: LSB is major release, MSB minor release.

Function: $0513
Name: PMReset
Resets the Print Manager.
Push: nothing
Pull: nothing
Errors: none
Comments: Do not make this call.

Function: $0613
Name: PMStatus
Determines if the Print Manager is active.
Push: Result Space (W)
Pull: Active (W)
Errors: none
Comments: A nonzero value is returned if active.

Function: $0913
Name: PrDefault
Fills the Print Record with standard values.
Push: Print Record Handle (L)
Pull: nothing
Errors: none
Comments:

Function: $0A13
Name: PrValidate
Determines if the contents of the Print Record are compatible with the current Print Manager.
Push: Result Space (W); Print Record Handle (L)
Pull: Invalid (W)
Errors: none
Comments: Invalid will be nonzero if the contents are incompatible.

Function: $0B13
Name: PrStlDialog
Brings up a dialog allowing the user to set page dimensions.
Push: Result Space (W); Print Record Handle (L)
Pull: Continue (W)
Errors: none
Comments: Continue is nonzero if the user did not cancel this operation.

Function: $0C13
Name: PrJobDialog
Brings up a dialog asking the user to choose print quality, page ranges, and so on.
Push: Result Space (W); Print Record Handle (L)
Pull: Continue (W)
Errors: none
Comments: Continue is nonzero if the user wishes to start the print job. A zero indicates the user has canceled.

Function: $0E13
Name: PrOpenDoc
Opens a GrafPort in which to print a document.
Push: Result Space (L); Print Record Handle (L); Old GrafPort (L)
Pull: New GrafPort (L)
Errors: none
Comments: If Old GrafPort is zero, PrOpenDoc will allocate a new port and return a pointer to it in New GrafPort.

Function: $0F13
Name: PrCloseDoc
Closes the GrafPort currently opened for printing.
Push: GrafPort (L)
Pull: nothing
Errors: none
Comments:

Function: $1013
Name: PrOpenPage
Begins printing a new page.
Push: GrafPort (L); Page Scaling (L)
Pull: nothing
Errors: none
Comments: Use zero to specify no scaling parameter.

Function: $1113
Name: PrClosePage
Signals the end of the printing of the current page.
Push: GrafPort (L)
Pull: nothing
Errors: none
Comments:

Function: $1213
Name: PrPicFile
Prints a spooled document.
Push: Print Record Handle (L); GrafPort (L); Status Record (L)
Pull: nothing
Errors: none
Comments: Usually, the GrafPort pointer is zero.

Function: $1313
Name: PrControl
Passes control to the low-level printer functions.
Push: Appropriate parameters; Control Value (W)
Pull: Appropriate results, if any
Errors: none
Comments: Parameters to and from the stack are dependent on the type of control call being made. See the end of this section for a list of low-level printer controls.

Function: $1413
Name: PrError
Returns the error code of the most recent Print Manager function.
Push: Result Space (W)
Pull: Error (W)
Errors: none
Comments: Error codes are: 0 = No Error, -27 = I/O Abort, -128 = Memory Fault Error, 128 = Printer Abort.

Function: $1513
Name: PrSetError
Places an error value into the Print Manager's result code variable.
Push: Error (W)
Pull: nothing
Errors: none
Comments: This is used to force a print job to cancel, for example.

Function: $1613
Name: PrChooser
Brings up a dialog to allow the user to choose a printing device and driver.
Push: Result Space (W)
Pull: Changed (W)
Errors: none
Comments: Changed is nonzero if the user has changed to a driver different from the current driver.

Low-Level Print Driver Controls:

Control: $00
Name: LLDStartup
Starts the low-level driver.
Push: Direct Page (W); User ID (W)
Pull: nothing
Errors: none
Comments:

Control: $01
Name: LLDShutDown
Shuts down the low-level driver.
Push: User ID (W)
Pull: nothing
Errors: none
Comments:

Control: $04
Name: PrBitMap
Prints the specified region of a QuickDraw II bit map.
Push: Bit Map (L); Rectangle (L); User ID (W)
Pull: nothing
Errors: none
Comments:

Control: $06
Name: PrText
Sends a stream of text directly to the printer.
Push: Text (L); Length (W); User ID (W)
Pull: nothing
Errors: none
Comments:

Control: $08
Name: LLDControl
Controls various printer functions.
Push: Control (W)
Pull: nothing
Errors: none
Comments: Control values are: 1 = Reset Printer, 2 = Form Feed, 3 = Line Feed.

Summary of Tool Set $13 Error Codes

none

Tool Set $14: LineEdit

Tool Set: $14
Tool Set Name: LineEdit
Version Number: 1.0

Function: $0114
Name: LEBootInit
Initializes the LineEdit tool set.
Push: nothing
Pull: nothing
Errors: none
Comments: Do not make this call.

Function: $0214
Name: LEStartUp
Starts the LineEdit tool set.
Push: User ID (W); Direct Page (W)
Pull: nothing
Errors: $1401, possible Memory Manager errors
Comments:

Function: $0314
Name: LEShutDown
Shuts down the LineEdit tool set.
Push: nothing
Pull: nothing
Errors: none
Comments: Make this call when your application is finished.

Function: $0414
Name: LEVersion
Returns the version number of the LineEdit tool set.
Push: Result Space (W)
Pull: Version (W)
Errors: none
Comments: LSB is major release, MSB minor release.

Function: $0514
Name: LEReset
Resets the LineEdit tool set.
Push: nothing
Pull: nothing
Errors: none
Comments: Do not make this call.

Function: $0614
Name: LEStatus
Determines if the LineEdit tool set is active.
Push: Result Space (W)
Pull: Active (W)
Errors: none
Comments: A nonzero value is returned if active.

Function: $0914
Name: LENew
Creates a new edit record.
Push: Result Space (L); Destination Rectangle (L); View Rectangle (L); Maximum Length (W)
Pull: Edit Record Handle (L)
Errors: Possible Memory Manager errors
Comments:

Function: $0A14
Name: LEDispose
Frees the memory which was allocated for an edit record.
Push: Edit Record Handle (L)
Pull: nothing
Errors: Possible Memory Manager errors
Comments: An application must make this call to dispose any edit records before calling LEShutDown.

Function: $0B14
Name: LESetText
Adds text to an edit record.
Push: Text (L); Length (W); Edit Record Handle (L)
Pull: nothing
Errors: Possible Memory Manager and QuickDraw II errors
Comments: Call InvalRect (Window Manager) after using LESetText.

Function: $0C14
Name: LEIdle
Regulates the blinking of the insertion point caret.
Push: Edit Record Handle (L)
Pull: nothing
Errors: Possible Memory Manager and QuickDraw II errors
Comments: LEIdle should be called whenever there is an active LineEdit item in a dialog box.

Function: $0D14
Name: LEClick
Manages selected text determined by mouse events.
Push: Event Record (L); Edit Record Handle (L)
Pull: nothing
Errors: Possible Memory Manager and QuickDraw II errors
Comments:

Function: $0E14
Name: LESetSelect
Sets the range of selected text.
Push: Start (W); End (W); Edit Record Handle (L)
Pull: nothing
Errors: Possible Memory Manager and QuickDraw II errors
Comments:

Function: $0F14
Name: LEActivate
Highlights a specified range of text.
Push: Edit Record Handle (L)
Pull: nothing
Errors: Possible Memory Manager and QuickDraw II errors
Comments:

Function: $1014
Name: LEDeactivate
Unhighlights a specified range of text.
Push: Edit Record Handle (L)
Pull: nothing
Errors: Possible Memory Manager and QuickDraw II errors
Comments:

Function: $1114
Name: LEKey
Replaces the selection range with a character.
Push: Character (W); Event Modifiers (W); Edit Record Handle (L)
Pull: nothing
Errors: Possible Memory Manager and QuickDraw II errors
Comments:

Function: $1214
Name: LECut
Moves selected text to the LineEdit scrap.
Push: Edit Record Handle (L)
Pull: nothing
Errors: Possible Memory Manager and QuickDraw II errors
Comments:

Function: $1314
Name: LECopy
Copies selected text to the LineEdit scrap.
Push: Edit Record Handle (L)
Pull: nothing
Errors: Possible Memory Manager and QuickDraw II errors
Comments:

Function: $1414
Name: LEPaste
Replaces selected text with contents of the LineEdit scrap.
Push: Edit Record Handle (L)
Pull: nothing
Errors: Possible Memory Manager and QuickDraw II errors
Comments:

Function: $1514
Name: LEDelete
Deletes a selected range of text.
Push: Edit Record Handle (L)
Pull: nothing
Errors: Possible Memory Manager and QuickDraw II errors
Comments:

Function: $1614
Name: LEInsert
Inserts text before the selection range.
Push: Text (L); Insertion Length (W); Edit Record Handle (L)
Pull: nothing
Errors: Possible Memory Manager and QuickDraw II errors
Comments:

Function: $1714
Name: LEUpdate
Redraws the text of an EditLine record.
Push: Edit Record Handle (L)
Pull: nothing
Errors: none
Comments:

Function: $1814
Name: LETextBox
Places text into a rectangle with desired justification.
Push: Text (L); Length (W); Rectangle (L); Justify Mode (W)
Pull: nothing
Errors: Possible Memory Manager and QuickDraw II errors
Comments: Justify Modes are 0 for left-justified, 1 for centered, and -1 for right-justified text.

Function: $1914
Name: LEFromScrap
Fills the LineEdit scrap with data from the desk scrap.
Push: nothing
Pull: nothing
Errors: $1404, possible Scrap Manager errors
Comments: The Scrap Manager must be active.

Function: $1A14
Name: LEToScrap
Copies the LineEdit scrap to the desk scrap.
Push: nothing
Pull: nothing
Errors: Possible Scrap Manager errors
Comments: The Scrap Manager must be active.

Function: $1B14
Name: LEScrapHandle
Returns a handle to the LineEdit scrap.
Push: Result Space (L)
Pull: Scrap Handle (L)
Errors: none
Comments:

Function: $1C14
Name: LEGetScrapLen
Returns a count of the number of bytes in the LineEdit scrap.
Push: Result Space (W)
Pull: Scrap Length (W)
Errors: none
Comments:

Function: $1D14
Name: LESetScrapLen
Sets the size of the LineEdit scrap.
Push: Scrap Size (W)
Pull: nothing
Errors: none
Comments: Any sizes greater than 256 will be treated as 256.

Function: $1E14
Name: LESetHilite
Specifies the highlight and unhighlight procedures.
Push: Procedure (L); Edit Record Handle (L)
Pull: nothing
Errors: none
Comments:

Function: $1F14
Name: LESetCaret
Specifies the caret drawing procedure.
Push: Procedure (L); Edit Record Handle (L)
Pull: nothing
Errors: none
Comments:

Function: $2014
Name: LETextBox2
Places text into a rectangle with desired justification.
Push: Text (L); Length (L); Rectangle (L); Justify Mode (W)
Pull: nothing
Errors: Possible Memory Manager and QuickDraw II errors
Comments: Justify Modes are 0 for left, 1 for centered, -1 for right, and 2 for fill justified text.

Summary of Tool Set $14 Error Codes

$1401 The LEStartUp call has already been made
$1402 Reset error
$1404 The desk scrap is too big

Tool Set $15: Dialog Manager

Tool Set: $15
Tool Set Name: Dialog Manager
Version Number: 1.1

Function: $0115
Name: DialogBootInit
Initialize the Dialog Manager.
Push: nothing
Pull: nothing
Errors: none
Comments: Do not make this call.

Function: $0215
Name: DialogStartUp
Starts the Dialog Manager.
Push: UserID (W)
Pull: nothing
Errors: none
Comments: The Control Manager must be started before making this call.

Function: $0315
Name: DialogShutDown
Shuts down the Dialog Manager.
Push: nothing
Pull: nothing
Errors: none
Comments:

Function: $0415
Name: DialogVersion
Returns version number of the Dialog Manager.
Push: Result Space (W)
Pull: Version Number (W)
Errors: none
Comments: LSB is major release, MSB minor release.

Function: $0515
Name: DialogReset
Called when the computer is reset.
Push: nothing
Pull: nothing
Errors: none
Comments: Do not make this call.

Function: $0615
Name: DialogStatus
Returns activity status of the Dialog Manager.
Push: Result Space (W)
Pull: Status (W)
Errors: none
Comments: $0000 indicates the Dialog Manager is inactive.

Function: $0915
Name: ErrorSound
Install an error sound procedure.
Push: Sound Procedure (L)
Pull: nothing
Errors: none
Comments: Your routine is called during dialog alerts and when the mouse is clicked outside of a dialog box.

Function: $0A15
Name: NewModalDialog
Creates a Modal dialog box on the screen.
Push: Result Space (L); Rectangle (L); Visible Flag (W); Window Reference (L)
Pull: Dialog Port (L)
Errors: Possible Memory Manager errors
Comments: See chapter 17.

Function: $0B15
Name: NewModelessDialog
Creates a Modeless dialog box.
Push: Result Space (L); Rectangle (L); Title String (L); Window Plane (L); Frame Info (W); Reference Value (L); Zoom Rectangle (L)
Pull: Dialog Port (L)
Errors: Possible Memory Manager errors
Comments:

Function: $0C15
Name: CloseDialog
Removes a dialog from the screen.
Push: Dialog Port (L)
Pull: nothing
Errors: Possible Window Manager errors
Comments:

Function: $0D15
Name: NewDItem
Places an item into a dialog box.
Push: Dialog Pointer (L); Item Reference (W); Rectangle (L); Item Type (W); Item Pointer (L); Item Value (W); Visible Flag (W); Color Table (L)
Pull: nothing
Errors: $150A, $150B
Comments:

Function: $0E15
Name: RemoveDItem
Removes an item from a dialog box.
Push: Dialog Port (L); Item ID (W)
Pull: nothing
Errors: $150C
Comments:

Function: $0F15
Name: ModalDialog
Handles events in the frontmost dialog window.
Push: Result Space (W); Filter Procedure (L)
Pull: Item Hit (W)
Errors: $150D
Comments: A long word of zero is used for the standard filter procedure.

Function: $1015
Name: IsDialogEvent
Returns a flag indicating whether an event is a dialog event.
Push: Result Space (W); Event Record (L)
Pull: Logical Result (W)
Errors: none
Comments: Zero is returned if the event is not a dialog event.

Function: $1115
Name: DialogSelect
Handles the events of a Modeless Dialog box.
Push: Result Space (W); Event Record (L); Dialog Pointer (L); Item ID (L)
Pull: Logical Result (W)
Errors: none
Comments:

Function: $1215
Name: DlgCut
Calls LECut for a selected EditLine item.
Push: Dialog Port (L)
Pull: nothing
Errors: none
Comments:

Function: $1315
Name: DlgCopy
Calls LECopy for a selected EditLine item.
Push: Dialog Port (L)
Pull: nothing
Errors: none
Comments:

Function: $1415
Name: DlgPaste
Calls LEPaste for a selected EditLine item.
Push: Dialog Port (L)
Pull: nothing
Errors: none
Comments:

Function: $1515
Name: DlgDelete
Calls LEDelete for a selected EditLine item.
Push: Dialog Port (L)
Pull: nothing
Errors: none
Comments:

Function: $1615
Name: DrawDialog
Draws a dialog box to the screen.
Push: Dialog Port (L)
Pull: nothing
Errors: none
Comments:

Function: $1715
Name: Alert
Brings up an Alert dialog.
Push: Result Space (W); Alert Template (L); Filter Procedure (L)
Pull: Item Hit (W)
Errors: none
Comments: The number of the selected item in the Alert dialog is returned after the call. If its value is -1, the dialog box was not drawn.

Function: $1815
Name: StopAlert
Brings up an Alert dialog with the stop icon.
Push: Result Space (W); Alert Template (L); Filter Procedure (L)
Pull: Item Hit (W)
Errors: none
Comments: (Same as Alert call). The stop icon is a stop-sign shape containing the image of an opened hand, and is placed in the upper left corner of the dialog box.

Function: $1915
Name: NoteAlert
Brings up an Alert dialog with the note icon.
Push: Result Space (W); Alert Template (L); Filter Procedure (L)
Pull: Item Hit (W)
Errors: none
Comments: (Same as Alert call). The note icon contains a face with an exclamation point inside a cartoon-like bubble, and is placed in the upper left corner of the dialog box.

Function: $1A15
Name: CautionAlert
Brings up an Alert dialog with the caution icon.
Push: Result Space (W); Alert Template (L); Filter Procedure (L)
Pull: Item Hit (W)
Errors: none
Comments: (Same as Alert call). The caution icon is a triangle with an exclamation point inside, and is placed in the upper left corner of the dialog box.

Function: $1B15
Name: ParamText
Replaces contents of StatText and LongStatText items.
Push: Parameter 0 (L); Parameter 1 (L); Parameter 2 (L); Parameter 3 (L)
Pull: nothing
Errors: none
Comments: Use a zero value for a parameter which should not be changed.

Function: $1C15
Name: SetDAFont
Specifies the font to be used by a dialog or alert.
Push: Font Handle (L)
Pull: nothing
Errors: none
Comments:

Function: $1E15
Name: GetControlDItem
Returns the handle to a control of a given dialog item.
Push: Result Space (L); Dialog Port (L); Item ID (W)
Pull: Control Handle (L)
Errors: $150C
Comments: Use with scroll bars is not recommended.

Function: $1F15
Name: GetIText
Returns the text of a StatText or EditLine item.
Push: Dialog Port (L); Item ID (W); String Storage (L)
Pull: nothing
Errors: $150A, $150C
Comments:

Function: $2015
Name: SetIText
Specifies text for a StatText or EditLine item.
Push: Dialog Port (L); Item ID (W); Text (L)
Pull: nothing
Errors: $150A, $150C
Comments:

Function: $2115
Name: SellText
Selects a portion of text in an EditLine.
Push: Dialog Port (L); Item ID (W); Start Position Value (W); End Position Value (W)
Pull: nothing
Errors: none
Comments:

Function: $2215
Name: HideDItem
Hides a dialog item from a specified dialog display.
Push: Dialog Port (L); Item ID (W)
Pull: nothing
Errors: $150C
Comments: The item can be made visible again with ShowDItem.

Function: $2315
Name: ShowDItem
Reveals a hidden dialog item.
Push: Dialog Port (L); Item ID (W)
Pull: nothing
Errors: $150C
Comments:

Function: $2415
Name: FindDItem
Finds the ID of a dialog item at specific coordinates.
Push: Result Space (W); Dialog Port (L); Coordinate Point (L)
Pull: Item ID (W)
Errors: none
Comments: The location is given in global coordinates. A zero result is returned if no item was found at the given coordinates.

Function: $2515
Name: UpdateDialog
Redraws the specified region of a dialog.
Push: Dialog Port (L); Update Region Handle (L)
Pull: nothing
Errors: none
Comments:

Function: $2615
Name: GetDItemType
Gets the type of a dialog item.
Push: Result Space (W); Dialog Port (L); Item ID (W)
Pull: Item Type (W)
Errors: $150C
Comments: If the item is disabled, the returned value will be the item's type plus the value of ItemDisable.

Function: $2715
Name: SetDItemType
Specifies the type of a dialog item.
Push: Item Type (W); Dialog Port (L); Item ID (W)
Pull: nothing
Errors: $150C
Comments:

Function: $2815
Name: GetDItemBox
Returns the display rectangle of a dialog item.
Push: Dialog Port (L); Item ID (W); Item Box Storage (L)
Pull: nothing
Errors: $150C
Comments:

Function: $2915
Name: SetDItemBox
Specifies a new rectangle size for an item.
Push: Dialog Port (L); Item ID (W); Rectangle (L)
Pull: nothing
Errors: none
Comments:

Function: $2A15
Name: GetFirstDItem
Returns the item ID of the first item in a given dialog.
Push: Result Space (W); Dialog Port (L)
Pull: First Item (W)
Errors: none
Comments: Zero is returned if there is no item.

Function: $2B15
Name: GetNextDItem
Returns the item ID of a proceeding item.
Push: Result Space (W); Dialog Port (L); Current Item ID (W)
Pull: Next Item ID (W)
Errors: none
Comments: Zero is returned if a next item is not found.

Function: $2C15
Name: ModalDialog2
Handles events in the frontmost dialog window, returning the Hit Item's ID and Part Code.
Push: Result Space (L); Filter Procedure (L)
Pull: Item ID and Part Code (L)
Errors: $150D
Comments: Same as ModalDialog except a Part Code is returned in the high order word and the Item Hit ID in the low order word of the result.

Function: $2E15
Name: GetDItemValue
Returns the value of a dialog item.
Push: Result Space (W); Dialog Port (L); Item ID (W)
Pull: Value (W)
Errors: $150C
Comments:

Function: $2F15
Name: SetDItemValue
Specifies the value of a dialog item.
Push: Item Value (W); Dialog Port (L); Item ID (W)
Pull: nothing
Errors: $150C
Comments:

Function: $3215
Name: GetNewModalDialog
Creates a modal dialog using a template.
Push: Result Space (L); Template (L)
Pull: Dialog Port (L)
Errors: none
Comments: Also see NewModalDialog.

Function: $3315
Name: GetNewDItem
Adds an item to a dialog using a template.
Push: Dialog Port (L); Template (L)
Pull: nothing
Errors: $150A, $150C
Comments: Also see NewDItem.

Function: $3415
Name: GetAlertStage
Returns the latest alert stage.
Push: Result Space (W)
Pull: Stage (W)
Errors: none
Comments: Stage will be a value from 0 to 3.

Function: $3515
Name: ResetAlertStage
Reset the current alert stage to zero.
Push: nothing
Pull: nothing
Errors: none
Comments:

Function: $3615
Name: DefaultFilter
Determines if an event is standard or requires handling by a user filter if specified.
Push: Result Space (W); Dialog Port (L); Event (L); Item Hit (L)
Pull: Flag (W)
Errors: none
Comments: The Flag is zero if the event requires custom handling; Apple keys for Cut, Copy, and Paste, and Return key as the default button are handled as standard event items and are denoted by a nonzero Flag value.

Function: $3715
Name: GetDefButton
Returns the Item ID of the default button.
Push: Result Space (W); Dialog Port (L)
Pull: Button ID (W)
Errors: none
Comments: Zero is returned if there is no default button.

Function: $3815
Name: SetDefButton
Specifies the default button in a dialog.
Push: Button ID (W); Dialog Port (L)
Pull: nothing
Errors: none
Comments:

Function: $3915
Name: DisableDItem
Disables a dialog item.
Push: Dialog Port (L); Item ID (W)
Pull: nothing
Errors: $150C
Comments:

Function: $3A15
Name: EnableDItem
Enables a dialog item.
Push: Dialog Port (L); Item ID (W)
Pull: nothing
Errors: $150C
Comments:

Summary of Tool Set $15 Error Codes

$150A Bad Item Type
$150B New Item Failed
$150C Item Not Found
$150D Not a Modal Dialog

Tool Set $16: Scrap Manager

Tool Set: $16
Tool Set Name: Scrap Manager
Version Number: 1.1

Function: $0116
Name: ScrapBootInit
Initializes the Scrap Manager.
Push: nothing
Pull: nothing
Errors: none
Comments: Do not make this call.

Function: $0216
Name: ScrapStartUp
Starts the Scrap Manager.
Push: nothing
Pull: nothing
Errors: none
Comments: Make this call before using this tool set.

Function: $0316
Name: ScrapShutDown
Shuts down the Scrap Manager.
Push: nothing
Pull: nothing
Errors: none
Comments: Make this call before your program quits.

Function: $0416
Name: ScrapVersion
Returns the version of the Scrap Manager.
Push: Result Space (W)
Pull: Version (W)
Errors: none
Comments:

Function: $0516
Name: ScrapReset
Resets the Scrap Manager.
Push: nothing
Pull: nothing
Errors: none
Comments:

Function: $0616
Name: ScrapStatus
Determines if Scrap Manager is active.
Push: Result Space (W)
Pull: Active (W)
Errors: none
Comments: A nonzero value is returned if active.

Function: $0916
Name: UnloadScrap
Writes the desk scrap in memory to the scrap file.
Push: nothing
Pull: nothing
Errors: Possible Memory Manager and ProDOS errors
Comments:

Function: $0A16
Name: LoadScrap
Reads the scrap file on disk into memory.
Push: nothing
Pull: nothing
Errors: Possible Memory Manager and ProDOS errors
Comments:

Function: $0B16
Name: ZeroScrap
Erases the desk scrap whether in memory or on disk.
Push: nothing
Pull: nothing
Errors: Possible Memory Manager and ProDOS errors
Comments:

Function: $0C16
Name: PutScrap
Adds data to the desk scrap.
Push: Byte Count (L); Scrap Type (W); Scrap (L)
Pull: nothing
Errors: Possible Memory Manager and ProDOS errors
Comments: Use ZeroScrap to avoid appending to existing data.

Function: $0D16
Name: GetScrap
Copies scrap data to a specified location.
Push: Destination Handle (L); Scrap Type (W)
Pull: nothing
Errors: $1610, possible Memory Manager and ProDOS errors
Comments:

Function: $0E16
Name: GetScrapHandle
Returns the handle of a specific type of desk scrap.
Push: Result Space (L); Scrap Type (W)
Pull: Scrap Handle (L)
Errors: $1610, possible Memory Manager and ProDOS errors
Comments:

Function: $0F16
Name: GetScrapSize
Returns the size of a specific type of desk scrap.
Push: Result Space (L); Scrap Type (W)
Pull: Scrap Size (L)
Errors: $1610, possible Memory Manager and ProDOS errors
Comments:

Function: $1016
Name: GetScrapPath
Returns the address of the Clipboard's pathname.
Push: Result Space (L)
Pull: Pathname (L)
Errors: none
Comments:

Function: $1116
Name: SetScrapPath
Sets the address of the Clipboard's pathname.
Push: Pathname (L)
Pull: nothing
Errors: none
Comments:

Function: $1216
Name: GetScrapCount
Returns the current scrap count identifier.
Push: Result Space (W)
Pull: Scrap Count (W)
Errors: none
Comments: The scrap count increments after ZeroScrap is called.

Function: $1316
Name: GetScrapState
Returns scrap state flag.
Push: Result Space (W)
Pull: State (W)
Errors: none
Comments: A nonzero value means the scrap is in memory while zero indicates it's on disk.

Summary of Tool Set $16 Error Codes

$1610 Unknown Scrap Type

Tool Set $17: Standard File Operations Toolset

Tool Set: $17
Tool Set Name: Standard File Operations Tool Set
Version Number: 1.1

Function: $0117
Name: SFBootInit
Initialize the Standard File Tool Set environment.
Push: nothing
Pull: nothing
Errors: none
Comments: Applications do not make this call.

Function: $0217
Name: SFStartup
Starts up the Standard File Operations tool set.
Push: User ID (W); Direct Page (W)
Pull: nothing
Errors: none
Comments: Call this before using Standard File functions.

Function: $0317
Name: SFShutdown
Shuts down the Standard Files tool set and frees some memory.
Push: nothing
Pull: nothing
Errors: none
Comments: Call this when your application is finished using Standard File Operations.

Function: $0417
Name: SFVersion
Get the current version of the Standard File tool set.
Push: Result Space (W)
Pull: Version number (W)
Errors: none
Comments:

Function: $0517
Name: SFReset
Reset the Standard File Operations tool set.
Push: nothing
Pull: nothing
Errors: none
Comments:

Function: $0617
Name: SFStatus
Determine if the Standard File Operations tool set is active.
Push: Result Space (W)
Pull: Active flag (W)
Errors: none
Comments: The flag is zero if false, nonzero if true.

Function: $0917
Name: SFGetFile
Lets the user choose a specific file from a dialog box.
Push: X position of dialog box (W); Y position of dialog box (W); Pointer to dialog box title string (L); Pointer to filtering subroutine (L); Pointer to list of valid file types (L); Pointer to returned pathname record structure (L)
Pull: nothing
Errors: none
Comments: Title string starts with a count byte. Calling of the filtering routine can be inhibited by using $00000000 as its address. The filtering routine should return via RTL. File type list starts with a count byte. Record structure of returned pathname is: Open Flag (W), File type (W), Auxiliary file type (W), filename (15 bytes), full pathname to file (128 bytes).

Function: $0A17
Name: SFPutFile
Lets the user choose a filename for saving information to disk.
Push: X position of dialog box (W); Y position of dialog box (W); Pointer to dialog box title string (L); Pointer to string containing original filename (L); Maximum length of name (W); Pointer to returned pathname record structure (L)
Pull: nothing
Errors: none
Comments: Returned pathname record structure is the same as SFGetFile.

Function: $0B17
Name: SFPGetFile
Allows user to choose a file name from a custom dialog box.
Push: X position of dialog box (W); Y position of dialog box (W); Pointer to title string (L); Pointer to filtering routine (L); Pointer to file type list (L); Pointer to dialog template structure (L); Pointer to modal dialog event handler (L); Pointer to returned pathname record structure (L)
Pull: nothing
Errors: none
Comments: Same as SFGetFile except for the template pointer and modal dialog activity handler (see Dialog Manager section for details).

Function: $0C17
Name: SFPPutFile
Gives the user a custom dialog box to choose a file name for saving information to disk.
Push: X position of dialog box (W); Y position of dialog box (W); Pointer to dialog box title string (L); Pointer to string containing original filename (L); Maximum length of name (W); Pointer to dialog template structure (L); Pointer to modal dialog event handler (L); Pointer to returned pathname record structure (L)
Pull: nothing
Errors: none
Comments: See SFPGetFile.

Function: $0D17
Name: SFAllCaps
Sets the case mode for filenames in dialog boxes.
Push: Case flag (W)
Pull: nothing
Errors: none
Comments: If case flag is true (nonzero), all filenames in SFO dialog boxes will be shown without conversion to lowercase.

Summary of Tool Set $17 Error Codes

none

Tool Set $18: Disk Utilities

Tool Set: $18
Tool Set Name: Disk Utilities
Version Number: 0.0

As this book goes to press, the Disk Utilities tool set has not been made available from Apple.

Summary of Tool Set $18 Error codes:

none

Tool Set $19: Note Synthesizer

Tool Set: $19
Tool Set Name: Note Synthesizer
Version Number: 1.0

Function: $0119
Name: NSBootInit
Initialize the Note Synthesizer.
Push: nothing
Pull: nothing
Errors: none
Comments: Do not make this call.

Function: $0219
Name: NSStartUp
Starts the Note Synthesizer.
Push: Update Rate (W); User Update Routine (L)
Pull: nothing
Errors: none
Comments: Starts up the Note Synthesizer; Update Rate is in hertz, #70 ($46) = 60 Hz updates.

Function: $0319
Name: NSShutDown
Shuts down the Note Synthesizer.
Push: nothing
Pull: nothing
Errors: none
Comments:

Function: $0419
Name: NSVersion
Returns version number of the Note Synthesizer.
Push: Result Space (W)
Pull: Version Number (W)
Errors: none
Comments: LSB is major release, MSB minor release.

Function: $0519
Name: NSReset
Called when the computer is reset.
Push: nothing
Pull: nothing
Errors: none
Comments: Do not make this call.

Function: $0619
Name: NSStatus
Returns activity status of the Note Synthesizer.
Push: Result Space (W)
Pull: Status (W)
Errors: none
Comments:

Function: $0919
Name: AllocGen
Returns a generator to be used for playing notes.
Push: Result Space (W); Request Priority (W)
Pull: Generator (W)
Errors: $1921
Comments:

Function: $0A19
Name: DeallocGen
Resets a generator used by the Note Synthesizer to zero.
Push: Generator (W)
Pull: nothing
Errors: $1922
Comments:

Function: $0B19
Name: NoteOn
Starts playing a note on a specified generator.
Push: Generator (W); Semitone (W); Volume (W); Instrument (L)
Pull: nothing
Errors: $1924
Comments:

Function: $0C19
Name: NoteOff
Stops playing a note on a specified generator.
Push: Generator (W); Semitone (W)
Pull: nothing
Errors: none
Comments: Generator and Semitone must be the same as when NoteOn was called.

$0D19

Function: $0D19
Name: AllNotesOff
Stops the sound made by all generators used by the Note Synthesizer.
Push: nothing
Pull: nothing
Errors: none
Comments:

Summary of Tool Set $19 Error Codes

$0000	No error
$1901	NS Already initialized
$1902	Sound tool set not initialized
$1921	No generator available
$1922	Invalid or bad generator number
$1923	NS not initialized
$1924	Note is already on

Tool Set $0A: SANE

Tool Set: $0A
Tool Set Name: SANE
Version Number: 0.9

Function: $010A
Name: SANEBootInit
Initialize the SANE.
Push: nothing
Pull: nothing
Errors: none
Comments: Do not make this call.

Function: $020A
Name: SANEStartUp
Starts the SANE.
Push: Direct Page (W)
Pull: nothing
Errors: none
Comments:

Function: $030A
Name: SANEShutDown
Shuts down the SANE.
Push: nothing
Pull: nothing
Errors: none
Comments:

Function: $040A
Name: SANEVersion
Returns version number of the SANE.
Push: Result Space (W)
Pull: Version Number (W)
Errors: none
Comments: LSB is major release, MSB minor release.

Function: $050A
Name: SANEReset
Called when the computer is reset.
Push: nothing
Pull: nothing
Errors: none
Comments: Do not make this call.

Function: $060A
Name: SANEStatus
Returns activity status of the SANE.
Push: Result Space (W)
Pull: Status (W)
Errors: none
Comments: The SANE is always active.

Function: $090A
Name: SANEEFP816
See NOTE below.
Push:
Pull:
Errors: none
Comments:

Function: $0A0A
Name: SANEDecStr816
See NOTE below.
Push:
Pull:
Errors: none
Comments:

Function: $0B0A
Name: SANEElems816
See NOTE below.
Push:
Pull:
Errors: none
Comments:

NOTE: Documentation for the 65C816 SANE is avialable in the Apple Numerics Manual. Complete information on the above functions can be found there.

Summary of Tool Set $0A Error Codes

None

Tool Set $0B: Integer Math

Tool Set: $0B
Tool Set Name: Integer Math
Version Number: 1.2

Function: $010B
Name: IMBootInit
Not used.
Push: nothing
Pull: nothing
Errors: none
Comments: Do not make this call.

Function: $020B
Name: IMStartUp
Not used.
Push: nothing
Pull: nothing
Errors: none
Comments: Does nothing.

Function: $030B
Name: IMShutDown
Not used.
Push: nothing
Pull: nothing
Errors: none
Comments: Does nothing.

Function: $040B
Name: IMVersion
Returns version number of the Integer Math Tool Set.
Push: Result Space (W)
Pull: Version Number (W)
Errors: none
Comments: LSB is major release, MSB minor release.

Function: $050B
Name: IMReset
Called when the computer is reset.
Push: nothing
Pull: nothing
Errors: none
Comments: Does nothing.

Function: $060B
Name: IMStatus
Returns activity status of the Integer Math Tool Set.
Push: Result Space (W)
Pull: Status (W)
Errors: none
Comments: This call always returns $FFFF for active.

Function: $090B
Name: Multiply
Multiplies two 16-bit integers for a 32-bit result.
Push: Result Space (L); Int1 (W); Int2 (W)
Pull: Result (L)
Errors: none
Comments:

Function: $0A0B
Name: SDivide
Divides two 16-bit integers for a 16-bit result.
Push: Result Space (W); Result Space (W); Numerator (W); Denominator (W)
Pull: Quotient (W); Remainder (W)
Errors: none
Comments: Result is signed.

Function: $0B0B
Name: UDivide
Divides two 16-bit integers for a 16-bit result.
Push: Result Space (W); Result Space (W); Numerator (W); Denominator (W)
Pull: Quotient (W); Remainder (W)
Errors: none
Comments: Result is unsigned.

Function: $0C0B
Name: LongMul
Multiplies two 32-bit integer for a 64-bit result.
Push: Result Space (L); Result Space (L); Int1 (L); Int2 (L)
Pull: Result—least significant (L); most significant (L)
Errors: none
Comments:

Function: $0D0B
Name: LongDivide
Divides two 32-bit integers.
Push: Result Space (L); Result Space (L); Numerator (L); Denominator (L)
Pull: Quotient (L); Remainder (L)
Errors: none
Comments: Results are unsigned.

Function: $0E0B
Name: FixRatio
Produces Fixed ratio of numerator and denominator.
Push: Result Space (L); Numerator (W); Denominator (W)
Pull: Fixed result (L)
Errors: none
Comments:

Function: $0F0B
Name: FixMul
Multiplies two 32-bit Fixed values for a 32-bit Fixed result.
Push: Result Space (L); Fixed1 (L); Fixed2 (L)
Pull: Fixed Result (L)
Errors: none
Comments:

Function: $100B
Name: FracMul
Multiplies two 32-bit Frac values for a 32-bit Frac result.
Push: Result Space (L); Frac1 Address (L); Frac2 Address (L)
Pull: Result Address (L)
Errors: none
Comments:

Function: $110B
Name: FixDiv
Divides two 32-bit Fixed values for a Fixed result.
Push: Result Space (L); Fixed1 (L); Fixed2 (L)
Pull: Fixed Result (L)
Errors: none
Comments: Result is rounded; a remainder is not calculated.

Function: $120B
Name: FracDiv
Divides two 32-bit Frac values for a 32-bit Frac result.
Push: Result Space (L); Frac1 (L); Frac2 (L)
Pull: Frac Result (L)
Errors: none
Comments: Result is rounded; a remainder is not calculated.

Function: $130B
Name: FixRound
Produces a rounded integer from a Fixed input.
Push: Result Space (W); Fixed input (L)
Pull: Integer Result (W)
Errors: none
Comments: Result is rounded.

Function: $140B
Name: FracSqrt
Produces the Frac square root of a 32-bit Frac input.
Push: Result Space (L); Frac input (L)
Pull: Square Root (L)
Errors: none
Comments: Result is rounded.

Function: $150B
Name: FracCos
Calculates the cosine of a 32-bit Frac value.
Push: Result Space (L); Frac input (L)
Pull: Frac Cosine (L)
Errors: none
Comments: Frac input is an angle as measured in radians.

Function: $160B
Name: FracSin
Calculates the sine of a 32-bit Frac value.
Push: Result Space (L); Frac input (L)
Pull: Frac Sine (L)
Errors: none
Comments: Frac input is an angle as measured in radians.

Function: $170B
Name: FixATan2
Calculates the arctangent of two angle values.
Push: Result Space (L); Angle1 (L); Angle2 (L)
Pull: Fixed Arctangent (L)
Errors: none
Comments: Angles are in radians; Angle1 and Angle2 must both be integer, Fixed, or Frac.

Function: $180B
Name: HiWord
Returns the high order word of a 32-bit value.
Push: Result Space (W); Value (L)
Pull: High order word (W)
Errors: none
Comments: Undoubtedly an internal toolbox call, as there are more efficient ways to do this.

Function: $190B
Name: LoWord
Returns the low order word of a 32-bit value.
Push: Result Space (W); Value (L)
Pull: Low order word (W)
Errors: none
Comments: See function 18.

Function: $1A0B
Name: Long2Fix
Translates a long integer to a Fixed value.
Push: Result Space (L); Integer value (L)
Pull: Fixed Result (L)
Errors: none
Comments:

Function: $1B0B
Name: Fix2Long
Translates a Fixed value to a long integer.
Push: Result Space (L); Fixed value (L)
Pull: Integer Result (L)
Errors: none
Comments: The result is rounded.

Function: $1C0B
Name: Fix2Frac
Converts a Fixed value to a Frac value.
Push: Result Space (L); Fixed value (L)
Pull: Frac Result (L)
Errors: none
Comments: The result is rounded.

Function: $1D0B
Name: Frac2Fix
Converts a Frac value to a Fixed value.
Push: Result Space (L); Frac value (L)
Pull: Fixed Result (L)
Errors: none
Comments: The result is rounded.

Function: $1E0B
Name: Fix2X
Converts a Fixed value to an Extended value.
Push: Fixed value (L); Extended Address (L)
Pull: nothing
Errors: none
Comments:

Function: $1F0B
Name: Frac2X
Converts a Frac value to an Extended value.
Push: Frac value (L); Extended Address (L)
Pull: nothing
Errors: none
Comments:

Function: $200B
Name: X2Fix
Converts an Extended value to a Fixed value.
Push: Result Space (L); Extended Address (L)
Pull: Fixed Result (L)
Errors: none
Comments: The result is rounded.

Function: $210B
Name: X2Frac
Converts an Extended value to a Frac value.
Push: Result Space (L); Extended Address (L)
Pull: Frac Result (L)
Errors: none
Comments: The result is rounded.

Function: $220B
Name: Int2Hex
Produces an ASCII string of hex characters for a 16-bit integer.
Push: Integer value (W); String Address (L); String Length (W)
Pull: nothing
Errors: $0B04
Comments: The integer value is unsigned; the string at String Address is right-justified with leading zeros.

Function: $230B
Name: Long2Hex
Produces an ASCII string of hex characters of a 32-bit integer.
Push: Integer value (L); String Address (L); String Length (W)
Pull: nothing
Errors: $0B04
Comments: See function 22.

Function: $240B
Name: Hex2Int
Converts an ASCII string of Hex numbers to a 16-bit integer.
Push: Result Space (W); String Pointer (L); String Length (W)
Pull: Integer Value (W)
Errors: $0B02, $0B03
Comments: Only converts strings from "0000" through "FFFF"; string can be upper- or lowercase.

Function: $250B
Name: Hex2Long
Converts an ASCII string of Hex numbers to a 32-bit integer.
Push: Result Space (L); String Pointer (L); String length (W)
Pull: Integer Value (L)
Errors: $0B02, $0B03
Comments: Converts strings from "00000000" through "FFFFFFFF"; string can be upper- or lowercase.

Function: $260B
Name: Int2Dec
Produces a string of ASCII numeric characters for a 16-bit integer input.
Push: Integer Value (W); String Address (L); String Length (W); Sign (W)
Pull: nothing
Errors: $0B04
Comments: The string at String Address is right-justified with leading spaces; if the Integer Value is unsigned, Sign should be zero.

Function: $270B
Name: Long2Dec
Produces a string of ASCII numeric characters for a 32-bit integer input.
Push: Integer Value (L); String Address (L); String Length (W); Sign (W)
Pull: nothing
Errors: $0B04
Comments: See function 26.

Function: $280B
Name: Dec2Int
Converts a string of ASCII numeric characters into a 16-bit integer value.
Push: Result Space (W); String Addres (L); String Length (W); Sign (W)
Pull: Integer Result (W).
Errors: $0B02, $0B03
Comments: The string may have a leading + or − sign and may have leading blanks or zeros; if the Integer Result is unsigned, Sign should be zero.

Function: $290B
Name: Dec2Long
Converts a string of ASCII numeric characters into a 32-bit integer value.
Push: Result Space (L); String Address (L); String Length (W); Sign (W)
Pull: Integer Result (L).
Errors: $0B02, $0B03
Comments: See function 29.

Function: $2A0B
Name: HexIt
Returns ASCII string representing 16-bit integer.
Push: Result Space (L); Integer Value (W)
Pull: String (L)
Errors: none
Comments: The String actually contains the ASCII characters starting with the LSB of the low order word.

Summary of Tool Set $0B Error Codes

$0B01	Bad input parameter
$0B02	Illegal character in input string
$0B03	Integer or Long Integer overflow
$0B04	String overflow

Tool Set $0C: Text Tool Set

Tool Set: $0C
Tool Set Name: Text tool set
Version Number: 1.2

Function: $010C
Name: TextBootInit
Initialize the Text Tools.
Push: nothing
Pull: nothing
Errors: none
Comments: Do not make this call.

Function: $020C
Name: TextStartUp
Does nothing.
Push: nothing
Pull: nothing
Errors: none
Comments: No need to make this call, as it does nothing.

Function: $030C
Name: TextShutDown
Does nothing.
Push: nothing
Pull: nothing
Errors: none
Comments: No need to make this call either.

Function: $040C
Name: TextVersion
Returns version number of the Text Tool Set.
Push: Result Space (W)
Pull: Version Number (W)
Errors: none
Comments: LSB is major release, MSB minor release.

Function: $050C
Name: TextReset
Resets and reinitialized the Text Tool Set.
Push: nothing
Pull: nothing
Errors: none
Comments:

Function: $060C
Name: TextStatus
Returns activity status of the Text Tool Set.
Push: Result Space (W)
Pull: Status (W)
Errors: none
Comments: This call always returns $FFFF for active.

Function: $090C
Name: SetInGlobals
Specifies AND and OR mask for the input device.
Push: AND mask (W); OR mask (W)
Pull: nothing
Errors: none
Comments: Only LSB of word pushed is significant. The logical AND is performed first.

Function: $0A0C
Name: SetOutGlobals
Specifies AND and OR masks for the output device.
Push: AND mask (W); OR mask (W)
Pull: nothing
Errors: none
Comments: See function $09.

Function: $0B0C
Name: SetErrGlobals
Specifies AND and OR masks for the error output device.
Push: AND mask (W); OR mask (W)
Pull: nothing
Errors: none
Comments: See function $09.

Function: $0C0C
Name: GetInGlobals
Returns AND and OR masks set for the input device.
Push: Result Space (W); Result Space (W)
Pull: OR mask (W); AND mask (W)
Errors: none
Comments: Only the LSB of the word returned is significant.

$0D0C

Function: $0D0C
Name: GetOutGlobals
Returns AND and OR masks set for the output device.
Push: Result Space (W); Result Space (W)
Pull: OR mask (W); AND mask (W)
Errors: none
Comments: See function $0C.

Function: $0E0C
Name: GetErrGlobals
Returns AND and OR masks for the error output device.
Push: Result Space (W); Result Space (W)
Pull: OR mask (W); AND mask (W);
Errors: none
Comments: See function $0C.

Function: $0F0C
Name: SetInputDevice
Redirects input from another device.
Push: Device Number (W); Input device slot number or address of a RAM device driver (L)
Pull: nothing
Errors: Only if the input device number is greater than two
Comments: Input device numbers: 0 = Basic, 1 = Pascal, 2 = RAM.

Function: $100C
Name: SetOutputDevice
Redirects output to another device.
Push: Device Number (W); Output device slot number or address of a RAM device driver (L)
Pull: nothing
Errors: Only if the input device number is greater than two
Comments: See function $0F.

Function: $110C
Name: SetErrDevice
Redirects error output to a specific device.
Push: Device Number (W); Error device slot number or address of a RAM device driver (L)
Pull: nothing
Errors: Only if the input device number is greater than two
Comments: See function $0F.

Function: $120C
Name: GetInputDevice
Returns the input device number and the slot number of that device or the address of a RAM-based driver.
Push: Result Space (W); Result Space (L)
Pull: Input device slot number or address of a RAM device driver (L); Device Number (W)
Errors: none
Comments: If the input device is less than seven, it's a slot number.

Function: $130C
Name: GetOutputDevice
Returns the output device number and the slot number of that device or the address of a RAM-based driver.
Push: Result Space (W); Result Space (L)
Pull: Output device slot number or address of a RAM device driver (L); Device Number (W)
Errors: none
Comments: See function $12.

Function: $140C
Name: GetErrorDevice
Returns the error device number and the slot number of that device or the address of a RAM-based driver.
Push: Result Space (W); Result Space (L)
Pull: Error device slot number or address of a RAM device driver (L); Device Number (W).
Errors: none
Comments: See function $12.

Function: $150C
Name: InitTextDev
Initializes the indicated text device.
Push: Device Number (W)
Pull: nothing
Errors: $0C01
Comments: Text device numbers are 0 = input, 1 = output, 2 = error.

Function: $160C
Name: CtrlTextDev
Sends control code to a text device.
Push: Device Number (W); Control code (W)
Pull: nothing
Errors: Possible Pascal Errors, Fatal errors if used with Basic devices
Comments: The control code is in the LSB of the word pushed; Text device numbers are 0 = input, 1 = output, 2 = error. This routine should not be used with Basic devices.

Function: $170C
Name: StatusTDev
Sends a status request to a device.
Push: Device Number (W); Request Code (W)
Pull: nothing
Errors: Possible Pascal Errors
Comments: See function $16 for device numbers; the request code is the LSB of the word pushed. This routine is not used with Basic devices.

Function: $180C
Name: WriteChar
Sends a character to the output device.
Push: Character (W)
Pull: nothing
Errors: Possible Pascal Errors
Comments: The character is in the LSB of the word pushed; it is affected by the AND and OR masks of function $0A.

Function: $190C
Name: ErrWriteChar
Sends a character to the error output device.
Push: Character (W)
Pull: nothing
Errors: Possible Pascal Errors
Comments: The character is in the LSB of the word pushed; it is affected by the AND and OR masks of function 0B.

Function: $1A0C
Name: WriteLine
Displays a line of text to the output device and adds a carriage return.
Push: String Pointer (L)
Pull: nothing
Errors: Possible Pascal Errors
Comments: First character of the string is a count byte; characters in the string are affected by the AND and OR masks of function $0A; Pascal also adds a linefeed.

Function: $1B0C
Name: ErrWriteLine
Sends a line of text to the error output device.
Push: String Pointer (L)
Pull: nothing
Errors: Possible Pascal Errors
Comments: First character of the string is a count byte; characters in the string are affected by the AND and OR masks of function $0B; Pascal also adds a linefeed.

Function: $1C0C
Name: WriteString
Displays a line of text to the output device.
Push: String Pointer (L)
Pull: nothing
Errors: Possible Pascal Errors
Comments: First character of the string is a count byte; characters in the string are affected by the AND and OR masks of function $0A; no carriage return is added.

Function: $1D0C
Name: ErrWriteString
Sends a line of text to the error output device.
Push: String Pointer (L)
Pull: nothing
Errors: Possible Pascal Errors
Comments: First character of the string is a count byte; characters in the string are affected by the AND and OR masks of function $0B; no carriage return is added.

Function: $1E0C
Name: WriteBlock
Displays characters at a given address and offset.
Push: Text Address (L); Offset (W); Length (W)
Pull: nothing
Errors: Possible Pascal Errors
Comments: Characters in the block are affected by the AND and OR masks of function $0A.

Function: $1F0C
Name: ErrWriteBlock
Sends characters at a given address and offset to the error output device.
Push: Text Address (L); Offset (W); Length (W)
Pull: nothing
Errors: Possible Pascal Errors
Comments: Characters in the block are affected by the AND and OR masks of function $0A.

Function: $200C
Name: WriteCString
Displays a string of text to the output device.
Push: String Address (L)
Pull: nothing
Errors: Possible Pascal Errors
Comments: The string ends with the byte $00; characters in the string are affected by the AND and OR masks of function $0A.

Function: $210C
Name: ErrWriteCString
Sends a string of text to the error output device.
Push: String Address (L)
Pull: nothing
Errors: Possible Pascal Errors
Comments: The string ends with the byte $00; characters in the string are affected by the AND and OR masks of function $0B.

Function: $220C
Name: ReadChar
Reads one character from the input device.
Push: Result Space (W); Echo flag (W);
Pull: ASCII Character (W)
Errors: Possible Pascal errors
Comments: Echo flag is $0001 to echo, $0000 no echo. The character returned is the LSB of the word, its high bit is clear; the character is affected by the AND and OR masks of function $09.

Function: $230C
Name: ReadBlock
Reads characters from the input device.
Push: Block Address (L); Offset (W); Length (W); Echo flag (W)
Pull: nothing
Errors: Possible Pascal errors
Comments: Echo flag is $0001 to echo, $0000 no echo.

Function: $240C
Name: ReadLine
Reads a string from the input device.
Push: Result Space (W); Buffer Address (L); Line length (W); End of line (EOL) character (W) Echo Flag (W)
Pull: Character Count (W)
Errors: Possible Pascal errors
Comments: EOL character is in LSB of word pushed; EOL is not written to buffer; Echo flag is $0001 to echo, $0000 no echo.

Summary of Tool Set $0C Error Codes

$0C01 Illegal device type
$0C02 Illegal device number
$0C03 Bad mode
$0C04 Undefined hardware error
$0C05 Lost device, or device not online
$0C06 Lost file, no longer in directory
$0C07 Bad filename
$0C08 Disk is full
$0C09 Volume not found, or not online
$0C0A File not found
$0C0B Duplicate filename, file already exist
$0C0C Attempt to open already open file
$0C0D Attempt to close a not open file
$0C0E Bad format, either real or integer
$0C0F Ring buffer overflow
$0C10 Disk is write protected
$0C11 Device error, read or write operation failed

NOTE: Errors $0C02 and greater are only produced by Pascal.

Tool Set $0E: Window Manager

Tool Set: $0E
Tool Set Name: Window Manager
Version Number: 1.3

Function: $010E
Name: WindBootInit
Initialize the Window Manager.
Push: nothing
Pull: nothing
Errors: none
Comments: Do not make this call.

Function: $020E
Name: WindStartUp
Starts the Window Manager.
Push: UserID (W)
Pull: nothing
Errors: none
Comments: The Event Manager should be started before this call is made.

Function: $030E
Name: WindShutDown
Shuts down the Window Manager.
Push: nothing
Pull: nothing
Errors: none
Comments: This call must be made before the Control Manager is shutdown.

Function: $040E
Name: WindVersion
Returns version number of the Window Manager.
Push: Result Space (W)
Pull: Version Number (W)
Errors: none
Comments: LSB is major release, MSB minor release.

Function: $050E
Name: WindReset
Called when the computer is reset.
Push: nothing
Pull: nothing
Errors: none
Comments: Do not make this call.

Function: $060E
Name: WindStatus
Returns activity status of the Window Manager.
Push: Result Space (W)
Pull: Status (W)
Errors: none
Comments: $0000 indicates the Window Manager is inactive.

Function: $090E
Name: NewWindow
Creates and displays (if specified) a new window on the screen.
Push: Result Space (L); Window Record (L)
Pull: Window Pointer (L)
Errors: $0E01, $0E02
Comments: See Chapter 15.

Function: $0A0E
Name: CheckUpdate
Called by the Event Manager to see if a window needs updating.
Push: Result Space (W); Event Record (L)
Pull: Logical Result (W)
Errors: none
Comments: A true result indicates an update event was found.

Function: $0B0E
Name: CloseWindow
Removes a window from the display, releasing all memory, controls and other items associated with the window.
Push: Window Pointer (L)
Pull: nothing
Errors: none
Comments:

Function: $0C0E
Name: Desktop
Controls a variety of things dealing with the desktop.
Push: Result Space (L); Command (W); Parameter (L)
Pull: Result (L)
Errors: none
Comments: See chapter 15.

Function: $0D0E
Name: SetWTitle
Sets or changes a window's title string.
Push: Title (L); Window Pointer (L)
Pull: nothing
Errors: none
Comments: The string at address title is a Pascal string.

Function: $0E0E
Name: GetWTitle
Returns the address of a window's title string.
Push: Result Space (L); Window Pointer (L)
Pull: Title (L)
Errors: none
Comments:

Function: $0F0E
Name: SetFrameColor
Changes the colors used to draw a window's frame to those in an eight-word table.
Push: Table Pointer (L); Window Pointer (L)
Pull: nothing
Errors: none
Comments: Call function $12, and then $13 to change the window's colors.

Function: $100E
Name: GetFrameColor
Fills an eight-word table with the colors used for the specified window's frame.
Push: Table Pointer (L); Window Pointer (L)
Pull: nothing
Errors: none
Comments:

Function: $110E
Name: SelectWindow
Selects the specified window, making it the active window.
Push: Window Pointer (L)
Pull: nothing
Errors: none
Comments:

Function: $120E
Name: HideWindow
Makes a window invisible.
Push: Window Pointer (L)
Pull: nothing
Errors: none
Comments:

Function: $130E
Name: ShowWindow
Makes a window visible.
Push: Window Pointer (L)
Pull: nothing
Errors: none
Comments:

Function: $140E
Name: SendBehind
Sends the specified window behind one or all of the windows on the desktop.
Push: New Location (L); Window Pointer (L)
Pull: nothing
Errors: none
Comments: New Location ranges from 0 to $FFFFFFFE. A value of $FFFFFFFF (-1) puts the window in front.

Function: $150E
Name: FrontWindow
Returns the window pointer of the window in front.
Push: Result Space (L)
Pull: Window Pointer (L)
Errors: none
Comments:

Function: $160E
Name: SetInfoDraw
Sets the routine which draws a window's info bar.
Push: Routine's Address (L); Window Pointer (L)
Pull: nothing
Errors: none
Comments:

Function: $170E
Name: FindWindow
Returns that part of the window where the mouse was pressed.
Push: Result Space (W); Window Pointer (L); X Location (W); Y Location (W)
Pull: Location of Mouse Down event (W)
Errors: none
Comments: X and Y Locations refer to where the mouse was clicked.

Function: $180E
Name: TrackGoAway
Determines if the mouse button was clicked in a window's goaway box.
Push: Result Space (W); X Position (W); Y Position (W); Window Pointer (L)
Pull: Logical Result (W)
Errors: none
Comments: X and Y Positions are of the mouse. A logical True is returned if the goaway was clicked upon.

Function: $190E
Name: MoveWindow
Moves a window to another location, the window's size is not changed.
Push: X Location (W); Y Location (W); Window Pointer (L)
Pull: nothing
Errors: none
Comments:

Function: $1A0E
Name: DragWindow
Called when a window is dragged, it displays a dotted outline of the window until the mouse button is released.
Push: Drag Resolution (W); X Pos (W); Y Pos (W); Grace limit (W); Boundary Rectangle (L); Window Pointer (L)
Pull: nothing
Errors: none
Comments:

Function: $1B0E
Name: GrowWindow
Called when a window is resized using its grow box.
Push: Result Space (W); (W); Max width of contents (W); Max height of contents (W); X Pos (W); Y Pos (W); Window Pointer (L)
Pull: New Width (W); New Height (W)
Errors: none
Comments:

Function: $1C0E
Name: SizeWindow
Changes a window's size to the specified values.
Push: Width (W); Height (W); Window Pointer (L)
Pull: nothing
Errors: none
Comments:

Function: $1D0E
Name: TaskMaster
Returns status of the event queue as well as checks for certain window/menu events.
Push: Result Space (W); Event Mask (W); Event Record (L)
Pull: Extended Event Code (W)
Errors: $0E03
Comments: See Chapter 12.

Function: $1E0E
Name: BeginUpdate
Called when an update event occurs in a window.
Push: Window Pointer (L)
Pull: nothing
Errors: none
Comments:

Function: $1F0E
Name: EndUpdate
Restores the region changed by the BeginUpdate function.
Push: Window Port (L)
Pull: nothing
Errors: none
Comments:

Function: $200E
Name: GetWMgrPort
Returns the address of the Window Manager's port.
Push: Result Space (L)
Pull: WM's Port (L)
Errors: none
Comments:

Function: $210E
Name: PinRect
Determines if a point is inside a specific rectangle.
Push: Result Space (W); (W); X Location (W); Y Location (W); Rectangle (L)
Pull: X (W); Y (W)
Errors: none
Comments: X and Y are the locations of the point.

Function: $220E
Name: HiliteWindow
Highlights or unhighlights a window.
Push: Highlight (W); Window Pointer (L)
Pull: nothing
Errors: none
Comments: If Highlight is a logical True, the window is highlighted; if it's a logical False, the window is unhighlighted.

Function: $230E
Name: ShowHide
Makes a window visible or invisible.
Push: Show Flag (W); Window Pointer (L)
Pull: nothing
Errors: none
Comments: If Show Flag is a logical True, the window is made visible, if a logical False, the window is hidden.

Function: $240E
Name: BringToFront
Places the specified window "on top" of all others on the desktop.
Push: Window Pointer (L)
Pull: nothing
Errors: none
Comments: Used by function $11.

Function: $250E
Name: WindNewRes
Resets the Window Manager's port when the screen size changes.
Push: nothing
Pull: nothing
Errors: none
Comments:

Function: $260E
Name: TrackZoom
Determines if the mouse button was clicked in a window's zoom box.
Push: Result Space (W); X Position (W); Y Position (W); Window Pointer (L)
Pull: Logical Result (W)
Errors: none
Comments: X and Y Positions are of the mouse. A logical True is returned if the zoom was clicked.

Function: $270E
Name: ZoomWindow
Zooms a window out to its zoom size as specified when the window was created.
Push: Window Pointer (L)
Pull: nothing
Errors: none
Comments:

Function: $280E
Name: SetWRefCon
Sets or changes the wRefCon value for a specified window.
Push: wRefCon Value (L); Window Pointer (L)
Pull: nothing
Errors: none
Comments:

Function: $290E
Name: GetWRefCon
Returns the wRefCon value specified when the window was created.
Push: Result Space (L); Window Pointer (L)
Pull: wRefCon Value (L)
Errors: none
Comments:

Function: $2A0E
Name: GetNextWindow
Returns a Window Pointer in the window list after the specified window.
Push: Result Space (L); Window Pointer (L)
Pull: Next window in list (L)
Errors: none
Comments:

Function: $2B0E
Name: GetWKind
Determines if a window is a system window or not.
Push: Result Space (W); Window Pointer (L)
Pull: Logical Result (W)
Errors: none
Comments: $8000 = application window, $0000 = system window.

Function: $2C0E
Name: GetWFrame
Returns the word used to define a window's frame.
Push: Result Space (W); Window Pointer (L)
Pull: Frame Word (W)
Errors: none
Comments: See Chapter 15 for information on the bit values of the Frame Word.

Function: $2D0E
Name: SetWFrame
Sets or Changes the word used to define a window's frame.
Push: Frame Word (W); Window Pointer (L)
Pull: nothing
Errors: none
Comments: See Chapter 15.

Function: $2E0E
Name: GetStructRgn
Returns a handle to the specified window's structure region.
Push: Result Space (L); Window Pointer (L)
Pull: Structure Region's Handle (L)
Errors: none
Comments:

Function: $2F0E
Name: GetContentRgn
Returns the handle of a window's content region.
Push: Result Space (L); Window Pointer (L)
Pull: Content's Handle (L)
Errors: none
Comments:

Function: $300E
Name: GetUpdateRgn
Returns a window's update region handle.
Push: Result Space (L); Window Pointer (L)
Pull: Region's Handle (L)
Errors: none
Comments:

Function: $310E
Name: GetDefProc
Returns the address of the routine that controls the window's behavior.
Push: Result Space (L); Window Pointer (L)
Pull: Routine's Address (L)
Errors: none
Comments:

Function: $320E
Name: SetDefProc
Sets the address of the routine that controls the window's behavior.
Push: Routine's Address (L); Window Pointer (L)
Pull: nothing
Errors: none
Comments:

Function: $330E
Name: GetWControls
Examines a window's Control List and returns the first control's handle.
Push: Result Space (L); Window Pointer (L)
Pull: First Control's Handle (L)
Errors: none
Comments:

Function: $340E
Name: SetOriginMask
Sets a mask to assist windows used on a "dithered" 640-mode screen.
Push: Mask (W); Window Pointer (L)
Pull: nothing
Errors: none
Comments:

Function: $350E
Name: GetInfoRefCon
Returns the value used by a window's info bar routine.
Push: Result Space (L); Window Pointer (L)
Pull: Info Bar Reference (L)
Errors: none
Comments:

Function: $360E
Name: SetInfoRefCon
Sets the value used by a window's info bar routine.
Push: Info Bar Reference (L); Window Pointer (L)
Pull: nothing
Errors: none
Comments:

Function: $370E
Name: GetZoomRect
Returns the zoom size for a specified window.
Push: Result Space (L); Window Pointer (L)
Pull: Rectangle (L)
Errors: none
Comments:

Function: $380E
Name: SetZoomRect
Sets or changes the zoom size of window.
Push: Rectangle (L); Window Pointer (L)
Pull: nothing
Errors: none
Comments:

Function: $390E
Name: RefreshDesktop
Redraws the entire screen.
Push: Rectangle (L)
Pull: nothing
Errors: none
Comments: If Rectangle is a long word of zero, the entire screen is redrawn.

Function: $3A0E
Name: InvalRect
Called after SizeWindow to update the window's contents.
Push: Rectangle (L)
Pull: nothing
Errors: none
Comments:

Function: $3B0E
Name: InvalRgn
Places the specified region into the current window.
Push: Region's Handle (L)
Pull: nothing
Errors: none
Comments:

Function: $3C0E
Name: ValidRect
Removes a rectangle from the current window.
Push: Rectangle (L)
Pull: nothing
Errors: none
Comments:

Function: $3D0E
Name: ValidRgn
Removes a specific region from the current window.
Push: Region's Handle (L)
Pull: nothing
Errors: none
Comments:

Function: $3E0E
Name: GetContentOrgin
Returns the Y and X origins of a window's port.
Push: Result Space (W); (W); Window Pointer (L)
Pull: Y Origin (W); X Origin (W)
Errors: none
Comments: Values are in global coordinates.

Function: $3F0E
Name: SetContentOrigin
Sets or changes the origin of a window's content.
Push: Horizontal Offset (W); Vertical Offset (W); Window Pointer (L)
Pull: nothing
Errors: none
Comments:

Function: $400E
Name: GetDataSize
Returns the size of a window's data area.
Push: Result Space (W); (W); Window Pointer (L)
Pull: Height (W); Width (W)
Errors: none
Comments: Values are in pixels.

Function: $410E
Name: SetDataSize
Sets or changes the size of the data area in a specified window.
Push: Data Area Width (W); Data Area Height (W); Window Pointer (L)
Pull: nothing
Errors: none
Comments:

Function: $420E
Name: GetMaxGrow
Returns the maximum size allowed for a window.
Push: Result Space (W); (W); Window Pointer (L)
Pull: Max Height (W); Max Width (W)
Errors: none
Comments: The Height and Width are in pixels.

Function: $430E
Name: SetMaxGrow
Sets or changes the maximum size allowed for a window.
Push: Max Width (W); Max Height (W); Window Pointer (L)
Pull: nothing
Errors: none
Comments:

Function: $440E
Name: GetScroll
Returns the number of pixels the window scrolls when the buttons are clicked on the scroll bar.
Push: Result Space (W); (W); Window Pointer (L)
Pull: Vertical Distance (W); Horizontal Distance (W)
Errors: none
Comments:

Function: $450E
Name: SetScroll
Sets or changes the number of pixels the window scrolls when the buttons are clicked on the scroll bar.
Push: Horizontal Distance (W); Vertical Distance (W); Window Pointer (L)
Pull: nothing
Errors: none
Comments:

Function: $460E
Name: GetPage
Returns the number of pixels the window will scroll when the window is paged using the scroll bar.
Push: Result Space (W); (W); Window Pointer (L)
Pull: Vertical Distance (W); Horizontal Distance (W)
Errors: none
Comments:

Function: $470E
Name: SetPage
Sets or changes the number of pixels the window scrolls when the window is paged using the scroll bar.
Push: Horizontal Distance (W); Vertical Distance (W); Window Pointer (L)
Pull: nothing
Errors: none
Comments:

Function: $480E
Name: GetContentDraw
Returns the address of the routine which draws a window's contents.
Push: Result Space (L); Window Pointer (L)
Pull: Routine's Address (L)
Errors: none
Comments:

Function: $490E
Name: SetContentDraw
Sets the address of a routine which draws the window's content.
Push: Routine's Address (L); Window Pointer (L)
Pull: nothing
Errors: none
Comments:

Function: $4A0E
Name: GetInfoDraw
Returns the address of the routine which draws a window's info bar.
Push: Result Space (L); Window Pointer (L)
Pull: Routine's Address (L)
Errors: none
Comments:

Function: $4B0E
Name: SetSysWindow
Changes the window to a system window.
Push: Window Pointer (L)
Pull: nothing
Errors: none
Comments:

Function: $4C0E
Name: GetSysWFlag
Determines if a given window is a system window.
Push: Result Space (W); Window Pointer (L)
Pull: Logical Result (W)
Errors: none
Comments: If the result is true, it's a system window.

Function: $4D0E
Name: StartDrawing
Sets the current port to the window's port, allowing the window's area to be used for drawing.
Push: Window Pointer (L)
Pull: nothing
Errors: none
Comments:

Function: $4E0E
Name: SetWindowIcons
Sets or changes the icon font used by the Window Manager.
Push: Result Space (L); Icon Font Handle (L)
Pull: Previous Icon Font Handle (L)
Errors: none
Comments:

Function: $4F0E
Name: GetRectInfo
Returns the contents of the window's info bar to a rectangle.
Push: Destination Rectangle (L); Window Pointer (L)
Pull: nothing
Errors: none
Comments:

Function: $500E
Name: StartInfoDrawing
Used to draw information inside a window's info bar.
Push: Destination Rectangle (L); Window Pointer (L)
Pull: nothing
Errors: none
Comments:

Function: $510E
Name: EndInfoDrawing
Used after function $50 to return the Window Manager to global coordinates.
Push: nothing
Pull: nothing
Errors: none
Comments:

Function: $520E
Name: GetFirstWindow
Returns a pointer to the first window in the window list.
Push: Result Space (L)
Pull: Window Pointer (L)
Errors: none
Comments: The first window is not necessarily the top window. See functions $15 and $17.

Function: $530E
Name: WindDragRect
Drags a dotted rectangle around the screen until the mouse is released.
Push: Result Space (W); (W); Routine (W); Drag Pattern (L); X Start (W); Y Start (W); Rectangle (L); Limit Rectangle (L); Slop Rectangle (L); Movement Constraint (W); Flag (W)
Pull: X Change (W); Y Change (W)
Errors: none
Comments:

Summary of Tool Set $0E Error Codes

$0E01 First word of parameter list is the wrong size
$0E02 Unable to allocate window record
$0E03 Bits 14–31 not clear in task mask

Tool Set $0F: Menu Manager

Tool Set: $0F
Tool Set Name: Menu Manager
Version Number: 1.3

Function: $010F
Name: MenuBootInit
Initializes the Menu Manager.
Push: nothing
Pull: nothing
Errors: none
Comments: Do not make this call.

Function: $020F
Name: MenuStartUp
Starts the Menu Manager.
Push: User ID (W); Direct Page (W)
Pull: nothing
Errors: none
Comments:

Function: $030F
Name: MenuShutDown
Shuts down the Menu Manager.
Push: nothing
Pull: nothing
Errors: none
Comments: Make this call when your application is finished.

Function: $040F
Name: MenuVersion
Returns the version number of the Menu Manager.
Push: Result Space (W)
Pull: Version (W)
Errors: none
Comments: LSB is major release, MSB minor release.

Function: $050F
Name: MenuReset
Resets the Menu Manager.
Push: nothing
Pull: nothing
Errors: none
Comments: Do not make this call.

Function: $060F
Name: MenuStatus
Determines if the Menu Manager is active.
Push: Result Space (W)
Pull: Active (W)
Errors: none
Comments: A nonzero value is returned if active.

Function: $090F
Name: MenuKey
Binds an Apple key event to a menu item.
Push: Task Record (L); Menu Bar Handle (L)
Pull: nothing
Errors: none
Comments:

Function: $0A0F
Name: GetMenuBar
Returns the handle of the menu bar.
Push: Result Space (L)
Pull: Menu Bar Handle (L)
Errors: none
Comments:

Function: $0B0F
Name: MenuRefresh
Restores the screen under a menu.
Push: Redraw Routine (L)
Pull: nothing
Errors: none
Comments: An application makes this call if the Window Manager is not in use.

Function: $0C0F
Name: FlashMenuBar
Flashes the menu bar.
Push: nothing
Pull: nothing
Errors: none
Comments: The menu is quickly inversed and restored to normal.

Function: $0D0F
Name: InsertMenu
Inserts a menu into the menu bar.
Push: Menu Handle (L); Insert After (W)
Pull: nothing
Errors: none
Comments: If Insert After is zero, the menu becomes the first in the menu bar.

Function: $0E0F
Name: DeleteMenu
Removes a menu from the menu list.
Push: Menu Number (W)
Pull: nothing
Errors: none
Comments: Use DrawMenuBar to update the screen. The menu is not fully disposed, just deleted from the list.

Function: $0F0F
Name: InsertMItem
Inserts a menu item into a menu.
Push: Item (L); Insert After (W); Menu Number (W)
Pull: nothing
Errors: none
Comments: If Insert After is zero, the item becomes the first in the menu.

Function: $100F
Name: DeleteMItem
Removes an item from a menu.
Push: Item (W)
Pull: nothing
Errors: none
Comments: Use CalcMenuSize after making this call.

Function: $110F
Name: GetSysBar
Returns the handle of the system menu bar.
Push: Result Space (L)
Pull: Bar Handle (L)
Errors: none
Comments:

Function: $120F
Name: SetSysBar
Specifies the current system bar.
Push: System Bar Handle (L)
Pull: nothing
Errors: none
Comments:

Function: $130F
Name: FixMenuBar
Standardizes the menu bar's sizes and returns its height.
Push: Result Space (W)
Pull: Heigth (W)
Errors: none
Comments: The returned Height is in pixels and is usually 13.

Function: $140F
Name: CountMItems
Returns the number of items in a menu.
Push: Result Space (W); Menu Number (W)
Pull: Count (W)
Errors: none
Comments: Dividing lines are considered items.

Function: $150F
Name: NewMenuBar
Creates an empty menu bar.
Push: Result Space (L); Window (L)
Pull: Menu Bar Handle (L)
Errors: none
Comments:

Function: $160F
Name: GetMHandle
Returns the handle of a menu record.
Push: Result Space (L); Menu Number (W)
Pull: Menu Handle (L)
Errors: none
Comments:

Function: $170F
Name: SetBarColors
Specifies the colors of the menu bar.
Push: Normal Color (W); Selected Color (W); Outline Color (W)
Pull: nothing
Errors: none
Comments:

Function: $180F
Name: GetBarColors
Returns the colors of the menu bar.
Push: Result Space (L)
Pull: Color Values (L)
Errors: none
Comments: The result is a bit array, not an address.

Function: $190F
Name: SetMTitleStart
Sets the horizontal position of the first menu title.
Push: X Start (W)
Pull: nothing
Errors: none
Comments:

Function: $1A0F
Name: GetMTitleStart
Returns the pixel column of the leftmost menu bar title.
Push: Result Space (W)
Pull: X Start (W)
Errors: none
Comments:

Function: $1B0F
Name: GetMenuMgrPort
Returns the address of the Menu Manager's port.
Push: Result Space (L)
Pull: Menu Manager Port (L)
Errors: none
Comments: This is used when changing fonts.

Function: $1C0F
Name: CalcMenuSize
Calculates the new dimensions of a menu.
Push: Width (W); Height (W); Menu Number (W)
Pull: nothing
Errors: none
Comments:

Function: $1D0F
Name: SetMTitleWidth
Selects the width in pixels of a menu title.
Push: Width (W); Menu Number (W)
Pull: nothing
Errors: none
Comments:

Function: $1E0F
Name: GetMTitleWidth
Returns the width in pixels of a menu title.
Push: Result Space (W); Menu Number (W)
Pull: Width (W)
Errors: none
Comments:

Function: $1F0F
Name: SetMenuFlag
Specifies the attributes of a menu.
Push: Attributes (W); Menu Number (W)
Pull: nothing
Errors: none
Comments: Attributes are: $FF7F = Enable, $0080 = Disable; $FFDF = Color Replace; $0020 = XOR Highlight; $FFEF = Standard; $0010 = Custom.

Function: $200F
Name: GetMenuFlag
Returns the state flag for a menu.
Push: Result Space (W); Menu Number (W)
Pull: State (W)
Errors: none
Comments:

Function: $210F
Name: SetMenuTitle
Selects the title for a menu.
Push: Title (L); Menu Number (W)
Pull: nothing
Errors: none
Comments:

Function: $220F
Name: GetMenuTitle
Returns a menu title's address.
Push: Result Space (L); Menu Number (W)
Pull: Title (L)
Errors: none
Comments:

Function: $240F
Name: SetMItem
Selects the name for an item.
Push: Name (L); Item Number (W)
Pull: nothing
Errors: none
Comments:

Function: $250F
Name: GetMItem
Returns the address of a menu item's name.
Push: Result Space (L); Item Number (W)
Pull: Name (L)
Errors: none
Comments:

Function: $260F
Name: SetMItemFlag
Sets the attributes of a menu item such as being underlined, enabled, and so on.
Push: Attributes (W); Item Number (W)
Pull: nothing
Errors: none
Comments: Attributes are: $0040 = Underline, $FFBF = No Underline, $0020 = XOR Highlight; $FFDF = Redraw Highlight; $FF7F = Enable; $0080 = Disable.

Function: $270F
Name: GetMItemFlag
Determines the attributes of a menu item, such as being disabled, underlined, and so on.
Push: Result Space (W); Item Number (W)
Pull: Item Flag (W)
Errors: none
Comments:

Function: $280F
Name: SetMItemBlink
Sets the blink rate for selected items.
Push: Blink Count (W)
Pull: nothing
Errors: none
Comments:

Function: $290F
Name: MenuNewRes
Updates the menu bar after a screen resolution change.
Push: nothing
Pull: nothing
Errors: none
Comments: Call this after changing screen modes.

Function: $2A0F
Name: DrawMenuBar
Draws the menu bar and its titles.
Push: nothing
Pull: nothing
Errors: none
Comments:

Function: $2B0F
Name: MenuSelect
Manages interaction with a pull-down menu.
Push: Task Record (L); Menu Bar Handle (L)
Pull: nothing
Errors: none
Comments: An application makes this call when the Window Manager's TaskMaster is not used.

Function: $2C0F
Name: HiliteMenu
Determines if a menu title is highlighted.
Push: Hilite Flag (W); Menu Number (W)
Pull: nothing
Errors: none
Comments: If Hilite Flag is nonzero, the title is highlighted, otherwise its unhighlighted.

Function: $2D0F
Name: NewMenu
Creates a new menu.
Push: Result Space (L); Menu Structure (L)
Pull: nothing
Errors: none
Comments: This creates the menu internally and does not display or insert it into a menu bar.

Function: $2E0F
Name: DisposeMenu
Disposes of the memory allocated for a menu.
Push: Menu Handle (L)
Pull: nothing
Errors: none
Comments:

Function: $2F0F
Name: InitPalette
Sets the standard color palette for the Apple logo.
Push: nothing
Pull: nothing
Errors: none
Comments:

Function: $300F
Name: EnableMItem
Enables a disabled menu item.
Push: Item (W)
Pull: nothing
Errors: none
Comments:

Function: $310F
Name: DisableMItem
Disables a menu item, making it dimmed.
Push: Item (W)
Pull: nothing
Errors: none
Comments: The item will no longer be available for selection.

Function: $320F
Name: CheckMItem
Manages check marks for a menu item.
Push: Check Flag (W); Item (W)
Pull: nothing
Errors: none
Comments: An item will be marked with a check if Check Flag is true; otherwise, a check will be removed if false.

Function: $330F
Name: SetMItemMark
Sets the marking character (or none) for an item.
Push: Mark Character (W); Item Number (W)
Pull: nothing
Errors: none
Comments: Use zero for no mark.

Function: $340F
Name: GetMItemMark
Returns the mark character for an item.
Push: Result Space (W); Item Number (W)
Pull: Mark (W)
Errors: none
Comments: Mark is zero if the item is not currently marked.

Function: $350F
Name: SetMItemStyle
Sets the text style of a menu item.
Push: Text Style (W); Item Number (W)
Pull: nothing
Errors: none
Comments:

Function: $360F
Name: GetMItemStyle
Returns the text style of a menu item.
Push: Result Space (W); Item Number (W)
Pull: Text Style (W)
Errors: none
Comments:

Function: $370F
Name: SetMenuID
Selects a new menu number.
Push: New Number (W); Current Number (W)
Pull: nothing
Errors: none
Comments:

Function: $380F
Name: SetMItemID
Selects a new menu item number.
Push: New Number (W); Current Number (W)
Pull: nothing
Errors: none
Comments:

Function: $390F
Name: SetMenuBar
Specifies the current menu bar.
Push: Menu Bar Handle (L)
Pull: nothing
Errors: none
Comments:

$3A0F

Function: $3A0F
Name: SetMItemName
Selects a name for a menu item.
Push: Name (L); Item Number (W)
Pull: nothing
Errors: none
Comments: Name is a Pascal-type string.

Summary of Tool Set $0F Error Codes:

none

Appendices

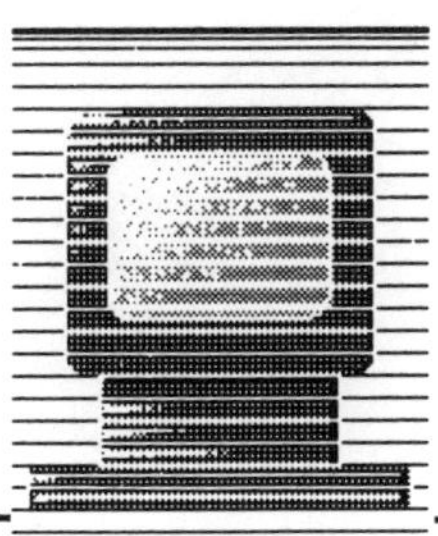

Appendix A

ASCII Character Codes

ASCII Chart with Codes and Values

ASCII, pronounced ask-ee, is an acronym for the American Standard Code for Information Interchange. The ASCII codes 0–127 are assigned to letters, numbers, special characters, and other symbols.

Char	Dec	Hex	Binary	Code
^@	0	$00	00000000	NUL
^A	1	$01	00000001	SOH
^B	2	$02	00000010	STX
^C	3	$03	00000011	ETX
^D	4	$04	00000100	EOT
^E	5	$05	00000101	ENQ
^F	6	$06	00000110	ACK
^G	7	$07	00000111	BEL
^H	8	$08	00001000	BS
^I	9	$09	00001001	HT
^J	10	$0A	00001010	LF
^K	11	$0B	00001011	VT
^L	12	$0C	00001100	FF
^M	13	$0D	00001101	CR
^N	14	$0E	00001110	SO
^O	15	$0F	00001111	SI
^P	16	$10	00010000	DLE
^Q	17	$11	00010001	DC1
^R	18	$12	00010010	DC2
^S	19	$13	00010011	DC3
^T	20	$14	00010100	DC4
^U	21	$15	00010101	NAK
^V	22	$16	00010110	SYN
^W	23	$17	00010111	ETB
^X	24	$18	00011000	CAN
^Y	25	$19	00011001	EM
^Z	26	$1A	00011010	SUB
^[	27	$1B	00011011	ESC
^\	28	$1C	00011100	FS
^]	29	$1D	00011101	GS
^^	30	$1E	00011110	RS
^_	31	$1F	00011111	US
SPC	32	$20	00100000	
!	33	$21	00100001	
"	34	$22	00100010	
#	35	$23	00100011	
$	36	$24	00100100	
%	37	$25	00100101	
&	38	$26	00100110	
'	39	$27	00100111	
(	40	$28	00101000	
)	41	$29	00101001	
*	42	$2A	00101010	
+	43	$2B	00101011	
,	44	$2C	00101100	
-	45	$2D	00101101	
.	46	$2E	00101110	
/	47	$2F	00101111	
0	48	$30	00110000	
1	49	$31	00110001	
2	50	$32	00110010	
3	51	$33	00110011	
4	52	$34	00110100	
5	53	$35	00110101	
6	54	$36	00110110	
7	55	$37	00110111	
8	56	$38	00111000	
9	57	$39	00111001	
:	58	$3A	00111010	
;	59	$3B	00111011	
<	60	$3C	00111100	
=	61	$3D	00111101	
>	62	$3E	00111110	
?	63	$3F	00111111	
@	64	$40	01000000	
A	65	$41	01000001	
B	66	$42	01000010	
C	67	$43	01000011	
D	68	$44	01000100	
E	69	$45	01000101	
F	70	$46	01000110	
G	71	$47	01000111	

Char	Dec	Hex	Binary	Code	Char	Dec	Hex	Binary	Code
H	72	$48	01001000		d	100	$64	01100100	
I	73	$49	01001001		e	101	$65	01100101	
J	74	$4A	01001010		f	102	$66	01100110	
K	75	$4B	01001011		g	103	$67	01100111	
L	76	$4C	01001100		h	104	$68	01101000	
M	77	$4D	01001101		i	105	$69	01101001	
N	78	$4E	01001110		j	106	$6A	01101010	
O	79	$4F	01001111		k	107	$6B	01101011	
P	80	$50	01010000		l	108	$6C	01101100	
Q	81	$51	01010001		m	109	$6D	01101101	
R	82	$52	01010010		n	110	$6E	01101110	
S	83	$53	01010011		o	111	$6F	01101111	
T	84	$54	01010100		p	112	$70	01110000	
U	85	$55	01010101		q	113	$71	01110001	
V	86	$56	01010110		r	114	$72	01110010	
W	87	$57	01010111		s	115	$73	01110011	
X	88	$58	01011000		t	116	$74	01110100	
Y	89	$59	01011001		u	117	$75	01110101	
Z	90	$5A	01011010		v	118	$76	01110110	
[	91	$5B	01011011		w	119	$77	01110111	
\	92	$5C	01011100		x	120	$78	01111000	
]	93	$5D	01011101		y	121	$79	01111001	
^	94	$5E	01011110		z	122	$7A	01111010	
_	95	$5F	01011111		{	123	$7B	01111011	
`	96	$60	01100000		|	124	$7C	01111100	
a	97	$61	01100001		}	125	$7D	01111101	
b	98	$62	01100010		~	126	$7E	01111110	
c	99	$63	01100011		DEL	127	$7F	01111111	

Codes

NUL - NULL
SOH - Start Of Heading
STX - Start of TeXt
ETX - End of TeXt
EOT - End Of Transmission
ENQ - ENQuiry
ACK - ACKnowledge
BEL - BELL
BS - Back Space
HT - Horizontal Tab
LF - Line Feed
VT - Vertical Tab
FF - Form Feed
CR - Carriage Return
SO - Shift Out
SI - Shift In
DLE - Data Link Escape
DC1 - Device Control 1 (XON)
DC2 - Device Control 2 (AUXON)
DC3 - Device Control 3 (XOFF)
DC4 - Device Control 4 (AUXOFF)
NAK - Negative AcKnowledgement
SYN - SYNchronus file
ETB - End of Tranmission Block
CAN - CANcel
EM - End of Medium
SUB - SUBstitute
ESC - ESCape
FS - File (or Form) Separator
GS - Group Separator
RS - Record Separator
US - Unit Separator
SPC - SPaCe
DEL - DELete, rubout

Appendix B

Firmware Entry Points and Vectors

Bank $00 Entry Points

All calls to the following entry points must be made in the 65816 processor's 65C02 emulation mode, with the decimal mode turned off. In addition, the program bank register, data bank register, and direct page register must all be set to $00. The call should be made with a JSR since all the bank $00 routines return via RTS. All Entry Points are in bank $00.

Entry Point		Notes
C311	AUXMOVE	Move a range of memory between main and auxiliary RAM
C314	XFER	Transfer program control between main and auxiliary RAM
F800	PLOT	Place a block on the low-resolution screen
F80E	PLOT1	(Alternate entry point in PLOT)
F819	HLINE	Draw a horizontal line on the low-res screen
F828	VLINE	Draw a vertical line on the low-res screen
F832	CLRSCR	Clear the low-resolution display to black
F836	CLRTOP	Clear only the top 40 lines of the low-res screen
F847	GBASCALC	Calculate a low-res plot position
F85F	NXTCOL	Add 3 to the current low-res color setting
F864	SETCOL	Set the low-resolution graphics color mode
F871	SCRN	Determine the color of a low-res block
F882	INSDS1	Print the monitor's current PC (program counter)
F88C	INSDS1.2	Load accumulator with the opcode at the PC
F88E	INSDS2	Calculate length of 65C02 instruction in accumulator
F890	INSDS816	Calculate length of 65816 instruction in A register
F8D0	INSTDSP	Display one disassembled instruction at the PC
F940	PRNTYX	Print X and Y in hexadecimal to COUT
F941	PRNTAX	Print A and X in hexadecimal to COUT
F944	PRNTX	Print X in hexadecimal to COUT
F948	PRBLNK	Print three spaces to COUT
F94A	PRBL2	Print X spaces to COUT
F953	PCADJ	Adjust the monitor's program counter (PC)
F962	TEXT2COPY	Manipulate shadowing of text page 2
FA40	OLDIRQ	Save registers and call interrupt handler (NEWIRQ)

FA4C	BREAK	Save registers and jump through the BRK vector ($03F0)
FA59	OLDBRK	Prints address of 65816 BRK instruction and all registers
FA62	RESET	Reset key handler
FAA6	PWRUP	Reboot the computer
FABA	SLOOP	Search the slots for a bootable device
FAD7	REGDSP	Display the A, X, Y and system registers
FB1E	PREAD	Return paddle X value in Y register
FB21	PREAD4	(Alternate entry point in PREAD)
FB2F	INIT	Initialize video display
FB39	SETTXT	Set text mode and a full-width text window
FB40	SETGR	Set low-resolution graphics mode
FB4B	SETWND	Set the text window determined by zero page bounds
FB51	SETWND2	(Alternate entry point in SETWND)
FB5B	TABV	Tab to the screen row in the A register
FB60	APPLEII	Display "Apple IIGS"
FB6F	SETPWRC	Calculate reset vector's power-up complement
FB78	VIDWAIT	Check keyboard for a Control-S when $8D is printed
FB88	KBDWAIT	Wait for a keypress, then print it
FBC1	BASCALC	Determine cursor's address in video RAM
FBDD	BELL1	Beep the speaker
FBE2	BELL1.2	Beep the speaker
FBE4	BELL2	Beep the speaker
FBF0	STORADV	Print A register to screen at the base index
FBF4	ADVANCE	Increment the cursor's position
F8FD	VIDOUT	Print A register to screen, with format control
FC10	BS	Move cursor left (backspace)
FC1A	UP	Move cursor up
FC22	VTAB	Tab to row given in location $25
FC24	VTABZ	Tab to row given in accumulator
FC42	CLREOP	Clear screen from cursor to end of page
FC58	HOME	Clear screen and home cursor
FC62	CR	Perform a carriage return and linefeed
FC66	LF	Perform a linefeed only
FC70	SCROLL	Scroll screen up one line
FC9C	CLREOL	Clear from cursor to end of line
FC9E	CLEOLZ	Clear from the base index plus Y to end of line
FCA8	WAIT	Wait 13 + (11*A) + (5*A*A) microseconds
FCB4	NXTA4	16-bit increment of location $42/$43
FCBA	NXTA1	16-bit compare of $3C/$3D with $3E/$3F
FD0C	RDKEY	Show cursor, get keypress, return in A register
FD10	FD10	Get keypress, return in A register
FD18	RDKEY1	Jump to vector at $38/$39, return keypress in A

FD1B	KEYIN	Standard low-level keypress input handler
FD35	RDCHAR	Read keyboard and perform Escape-key commands
FD67	GETLNZ	Perform a carriage return and fall into GETLN
FD6A	GETLN	Load A register with character at $33, fall into GETLN0
FD6C	GETLN0	Display character in A register and fall into GETLN1
FD6F	GETLN1	Get a line of input
FD8B	CROUT1	Clear to end of line and perform a carriage return
FD8E	CROUT	Send a carriage return to COUT
FD92	PRA1	Call CROUT and print $3C/$3D in hexadecimal
FDDA	PRBYTE	Print accumulator in hexadecimal
FDE3	PRHEX	Print lower four bits of accumulator in hexadecimal
FDED	COUT	Send accumulator to the vector at $36/$37
FDF0	COUT1	Print character to screen with format control
FDF6	COUTZ	Print character to screen, ignoring inverse video
FE1F	IDROUTINE	Determine machine type and system information
FE2C	MOVE	Move a block of memory
FE80	SETINV	Set inverse video mode
FE84	SETNORM	Set normal video mode
FE89	SETKBD	Reset standard input vectors to the keyboard
FE8B	INPORT	Reset input to the slot determined by the A register
FE93	SETVID	Reset standard output vectors to the screen
FE95	OUTPORT	Reset output to the slot determined by the A register
FEB6	GO	Run instructions determined by the address at $3C/$3D
FF2D	PRERR	Print "ERR" to COUT, fall into BELL
FF3A	BELL	Load accumulator with $87 and call COUT
FF3F	RESTORE	Restore processor registers
FF4A	SAVE	Save processor registers
FF58	IORTS	Does nothing (a known RTS instruction)
FF59	OLDRST	Enter the monitor (old)
FF65	MON	Enter the monitor with a bell tone
FF69	MONZ	Enter the monitor, reset register storage areas
FF6C	MONZ2	Enter the monitor, leave register storage areas intact
FF70	MONZ4	Same as MONZ2, but does not display the * prompt
FF8A	DIG	Put hex version of A register into $3E/$3F, branch to NXTCHR
FFA7	GETNUM	Convert hex input to 16-bit value, fall into NXTCHR
FFAD	NXTCHR	Parse input buffer characters
FFC7	ZMODE	Zero monitor's MODE flag

Bank $00 Vectors

Vectors in bank $00 usually consist of two bytes which consistute a 16-bit address. By using an indirect jump, such as "JMP (vector)", execution can resume at that address. However, some bank $00 vector points consist of three bytes, and should be called using an absolute jump, such as "JMP vector." These are documented below.

Vector or Entry Point		Notes
03F0-03F1	BRKV	User's break (BRK) instruction vector
03F2-03F3	SOFTEV	Soft entry (RESET) vector
03F5	AMPERV	Applesoft's ampersand JMP vector
03F8	USRADR	Monitor's Control-Y JMP vector
03FB	NMI	User's nonmaskable interrupt (NMI) JMP vector
03FE-03FF	IRQLOC	User's processor interrupt vector
FFE4-FFE5	NCOP	Native mode coprocessor (COP) vector
FFE6-FFE7	NBREAK	Native mode BRK vector
FFE8-FFE9	NABORT	Native mode ABORT vector
FFEA-FFEB	NNMI	Native mode NMI vector
FFEE-FFEF	NIRQ	Native mode interrupt request (IRQ) vector
FFF4-FFF5	ECOP	Emulation mode COP vector
FFF8-FFF9	EABORT	Emulation mode ABORT vector
FFFA-FFFB	ENMI	Emulation mode NMI vector
FFFC-FFFD	ERESET	Reset vector
FFFE-FFFF	EBRKIRQ	Emulation mode BRK/IRQ vector

Bank $E1 Entry Points

The following 24-bit addresses can be called directly via absolute long JSL or JML instructions in full native mode.

Entry Point		Notes
E10000	DISPATCH1	Tool locator (1 return address on stack)
E10004	DISPATCH2	Tool locator (2 return addresses on stack)
E10008	UDISPATCH1	User's tool locator (1 return address on stack)
E1000C	UDISPATCH2	User's tool locator (2 return addresses on stack)
E10010	INTMGRV	System interrupt handler/manager
E10014	COPMGRV	Coprocessor manager
E10018	ABORTMGRV	Abort manager
E1001C	SYSDMGRV	System death manager
E10020	IRQ.APTALK	AppleTalk interrupt handler
E10024	IRQ.SERIAL	Serial port interrupt handler
E10028	IRQ.SCAN	Scanline interrupt handler
E1002C	IRQ.SOUND	Sound interrupt handler

E10030	IRQ.VBL	Vertical blanking interrupt handler
E10034	IRQ.MOUSE	Mouse interrupt handler
E10038	IRQ.QTR	Quarter second interrupt handler
E1003C	IRQ.KBD	Keyboard interrupt handler
E10040	IRQ.RESPONSE	ADB response interrupt handler
E10044	IRQ.SRQ	ADB service request interrupt handler
E10048	IRQ.DSKACC	Desk accessory interrupt handler
E1004C	IRQ.FLUSH	Keyboard FLUSH interrupt handler
E10050	IRQ.MICRO	Keyboard micro abort interrupt handler
E10054	IRQ.1SEC	One second interrupt handler
E10058	IRQ.EXT	VGC external interrupt handler
E1005C	IRQ.OTHER	Other interrupt handler
E10060	CUPDATE	Update cursor
E10064	INCBUSYFLG	Increment busy flag
E10068	DECBUSYFLG	Decrement busy flag
E1006C	BELLVECTOR	Call system's bell routine
E10070	BREAKVECTOR	Break vector
E10074	TRACEVECTOR	Monitor's trace routine vector
E10078	STEPVECTOR	Monitor's step routine vector
E1007C	...	(Reserved)
E10080	TOWRITEBR	Write battery RAM routine
E10084	TOREADBR	Read battery RAM routine
E10088	TOWRITETIME	Write to realtime clock routine
E1008C	TOREADTIME	Read realtime clock routine
E10090	TOCTRLPANEL	Invoke the Control Panel
E10094	TOBRAMSETUP	Match system parameters to those in battery RAM
E10098	TOPRINTMSG8	Print string indexed by 8-bit A register + $E100C0 (long)
E1009C	TOPRINTMSG16	Print string indexed by 16-bit A register + $E100C0 (long)
E100A0	CTRLYVECTOR	User's Control-Y vector
E100A4	TOTEXTPG2DA	Alternate Display mode program (from Control Panel)
E100A8	PRODOS16MLI	ProDOS 16 Machine Language Interface

Appendix C

Hardware Registers and Softswitches

Description of Access Modes

Read - Any read/fetch instruction
Read2 - Two successive reads
Write - Any write, modify, or zero instruction
Test - Read and test bit 7 to see if true
Modify - Read, modify certain bits, then write

Address		Access Modes	Notes
C000	KBD	Read/Test	Keyboard input latch
C000	CLR80COL	Write	Disable 80-column store
C001	SET80COL	Write	Enable 80-column store
C002	RDMAINRAM	Write	Read main 48K RAM
C003	RDCARDRAM	Write	Read aux. 48K RAM
C004	WRMAINRAM	Write	Write main 48K RAM
C005	WRCARDRAM	Write	Write aux. 48K RAM
C006	SETSLOTCXROM	Write	Use peripheral ROM
C007	SETINTCXROM	Write	Use internal ROM
C008	SETSTDZP	Write	Use main zero page and stack
C009	SETALTZP	Write	Use aux. zero page and stack
C00A	SETINTC3ROM	Write	Use internal slot 3 ROM
C00B	SETSLOTC3ROM	Write	Use external slot 3 ROM
C00C	CLR80VID	Write	Disable 80-column video
C00D	SET80VID	Write	Enable 80-column video
C00E	CLRALTCHAR	Write	Disable alternate character set
C00F	SETALTCHAR	Write	Enable alternate character set
C010	KBDSTRB	Write	Clear keypress pending flag
C011	RDLCBNK2	Test	Language Card installed
C012	RDLCRAM	Test	Language Card read-enabled
C013	RDRAMRD	Test	Reading auxiliary 48K RAM
C014	RDRAMWRT	Test	Writing auxiliary 48K RAM

Address		Access Modes	Notes
C015	RDCXROM	Test	Using internal ROM
C016	RDALTZP	Test	Using alternate zero page and stack
C017	RDC3ROM	Test	Slot 3 ROM enabled
C018	RD80COL	Test	80-column store enabled
C019	RDVBLBAR	Test	In vertical blanking cycle
C01A	RDTEXT	Test	In text mode
C01B	RDMIX	Test	Mixed mode enabled
C01C	RDPAGE2	Test	TXTPAGE2 enabled
C01D	RDHIRES	Test	High-resolution graphics enabled
C01E	ALTCHARSET	Test	Alternate character set enabled
C01F	RD80VID	Test	80-column video enabled
C020	—	—	(Reserved)
C021	MONOCOLOR	Read/Modify	Monochrome/color selector
C022	TBCOLOR	Read/Modify	Text/background color selector
C023	VGCINT	Read/Modify	VGC interrupt selector
C024	MOUSEDATA	Read	X or Y mouse data
C025	KEYMODREG	Read	Key modifier information
C026	DATAREG	Read/Modify	GLU data register
C027	KMSTATUS	Read	Keyboard/mouse status
C028	ROMBANK	Read	(Not used in Apple IIGS)
C029	NEWVIDEO	Read/Modify	Miscellaneous video mode selector
C02A	—	—	(Reserved)
C02B	LANGSEL	Read/Modify	Language/PAL/NTSC selector
C02C	CHARROM	Read	Test character ROM
C02D	SLTROMSEL	Read/Modify	Slot ROM selector
C02E	VERTCNT	Read	Video control bits V5-VB
C02F	HORIZCNT	Read	Video control bits VA-H0
C030	SPKR	Read	Speaker toggle
C031	DISKREG	Read/Modify	3.5-inch drive enable/head selector
C032	SCANINT	Read/Modify	Scan line interrupts/1-sec int. reset
C033	CLOCKDATA	Read/Write	Real time clock data register
C034	CLOCKCTL	Read/Modify	Clock control/border color selector
C035	SHADOW	Read/Modify	Shadow register
C036	CYAREG	Read/Modify	CPU speed control/drive motor detect

Address		Access Modes	Notes
C037	DMAREG	Read	Bank address during DMA
C038	SCCBREG	Write	SCC command register B
C039	SCCAREG	Write	SCC command register A
C03A	SCCBDATA	Read	SCC data register B
C03B	SCCADATA	Read	SCC data register A
C03C	SOUNDCTL	Read/Modify	Sound control register
C03D	SOUNDDATA	Read/Write	Sound data register
C03E	SOUNDADRL	Read/Write	Sound address pointer (low byte)
C03F	SOUNDADRH	Read/Write	Sound address pointer (high byte)
C040	—	—	(Reserved)
C041	INTEN	Read/Modify	Interrupt enable register
C042	—	—	(Reserved)
C043	—	—	(Reserved)
C044	MMDELTAX	Read	Mega II mouse delta X register
C045	MMDELTAY	Read	Mega II mouse delta Y register
C046	DIAGTYPE	Test	Self- or burned-in diagnostics select
C046	INTFLAG	Read	Mouse button/interrupt flag register
C047	CLRVBLINT	Write	Clear VBL/3.75Hz interrupt flags
C048	CLRXYINT	Write	Clear Mega II mouse interrupt flags
C049-C04F	—	(Reserved)	
C050	TXTCLR	Write	Clear text mode (select graphics)
C051	TXTSET	Write	Set text mode
C052	MIXCLR	Write	Clear mixed text/graphics mode
C053	MIXSET	Write	Set mixed text/graphics mode
C054	TXTPAGE1	Write	Enable text page 1
C055	TXTPAGE2	Write	Enable text page 2
C056	LORES	Write	Select low-resolution graphics
C057	HIRES	Write	Select high-resolution graphics
C058	CLRAN0	Write	Clear annunciator 0
C059	SETAN0	Write	Set annunciator 0
C05A	CLRAN1	Write	Clear annunciator 1
C05B	SETAN1	Write	Set annunciator 1
C05C	CLRAN2	Write	Clear annunciator 2

Address		Access Modes	Notes
C05D	SETAN2	Write	Set annunciator 2
C05E	CLRAN3	Write	Clear annunciator 3
C05F	SETAN3	Write	Set annunciator 3
C060	BUTN3	Read/Test	Switch 3
C061	BUTN0	Read/Test	Switch 0 (Apple/Command key)
C062	BUTN1	Read/Test	Switch 1 (Option key)
C063	BUTN2	Read/Test	Switch 2
C064	PADDL0	Read	Paddle 0
C065	PADDL1	Read	Paddle 1
C066	PADDL2	Read	Paddle 2
C067	PADDL3	Read	Paddle 3
C068	STATEREG	Read/Modify	Memory management state register
C069-C06C	—	(Reserved)	
C06D	TESTREG	Test	Test mode enabled
C06E	CLRTM	Write	Disable test mode
C06F	ENTM	Write	Enable test mode
C070	PTRIG	Write	Trigger the paddle timer
C071-C07F	Read	ROM interrupt code jump table	
C080		Read	Read LC RAM bank 2, no write
C081	ROMIN	Read2	Read ROM, write to LC RAM bank 2
C082		Read	Read ROM, no write to LC RAM
C083	LCBANK2	Read2	Read and write LC RAM bank 2
C084		Read	Read LC RAM bank 2, no write
C085		Read2	Read ROM, write LC RAM bank 2
C086		Read	Read ROM, no write to LC RAM
C087		Read2	Read and write LC RAM bank 2
C088		Read	Read LC RAM bank 1, no write
C089		Read2	Read ROM, write to LC RAM bank 1
C08A		Read	Read ROM, no write to LC RAM
C08B	LCBANK1	Read2	Read and write LC RAM bank 1

Address		Access Modes	Notes
C08C		Read	Read LC RAM bank 1, no write
C08D		Read2	Read ROM, write LC RAM bank 1
C08E		Read	Read ROM, no write to LC RAM
C08F		Read2	Read and write LC RAM bank 1
CFFF	CLRROM	Write	Swap out $C800 ROMs

Appendix D

ProDOS 16 Function Calls

Though the scope of this book does not encompass working with ProDOS 16, this appendix is provided as a brief reference. It would be valuable to study the ProDOS 16 operating environment further once the toolbox has been mastered.

For the sake of completeness, making a call to the ProDOS 16 command dispatcher is illustrated in the following example.

```
        JSL   $E100A8        ;PRODOS 16 DISPATCH VECTOR
        DC    I'$29'         ;COMMAND NUMBER
        DC    I4'QPARMS'     ;PARAMETER LIST
        BCS   UHOH           ;BRANCH IF ERROR OCCURRED
        ...
QPARMS  DC    I4'0'          ;NO RETURN PATHNAME
        DC    I'0'           ;CAN'T BE RE-RUN FROM MEMORY
```

You've seen this before. Many of the sample programs in this book call ProDOS 16's Quit function ($29) when the application is finished. All other ProDOS 16 commands are made in exactly the same fashion, the only difference being the command number and the structure of the parameter list.

After a call is made, the C (carry) flag tells if an error occurred. If set, the error code is returned in the A register, and your program can act on it accordingly. (See Appendix E for a list of error codes and their descriptions.)

The following section lists the structure of the parameter table for each ProDOS 16 call. The size of each parameter is denoted by (L) for long word sizes, (W) for word sizes, and (B) for byte sizes. Fields modified with information from ProDOS are noted as "Result" fields.

Function and Parameter List

Function	Parameter List
$01 Create	Pathname (L) Access (W) File Type (W) Auxiliary Type (L) Storage Type (W) Create Date (W) Create Time (W)
$02 Destroy	Pathname (L)
$04 Change_Path	Pathname (L) New Pathname (L)
$05 Set_File_Info	Pathname (L) Access (W) File Type (W) Auxiliary Type (L) Null Field (W) Create Date (W) Create Time (W) Modification Date (W) Modification Time (W)
$06 Get_File_Info	Pathname (L) Result: Access (W) Result: File Type (W) Result: Auxiliary Type (L) Result: Storage Type (W) Result: Create Date (W) Result: Create Time (W) Result: Modification Date (W) Result: Modification Time (W) Result: Blocks Used (L)
$08 Volume	Device Name (L) Result: Volume Name (L) Result: Total Blocks (L) Result: Free Blocks (L) Result: File System ID (W)
$09 Set_Prefix	Prefix Number (W) Prefix (L)
$0A Get_Prefix	Prefix Number (W) Prefix (L)
$0B Clear_Backup_Bit	Pathname (L)
$10 Open	Result: Reference Number (W) Pathname (L) Result: I/O Buffer Handle (L)
$11 Newline	Reference Number (W) Enable Mask (W) Newline Character (W)

Function	Parameter List
$12 Read	Reference Number (W) Data Buffer (L) Request Count (L) Result: Transfer Count (L)
$13 Write	Reference Number (W) Data Buffer (L) Request Count (L)
$14 Close	Reference Number (W)
$15 Flush	Reference Number (W)
$16 Set_Mark	Reference Number (W) Position (L)
$17 Get_Mark	Reference Number (W) Result: Position (L)
$18 Set_EOF	Reference Number (W) EOF Position (L)
$19 Get_EOF	Reference Number (W) Result: EOF Position (L)
$1A Set_Level	Level (W)
$1B Get_Level	Result: Level (W)
$20 Get_Dev_Num	Device Name (L) Result: Device Number (W)
$21 Get_Last_Dev	Result: Device Number (W)
$22 Read_Block	Device Number (W) Data Buffer (L) Block Number (L)
$23 Write_Block	Device Number (W) Data Buffer (L) Block Number (L)
$24 Format	Device Name (L) Volume Name (L) File System ID (W)
$27 Get_Name	Data Buffer (L)
$28 Get_Boot_Vol	Data Buffer (L)
$29 Quit	Pathname (L) Flags (W)
$2A Get_Version	Result: Version (W)
$31 Alloc_Interrupt	Result: Interrupt Number (W) Interrupt Code (L)
$32 Dealloc_Interrupt	Interrupt Number (W)

Functions Arranged by Name

Function	Location
Alloc_Interrupt	$31
Change_Path	$04
Clear_Backup_Bit	$0B
Close	$14
Create	$01
Dealloc_Interrupt	$32
Destroy	$02
Flush	$15
Format	$24
Get_Boot_Vol	$28
Get_Dev_Num	$20
Get_EOF	$19
Get_File_Info	$06
Get_Last_Dev	$21
Get_Level	$1B
Get_Mark	$17
Get_Name	$27
Get_Prefix	$0A
Get_Version	$2A
Newline	$11
Open	$10
Quit	$29
Read	$12
Read_Block	$22
Set_EOF	$18
Set_File_Info	$05
Set_Level	$1A
Set_Mark	$16
Set_Prefix	$09
Volume	$08
Write	$13
Write_Block	$23

Appendix E

Error Codes

Fatal System Errors

Error Number	Message
$01	Unclaimed interrupt
$0A	Volume Control Block unusable
$0B	File Control Block unusable
$0C	Block zero allocated illegally
$0D	Interrupt occurred while I/O shadowing off
$11	Wrong OS Version

Errors Returned from ProDOS

Error Number	Message
$00	No error
$01	Invalid call number
$07	ProDOS is busy
$10	Device not Found
$11	Invalid device request
$25	Interrupt vector table full
$27	I/O Error
$28	No device connected
$2B	Disk is write protected
$2E	Disk switched, files open
$2F	Device not online
$30–$3F	Device-specific errors
$40	Invalid Pathname
$42	File control block table full
$43	Invalid reference number
$44	Path not found
$45	Volume not found
$46	File not found
$47	Duplicate pathname
$48	Volume full
$49	Volume directory full
$4A	Version error
$4B	Unsupported storage type
$4C	EOF encountered, out of data
$4D	Position out of range
$4E	Access: file not rename enabled
$50	File is open

Error Number	Message
$51	Directory structure damaged
$52	Unsupported volume type
$53	Invalid parameter
$54	Out of memory
$55	Volume control block full
$57	Duplicate volume
$58	Not a block device
$59	Invalid file level
$5A	Block number out of range
$5B	Illegal pathname change
$5C	Not an executable file
$5D	File system not available
$5E	Cannot deallocate /RAM
$5F	Return stack overflow
$60	Data unavailable

Errors Returned from the Toolbox

Error Number	Message
$0100	Unable to mount system startup volume
$0110	Bad tool set version number
$0201	Unable to allocate block
$0202	Illegal operation on an empty handle
$0203	Empty handle expected for this operation
$0204	Illegal operation on a lock or immovable block
$0205	Attempt to purge an unpurgeable block
$0206	Invalid handle given
$0207	Invalid User ID given
$0208	Operation illegal on block specified attributes
$0301	Bad Input Parameter
$0302	No device for input parameter
$0303	Task is already in the Heartbeat queue
$0304	No signature in Task Header was detected
$0305	Damaged Queue was detected during insert or delete
$0306	Task was not found during delete
$0307	Firmware task was unsuccessful
$0308	Detected damaged Heartbeat queue
$0309	Attempted dispatch to a device that is disconnected
$030B	ID tag not available
$0401	QuickDraw already initialized
$0402	Cannot Reset
$0403	QuickDraw is not initialized
$0410	Screen is reserved
$0411	Bad Rectangle
$0420	Chunkiness is not equal
$0430	Region is already open

Error Number	Message
$0431	Region is not open
$0432	Region scan overflow
$0433	Region is full
$0440	Poly is already open
$0441	Poly is not open
$0442	Poly is too big
$0450	Bad table number
$0451	Bad color number
$0452	Bad scan line
$0510	Desk Accessory is not available
$0511	Window pointer does not belong to the NDA
$0601	The Event Manager has already been started
$0602	Reset error
$0603	The Event Manager is not active
$0604	Bad event code number (greater than 15)
$0605	Bad button number value
$0606	Queue size greater than 3639
$0607	No memory for event queue
$0681	Fatal error: event queue is damaged
$0682	Fatal error: event queue handle damaged
$0810	No DOC chip or RAM found
$0811	DOC address range error
$0812	No SAppInt call made
$8013	Invalid generator number
$0814	Synthesizer mode error
$0815	Generator busy error
$8017	Master IRQ not assigned
$0818	Sound Tools already started
$08FF	Fatal Error—Unclaimed sound interrupt
$0910	Command not completed
$0982	Busy, command pending
$0983	Device not present at address
$0984	List is full
$0B01	Bad input parameter
$0B02	Illegal character in input string
$0B03	Integer or Long Integer overflow
$0B04	String overflow
$0E01	First word of parameter list is the wrong size
$0E02	Unable to allocate window record
$0E03	Bits 14–31 not clear in task mask
$1101	Segment or Entry not found
$1102	Incompatible object module format (OMF) version
$1104	File is not a load file
$1105	System Loader is busy
$1107	File version error
$1108	UserID error

Error Number	Message
$1109	Segment number is out of sequence
$110A	Illegal load record found
$110B	Load segment is foreign
$1401	The LEStartUp call has already been made
$1402	Reset error
$1404	The desk scrap is too big
$150A	Bad Item Type
$150B	New Item Failed
$150C	Item Not Found
$150D	Not a Modal Dialog
$1610	Unknown Scrap Type
$1B01	Font Manager has already been started
$1B02	Can't reset Font Manager
$1B03	Font Manager is not active
$1B04	Family not found
$1B05	Font not found
$1B06	Font is not in memory
$1B07	System font cannot be purgeable
$1B08	Illegal Family number
$1B09	Illegal size
$1B0A	Illegal name length
$1B0B	FixFontMenu never called
$1C01	Unable to create list control or scroll bar control

Appendix F

65816 Opcode Chart

Addressing Modes

Mode	Meaning
#imm	immediate value
relb	relative byte displacement
relw	relative word displacement
addr	absolute address
long	absolute long address
byte	byte constant
dp	direct page
( )	indirect address
[ ]	long indirect address
,X	indexed by X
,Y	indexed by Y
,S	stack relative index

Status Register Map

Flag	Meaning
n	negative result
v	overflow
m	memory/accumulator
x	index register
d	decimal mode
i	interrupt disable
z	zero result
c	carry
b	BRK interrupt (emulation)

Status Register Bit Settings

Code	Meaning
x	may be affected
-	not affected
0	reset to zero
1	set to one

Bytes/Cycles Adjustment Notes

Note	Meaning
A	Add 1 if using 16-bit memory/accumulator
B	Add 1 if low byte of DP reg. is not zero
C	Add 1 if index crosses page boundary
D	Add 1 if decimal bit set in emulation mode
E	Add 2 if using 16-bit memory/accumulator
F	Add 1 if branch is taken
G	Add 1 if branch taken over boundary in emulation mode
H	Add 1 if in native mode
I	Add 1 if using 16-bit index registers
J	Add 7 cycles for each byte moved
K	Add 1 if using optional signature byte
L	Unknown—subject to change

65816 Opcodes

Instruction		Object Code (#bytes)	Cycles	Status Register nv—bdizc nvmxdizc	Comments
ADC	#imm	69 __ A	2 + AD	xx----xx	Add memory to accumulator with carry
ADC	addr	6D __ __	4 + AD		
ADC	long	6F __ __ __	5 + AD		
ADC	dp	65 __	3 + ABD		
ADC	(dp)	72 __	5 + ABD		
ADC	[dp]	67 __	6 + ABD		
ADC	addr,X	7D __ __	4 + ACD		
ADC	long,X	7F __ __ __	5 + AD		
ADC	addr,Y	79 __ __	4 + ACD		
ADC	dp,X	75 __	4 + ABD		
ADC	(dp,X)	61 __	6 + ABD		
ADC	(dp),Y	71 __	5 + ABCD		
ADC	[dp],Y	77 __	6 + ABD		
ADC	byte,S	63 __	4 + AD		
ADC	(byte,S),Y	73 __	7 + AD		
AND	#imm	29 __ A	2 + A	x-----x-	And accumulator with memory
AND	addr	2D __ __	4 + A		
AND	long	2F __ __ __	5 + A		
AND	dp	25 __	3 + AB		
AND	(dp)	32 __	5 + AB		
AND	[dp]	27 __	6 + AB		
AND	addr,X	3D __ __	4 + AC		
AND	long,X	3F __ __ __	5 + A		
AND	addr,Y	39 __ __	4 + AC		
AND	dp,X	35 __	4 + AB		
AND	(dp,X)	21 __	6 + AB		
AND	(dp),Y	31 __	5 + ABC		
AND	[dp],Y	37 __	6 + AB		
AND	byte,S	23 __	4 + A		
AND	(byte,S),Y	33 __	7 + A		
ASL		0A	2	x-----xx	Shift left memory or accumulator

Instruction		Object Code (#bytes)	Cycles	Status Register nv— bdizc nvmxdizc	Comments
ASL	addr	0E ___ ___	6 + E		
ASL	dp	06 ___	5 + EB		
ASL	addr,X	1E ___ ___	7 + E		
ASL	dp,X	16 ___	6 + EB		
BCC	relb	90 ___	2 + FG	--------	Branch if carry clear
BCS	relb	B0 ___	2 + FG	--------	Branch if carry set
BEQ	relb	F0 ___	2 + FG	--------	Branch if equal
BIT	#imm	89 ___ A	2 + A	------x-	Test memory bits with accumulator
BIT	addr	2C ___ ___	4 + A	xx----x-	
BIT	dp	24 ___	3 + AB	xx----x-	
BIT	addr,X	3C ___ ___	4 + AC	xx----x-	
BIT	dp,X	34 ___	4 + AB	xx----x-	
BMI	relb	30 ___	2 + FG	--------	Branch if minus
BNE	relb	D0 ___	2 + FG	--------	Branch if not equal
BPL	relb	10 ___	2 + FG	--------	Branch if plus
BRA	relb	80 ___	3 + G	--------	Branch always
BRK	byte	00 K	7 + H	----01--	Software break interrupt
BRK		00		---101--	(sets b flag in emulation mode)
BRL	relw	82 ___ ___	4	--------	Branch always long
BVC	relb	50 ___	2 + FG	--------	Branch if overflow clear
BVS	relb	70 ___	2 + FG	--------	Branch if overflow set
CLC		18	2	-------0	Clear carry flag
CLD		D8	2	----0---	Clear decimal flag
CLI		58	2	-----0--	Clear interrupt disable flag
CLV		B8	2	-0------	Clear overflow flag
CMP	#imm	C9 ___ A	2 + A	x-----xx	Compare accumulator with memory
CMP	addr	CD ___ ___	4 + A		
CMP	long	CF ___ ___ ___	5 + A		
CMP	dp	C5 ___	3 + AB		
CMP	(dp)	D2 ___	5 + AB		
CMP	[dp]	C7 ___	6 + AB		
CMP	addr,X	DD ___ ___	4 + AC		
CMP	long,X	DF ___ ___ ___	5 + A		
CMP	addr,Y	D9 ___ ___	4 + AC		
CMP	dp,X	D5 ___	4 + AB		
CMP	(dp,X)	C1 ___	6 + AB		
CMP	(dp),Y	D1 ___	5 + ABC		
CMP	[dp],Y	D7 ___	6 + AB		
CMP	byte,S	C3 ___	4 + A		
CMP	(byte,S),Y	D3 ___	7 + A		
COP	byte	02 K	7 + H	----01--	Coprocessor enable
CPX	#imm	E0 ___ I	2 + I	x-----xx	Compare X register with memory
CPX	addr	EC ___ ___	4 + I		
CPX	dp	E4 ___	3 + IB		
CPY	#imm	C0 ___ I	2 + I	x-----xx	Compare Y register with memory
CPY	addr	CC ___ ___	4 + I		
CPY	dp	C4 ___	3 + IB		
DEC		3A	2	x-----x-	Decrement accumulator or memory
DEC	addr	CE ___ ___	6 + E		

Appendix F

Instruction	Object Code (#bytes)	Cycles	Status Register nv—bdizc nvmxdizc	Comments
DEC dp	C6 __	5 + EB		
DEC addr,X	DE __ __	7 + E		
DEC dp,X	D6 __	6 + EB		
DEX	CA	2	x-----x-	Decrement X register
DEY	88	2	x-----x-	Decrement Y register
EOR #imm	49 __ A	2 + A	x-----x-	Exclusive-OR accumulator with memory
EOR addr	4D __ __	4 + A		
EOR long	4F __ __ __	5 + A		
EOR dp	45 __	3 + AB		
EOR (dp)	52 __	5 + AB		
EOR [dp]	47 __	6 + AB		
EOR addr,X	5D __ __	4 + AC		
EOR long,X	5F __ __ __	5 + A		
EOR addr,Y	59 __ __	4 + AC		
EOR dp,X	55 __	4 + AB		
EOR (dp,X)	41 __	6 + AB		
EOR (dp),Y	51 __	5 + ABC		
EOR [dp],Y	57 __	6 + AB		
EOR byte,S	43 __	4 + A		
EOR (byte,S),Y	53 __	7 + A		
INC	1A	2	x-----x-	Increment accumulator or memory
INC addr	EE __ __	6 + E		
INC dp	E6 __	5 + EB		
INC addr,X	FE __ __	7 + E		
INC dp,X	F6 __	6 + EB		
INX	E8	2	x-----x-	Increment X register
INY	C8	2	x-----x-	Increment Y register
JMP addr	4C __ __	3	--------	Jump
JMP (addr)	6C __ __	5		
JMP (addr,X)	7C __ __	6		
JML long	5C __ __ __	4	--------	Jump long
JML [addr]	DC __ __	6		
JSL long	22 __ __ __	8	--------	Jump to subroutine long
JSR addr	20 __ __	6	--------	Jump to subroutine
JSR (addr,X)	FC __ __	8		
LDA #imm	A9 __ A	2 + A	x-----x-	Load accumulator with memory
LDA addr	AD __ __	4 + A		
LDA long	AF __ __ __	5 + A		
LDA dp	A5 __	3 + AB		
LDA (dp)	B2 __	5 + AB		
LDA [dp]	A7 __	6 + AB		
LDA addr,X	BD __ __	4 + AC		
LDA long,X	BF __ __ __	5 + A		
LDA addr,Y	B9 __ __	4 + AC		
LDA dp,X	B5 __	4 + AB		
LDA (dp,X)	A1 __	6 + AB		
LDA (dp),Y	B1 __	5 + ABC		
LDA [dp],Y	B7 __	6 + AB		
LDA byte,S	A3 __	4 + A		
LDA (byte,S),Y	B3 __	7 + A		
LDX #imm	A2 __	2 + I	x-----x-	Load X register with memory
LDX addr	AE __ __	4 + I		

Instruction		Object Code (#bytes)	Cycles	Status Register nv—bdizc nvmxdizc	Comments
LDX	dp	A6 __	3 + IB		
LDX	addr,Y	BE __ __	4 + IC		
LDX	dp,Y	B6 __	4 + IB		
LDY	#imm	A0 __	2 + I	x-----x-	Load Y register with memory
LDY	addr	AC __ __	4 + I		
LDY	dp	A4 __	3 + IB		
LDY	addr,X	BC __ __	4 + IC		
LDY	dp,X	B4 __	4 + IB		
LSR		4A	2	x-----xx	Logical shift accumulator or memory right
LSR	addr	4E __ __	6 + A		
LSR	dp	46 __	5 + AB		
LSR	addr,X	5E __ __	7 + A		
LSR	dp,X	56 __	6 + AB		
MVN	byte,byte	54 __ __	J	--------	Move memory negative (srcbank,trgbank)
MVP	byte,byte	44 __ __	J	--------	Move memory positive (srcbank,trgbank)
NOP		EA	2	--------	No operation
ORA	#imm	09 __ A	2 + A	x-----x-	OR accumulator with memory
ORA	addr	0D __ __	4 + A		
ORA	long	0F __ __ __	5 + A		
ORA	dp	05 __	3 + AB		
ORA	(dp)	12 __	5 + AB		
ORA	[dp]	07 __	6 + AB		
ORA	addr,X	1D __ __	4 + AC		
ORA	long,X	1F __ __ __	5 + A		
ORA	addr,Y	19 __ __	4 + AC		
ORA	dp,X	15 __	4 + AB		
ORA	(dp,X)	01 __	6 + AB		
ORA	(dp),Y	11 __	5 + ABC		
ORA	[dp],Y	17 __	6 + AB		
ORA	byte,S	03 __	4 + A		
ORA	(byte,S),Y	13 __	7 + A		
PEA	addr	F4 __ __	5	--------	Push effective absolute address
PEI	(dp)	D4 __	6 + B	--------	Push effective indirect address
PER	relw	62 __ __	6	--------	Push effective PC relative address
PHA		48	3 + A	--------	Push accumulator
PHB		8B	3	--------	Push data bank register
PHD		0B	4	--------	Push direct page register
PHK		4B	3	--------	Push program bank register
PHP		08	3	--------	Push processor status register
PHX		DA	3 + I	--------	Push X register
PHY		5A	3 + I	--------	Push Y register
PLA		68	4 + A	x-----x-	Pull accumulator
PLB		AB	4	x-----x-	Pull data bank register
PLD		2B	5	x-----x-	Pull direct page register
PLP		28	4	xxxxxxxx	Pull processor status
PLX		FA	4 + I	x-----x-	Pull X register
PLY		7A	4 + I	x-----x-	Pull Y register
REP	#imm	C2 __	3	00000000	Reset processor status bits

Instruction		Object Code (#bytes)	Cycles	Status Register nv—bdizc nvmxdizc	Comments
ROL		2A	2	x-----xx	Rotate accumulator or memory right
ROL	addr	2E __ __	6 + A		
ROL	dp	26 __	5 + AB		
ROL	addr,X	3E __ __	7 + A		
ROL	dp,X	36 __	6 + AB		
RTI		40	6 + H	xxxxxxxx	Return from interrupt
RTI		40	6	xx--xxxx	(emulation mode)
RTL		6B	6	--------	Return from subroutine long
RTS		60	6	--------	Return from subroutine
SBC	#imm	E9 __ A	2 + AD	xx----xx	Subtract memory from accumulator with borrow
SBC	addr	ED __ __	4 + AD		
SBC	long	EF __ __ __	5 + AD		
SBC	dp	E5 __	3 + ABD		
SBC	(dp)	F2 __	5 + ABD		
SBC	[dp]	E7 __	6 + ABD		
SBC	addr,X	FD __ __	4 + ACD		
SBC	long,X	FF __ __ __	5 + AD		
SBC	addr,Y	F9 __ __	4 + ACD		
SBC	dp,X	F5 __	4 + ABD		
SBC	(dp,X)	E1 __	6 + ABD		
SBC	(dp),Y	F1 __	5 + ABCD		
SBC	[dp],Y	F7 __	6 + ABD		
SBC	byte,S	E3 __	4 + AD		
SBC	(byte,S),Y	F3 __	7 + AD		
SEC		38	2	-------1	Set carry flag
SED		F8	2	----1---	Set decimal flag
SEI		78	2	-----1--	Set interrupt disable flag
SEP	#imm	E2 __	3	11111111	Set processor status bits
STA	addr	8D __ __	4 + A	--------	Store accumulator to memory
STA	long	8F __ __ __	5 + A		
STA	dp	85 __	3 + AB		
STA	(dp)	92 __	5 + AB		
STA	[dp]	87 __	6 + AB		
STA	addr,X	9D __ __	5 + A		
STA	long,X	9F __ __ __	5 + A		
STA	addr,Y	99 __ __	5 + A		
STA	dp,X	95 __	4 + AB		
STA	(dp,X)	81 __	6 + AB		
STA	(dp),Y	91 __	6 + AB		
STA	[dp],Y	97 __	6 + AB		
STA	byte,S	83 __	4 + A		
STA	(byte,S),Y	93 __	7 + A		
STP		DB	3	--------	Stop the processor
STX	addr	8E __ __	4 + I	--------	Store X register to memory
STX	dp	86 __	3 + IB		
STX	dp,Y	96 __	4 + IB		
STY	addr	8C __ __	4 + I	--------	Store Y register to memory
STY	dp	84 __	3 + IB		
STY	dp,X	94 __	4 + IB		
STZ	addr	9C __ __	4 + A	--------	Store zero to memory
STZ	dp	64 __	3 + AB		
STZ	addr,X	9E __ __	5 + A		
STZ	dp,X	74 __	4 + AB		

Instruction	Object Code (#bytes)	Cycles	Status Register nv—bdizc nvmxdizc	Comments
TAX	AA	2	x-----x-	Transfer accumulator to X register
TAY	A8	2	x-----x-	Transfer accumulator to Y register
TCD	5B	2	x-----x-	Transfer 16-bit accumulator to direct page register
TCS	1B	2	--------	Transfer accumulator to stack pointer
TDC	7B	2	x-----x-	Transfer direct page register to 16-bit accumulator
TRB addr	1C ___ ___	6 + E	------x-	Test and reset memory bits against accumulator
TRB dp	14 ___	5 + EB		
TSB addr	0C ___ ___	6 + E	------x-	Test and set memory bits against accumulator
TSB dp	04 ___	5 + EB		
TSC	3B	2	x-----x-	Transfer stack pointer to 16–bit accumulator
TSX	BA	2	x-----x-	Transfer stack pointer to X register
TXA	8A	2	x-----x-	Transfer X register to accumulator
TXS	9A	2	--------	Transfer X register to stack pointer
TXY	9B	2	x-----x-	Transfer X to Y register
TYA	98	2	x-----x-	Transfer Y register to accumulator
TYX	BB	2	x-----x-	Transfer Y to X register
WAI	CB	3	--------	Wait for interrupt
WDM	42 L	L	--------	Reserved (William D. Mensch)
XBA	EB	3	x-----x-	Exchange the B and A accumulators
XCE	FB	2	--xx---x	Exchange carry and emulation bits

Appendix G

Apple IIGS Monitor Command Summary

The following commands are available from the Apple IIGS's built-in monitor program. You can get to the monitor in many ways. From Applesoft BASIC, use the CALL-151 instruction. From the DEBUG program, use MON. The monitor uses the asterisk, *, when prompting you for commands.

Symbols Used in Summary

The symbol [addr] is used to denote a hexadecimal address. All addresses are considered 16-bit values unless a bank qualifier is used. For example, C58 represents location $0C58 in the current bank, but 2/C58 is location $020C58.

The symbol [range] consists of two addresses, separated by a period. For example, [addr].[addr] is the same as [range]. The first address in the range always comes before the second address in memory.

The symbol [val] refers to a single hexadecimal value (unless decimal is specified). Other symbols will be shown, but their meanings are explained immediately after use.

Complex Arguments

Complex arguments of hexadecimal values, characters, and so forth, can be specified in the monitor. These are denoted by [args] in the next section. Example:

300:0A C58 "Apple IIGS" 'XYZ'

The above would store $0A, $58, and $0C starting at location $0300, followed by the values of the string *Apple IIGS* in high-order ASCII, and finally, the letters Z, Y, and X in that order. (Strings between single quotation marks are treated in reverse order by the monitor.)

Apple IIGS Monitor Command Summary

The monitor is sensitive to the case of the character used to denote a register. However, all other monitor commands can be entered in either upper- or lowercase.

Commands Available from Monitor

Command	Description
CONTROL-B	Cold starts Applesoft BASIC
CONTROL-C	Warm starts BASIC
CONTROL-E	Displays registers
[val] CONTROL-P	Sends output to the specified slot
[val] CONTROL-K	Directs input from the specified slot
CONTROL-M	(Return key) Shows 16 consecutive bytes
CONTROL-R	Resets standard register values
CONTROL-T	Asserts text page 1
CONTROL-Y	Jumps to the vector at $03F8
CONTROL-^ [char]	Changes the cursor to the character typed
[addr]	Displays a byte
[range]	Displays a range of bytes (Control-X cancels)
[addr]G	JSR to address in bank $00
[addr]X	JSL to address
[addr]R	Resume execution after interrupt
[addr]S	Step through instructions
[addr]T	Trace through instructions
[addr]L	Disassemble instructions
[addr]:[args]	Stores values into consecutive locations
[addr]<[range]M	Moves a range of memory to another address
[addr]<[range]V	Verifies a range with that at another address
[val]<[range]Z	Zaps a range of memory with a single value
\[args] \[range]P	Finds patterns of values within a range
\[args] \U	Perform a toolbox call (see Chapter 5)
[val] + [val]	Add
[val] - [val]	Subtract
[val] * [val]	Multiply
[val] _ [val]	Divide (underscore)
[val] = A	Define A register
[val] = X	Define X register
[val] = Y	Define Y register
[val] = D	Define direct page register
[val] = B	Define data bank register
[val] = K	Define code bank register
[val] = S	Define stack pointer
[val] = P	Define processor status register

Command	Description
[val] = M	Define machine (bankswitched memory) state
[val] = Q	Define quagmire (shadowing) state
[val] = m	Define memory/accumulator width
[val] = x	Define index register width
[val] = e	Define emulation mode
[val] = L	Define language card bank
[val] = F	Define filter mask
[val] =	Convert a hex value to decimal
= [val]	Convert a decimal value to hex
= T	Display date and time
=T = mm/dd/yy hh:mm:ss	Change date and time
I	Inverse video
N	Normal video
!	Enter Mini-Assembler
Q	Quit monitor

Appendix H

Apple Desktop Bus Keycodes

The following codes are used by the Apple Desktop Bus to represent keys on the keyboard.

Abbreviations:

L. = Left
R. = Right
D. = Down

Keycodes

No.	Legend	Code	No.	Legend	Code	No.	Legend	Code
1	ESC	$35	36	=	$51	71	'	$27
2	F1	$7A	37	/	$4B	72	RETURN	$24
3	F2	$7B	38	*	$43	73	4	$56
4	F3	$63	39	TAB	$30	74	5	$57
5	F4	$76	40	Q	$0C	75	6	$58
6	F5	$60	41	W	$0D	76	+	$45
7	F6	$61	42	E	$0E	77	L. SHIFT	$38
8	F7	$62	43	R	$0F	78	Z	$06
9	F8	$64	44	T	$11	79	X	$07
10	F9	$65	45	Y	$10	80	C	$08
11	F10	$6D	46	U	$20	81	V	$09
12	F11	$67	47	I	$22	82	B	$0B
13	F12	$6F	48	O	$1F	83	N	$2D
14	F13	$69	49	P	$23	84	M	$2E
15	F14	$6B	50	[	$21	85	,	$2B
16	F15	$71	51	]	$1E	86	.	$2F
17	RESET	$7F	52	\	$2A	87	/	$2C
18	'	$32	53	DEL	$75	88	R. SHIFT	$38 ($7B)
19	1	$12	54	END	$77	89	UP ARROW	$3E
20	2	$13	55	PAGE DOWN	$79	90	1	$53
21	3	$14	56	7	$59	91	2	$54
22	4	$15	57	8	$5B	92	3	$55
23	5	$17	58	9	$5C	93	L. CONTROL	$36
24	6	$16	59	-	$4E	94	L. OPTION	$3A
25	7	$1A	60	CAPS LOCK	$39	95	L. APPLE	$37
26	8	$1C	61	A	$00	96	SPACE	$31
27	9	$19	62	S	$01	97	R. APPLE	$37
28	0	$1D	63	D	$02	98	R. OPTION	$3A ($7C)
29	-	$1B	64	F	$03	99	R. CONTROL	$36 ($7D)
30	=	$18	65	G	$05	100	L. ARROW	$3B
31	DELETE	$33	66	H	$04	101	D. ARROW	$3D
32	HELP	$72	67	J	$26	102	R. ARROW	$3C
33	HOME	$73	68	K	$28	103	0	$52
34	PAGE UP	$74	69	L	$25	104	.	$41
35	CLEAR	$47	70	;	$29	105	ENTER	$4C

Appendix I

Tool Set Cross Reference

This appendix contains a cross reference list of tool sets which require other tool sets to function.

Just because a second tool set is listed does not imply it should be started up before the first tool set is used. Sometimes you will be able to perform all the functions you want without starting up the other tool set. However, if you are unsuccessful at accomplishing your task, you should try starting up the other tool set. That may solve your problem. The reason for this is that routines in the other tool set may be called only to perform specific tasks. At this point in the development of the toolbox, the best policy is to experiment. When new versions are released, this vague area may be clarified.

Tool Set Cross Reference Chart

To determine which ones need to be used, refer to the functions you're using. If an asterisk (*) follows the second tool set's name, its use is optional depending on the functions used by the first tool set.

ID	Tool Set Name	Other Tool Sets Used
$01	Tool Locator	<none>
$02	Memory Manager	Tool Locator ($01)
$03	Miscellaneous Tools	Tool Locator ($01)
		Memory Manager ($02)
$04	QuickDraw II	Tool Locator ($01)
		Memory Manager ($02)
		Miscellaneous Tools ($03)
$05	Desk Manager	Tool Locator ($01)
		Memory Manager ($02)
		Miscellaneous Tools ($03)
		QuickDrawII ($04)
		Event Manager ($06)
		Window Manager ($0E)
		Control Manager ($10)
		Menu Manager ($0F)
		Line Edit ($14)
		Dialog Manager ($15)
		Scrap Manager ($16)

ID	Tool Set Name	Other Tool Sets Used
$06	Event Manager	Tool Locator ($01)
		Memory Manager ($02)
		Miscellaneous Tools ($03)
		QuickDrawII ($04)*
		Desk Manager ($05)*
		ADB tool set ($09)*
$07	Scheduler	Tool Locator ($01)
		Memory Manager ($02)
		Miscellaneous Tools ($03)
$08	Sound Manager	Tool Locator ($01)
		Memory Manager ($02)
		Miscellaneous Tools ($03)
$09	Apple Desktop Bus	Tool Locator ($01)
$0A	SANE	Tool Locator ($01)
		Memory Manager ($02)
$0B	Integer Math	Tool Locator ($01)*
$0C	Text Tools	Tool Locator ($01)*
$0E	Window Manager	Tool Locator ($01)
		Memory Manager ($02)
		Miscellaneous Tools ($03)
		QuickDrawII ($04)
		Event Manager ($06)
		Control Manager ($10)
		Menu Manager ($0F)
$0F	Menu Manager	Tool Locator ($01)
		Memory Manager ($02)
		Miscellaneous Tools ($03)
		QuickDrawII ($04)
		Event Manager ($06)
		Window Manager ($0E)
		Control Manager ($10)
$10	Control Manager	Tool Locator ($01)
		Memory Manager ($02)
		Miscellaneous Tools ($03)
		QuickDrawII ($04)
		Event Manager ($06)
		Window Manager ($0E)
		Menu Manager ($0F)*
$11	System Loader	Tool Locator ($01)
		Memory Manager ($02)
		Miscellaneous Tools ($03)
$12	QuickDrawAux	Tool Locator ($01)
		Memory Manager ($02)
		Miscellaneous Tools ($03)
		QuickDrawII ($04)

ID	Tool Set Name	Other Tool Sets Used
$13	Print Manager	Tool Locator ($01)
		Memory Manager ($02)
		Miscellaneous Tools ($03)
		QuickDrawII ($04)
		QuickDrawAux ($12)
		Event Manager ($06)
		Window Manager ($0E)
		Control Manager ($10)
		Menu Manager ($0F)*
		Line Edit ($14)
		Dialog Manager ($15)*
		List Manager ($1C)
		Font Manager ($1B)
$14	Line Edit	Tool Locator ($01)
		Memory Manager ($02)
		Miscellaneous Tools ($03)
		QuickDrawII ($04)
		Event Manager ($06)*
		Scrap Manager ($16)*
$15	Dialog Manager	Tool Locator ($01)
		Memory Manager ($02)
		Miscellaneous Tools ($03)
		QuickDrawII ($04)
		Event Manager ($06)
		Window Manager ($0E)
		Control Manager ($10)*
		Menu Manager ($0F)*
		Line Edit ($14)*
$16	Scrap Manager	Tool Locator ($01)
		Memory Manager ($02)
$17	Stadard File	Tool Locator ($01)
		Memory Manager ($02)
		Miscellaneous Tools ($03)
		QuickDrawII ($04)
		Event Manager ($06)
		Window Manager ($0E)
		Control Manager ($10)
		Menu Manager ($0F)*
		Line Edit ($14)
		Dialog Manager ($15)
$19	Note Synthesizer	Tool Locator ($01)
		Memory Manager ($02)
		Sound Tools ($08)

ID	Tool Set Name	Other Tool Sets Used
$1B	Font Manager	Tool Locator ($01)
		Memory Manager ($02)
		Miscellaneous Tools ($03)
		QuickDrawII ($04)
		Integer Math ($0B)*
		Window Manager ($0E)
		Control Manager ($10)
		Menu Manager ($0F)
		List Manager ($1C)
		Line Edit ($14)
		Dialog Manager ($15)
$1C	List Manager	Tool Locator ($01)
		Memory Manager ($02)
		Miscellaneous Tools ($03)
		QuickDrawII ($04)
		Event Manager ($06)
		Window Manager ($0E)
		Control Manager ($10)
		Menu Manager ($0F)

Appendix J

ProDOS Filetypes

ProDOS Filetype Codes

Type	Hex	Dec	Description
	00	0	Typeless File
BAD	01	1	Bad Block File
PCD	02	2	Pascal Code File
PTX	03	3	Pascal Text File
TXT	04	4	ASCII Text File
PDA	05	5	Pascal Data File
BIN	06	6	General Binary File
FNT	07	7	SOS Font File
FOT	08	8	Graphics Screen File
BA3	09	9	Business BASIC Program
DA3	0A	10	Business BASIC Data File
WPF	0B	11	Word Processor File
SOS	0C	12	SOS System File
DIR	0F	15	Subdirectory File
RPD	10	16	RPS Data File
RPI	11	17	RPS Index File
	12	18	AppleFile Discard File
	13	19	AppleFile Model File
	14	20	AppleFile Report Format File
	15	21	Screen Library File
ADB	19	25	AppleWorks Data Base File
AWP	1A	26	AppleWorks Word Processor File
ASP	1B	27	AppleWorks Spread Sheet File
HLP	A2	162	*WordPerfect* Help File
DAT	A3	163	*WordPerfect* Data File
LEX	A5	165	*WordPerfect* Dictionary File
SRC	B0	176	APW Source File
OBJ	B1	177	APW Object File
LIB	B2	178	APW Library File
S16	B3	179	ProDOS 16 System Application File
RTL	B4	180	APW Runtime Library File
EXE	B5	181	ProDOS 16 Shell Application File
STR	B6	182	ProDOS 16 Permanent Initialization File
TSF	B7	183	ProDOS 16 Temporary Initialization File
NDA	B8	184	New Desk Accessory
CDA	B9	185	Classic Desk Accessory
TOL	BA	186	ProDOS 16 Tool Set File

Type	Hex	Dec	Description
DRV	BB	187	ProDOS 16 Driver File
DOC	BF	191	ProDOS Document File
FNT	C8	200	ProDOS 16 Font File
LBR	E0	224	Library File
DTS	E2	226	
PAS	EF	239	Pascal Area on Partitioned Disk File
CMD	F0	240	Added Command File
MAC	F4	244	Macro File
BAT	F5	245	Shell Batch Command File
LNK	F8	248	EDASM Linker File
P16	F9	249	
INT	FA	250	Integer BASIC Program
IVR	FB	251	Integer BASIC Variables File
BAS	FC	252	BASIC Program
VAR	FD	253	BASIC Variables File
REL	FE	254	Relocatable Code File
SYS	FF	255	ProDOS 8 System Application File

Appendix K

List of Tools by Function Name

All the tool set functions are listed below alphabetically. This list is provided to help you look up functions which may be listed by their name, rather than function number. An example would be a program written using macros that are named after the function.

Function Name	Function/Tool Set
ABSOFF	$1009
ABSON	$0F09
ADBBootInit	$0109
ADBReset	$0509
ADBShutDown	$0309
ADBStartUp	$0209
ADBStatus	$0609
ADBVersion	$0409
ADBpoll	$0D09
ADBrcv	$0E09
AddFamily	$0D1B
AddFontVar	$141B
AddPt	$8004
Alert	$1715
AllNotesOff	$0D19
AllocGen	$0919
BeginUpdate	$1E0E
BlockMove	$2B02
BringToFront	$240E
Button	$0D06
CLRSRQTBL	$1609
CStringBounds	$AE04
CStringWidth	$AA04
CalcMenuSize	$1C0F
CautionAlert	$1A15
CharBounds	$AC04
CharWidth	$A804
CheckHandle	$1E02
CheckMItem	$320F
CheckUpdate	$0A0E
ChooseCDA	$1105

Function Name	Function/Tool Set
ChooseFont	$161B
ClampMouse	$1C03
ClearMouse	$1B03
ClearScreen	$1504
ClipRect	$2604
CloseAllNDAs	$1D05
CloseDialog	$0C15
CloseNDA	$1605
CloseNDAbyWinPtr	$1C05
ClosePoly	$C204
ClosePort	$1A04
CloseRgn	$6E04
CloseWindow	$0B0E
ClrHeartBeat	$1403
CompactMem	$1F02
CopyPixels	$0912
CopyRgn	$6904
CountFamilies	$091B
CountFonts	$101B
CountMItems	$140F
CreateList	$091C
CtlBootInit	$0110
CtlReset	$0510
CtlShutDown	$0310
CtlStartUp	$0210
CtlStatus	$0610
CtlVersion	$0410
CtrlTextDev	$160C
DeallocGen	$0A19
Dec2Int	$280B
Dec2Long	$290B
DefaultFilter	$3615
DelHeartBeat	$1303
DeleteID	$2103
DeleteMItem	$100F
DeleteMenu	$0E0F
DeskBootInit	$0105
DeskReset	$0505
DeskShutDown	$0305
DeskStartUp	$0205
DeskStatus	$0605
DeskVersion	$0405
Desktop	$0C0E
DialogBootInit	$0115
DialogReset	$0515
DialogSelect	$1115

Function Name	Function/Tool Set
DialogShutDown	$0315
DialogStartUp	$0215
DialogStatus	$0615
DialogVersion	$0415
DiffRgn	$7304
DigCopy	$1315
DigCut	$1215
DigDelete	$1515
DigPaste	$1415
DisableDItem	$3915
DisableMItem	$310F
Dispose Handle	$1002
DisposeAll	$1102
DisposeControl	$0A10
DisposeMenu	$2E0F
DisposeRgn	$6804
DoWindows	$0906
DragControl	$1710
DragRect	$1D10
DragWindow	$1A0E
DrawCString	$A604
DrawChar	$A404
DrawControls	$1010
DrawDialog	$1615
DrawMember	$0C1C
DrawMenuBar	$2A0F
DrawOneCtl	$2510
DrawString	$A504
DrawText	$A704
EMBootInit	$0106
EMReset	$0506
EMShutDown	$0306
EMStartUp	$0206
EMStatus	$0606
EMVersion	$0406
EmptyRect	$5204
EmptyRgn	$7804
EnableDItem	$3A15
EnableMItem	$300F
EndInfoDrawing	$510E
EndUpdate	$1F0E
EqualPt	$8304
EqualRect	$5104
EqualRgn	$7704
EraseArc	$6404
EraseControl	$2410

Function Name	Function/Tool Set
EraseOval	$5A04
ErasePoly	$BE04
EraseRRect	$5F04
EraseRect	$5504
EraseRgn	$7B04
ErrWriteBlock	$1F0C
ErrWriteCString	$210C
ErrWriteChar	$190C
ErrWriteLine	$1B0C
ErrWriteString	$1D0C
ErrorSound	$0915
EventAvail	$0B06
FFGeneratorStatus	$1108
FFSoundDoneStatus	$1408
FFSoundStatus	$1008
FFStartSound	$0E08
FFStopSound	$0F08
FMBootInit	$011B
FMGetCurFID	$1A1B
FMGetSysFID	$191B
FMReset	$051B
FMSetSysFont	$181B
FMShutDown	$031B
FMStartup	$021B
FMStatus	$061B
FMVersion	$041B
FWEntry	$2403
FakeMouse	$1906
FamNum2ItemID	$1B1B
FillArc	$6604
FillOval	$5C04
FillPoly	$C004
FillRRect	$6104
FillRect	$5704
FillRgn	$7D04
FindControl	$1310
FindDItem	$2415
FindFamily	$0A1B
FindFontStats	$111B
FindHandle	$1A02
FindWindow	$170E
Fix2Frac	$1C0B
Fix2Long	$1B0B
Fix2X	$1E0B
FixATan2	$170B
FixAppleMenu	$1E05

Function Name	Function/Tool Set
FixDiv	$110B
FixFontMenu	$151B
FixMenuBar	$130F
FixMul	$0F0B
FixRatio	$0E0B
FixRound	$130B
FlashMenuBar	$0C0F
FlushEvents	$1506
ForceBufDims	$CC04
Frac2Fix	$1D0B
Frac2X	$1F0B
FracCos	$150B
FracDiv	$120B
FracMul	$100B
FracSin	$160B
FracSqrt	$140B
FrameArc	$6204
FrameOval	$5804
FramePoly	$BC04
FrameRRect	$5D04
FrameRect	$5304
FrameRgn	$7904
FreeMem	$1B02
FrontWindow	$150E
GetAbsClamp	$2B03
GetAddr	$1603
GetAddress	$0904
GetAlertStage	$3415
GetBackColor	$A304
GetBackPat	$3504
GetBarColors	$180F
GetCaretTime	$1206
GetCharExtra	$D504
GetClip	$2504
GetClipHandle	$C704
GetColorEntry	$1104
GetColorTable	$0F04
GetContentDraw	$480E
GetContentOrgin	$3E0E
GetContentRgn	$2F0E
GetControlDItem	$1E15
GetCtlAction	$2110
GetCtlDpage	$1F10
GetCtlParams	$1C10
GetCtlRefCon	$2310
GetCtlTitle	$0D10

Function Name	Function/Tool Set
GetCtlValue	$1A10
GetCursorAdr	$8F04
GetDAStrPtr	$1405
GetDItemBox	$2815
GetDItemType	$2615
GetDItemValue	$2E15
GetDataSize	$400E
GetDblTime	$1106
GetDefButton	$3715
GetDefProc	$310E
GetErrGlobals	$0E0C
GetErrorDevice	$140C
GetFGSize	$CF04
GetFamInfo	$0B1B
GetFamNum	$0C1B
GetFirstDItem	$2A15
GetFirstWindow	$520E
GetFont	$9504
GetFontFlags	$9904
GetFontGlobals	$9704
GetFontID	$D104
GetFontInfo	$9604
GetFontLore	$D904
GetForeColor	$A104
GetFrameColor	$100E
GetFuncPtr	$0B01
GetGrafProcs	$4504
GetHandleSize	$1802
GetIRQ Enable	$2903
GetIText	$1F15
GetInGlobals	$0C0C
GetInfoDraw	$4A0E
GetInfoRefCon	$350E
GetInputDevice	$120C
GetListDefProc	$0E1C
GetLoadSegInfo	$0F11
GetMHandle	$160F
GetMItem	$250F
GetMItemFlag	$270F
GetMItemMark	$340F
GetMItemStyle	$360F
GetMTitleStart	$1A0F
GetMTitleWidth	$1E0F
GetMasterSCB	$1704
GetMaxGrow	$420E
GetMenuBar	$0A0F

Function Name	Function/Tool Set
GetMenuFlag	$200F
GetMenuMgrPort	$1B0F
GetMenuTitle	$220F
GetMouse	$0C06
GetMouseClamp	$1D03
GetNewDItem	$3315
GetNewID	$2003
GetNewModalDialog	$3215
GetNextDItem	$2B15
GetNextEvent	$0A06
GetNextWindow	$2A0E
GetNumNDAs	$1B05
GetOSEvent	$1606
GetOutGlobals	$0D0C
GetOutputDevice	$130C
GetPage	$460E
GetPathname	$1111
GetPen	$2904
GetPenMask	$3304
GetPenMode	$2F04
GetPenPat	$3104
GetPenSize	$2D04
GetPenState	$2B04
GetPicSave	$3F04
GetPixel	$8804
GetPolySave	$4304
GetPort	$1C04
GetPortLoc	$1E04
GetPortRect	$2004
GetRectInfo	$4F0E
GetRgnSave	$4104
GetRomFont	$D804
GetSCB	$1304
GetScrap	$0D16
GetScrapCount	$1216
GetScrapHandle	$0E16
GetScrapPath	$1016
GetScrapSize	$0F16
GetScrapState	$1316
GetScroll	$440E
GetSoundVolume	$0C08
GetSpaceExtra	$9F04
GetStandardSCB	$0C04
GetStructRgn	$2E0E
GetSysBar	$110F
GetSysField	$4904

Function Name	Function/Tool Set
GetSysFont	$B304
GetSysWFlag	$4C0E
GetTSPtr	$0901
GetTableAddress	$0B08
GetTextFace	$9B04
GetTextMode	$9D04
GetTick	$2503
GetUpdateRgn	$300E
GetUserField	$4704
GetUserID	$1011
GetVector	$1103
GetVisHandle	$C904
GetVisRgn	$B504
GetWAP	$0C01
GetWControls	$330E
GetWFrame	$2C0E
GetWKind	$2B0E
GetWMgrPort	$200E
GetWRefCon	$290E
GetWTitle	$0E0E
GetZoomRect	$370E
GlobalToLocal	$8504
GrafOff	$0B04
GrafOn	$0A04
GrowSize	$1E10
GrowWindow	$1B0E
HLock	$2002
HLockAll	$2102
HUnLock	$2202
HUnLockAll	$2302
HandToHand	$2A02
HandToPtr	$2902
Hex2Int	$240B
Hex2Long	$250B
HexIt	$2A0B
HiWord	$180B
HideControl	$0E10
HideCursor	$9004
HideDItem	$2215
HidePen	$2704
HideWindow	$120E
HiliteControl	$1110
HiliteMenu	$2C0F
HiliteWindow	$220E
HomeMouse	$1A03
IMBootInit	$010B

Function Name	Function/Tool Set
IMReset	$050B
IMShutDown	$030B
IMStartUp	$020B
IMStatus	$060B
IMVersion	$040B
InflateTextBuffer	$D704
InitColorTable	$0D04
InitCursor	$CA04
InitMouse	$1803
InitPalette	$2F0F
InitPort	$1904
InitTextDev	$150C
InitialLoad	$0711
InsertMItem	$0F0F
InsertMenu	$0D0F
InsetRect	$4C04
InsetRgn	$7004
InstallCDA	$0F05
InstallFont	$0E1B
InstallNDA	$0E05
Int2Dec	$260B
Int2Hex	$220B
IntSource	$2303
InvalRect	$3A0E
InvalRgn	$3B0E
InvertArc	$6504
InvertOval	$5B04
InvertPoly	$BF04
InvertRRect	$6004
InvertRect	$5604
InvertRgn	$7C04
IsDialogEvent	$1015
ItemID2FamNum	$171B
KillControls	$0B10
KillPoly	$C304
LEActivate	$0F14
LEBootInit	$0114
LEClick	$0D14
LECopy	$1314
LECut	$1214
LEDeactivate	$1014
LEDelete	$1514
LEDispose	$0A14
LEFromScrap	$1914
LEGetScrapLen	$1C14
LEIdle	$0C14

Function Name	Function/Tool Set
LEInsert	$1614
LEKey	$1114
LENew	$0914
LEPaste	$1414
LEReset	$0514
LEScrapHandle	$1B14
LESetCaret	$1F14
LESetHilite	$1E14
LESetScrapLen	$1D14
LESetSelect	$0E14
LESetText	$0B14
LEShutDown	$0314
LEStartUp	$0214
LEStatus	$0614
LETextBox	$1814
LETextBox2	$2014
LEToScrap	$1A14
LEUpdate	$1714
LEVersion	$0414
Line	$3D04
LineTo	$3C04
ListBootInit	$011C
ListReset	$051C
ListShutDown	$031C
ListStartUp	$021C
ListStatus	$061C
ListVersion	$041C
LoWord	$190B
LoadFont	$121B
LoadOneTool	$0F01
LoadScrap	$0A16
LoadSegName	$0D11
LoadSegNum	$0B11
LoadSysFont	$131B
LoadTools	$0E01
LoaderInit	$0111
LoaderReset	$0511
LoaderShutDown	$0311
LoaderStartUp	$0211
LoaderStatus	$0611
LoaderVersion	$0411
LocalToGlobal	$8404
Long2Dec	$270B
Long2Fix	$1A0B
Long2Hex	$230B
LongDivide	$0D0B

Function Name	Function/Tool Set
LongMul	$0C0B
MMBootInit	$0102
MMReset	$0502
MMShutDown	$0302
MMStartUp	$0202
MMStatus	$0602
MMVersion	$0402
MTBootInit	$0103
MTReset	$0503
MTShutDown	$0303
MTStartup	$0203
MTStatus	$0603
MTVersion	$0403
MapPoly	$C504
MapPt	$8A04
MapRect	$8B04
MapRgn	$8C04
MaxBlock	$1C02
MenuBootInit	$010F
MenuKey	$090F
MenuNewRes	$290F
MenuRefresh	$0B0F
MenuReset	$050F
MenuSelect	$2B0F
MenuShutDown	$030F
MenuStartUp	$020F
MenuStatus	$060F
MenuVersion	$040F
ModalDialog	$0F15
ModalDialog2	$2C15
Move	$3B04
MoveControl	$1610
MovePortTo	$2204
MoveTo	$3A04
MoveWindow	$190E
Multiply	$090B
Munger	$2803
NSBootInit	$0119
NSReset	$0519
NSShutDown	$0319
NSStartUp	$0219
NSStatus	$0619
NSVersion	$0419
NewControl	$0910
NewDItem	$0D15
NewHandle	$0902

Function Name	Function/Tool Set
NewList	$101C
NewMenu	$2D0F
NewMenuBar	$150F
NewModalDialog	$0A15
NewModelessDialog	$0B15
NewRgn	$6704
NewWindow	$090E
NextMember	$0B1C
NoteAlert	$1915
NoteOff	$0C19
NoteOn	$0B19
OSEventAvail	$1706
ObscureCursor	$9204
OffsetPoly	$C404
OffsetRect	$4B04
OffsetRgn	$6F04
OpenNDA	$1505
OpenPoly	$C104
OpenPort	$1804
OpenRgn	$6D04
PMBootInit	$0113
PMReset	$0513
PMShutDown	$0313
PMStartUp	$0213
PMStatus	$0613
PMVersion	$0413
PPToPort	$D604
PackBytes	$2603
PaintArc	$6304
PaintOval	$5904
PaintPixels	$7F04
PaintPoly	$BD04
PaintRRect	$5E04
PaintRect	$5404
PaintRgn	$7A04
ParamText	$1B15
PenNormal	$3604
PinRect	$210E
PosMouse	$1E03
PostEvent	$1406
PrChooser	$1613
PrCloseDoc	$0F13
PrClosePage	$1113
PrControl	$1313
PrDefault	$0913
PrError	$1413

Function Name	Function/Tool Set
PrJobDialog	$0C13
PrOpenDoc	$0E13
PrOpenPage	$1013
PrPicFile	$1213
PrSetError	$1513
PrStlDialog	$0B13
PrValidate	$0A13
Pt2Rect	$5004
PtInRect	$4F04
PtInRgn	$7504
PtrToHand	$2802
PurgeAll	$1302
PurgeHandle	$1202
PutScrap	$0C16
QDAuxBootInit	$0112
QDAuxReset	$0512
QDAuxShutDown	$0312
QDAuxStartUp	$0212
QDAuxStatus	$0612
QDAuxVersion	$0412
QDBootInit	$0104
QDReset	$0504
QDShutDown	$0304
QDStartUp	$0204
QDStatus	$0604
QDVersion	$0404
RCV	$0A09
RDABS	$1109
RDScale	$1309
RDmem	$0B09
Random	$8604
ReAllocHandle	$0A02
ReadASCIITime	$0F03
ReadBParam	$0C03
ReadBRAM	$0A03
ReadBlock	$230C
ReadChar	$220C
ReadLine	$240C
ReadMouse	$1703
ReadRAMBlock	$0A08
ReadTimeHex	$0D03
RectInRgn	$7604
RectRgn	$6C04
RefreshDesktop	$390E
RemoveDItem	$0E15
ResetAlertStage	$3515

Function Name	Function/Tool Set
ResetMember	$0F1C
RestAll	$0C05
RestScrn	$0A05
Restart	$0A11
RestoreBufDims	$CE04
RestoreHandle	$0B02
SANEBootInit	$010A
SANEDecStr816	$0A0A
SANEEFP816	$090A
SANEElems816	$0B0A
SANEShutDown	$030A
SANEStartUp	$020A
SANEStatus	$060A
SANEVersion	$040A
SDivide	$0A0B
SEND	$0909
SFAllCaps	$0D17
SFBootInit	$0117
SFGetFile	$0917
SFPGetFile	$0B17
SFPPutFile	$0C17
SFPutFile	$0A17
SFReset	$0517
SFShutdown	$0317
SFStartup	$0217
SFStatus	$0617
SFVersion	$0417
SRQPL	$1409
SRQRMV	$1509
SaveAll	$0B05
SaveBufDims	$CD04
SaveScrn	$0905
Scale	$1209
ScalePt	$8904
SchAddTask	$0907
SchBootInit	$0107
SchFlush	$0A07
SchReset	$0507
SchShutDown	$0307
SchStartUp	$0207
SchStatus	$0607
SchVersion	$0407
ScrapBootInit	$0116
ScrapReset	$0516
ScrapShutDown	$0316
ScrapStartUp	$0216

Function Name	Function/Tool Set
ScrapStatus	$0616
ScrapVersion	$0416
ScrollRect	$7E04
SectRect	$4D04
SectRgn	$7104
SelectMember	$0D1C
SelectWindow	$110E
SellText	$2115
SendBehind	$140E
ServeMouse	$1F03
SetAbsClamp	$2A03
SetAllSCBs	$1404
SetBackColor	$A204
SetBackPat	$3404
SetBarColors	$170F
SetBufDims	$CB04
SetCharExtra	$D404
SetClip	$2404
SetClipHandle	$C604
SetColorEntry	$1004
SetColorTable	$0E04
SetContentDraw	$490E
SetContentOrigin	$3F0E
SetCtlAction	$2010
SetCtlIcons	$1810
SetCtlParams	$1B10
SetCtlRefCon	$2210
SetCtlTitle	$0C10
SetCtlValue	$1910
SetCursor	$8E04
SetDAFont	$1C15
SetDAStrPtr	$1305
SetDItemBox	$2915
SetDItemType	$2715
SetDItemValue	$2F15
SetDataSize	$410E
SetDefButton	$3815
SetDefProc	$320E
SetEmptyRgn	$6A04
SetErrDevice	$110C
SetErrGlobals	$0B0C
SetEventMask	$1806
SetFont	$9404
SetFontFlags	$9804
SetFontID	$D004
SetForeColor	$A004

Function Name	Function/Tool Set
SetFrameColor	$0F0E
SetGrafProcs	$4404
SetHandleSize	$1902
SetHeartBeat	$1203
SetIText	$2015
SetInGlobals	$090C
SetInfoDraw	$160E
SetInfoRefCon	$360E
SetInputDevice	$0F0C
SetMItem	$240F
SetMItemBlink	$280F
SetMItemFlag	$260F
SetMItemID	$380F
SetMItemMark	$330F
SetMItemName	$3A0F
SetMItemStyle	$350F
SetMTitleStart	$190F
SetMTitleWidth	$1D0F
SetMasterSCB	$1604
SetMaxGrow	$430E
SetMenuBar	$390F
SetMenuFlag	$1F0F
SetMenuID	$370F
SetMenuTitle	$210F
SetMouse	$1903
SetOrigin	$2304
SetOriginMask	$340E
SetOutGlobals	$0A0C
SetOutputDevice	$100C
SetPage	$470E
SetPenMask	$3204
SetPenMode	$2E04
SetPenPat	$3004
SetPenSize	$2C04
SetPenState	$2A04
SetPicSave	$3E04
SetPolySave	$4204
SetPort	$1B04
SetPortLoc	$1D04
SetPortRect	$1F04
SetPortSize	$2104
SetPt	$8204
SetPurge	$2402
SetPurgeAll	$2502
SetPurgeStat	$0F1B
SetRandSeed	$8704

Function Name	Function/Tool Set
SetRect	$4A04
SetRectRgn	$6B04
SetRgnSave	$4004
SetSCB	$1204
SetScrapPath	$1116
SetScroll	$450E
SetSolidBackPat	$3804
SetSolidPenPat	$3704
SetSoundMIRQV	$1208
SetSoundVolume	$0D08
SetSpaceExtra	$9E04
SetSwitch	$1306
SetSysBar	$120F
SetSysField	$4804
SetSysFont	$B204
SetSysWindow	$4B0E
SetTSPtr	$0A01
SetTextFace	$9A04
SetTextMode	$9C04
SetUserField	$4604
SetUserSoundIRQV	$1308
SetVector	$1003
SetVisHandle	$C804
SetVisRgn	$B404
SetWAP	$0D01
SetWFrame	$2D0E
SetWRefCon	$280E
SetWTitle	$0D0E
SetWindowIcons	$4E0E
SetZoomRect	$380E
ShowControl	$0F10
ShowCursor	$9104
ShowDItem	$2315
ShowHide	$230E
ShowPen	$2804
ShowWindow	$130E
SizeWindow	$1C0E
SolidPattern	$3904
SortList	$0A1C
SoundBootInit	$0108
SoundReset	$0508
SoundShutDown	$0308
SoundStartUp	$0208
SoundToolStatus	$0608
SoundVersion	$0408
StartDrawing	$4D0E

Function Name	Function/Tool Set
StartInfoDrawing	$500E
StatusID	$2203
StatusTDev	$170C
StillDown	$0E06
StopAlert	$1815
StringBounds	$AD04
StringWidth	$A904
SubPt	$8104
SysBeep	$2C03
SysFailMgr	$1503
SystemClick	$1705
SystemEdit	$1805
SystemEvent	$1A05
SystemTask	$1905
TLBootInit	$0101
TLMountVolume	$1101
TLReset	$0501
TLShutDown	$0301
TLStartUp	$0201
TLStatus	$0601
TLTextMountVolume	$1201
TLVersion	$0401
TaskMaster	$1D0E
TestControl	$1410
TextBootInit	$010C
TextBounds	$AF04
TextReset	$050C
TextShutDown	$030C
TextStartUp	$020C
TextStatus	$060C
TextVersion	$040C
TextWidth	$AB04
TickCount	$1006
TotalMem	$1D02
TrackControl	$1510
TrackGoAway	$180E
TrackZoom	$260E
UDivide	$0B0B
UnLoadSegNum	$0C11
UnionRect	$4E04
UnionRgn	$7204
UnloadOneTool	$1001
UnloadScrap	$0916
UnloadSeg	$0E11
UnpackBytes	$2703
UpdateDialog	$2515

Function Name	Function/Tool Set
UserShutdown	$1211
ValidRect	$3C0E
ValidRgn	$3D0E
WaitCursor	$0A12
WaitMouseUp	$0F06
WindBootInit	$010E
WindDragRect	$530E
WindNewRes	$250E
WindShutDown	$030E
WindStartUp	$020E
WindStatus	$060E
WindVersion	$040E
WriteBParam	$0B03
WriteBRAM	$0903
WriteBlock	$1E0C
WriteCString	$200C
WriteChar	$180C
WriteLine	$1A0C
WriteRAMBlock	$0908
WriteString	$1C0C
WriteTimeHex	$0E03
X2Fix	$200B
X2Frac	$210B
XorRgn	$7404
ZeroScrap	$0B16
ZoomWindow	$270E

Index

#INCLUDE C statement 55
6502 chip 11
65C02 chip 11
A register 11, 15, 36, 37, 44, 46, 141
About . . . menu item 265
accumulator. *See* A register
addressing modes, list of 603
Alert function 316
alerts 315–22
  example subroutine 319–22
  template 315, 317–18
AllocGen function 333
Apple Programmer's Workshop for the C language (*APW C*) 54
Apple's Human Interface Guidelines 265
applications, designing 75–92
APW (Apple Programmer's Workshop) assembler 4, 43–44, 51, 63, 130
Arc function 210
arguments, passing to and from the toolbox 36–44
ASCII code list 583–84
banks, of memory 18–21
BASIC programming language 49–51
BCC (Branch if Carry Clear) instruction 44–45, 142
BCS (Branch if Carry Set) instruction 44
BeepBeep program 63–65
BLOAD BASIC statement 49
block attributes 99–101
block strings 67, 136
Bombs Away! program 65–67
book, how to use 3–7
Boolean value 6
BootInit function 28
bottom scroll bar 235, 237
buttons 297–298
  placing in dialog box 306–8
byte 5
C flag 44, 46, 141, 142
C programming language 3, 35, 49, 51, 54–56
C strings 67, 135–36
CALL BASIC statement 49, 50
CautionAlert function 316
check boxes 295, 296
clamping values, mouse 91–92
CLC instruction 13, 50
close box 235–236
CloseWindow function 251
code optimization 351–61
colors
  setting in 320 mode 187–90
  setting in 640 mode 190–93
color tables 176, 187–201, 214
  locations of 187
CompactMem function 105
Control Manager tool set 235, 243–44
controls, in dialog boxes 235
CPU 11–15
cursor record 229–30
data bank register 11, 18–19, 130
DATA BASIC statement 50
Desktop function 237–41
  bus keycodes 613
  commands 238–39
  pattern and color parameters 239–40
dialog box 293–322
  building 300–306
  example subroutine 308–10
  example subroutine, modifying 310–12
  items 296–98
  modal 295
  modeless 295
dialog events, acting on 312–15
dialog example subroutine 313–15
Dialog Manager tool set
  order of starting tool sets for 299
  using in program 298–300
dialog port pointer 302
direct page
  buffer, calculating the next available 355
  buffers, programming efficiency 353–56
  register 11
  space, establishing 79
  tool sets and 113–21
  tool sets requiring, list of (table) 114
DisposeAll function 123
Dispose function 123
DisposeHandle function 105–6
DOC (Digital Oscillator Chip) 325
DOODLE.ASM program 216–24
drawing methods 205
DrawMenuBar function 278
Edit menu item 266
E flag 13
EmStartUp function 91, 92, 119, 146–47, 153

emulation 43, 50
65C02, 65816 chip and 13–18
Ensoniq sound chip 323, 325
envelope, sound 331
environment, establishing 77
equipment required 6–7
error codes 30–31, 599–602
toolbox calls and 44–45
error handlers
failsafe 146–48
general 143–45
general, making more specific 145–46
specific 141–43
error handling 65, 139–48
EVENT.ASM program 160–65, 178
modifying 165–66
event codes, taskmaster 167–68
Event Manager tool set 90–92, 118–19, 146, 149–70
program example 160–66
event mask 152, 155
event queues 152
event record 153–54, 156–60
mouse position and 211
What field 156–57
When field 158
Where field 158–59, 211–213
events
acting on 154–60
keyboard 151–52
mouse 152
types of 151
window 152
extended event codes, of TaskMaster 242
File menu item 266
filetypes, ProDOS 618–19
FillArc 229
FillOval function 228
FillRect function 226, 228
firmware entry points and vectors 585–89
FixMenuBar function 277
Frame, drawing a round rectangle 209–10
FrameArc function 210
FrameRRect function 209
FreeMem function 70
function
calls, ProDOS 16 595–98
of tool set 25
names, alphabetical list of 620–38
functions, list of 366–580
GetDeskPat command of Desktop 240
GetNewDItem function 307
GetNewID function 108
GetNewUserID function 25, 107
GetNextEvent function 154–55, 166, 216
GetPortRect function 225–26
GRAPH.ASM program 178–83, 185–87, 211
graphics
cursor, changing 229–31
modes 173–74
pointer 129
QuickDraw II and 171–99
toolbox and 133–34
Greetings program 67–70
Grow box 235, 237
handle 88, 96–99, 129, 131–32
hardware registers and softswitches 590–94
hexadecimal notation 4–5
HiliteMenu function 280
Hit Item ID 312
HLock function 103, 104
Info Bar 235–236
InitCursor function 183
Insertmenu function 276
instrument record 330–35
integer math tool set 70
intensities 188
interrupt-driven routines, replaced by the Event Manager 151
item reference number 302
item template 318–19
keyboard, reading 64
languages, accessing toolbox from other 47–60
LDX instruction 52
library, C 54–56
LineTo function 185
LoadOneTool function 148
LoadTools function 121–22, 148, 357
logical value. *See* Boolean value
long word 5–6, 40
machine language 35
macro, assembler 51–54
MaxBlock function 71
MemAttributes word 99–101
memory
allocation 101–2
available 70–73
block 85
block, purging 104–6
block, relocatable 95
block, securing 102–3
block, using 102–4
crunching 105
expansion card 6
management 93–108, 113
moving to block 103–4
organization 18–21
protection 95
Memory Manager tool set 70, 93–108, 117, 118
calling 113
shutdown 122–124
Memsize program 70–73

MENU.ASM program 281–91
menu item, Apple 265–66, 269
menu items
  describing 269–74
  multiple, managing 277
Menu Manager tool set 119–120, 355
  other tool sets to be loaded with 275
  using in programs 274–75
menu record 267, 268–75
menu selections, acting on 278–80
menus, pull-down 166, 263–91
  creating 276–78
  program efficiency and 359–60
message field, event record 157–58
M flag 15
Miscellaneous tool set 25, 41, 63, 65, 107, 142
ModalDialog function 312–13
modifiers field, event record 159–60
Monitor, Apple IIGS 43, 49
  accessing toolbox from 56–60
  command summary, Apple IIGS 610–12
mouse
  Event Manager and 153
  movement 90–92
  pointer. *See* graphics cursor
  QuickDraw II and 201–231
  using in programs 211–14
Music Construction Set 325
Music Studio, The 325
New Desk Accessories menu item, Apple 265
NewDItem function 306
NewHandle function 88, 101–2, 116, 147, 353–54
NewMenu function 276
NewModalDialog function 300
NewWindow function 245
NoteAlert function 316
NoteOff function 334
NoteOn function 333
Note Synthesiser tool set 325, 326
NSShutDown function 327
NSStartUp function 326
op codes 51
  list of 604–9
ORCA/M assembler 43, 63
PaintRect function 206
Pascal strings 67, 135
patterns 224–29
  setting 240–41
pen
  characteristics of 184
  modifying 209
  QuickDraw II and 184–87
PHONE.ASM program 335–42
PIANO.ASM program 342–49
pixel map size 172–77
pointers, 129–31
point, graphics 134
POKE BASIC statement 49, 50
previous handle 98
Print Manager tool set 114, 141
PROG1, modifying 90–92
PROG1 program 81–90
program bank register 18, 19
program skeleton example 78–81
PtrToHand function 103–4
PurgeAll function 105
PurgeHandle function 105
PushLong assembler macro 53
PushWord assembler macro 53
queue 151
QuickDraw II tool set 25, 114, 118–120, 171–231
  starting up 176–77
radio buttons 298
ramdisk 6–7
Random function 185
ReadASCIITime function 41–43, 54
ReadChar function 63
ReadLine function 68, 69
ReadRAMBlock function 328
rectangle 133–34, 203–5
redundancy, eliminating 353
release number 29
REP instruction 15–18
Reset function 29
resolution. *See* graphics modes
result space 38–40
result space, long 40–41
right scroll bar 235–236
RL.MYCOLOR program 193–99
ROM, Apple IIGS 49
roundness, rectangle and 210
SCB (Scan line Control Byte) 175–76, 214–16
screen mode, setting 177
SetColorTable function 189, 214
SetCursor function 229
SetDeskPat command of Desktop 241
SetPenPat function 227
SetPenSize function 209
SetPurgeAll function 106
SetPurge function 106
SetRect function 203–4
SetSCB function 175–76, 215
SetSolidPenPat function 184
shadow banks of memory 19
shape functions 205
SHAPES.ASM program 206–11
shortcuts, programming 351–61
shut down 80–81
  automatic 356–59
  general procedure 357–58
  importance of 78
  procedures 78
  tool sets not requiring 124

ShutDown function 28
sound 323–49
Sound Manager tool set 325
  limitations of 325
sound waves
  DOC and 327–30
  types of 327
StartUp function of tool set 28, 112–13
Status function 29
status register 13, 44
StopAlert function 316
strings, toolbox and 134–36
SysBeep function 63, 65
SysFailMgr function 65, 142
system death 142
TaskMaster function 166–70, 237, 241–42, 271, 278, 312
text blocks. *See* block strings
text, displaying on screen 67
text tool set 63, 67–69, 70
title bar 235–236
Tognazzini guide 265
toolbox, accessing 30, 33–46
toolbox examples, elementary 61–73
toolbox functions, common 28–29
toolbox, location of 29–30
Toolbox Tools (table) 26–27
ToolCall assembler macro 52–53
Tool Locator tool set 79, 121, 122, 124, 147
tools
  calling from C 54–56
  calling individual 36
  loading from disk 120–22
tool sets 25
  categories 111–12
  cross reference listing 615–17
  list of 26–27, 111–112, 365
  loading 77, 79–80
  locations, list of 28
  mathematical 112
  Mouse/Desktop Interface Tool Sets (table) 111–112
  requirements of 109–25
  shutting down 122–25
  starting 112–13
TotalMem function 71
User ID 79, 98, 101, 106–8, 153, 176, 353
vector 30
Version function 29
wavelist byte 333
window
  closing 251
  making 245–51
  order of starting tool sets for 244
  parts of 235–37
WINDOW.ASM program 251–60
Window Manager tool set 166, 233–61
window record 237, 246–50
  structure of 246
windows 233–61
  making and controlling 235–37
  multiple 260–61
WindShutDown function 243
WindStartUp function 243
WriteBlock function 67, 69, 70
WriteCString function 68, 69, 70
WriteRAMBlock function 328
WriteString function 67, 69, 71
X flag 15
X register 11, 15–18, 36, 46, 145
Y register 11, 15–18, 46
Zoom box 235, 236